GUIDO DE MARCO

The Politics
of Persuasion

an autobiography

Allied PUBLICATIONS
Valletta, Malta
2007

Allied Publications Limited,
341, St Paul Street, Valletta, Malta.
Copyright © 2007

Book Design: MediaMaker Limited, Valletta, Malta
Printed: Progress Press Limited, Valletta, Malta

ISBN 978-99909-3-118-1 (paperback)
978-99909-3-119-8 (hardback)

For Violet

Foreword

Before I put pen to paper to write this foreword, I went down memory lane. The first image of Guido I have in my mind is of a young schoolboy, a couple of years older than me, in a file going up from the lower to the upper ground at St Aloysius College on our way back to class after the mid-day break.

What made him very distinguishable was his thick, deep red hair. He has, however, become a very distinguished personality for much more valid reasons than the red hair of his youth.

I also have a very distinct recollection of my first meeting with Guido. It happened on stage at the college when Guido played the part of Shylock in Shakespeare's *Merchant of Venice* and I, in the part of a court attendant, had to hold him back when it appeared to me that he was becoming too aggressive towards Antonio, who, incidentally, was played by my eldest brother.

Guido must have learned his lesson because never again did he demand his pound of flesh. Indeed, as I can well attest, in his long public life, and as the title of the book suggests, he excelled in the politics of persuasion.

In the forty years we have worked together, Guido and I always sought to strike an acceptable balance, even when, in the difficult decision-making process, we started off having completely different positions.

In all the years I have known Guido, I have found him to be motivated by a very determined ambition to be outstanding in his service. He took pride in his work for his country. In all honesty, I have to agree with the assessment this book makes that we did achieve a lot for Malta.

My first eleven years as leader of the Nationalist Party, and, of course, Guido's first eleven years as my deputy, were indeed very difficult, as we sought to see Malta win back its democratic credentials in all aspects of life. The following years were years of achievement crowned with Malta's accession to the European Union. Guido was present in Athens on April 16, 2004 when Joe Borg and I signed the Treaty of Accession. It was a moment of personal satisfaction and fulfilment for both of us.

This book gives a fair description of the travails and achievements in which Guido was a protagonist and which shaped Malta's contemporary history.

EDWARD FENECH ADAMI
President of Malta

Introduction

I am no guru in the psychology of persuasion but I feel I can modestly say that I have practised the politics of persuasion for as long as I have been in public life. The term 'politics of persuasion' can mean various forms of persuasion, but in choosing it as title of my memoirs I did not have in mind such new techniques of persuasion as spin or image politics, much less what is known as coercive persuasion, manipulation, or indoctrination. I am using the term to mean bringing an opponent to agreement, or to share or conform to one's point of view, or to reach consensus without friction, or resorting to verbal or physical violence.

In politics, the strong language I often used at public meetings, particularly after the anomalous 1981 general election result, might have given the general impression among our supporters that I was tough in dealing with political opponents. I was indeed tough, but being politically tough showed only one side of my character. The other side showed a strong personal inclination to avoid confrontation and to settle differences by seeking common ground and consensus.

I think I have had this trait since childhood. Indeed, long before I made up my mind to study law, my schoolfriends were already calling me *l-avukat*, and nuns at St Joseph thought I argued too much. Not so the Jesuits at St Aloysius, who encouraged my interest in the sense of logic. When a debating society was formed at St Aloysius, I was among the first to be asked to take part.

I have always disliked violence in pursuit of personal, political, and national aims, believing that logic and the force of persuasion are more likely to bring opponents to my way of thinking. This principle has served me in good stead most of the times in my legal and political work as well as in every post I have held, both in Malta and abroad.

There were many instances in my political life, in and out of parliament, when the politics of persuasion carried the day. One was over the 1974 constitutional amendments under which the island changed its status from a monarchy to a republic. I took a very active part in the difficult talks we had with the Labour government's delegation and, directly, with Prime Minister Dom Mintoff.

The situation was made even more difficult because most of the Nationalist MPs found themselves in disagreement with the views of their own leader, George Borg Olivier, who was against turning Malta into a republic. Borg Olivier insisted on shelving the issue over the proposed change to a republic till after the elections. He renounced the right to the holding of a referendum on other issues that were being debated, but insisted that a referendum be held on the change to a republic.

It was a difficult moment for us but my politics of persuasion helped to get the majority of the parliamentary group to agree to the change. Disagreeing with the leader, whom I greatly respected, admired, and believed in, was one of the worst moments in my career as a member of parliament.

I was also involved in the difficult talks that led to the constitutional amendments aimed at avoiding a repetition of the 1981 anomalous election result. A parliamentary committee had been set up to go into the problem, but there did not appear to be much goodwill on the part of the Labour members for progress to be made.

In direct talks I had with Mintoff, I succeeded, through the force of persuasion, to help bring about a solution, one that guaranteed a majority of seats to the party winning an absolute majority of votes. Malta was saved from the brink of civil war. It was to Mintoff's credit that he started the talks between us. Tribute must also be paid to Dr Edgar Mizzi for his legal help. Together, we succeeded in finding a solution acceptable to both sides of the House.

I had also found the politics of persuasion particularly useful in my role as foreign minister, when my aim was to see the island become a member of the European Union. I hitched my wagon to a star, Malta in Europe. But the road to membership was uphill all the way, right from the time we applied to join on July 16, 1990. By 1995, Malta was in pole position for membership, but we received a great setback in 1996 when a Labour government froze the application as it said it preferred a partnership agreement to membership.

On the return to power of the Nationalist Party in 1998, Malta's application was immediately reactivated. A great deal of persuasion was required on our part to convince the EU that the island was back on track, and that the people really wanted to become part of the union, as the electorate later confirmed in a referendum and, again in no uncertain manner, in a subsequent general election.

I took on the presidency only when the EU commission decided to start membership negotiations with Malta. The commission had indeed confirmed that, in the course of its enlargement negotiations with other countries, Malta had won back the position it held before its membership application was frozen by the Labour government. Our persistence, insistence, and consistence paid off and eventually led to Malta taking its rightful place in the European community of nations.

Writing these memoirs has been a wonderful experience as, like others sharing my experiences, I have lived a most interesting time in the island's history. Thanks to the foresight and steadfastness of George Borg Olivier, the island won its independence from Britain in 1964, and set about building from scratch the required institutional infrastructure that in later years helped to usher in a most exciting era of social and economic development.

Borg Olivier strongly believed in a European Malta. Joining the Council of Europe signified our return 'home' and immediately firmly set our sense of direction towards Europe. After independence, Borg Olivier dedicated the rest of his political life to seeing Malta forging closer ties with Europe. We shared his belief, made it our own and worked until we convinced the majority of the people that our place is in the European Union.

My public life, from the time I first became a government minister to the time I served as president of the republic, is an open book, crammed with countless memories of events that give me great satisfaction. I owe a lot to the Nationalist Party and to the strong bond of friendship I have had for so long with Eddie Fenech Adami, and with so many others, such as Ċensu Tabone, Louis Galea, Ugo Mifsud Bonnici, George Bonello du Puis, and George Hyzler. These and so many others have all helped to make the Nationalist Party a national force dedicated to its mission to ensure democracy at all times, and steadfastly to keep to the sense of direction we had already set.

I have purposely avoided overloading my autobiography with too many details, particularly when I deal with the work involved in the talks that led to the amendments made to the constitution in 1974 and 1987, as my wish was to make the book as readable as possible. I have also sought to be as objective as possible, especially when I write about sensitive political issues, mindful of the fact that others may not share my interpretation of events as they occurred. They are, of course, entitled to hold on to their own interpretation. On my part, all I can say is that in writing these memoirs I have done my best to be faithful to myself and to history.

A public life as eventful as the one I have had would have been practically impossible without the help of others.

I owe a lot to my family, particularly to Violet who, even though she never liked politics, stood by me all my political life.

I feel a sense of gratitude, too, to my constituents who elected me to parliament in every election since 1966. We always felt as one big family. I thank the Maltese people who have given me this great honour of serving them for almost 40 years of my life. This book is also their story.

GUIDO DE MARCO

Acknowledgements

I would first like to pay particular acknowledgement to Victor Aquilina, former editor of *The Times*, for editing the manuscript, contributing towards ensuring a better portrayal of my autobiography. His was a major contribution towards the realisation of this autobiography. I would also like to thank Louis J. Scerri, who read the manuscript and made improvements; Paul Xuereb and Steve Mallia, for editing parts of the manuscript; Joe Tonna, who typed the manuscript – Joe is one of the very few who can decipher my handwriting; Joseph Schembri, of MediaMaker, who designed the book and put it together; Mark Sciberras, Progress Press; Department of Information; Tessa Baluci, director, Informa Library; Maurice Tanti Burlo; Joe Camilleri, printing manager, Progress Press; Joe Mizzi, director, Visual Trends; Maurizio D'Urso; and Vincent Buhagiar, managing director, Allied Newspapers Limited, and Adrian Hillman, managing director, Progress Press.

1

In Nerik Mizzi's footsteps

Politics is a mission. These words still ring in my ears, even though 57 years have passed since I heard them first straight from the lips of a man whom I greatly admired for his nationalism – Nerik Mizzi. I was a university student then, studying law, but he had already loomed large on my political horizon. Mizzi, son of Fortunato Mizzi, known to his generation as *pater patriae*, was no ordinary man.

As a law student already actively involved in student politics as a member of the Student Representative Council, I was very much interested in Nerik Mizzi. One day his son, Natolino, whom I knew from my childhood at St Joseph High School in Valletta – he was my captain at the Crusaders of the Blessed Sacrament (CBS) when I was only six – made arrangements for me to see his father.

When I went to their house in Strada San Giovanni, opposite the church of Ta' Giesu, Natolino, then a student of theology, opened the door for me and took me straight to his father's study. Mizzi, fairly tall with a prominent head, rather bald, received me warmly.

'What course are you following, young man?'

'I am taking law.'

'And how many are you in the course?'

'About twenty.'

Nerik Mizzi was hard of hearing and thought I had said a hundred and twenty.

'*Figlio mio*,' he said with some apparent concern, '*morirai di fame … morirai di fame.*'

When I told him we were actually only 20, not 120, he chuckled, pointing to his ears to explain away his hearing problem. I raised the pitch of my voice a bit and the little talk we had went on smoothly.

1

I can never forget the time he spent talking to us in his study. He spoke about politics, the political situation in the island, and, above all, about integrity in politics. Then he turned to me and to his son and said:

'Guido, you have taken up law... you know, that is a profession; Natolino, you have taken up the priesthood, that is a vocation.'

Turning directly to me again, he said, '... and politics is a mission'.

His words infused me with a political passion that has remained with me throughout my lifetime in politics.

Nerik Mizzi had been prime minister then for only two months. It was Mizzi who, together with Sir Ugo Mifsud, gave the Nationalist Party its modern structure in the late twenties. When Italy joined the war, in June 1940, Mizzi, an elected member of the Council of Government, was interned, together with a number of other Maltese, and later illegally exiled to Uganda. During the first world war, he had been arrested and court-martialled on a trumped-up charge and sentenced to one-year imprisonment, but the governor changed the sentence to a serious warning.

On his return from Uganda, he again took his place in the Council of Government, having become sole leader of the Nationalist Party on the death of Sir Ugo Mifsud in February, 1942. When the Labour Party split in 1950, the Nationalist Party found itself having a relative majority in the legislative assembly and Mizzi was asked by Governor Sir Gerald Creasy to form a government. Mizzi, for so many years considered an enemy of the colonial government, formed a minority government, thus becoming prime minister. To the Nationalists, and particularly to me as a young Nationalist who had admired Mizzi so much for his outstanding character and integrity, it was a dream come true.

But unfortunately for Malta he died on December 20, 1950, only four weeks after he ushered me into politics. The meeting I had with him when I was still a student has marked my life ever since. It was he who set me on a voyage with a mission.

*   *   *

I was born in Valletta on July 22, 1931, the year when the Carmelite Friars of Valletta were celebrating the fiftieth anniversary of the coronation of the painting of Our Lady of Mount Carmel above the high altar. As my mother was a great devotee of Our Lady, she was looking forward to taking part in the festivities and indeed prayed that my birth be delayed till after the feast. I was duly born six days after the event.

2

My parents lived in a flat in Strada San Cristoforo (street names were still in Italian then), Valletta, in an area known as 'Il-Biċċerija', for an abattoir the Knights of Malta had in their time. My father used to run St Rocco Baths, on the Marsamxett side of Valletta that belonged to my father's family on his mother's side. Public baths were a novelty at the time. They provided swimming facilities, changing rooms, a bar, and restaurant to people in Valletta and surroundings areas, as well as to Royal Navy personnel stationed in Malta.

My father was doing fairly well financially. The day before I was born, my mother had stayed at the restaurant of St Rocco Baths till late in the evening as it was a very hot day. I was born at six in the morning as recounted in detail in my baptism certificate. I was baptised at St Dominic Church or, to give it its proper name, the church Our Lady of Porto Salvo. I hold this church in great affection, knowing full well the sterling work the Dominican Fathers have done over the centuries in an area of the city where many lived in difficult financial circumstances. By tradition my family is linked to the parish of St Paul, and as a child I could never understand the keen rivalry that existed between the two parishes. Its root is possibly political in nature as shown by the fact, for example, that La Vallette Band Club is associated with the Nationalist Party while King's Own was linked with the now long extinct Constitutional Party, Strickland's party.

My family background provides an interesting study of Maltese society and politics in the 1930s. The de Marcos have been in Malta since the 1690s. According to family tradition, the first de Marco to have come to live in Malta was a medical doctor who had graduated from the medical schools in Salerno and Montpellier. He was a physician to the Grand Master. It appears that the Knights were at the time seeing prospects of establishing good relations with the Barbary States, so much so that when one day the Grand Master learned that the Bey of Tripoli was sick, he sent de Marco immediately to his aid. But, according to a document I traced at the Public Library in my student days, de Marco had no cure for him and '*dottor de Marco ritornò a Malta in disgrazia*'.

My grandfather, Salvatore, worked at the Palace in Valletta at the beginning of the twentieth century. He was responsible for its upkeep and was highly regarded by the governor and the colonial administration. I still keep a silver cigarette box donated to him by the governor's staff on his marriage in 1895, engraved with the signatures of the permanent members of the Palace staff. I also keep a silver inkpot donated to 'Mr Salvo de Marco' by the Duke of Connaught at Christmas in 1905. Who could have told him that his grandson would one day become president of Malta and have as his office the Palace where he worked and had his living quarters? Salvatore de Marco was married to Susanna Zammit. On the Zammit side, the family was in business and, by the standards of the time, was rather well off. Indeed, my grandmother was given as dowry a house in Prince of Wales Road (Triq Manwel Dimech) in Sliema. The rent from the house enabled her to employ a maid.

My father, Emanuele, was born in December 1902, the second son of five children. My grandfather died in 1908, leaving his family still very young; my father was looked after at times by his mother Susanna who was known to be rather capricious in nature, believing that, for a lady of her standing, her children need not be made to undertake any particular study because they could live off income from her property. As a child, my father preferred to stay with his uncle, Michele Zammit. Zio Kelin, as we called him, was a successful businessman, and after the First World War, could live off his earnings as a *benestante*. His marriage to a distinguished lady, Giovanna Schembri, was, as it were, on a 'hiccups' basis. Each time the couple broke away for any length of time, my father stayed with his mother. This appears to have disrupted his upbringing, at least in so far as schooling was concerned. Zio Kelin was a staunch Nationalist, a member for many years of La Vallette Band Club and therefore very close to the parish of St Paul Shipwrecked in Valletta. He had a lasting influence on my father, giving him a bearing and a sense of gentility that stood him up in difficult days.

As a child, my sister Carmen, who was 21 months older than me, was more inclined to mischief than I was. She had a sense of adventure and just loved pranks. On seeing a *karozzin* passing by, for example, she would run after it, climb to the back of the cab, and cling to it for a free ride to anywhere. I admired her daring spirit.

Father was a charming man. He was a pipe-smoker and friends called him 'Mr Pipe'. He just enjoyed running St Rocco Baths, which were built by the Zammit family on land taken on possession and use from the Admiralty. It was at the time he used to run the baths that he got to know my mother Giovanna, who was two years younger. Her parents were from Sicily. My grandfather, Francesco Raniolo, had settled in Malta in 1902, a young shoemaker who had married a Sicilian girl, Consolata Presti, some time before. Grandfather Raniolo came from Vittoria and grandmother from Gela. The young couple started their family life at Gela, where their first son, Salvatore Giovanni, was born in 1902. By that time, grandfather Raniolo had already decided to settle in Malta and, after finding a house in

Hamrun, brought his bride over. Grandmother Consolata had gone back to Gela for a time when she was about to give birth to my mother. It was not the custom at the time to give birth in hospital and grandmother did not find it acceptable either to stay in a place where she knew very few people. So she preferred Gela to Malta as a place where to give birth. Gela was then known as Terranova. She returned to the island on a schooner when the baby was three weeks old, and remained in Malta.

My grandparents on my mother's side had five children, two born in Sicily and three in Malta. After several years living in Hamrun, they moved to Valletta, in a house next to Palazzo Carafa in Strada Forni (Triq il-Fran). Palazzo Carafa then housed a very popular Italian school, Umberto Primo. My mother used to recall to me how the children at Umberto Primo used to walk down Strada Reale singing patriotic songs when in 1915 Italy joined the war allied to Great Britain and France against the 'Central Empires'. She would also endlessly describe to me the festivities held at the end of the war in 1918 when she was only 13.

My mother was very intelligent; her studies at Umberto Primo must have been very fruitful for, apart from speaking excellent Italian, she could also speak well in English, and had some knowledge of French, too. She was also a good businesswoman, assisting her father who had a fashionable shoe store in Strada Teatro, corner with Strada Forni, as well as a small haberdashery. Had she continued with her studies, I am sure she would have been a good scholar. A younger brother died in his youth. She had two sisters, Maria, who married an Italian, Vincenzo Benzoni, in 1938, and Ermelinda, who married a Maltese, Emanuel Xuereb, in 1935.

Mother and father were different in character. Mother could be stubborn, rather prudish in her beliefs; father was easier going, with a ready smile, always ready to oblige, and, in his younger days, had a zest for life. His upbringing with his uncle distanced him from the de Marco side, who were civil servants close to the colonial administration. His marriage to my mother, an Italian girl brought up in Malta, placed him in the classical Nationalist background of the thirties.

The thirties were difficult times for Malta and for my parents in particular. One day grandmother Susanna was in one of her capricious moods. She decided that if my father wanted to carry on running St Rocco Baths, he had to pay an annual rent, which, if I remember rightly, was of about £120. A top civil servant's salary rarely reached that amount and, besides, St Rocco Baths only opened for four months a year; clearly father could hardly accept the demand. So, he suddenly found himself jobless. He then ran a coffee shop, 'Haven Bar', in St Lucia Street, corner with Strada Stretta (Triq id-Dejqa) on a rental basis. Since it was close to the law courts, it became a haven for lawyers who frequented it on their breaks in between court sessions.

I was six when I started attending, together with my sister Carmen, St Joseph's High School in Strada Zaccaria in Valletta. It was run by the nuns of St Joseph of the Apparition. Out of my father's earnings, mother first used to put aside the money that had to be paid as tuition fees. During my school holidays, I used to go with my mother to see father at the coffee shop. I used to enjoy listening to lawyers talk law and politics. An artist who also frequented the coffee shop regularly and whom I distinctly remember from the time is Oscar Testa, who used to spend time drawing faces of people that held his attention. Testa later married a relative of Pope Pius XII in Rome. I remember seeing a beautiful portrait of the pope painted by the artist. After the war, he was brought to Malta, together with a number of other Maltese, and charged with treason. They were all found not guilty. Some years ago, a relative of his gave me some of his ink drawings, which I treasure.

There was a time when father was not doing well and I remember difficult moments when mother used to go and ask him for a few shillings before going to the market and father showing her an almost empty till. Grandmother Susanna had little regret for what she had done to her son and to us all in the family. Indeed, she used to tell mother not to continue sending me and my sister to St Joseph's High School, which, she said, was frequented by children of lawyers and doctors.

One day, when times were really hard, my mother asked Mother Superior if she could reduce the school fees. She did, but told her not to tell the nuns about it and to pay the reduced fee directly to her. But eventually one of the nuns appeared to have got wind of the arrangement and used to put my sister Carmen to endless embarrassment when she used to ask her in front of other children, 'Did you get the fee?' These are memories that last a lifetime. But I have no resentment. If anything, they made me strongly aware of the plight of those parents who, in spite of their limited financial means, do their very best to give their children the best education possible, as my parents did to us. We had very limited means; indeed, at times we were very close to poverty, but we were never poor in values. My parents gave me the best education possible – they taught me a sense of honesty and goodness, correctness, and integrity. Mother in particular made me appreciate the true values of the Catholic faith, its substance more than its form.

I grew up trilingual. We spoke Maltese and Italian at home, and of course we spoke Italian with my maternal grandparents. Even though grandmother Raniolo lived close to forty years in Malta, she never did master the 'ħ' in Maltese and 'ħabel' was always '*abel*'. I did not think that making childish fun of her, as we so very often did, helped her improve pronunciation. I grasped the English language from an early age. Financial considerations apart, I had a very happy childhood. In the space of five years after my birth, we moved house three times. We lived for a time in Floriana, in Strada Miratore (Triq il-Miratur), then in Strada Zecca (Triq iz-Zekka), and, the house I remember most, 17, Strada Stretta, corner with Strada San Giovanni.

My sister and I owe our self-discipline trait to mother. It was she who instilled in us the concept of doing what is right. For recreation she used to take us to Il-Biskuttin, the open space in front of the Hotel Phoenicia. My cousins from the Raniolo side used to be there, so were the children of Professor Arnaldo Fabriani. He used to teach Italian at the Lyceum and is the author of *Malta Fior del Mondo*, pubished under his pen-name Aldo Farini. He was known to be an anti-Fascist and, for some time after the war, he was a Christian Democrat member of the Italian House of Representatives.

At the Biskuttin, we used to play near the majestic statue of Christ the King by Antonio Sciortino. Whenever, in later years, I read Dun Karm's poem '*Waħdek, ġwejjed, b'mixjietek sabiħa, b'dik il-ħarsa mitfugħa 'l quddiem, fejn int sejjer, o Bniedem, o Alla, fommok mimli bil-kelma tas-sliem?*', it brought back memories of my younger days in Floriana. The figure of Malta at Christ's feet in this monument is quite realistic. When, as a child, I used to watch the procession of Christ the King, and see so many people, members of religious organisations, and personalities stop in front of this statue, to the singing of '*Noi vogliamo Dio che' è nostro padre, noi vogliamo Dio che' è nostro Re*', I used to feel a great sense of belonging to the faith of our fathers. At that time, I remember mother telling me about the persecution of the Catholics in Mexico and, later, about the Civil War in Spain. I used to be so impressed by the story of Padre Miguel Pro of Mexico who, on facing the firing squad, bravely responded to the bullets with the words '*Viva Cristo Re*'.

At the Biskuttin, we used to play the very simple games all children played at the time, such as hide and seek (*noli*), games now long discarded in preference to computer games. A boy from those times still firmly in my memory is Maurice Abela who in adulthood made his mark as chief government statistician and ambassador to Rome and Vienna. He used to test my arithmetic skills, making me recite for him countless number of tables. He was only three years older than me but he already had a great head for figures. But my strongest memory is of Padre Faustino, a Capuchin friar of great personal holiness. He belonged to a Maltese noble family and was a renowned painter of religious subjects. When I grew up and used to hear Mass at the Holy Trinity church in Marsa, I greatly admired his paintings in that church. Padre Faustino was a kind person and, whenever we saw him coming towards us at the Biskuttin, we all used to run to him. He would always have an orange or some other fruit for us.

On our way back home, we would first stop at St Francis church in Strada Reale (Triq ir-Repubblika). I love this church. My sister and I used to 'appropriate' an altar each; she would invariably opt for the altar of the Immaculate Conception and I for that of St Anthony. On the feast days of Our Lady and of the saint respectively, these two altars would be spectacularly decorated with flowers. I also particularly enjoyed the feast of St Francis. Giuseppe Calì's frescoes showing *The Glory of St Francis* are simply enchanting. Mother used to tell me that Calì had his *bottega* in Strada Forni, close to my grandfather's house. He was once keen to do a portrait of my mother. He used to say she had an angelic face.

The fresco of *The Death of St Francis* in the same church is indeed very touching. The Franciscan Conventuals, as the friars of this Order are known, were an interesting community. Padre Fiorini was a big man with a resounding voice; he came from an Italian family that had settled in Malta some decades earlier. The father provincial at the time was Padre Tabone but the friar I liked best was Padre Deguara because he helped me set up a small altar at home, complete with tabernacle and holy vestments. It was common for children in those days to build a model of a church at home. With my savings I used to buy small candlesticks and statuettes of the apostles from Bethlehem Bazaar in Strada Mercanti.

Mother also used to take Carmen and I to my maternal grandfather's shoe store. I used to enjoy it but grandfather Raniolo was not so keen on seeing us going in and out of his shop all the time. However, he was a kind man and, whenever I needed a new pair, he would let me have one. We used to just love going to grandfather's place on the feast day of Our Lady of Mount Carmel. When the statue of our beautiful Madonna arrived close to his shop, a searchlight would be directed towards it, making Our Lady appear beautiful and glorious. Every year, on her feast day, when I go for the Pontifical Mass, Our Lady appears as beautiful in my eyes as it did when I was a child.

These are memories of my childhood in Valletta at a time when the rumblings of World War II were getting closer. When Italy invaded Ethiopia, there was lively talk about it at grandfather's shop. Grandmother gave her wedding ring, *la fede*, for the war effort and had it substituted for one of ordinary metal. I am not sure if she was really pleased at this exchange. The rumblings grew with the Spanish Civil War. I have a feeling the family was pro-Franco. I remember seeing in the Church's newspaper, *Leħen is-Sewwa*, a picture of some 'Bolshevists', as they were described, holding the heads of some priests. Nor can I forget the story of the Siege of the Alcazar and the bravery shown by the son of its commander. When the 'Republicans' told him to persuade his father to give up the fort, as he would otherwise be shot, he told his father he would rather die than see him give up Alcazar. When I grew older, I could well understand that the Spanish Civil War had another dimension. It was the curtain raiser to World War II.

2

My childhood days

Who can ever forget one's first day at school! We went to the school in Strada Zaccaria, Valletta, run by the nuns of St Joseph of the Apparition. Even though I was only five, I felt so happy going to school. I even remember the name of my first teacher, Miss Miruzzi. She was a kind woman and looked at me quite favourably for being able to speak Italian. Like all children starting their school life, I struck new friendships, some of whom have lasted a lifetime.

The summer before I started going to school, mother used to take me for private lessons. The teacher's name was Italia Liberto but we all called her 'Miss Italia'. She must have surely been Italy's first Miss Italia! She also introduced me to the alphabet and sums. My first years at St Joseph's were easy and pleasant. My problem was my handwriting. It was, is, and will remain horrible.

Once I was kept after hours for an offence that was not, at least in my view, subject to school discipline. There was a boy, Louis, whom at school they used to call '*Louis Fellus*'. He must have been seven or thereabouts. One day I happened to be on the doorstep of my father's shop and saw this boy coming down Strada Santa Lucia with his mother. For some funny reason or other, I called him out loud by his nickname. His mother was not amused at all and reported me to the nuns. As I was about to leave school at 3.30 p.m. that day, eagerly looking forward to seeing mother, who used to take me to the Biskuttin after school, I was told I had to stay in class for calling the boy by his nickname. I felt humiliated and believed I was being punished unfairly. I had not misbehaved at school and, anyhow, all children were called by a nickname at some time or other. To make matters worse, a boy in my class went to my mother and told her in a loud voice '*Guido illum qieghed in penance.*' So, one of my first lessons in life was to avoid over-familiarity.

11

I received religious instruction in preparation for my First Holy Communion at St Joseph's. Apart from my wedding day, I think the day I received my First Holy Communion, in May 1937, at the church of Sta Caterina d'Italia, was the happiest in my life. I still remember the white suit, the armband in gold braid, and the religious medal I wore. After I had my picture taken at The Oxford Studio, just opposite our school, mother took me to see my grandparents. I was thrilled with the presents I got: a missal, rosary beads in a lovely box, and a half-crown.

I received Confirmation a year later. For a present, my godfather, Zio Johnny, gave me a fine wristwatch with a grey leather strap. As it happened, I smashed its glass face some time later when grandfather took me to an opera matinee show at the Royal Opera House and I slipped during the interval. Confirmation was administered by Bishop Michael Gonzi, then Bishop of Gozo, who was acting for Archbishop Maurus Caruana, who was indisposed. At the Confirmation, I was asked, together with a girl, to 'crown' a statue of Our Lady with a crown of roses. As the 'crowning' was taking place, the congregation sang 'O Mary, we crown thee with blossoms today, Queen of the angels and Queen of May.'

All in all, school was a pleasant experience. Doing my homework was no hardship. I had managed to do first and second class in one year. The nuns were highly dedicated and I particularly remember Sister Emma for her knowledge, teaching style, and affection. She was the sister of Father Savona, a Jesuit who would later teach me mathematics at St Aloysius College, and would become Father Provincial at one time. Sister Emma lived to an advanced age. She spent her last years at St Joseph's Convent in Rabat. I went to see her once at the time I was president and staying at Verdala Palace. She was frail but was still very clear in her mind and as loving as ever.

Another nun whom I used to hold in great affection was Sister Nellie. She had such a sweet face. When I learned she was terminally ill, I once made it a point of going to see her in hospital. I was still an MP then. On her death bed, she told me she was offering her sufferings for her country, Ireland, and for Malta, both of which were passing through difficult times in the late seventies. I also recall with affection Sister Christopher, an American with a ready twinkle in her eyes. Then there was an Irish nun whom I mostly remember for her beauty. Yes, Sister Imelda was one of the most beautiful women I have ever seen. Even at such an early age, I could already feel the magnetic pull of a beautiful woman.

The late thirties were difficult years internationally. It must have been during the Munich crisis when schoolchildren were taken in procession to

St John's co-cathedral to pray for peace. We sang beautiful hymns and the nuns prayed *'Parce domine, parce populum tuum'* (Have mercy, O Lord, have mercy on your people). We were Crusaders of the Blessed Sacrament and we used to refer to the abbreviated form of the name CBS as cruiser, battleship, and submarine. We were divided into groups, with a captain each as leader. As I said earlier, my captain was Natolino Mizzi, the boy who arranged my meeting with his father, Nerik Mizzi, when he was prime minister. Both Nerik Mizzi and his son had to pass through very difficult years. But at that time, the immediate concern was the oncoming war. Hitler had set his eyes on the Sudeten, the part of Czechoslovakia where Germans lived. He wanted to reunite all Germans in a Grossdeutchland and had also set his eyes on Eastern and Central Europe as the Lebansraum for the German people. Up till today, I still cannot fully understand how such a great people, as the Germans undoubtedly are, succumbed to Adolf Hitler and his doctrine. We are speaking of the country of Goethe and Wagner, of Beethoven and Hegel, a people that for the most part of them had Prussian discipline in them and, also, great sentiment as shown by their poetry.

I remember once raising the point with Duncan Sandys, the former secretary of state for the colonies and Commonwealth relations, whom I got to know fairly well when he led the UK delegation to the Council of Europe in Strasbourg. We were at the home of Charles Zaegel, for many years secretary of the cultural affairs committee of the parliamentary assembly, a person of great affability and culture, and I remember saying to him in conversation that I could never understand how Hitler had managed to persuade the German people to believe in him and to vote for him when he had made his ideas so clear in his *Mein Kampf*.

Duncan Sandys said he was a second secretary at the British Embassy in Berlin at the time and that, had he been a German, he, too, would have voted for Hitler. Many Germans saw in Hitler the only hope for national resurgence and for the country to win back the national pride lost after the defeat and humiliation of the Versailles Treaty and the failure of the German economy in the late twenties, when many of Germany's middle class were reduced to paupers. As against Stresemann, who stood for reconciliation with the French and membership of the League of Nations, Hitler brought the Saar back to Germany, suspended or cancelled war debts, rearmed Germany, solved the unemployment problem, and made Germany proud again of being *Uber Alles*. Great demonstrations and highly emotional meetings made the Germans proud at having *'Ein Volk, ein Reich, ein Führer'*.

Dictatorship, the horror of concentration camps, and the mass killing of the Jews, and all the disasters of war, came after, but in 1932 Hitler represented to the people the future of Germany, the rebirth of the German Reich.

I am not all that convinced Duncan Sandys was right. But eventually Duncan Sandys fought Hitler, was wounded in the war, and received the Military Cross. Sandys could see a side of Hitler that to this day I cannot accept. Mussolini was realising that Hitler had better be accommodated in some way or other and that anyhow Italy was not ready to go to war in spite of all his bombast and make-believe.

Chamberlain was a pragmatic conservative. He realised that for more than a decade successive British governments, far from arming Britain to face any possible German aggression, had moved towards a sheepish pacifism wilfully shutting eyes to the challenges posed by both Hitler and communism. Chamberlain realised he needed time to rearm Britain. Munich was for him the time-frame he needed for rearmament. His major mistake was, of course, that of giving the impression that at Munich he had succeeded in bringing 'peace in our time'. Edouard Deladier realised that France was not in a fighting mood, or prepared for war. The Maginot Line defence syndrome had completely taken over. For a brief time Mussolini gave the impression he was mediating to avert war. On his way from Munich to Rome by train, he was given a hero's welcome. After the war in Ethiopia and Spain, the Italian people were not in any war mood. But Hitler certainly was, and he galvanised the German people in their dream of a Grossdeutchland. Following Versailles and massive unemployment in the wake of the Wall Street crash, the German people truly believed that their moment of glory and power was worth the loss of democracy. The stage was set for one of the world's major wars in which millions of lives were lost.

The *dramatis personae* in all this were not foreign to me. Although I was only eight, I keenly followed Maltese newspapers, *Leħen is-Sewwa*, *Times of Malta*, as well as the Sunday edition of *Il Corriere della Sera* at my grandparents' house. I found it difficult finding the right wavelength on the radio we had at home, but father usually did in no time by banging on its top. At school, we were all so excited when we first tried on gas masks, looking ourselves in the mirror.

3

The day that changed my life

I was with grandfather Raniolo, going down Strada Forni, when an Italian friend of his told him, '*I tedeschi hanno sfrondato la linea Maginot.*' Grandfather turned white as he now realised that Mussolini would join Hitler in the war and turn the *Patto d'Acciaio* into a reality. The news put my family on high alert. I remember grandfather speaking to my grandmother about what this might mean to them all. How would their lives change if Italy joined Hitler's Germany? My mother and relatives shared the same concern. Would it spell the end of their forty years in Malta, with all that it had involved in setting up a family here and a profitable business? Would they be interned or deported? Some thought Malta would be taken by Italy *a giro di vapore*; by the time they were deported, they would be back, as Malta would have surrendered. Wishful thinking! Some days later I vividly remember someone telling me that Mussolini was scheduled to speak from Palazzo Venezia in Rome and that his speech would be transmitted on radio. It was June 10, 1940. I was not yet nine. I went to hear Mussolini's speech at my uncle Gianni's in Strada San Cristoforo. We were all very worried. The *Duce* then started his harangue and declared war with Britain and France.

It is difficult to describe the tension that gripped the family. The children in the room felt it too. Zia Elen, who was pregnant, was all in tears. We were overcome by a sense of an impending horror, for we were well aware by now of what was already happening in Poland, France, Holland, and Belgium. Barely an hour after Mussolini's declaration of war, the police were all over Valletta, rounding up people of Italian nationality. By that time, I had already gone to my grandparents' home. Mother was already there, too. The police called for grandfather who left us all putting on a brave face. He kissed each and every one of us, saying he would be back soon. He was devastated and in tears. We rushed to the balcony to see him get on the bus, but he had already got in and he waved to us from a window. Besides grandfather, the police had already rounded up some relatives.

Mother and grandmother Raniolo were concerned over the possible fate of Professor Arnaldo Fabriani as, being an anti-Fascist, they were sure he might have a difficult time returning to Italy. His wife was expecting a baby at any moment. Later that evening, my mother, sister, and I went to father's shop. The air was heavy. Weeks before, a number of Maltese of Nationalist sentiments, including the co-leader of the party, Nerik Mizzi, had also been rounded up and interned. Just a few days before the outbreak of war, when we were returning home from Floriana, we saw a crowd shouting slogans against the Nationalists. I later got to know from my mother that the crowd had first smashed a marble slab commemorating Fortunato Mizzi, the founder of the Nationalist Party, in retaliation for the putting up of a bust of him at the Pincio in Rome. All this helped raise the tension in the family even further. Would father also be interned for his Nationalist beliefs? Malta and the Nationalist Party were passing through difficult and conflicting times.

At this point, it may be useful to put these fears against a historical background. The Italian language and culture in Malta date back to around the twelfth century. At the dawn of the Italian language, when Latin was being supplanted by the *Volgare* in Sicily and in Italy, Italian was already spoken in Malta. It was used not only in the administration of the country but also in everyday life.

Maltese is a blend of basic words from the Semitic language and the richness of a Romance vocabulary. I find in the Maltese language a lasting evidence of our identity, a coagulant of our people, no matter their particular origin. Italian was the language of culture through which for centuries generations of Maltese communicated with the outside world. When the Spanish were in Malta, it was not the Spanish language that was used by those who administered the country, but Italian and, depending on the solemnity of the occasion, Latin. When the Knights of St John came to Malta in 1530, they followed the language used by the Università, the municipal authority, even though Italian knights were in a minority. When Napoleon Bonaparte took over Malta in 1798, proclamations were issued both in Italian and in French, and, when the British came, laws and regulations were issued in Italian first. Even the governor's invitations to balls and receptions at the Palace were in Italian. English was an alien language to the people. Imagine, hypothetically, what the situation would be

16

like today if Japan were to take over Malta! How many Maltese can speak Japanese? English had to be introduced gradually.

The historical position became more complicated for the British government when two events radically changed the strategic value of the island. The first was when Britain made of its political presence in Malta a determining factor in its global outreach, particularly when the Suez Canal was built in 1869. The Suez Canal radically reduced the time required to reach India, the subcontinent that made of Great Britain the world's leading naval power, with an empire over which the sun never set. In the geography books we had when we were young, British territories were all marked in red, whether they were in Africa, Asia, or the Americas. The red made clear the greatness of Britain. To the strains of 'Rule Britannia', the world was made aware of Britain's might and power and, in our case, of Malta's importance as a fortress and link to this great empire. When Winston Churchill, then secretary of state for the colonies, was told that the Maltese were demanding a self-government constitution, his terse reply was reported to have been, 'What, a constitution for a battleship?'

The movement for self-government had started in 1880 by a Maltese lawyer, Fortunato Mizzi. He was helped at first by a young aristocrat whose mother was a Maltese noble lady and his father an Englishman belonging to a Catholic noble family. His name was Gerald Strickland. But the nationalism of Gerald Strickland was short-lived. He was soon offered the post of chief secretary to the government by the colonial government, a post he took up with zest and with a certain competence but he renounced his Nationalist sympathies.

In June 1919, the Maltese workers who during the First World War had contributed so much, mainly through their hard work at HM Naval Dockyard, to make the Royal Navy supreme in the Mediterranean, found themselves facing unemployment and misery. At the *Giovane Malta* premises, a national assembly was meeting to draft a self-government constitution for Malta. The rest is history. The Maltese started demonstrating against British rule; students joined the workers and, in one protest, a British flag flying from a public building was pulled down from its mast. The crowd started getting out of hand. A reserve British armed detachment opened fire and Malta had its first martyrs under British rule. Four Maltese were killed. The printing press of the *Daily Chronicle*, an English-language newspaper owned by the Bartolo family, was ransacked; the house of the Francia family, importers of wheat, was also attacked, as well as other places considered by demonstrators as having been owned or run by sympathisers of the colonial administration. The crowd, believing that Nerik Mizzi was their leader in the fight against British imperialism, walked to his home for moral support. Both Dr (later Sir) Ugo Mifsud and Mizzi did their best to calm the crowd, as did the Bishop of Malta, Dom Maurus Caruana.

In the light of all this, the British government realised it had to change tactics. It appointed as governor Field Marshal Lord Plumer, a First World War hero. Plumer sensed the mood for change and reforms. Malta had its first self-government, complete with a cabinet and a bicameral assembly. The people's patriotism had prevailed and a great sense of moderation and ability had produced a political class able to put into practice a democracy, with a multi-party system.

We still consider the *Sette Giugno* as the event that set in motion Malta's parliamentary evolution. We passed through difficult times and although the constitution was suspended and revoked several times over the years, the Maltese people realised two very important principles. The first was that they were able to govern themselves with much better results than if they were under any foreign domination, and the second, that no constitution given by the British government could guarantee our sovereignty except one granting independence.

The road ahead was difficult indeed. Strickland tried to consolidate British dominance over Malta, politically, culturally and economically, and had a moderately successful career in the colonial service, ending up as governor of New South Wales in Australia. He came back to Malta four years before Malta was given its first self-government constitution. Strickland was determined to wipe out the Italian language in Malta in the interests of Britain's hold over the island. The Nationalist Party had great leaders; they represented Malta's intelligentsia, which had its roots in ordinary people. The clergy was also strong in its support for Maltese nationalism. Muscat Azzopardi, Ninu Cremona, Prof. Anastasio Cuschieri, and an up-and-coming student, Carmelo Mifsud Bonnici, were prolific writers in Maltese, ensuring a revival of our language. They were prominent in their support of the Nationalist Party and indeed some represented the party in the legislative assembly.

Strickland, on the other hand, managed to make the Nationalist Party appear hostile to the Maltese language in its defence of Italian culture. It was a political mistake, one that had serious repercussions. How could Italy accept, without any reaction, the British government's and Strickland's moves to stifle a culture that had been part of Malta's intellectual heritage for over seven centuries? The language issue divided the people, albeit artificially, into two camps, the pro-Italian and the pro-British. The division lasted for more than fifty years, covering the war years until the Nationalist leader and prime minister George Borg Olivier won Malta's independence from Britain in 1964. Independence was won mainly through the diplomatic skill of Borg Olivier and of the Nationalist Party, and, of course, through the popular support won in a cold war context, when the internal conflicts of yesterday became history and the future of an independent Malta, in friendship with Great Britain and its Nato allies, including Italy, beckoned.

My mother,
Giovanna.

My father,
Emanuele.

Grandfather Salvatore de Marco.

Grandfather Franceso Raniolo

Grandmother Susanna de Marco.

Adelaide Zammit, my great grandmother.

Great uncle Michele Zammit (Kelin).

Mother and father at St Rocco Baths.

Grandmother and grandfather Consolata and Francesco Raniolo with their three daughters, aunt Ermelinda, my mother, and aunt Maria at the entrance to St Rocco Baths in Valletta.

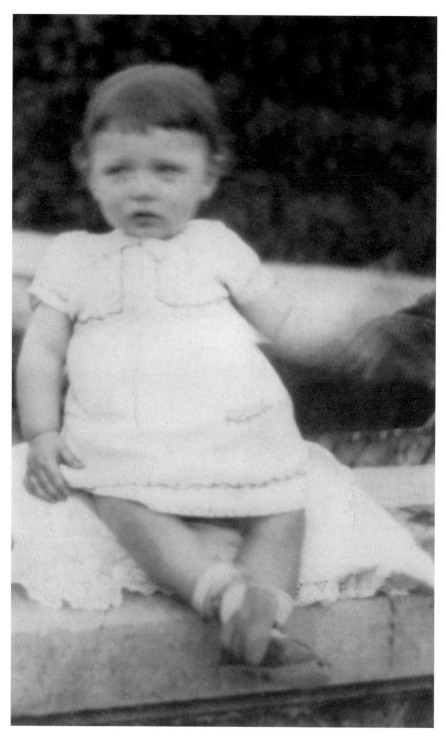

Not yet one.

My First Holy Communion.

My sister Carmen at il-Biskkutin in Floriana.

Wolf cubs, St Aloysius Scouts Group: first, clockwise, facing camera.

The matriculation class at St Aloysius College in 1946. I am first, left, standing. On right is Daniel Micallef, and third from left, front row, is Edwin Grech.

With Fr Gerald Seaston and members of the Classical Society.

The Royal Opera House shortly after it was destroyed in one of the heaviest raids during World War II.

Lord Gort handing over the George Cross to Chief Justice Sir George Borg at the Palace Square, Valletta, on September 13, 1942.

Reading a patriotic poem by V.M. Pellegrini at a commemoration marking September 8 at the Aula Magna at the University of Malta.

Receiving the Doctor of Laws degree on graduation day in 1955.

Carnival time when we were still students.

The Chamber of Legal Procurators in a celebratory mood.

On the reformation of the Societa' Universitaria di Litteratura Italiana in 1948.

Speaking as president of the Student Representative Council at a national congress of students.

Graduation day: First row, from left, Ronald Conti, Anthony H. Farrugia, Prof. Manche, rector,
myself, France Portanier; second row, Joseph Busuttil, Joseph Fenech, Ugo Mifsud Bonnici,
Mario Felice; third row, Joseph Fenech Adami, Rene Frendo Randon, Victor Caruana Colombo
and Joseph Cachia. Absent from the photo are Joseph Zammit Tabona and Gawdenz Borg.

With Ugo Mifsud Bonnici, Victor Caruana Colombo, France Portanier and Gaudenz Borg on the fiftieth anniversary of our graduation.

4

Malta at war

We were all gripped with tension when we went to sleep on the night of June 10/11, 1940. Some time after six in the morning, we heard the first wailing sound of the air-raid siren. Only a few hours after Mussolini had declared war against Britain and France, the *Regia Aeronautica* launched its first air raid over Malta. We took shelter under the staircase. My mother huddled us against her. Then we heard the sound of a bomb explosion. Father was already at his shop by then.

Someone must have informed my parents that grandparents, as well as Zio Gian and other relatives, were about to be deported. They had already boarded the ship that was to take them to Sicily by the time we arrived at Customs House in Valletta. There was great confusion. The early morning raid had disrupted all sense of order. One thing was certain in the mind of an eight-year-old boy: as from that moment his world would no longer be the same. As we waved goodbye, with tears blurring our sight, we tried to catch a glimpse of grandparents as they were leaving harbour. Some think children do not suffer, or tend to see the present without a sense of the past or the future. Well, it did not apply to me.

Il-Biskuttin in Floriana, where we loved to play so much, was no longer ours to go to; we could no longer go to grandfather's shop in Strada Forni to see the world go by; and, above all, we realised that the great sense of happiness and sheltered life we had had up till then was about to be shattered. In no time, Valletta turned into a ghost city, as people moved out. For some months we were allocated temporary housing in Fleur-de-Lys Road, Birkirkara. The house was called 'Costantino'. We stayed in a room upstairs, overlooking the street – my parents, my sister Carmen, and I, all in one room. Zia Ermelinda and Zio Manuel and cousins Lino and Maurice stayed in another room.

The Italian air raids were frequent but rarely effective in so far as the civilian population was concerned. The Savoia Marchetti and the other planes used to fly very high. They used to aim mainly at military targets but, of course, sometimes they missed, hitting houses and killing people. In the war Birkirkara turned into a very thriving city and Fleur-de-Lys became a meeting place. Many from Valletta and Cottonera used to meet there. After the first months, we started getting used to being at war. Like other boys in the area, we used to play in fields behind Fleur-de-Lys.

Also living in Costantino House were a blacksmith and his family and I used to go to his shop to see him at work. My father still ran his coffee shop and bar regularly. Though normal trade was disrupted, a large military presence helped boost business a bit at my father's shop. As my mother thought the war might disrupt our education, we then did what several others had done over time; we left the relative safety of Birkirkara to go back to our house in Valletta. Meanwhile, through the Red Cross, we started getting some letters from my grandparents who had by then settled in Catania, where grandfather opened up a shoe shop in Corso Vittorio Emmanuele; Zio Gian was staying with his parents. Zia Elena, who remained in Malta with her children Marion and Italo, had her baby, but it died some months after birth. I vividly remember when Zia Elena wrote to her husband about this.

Meanwhile, life in Valletta started to pick up again. At St Joseph's High School, lessons were being given as normally as possible. It was all so very strange; Britain was standing alone and enduring its finest hour. The loss of France made the British even more determined. The new prime minister, Winston Churchill, instilled a sense of bulldog resistance, which reveals itself best in adversity. I learned to admire this indomitable trait in the British character and I could well understand what they meant when they said, 'There will always be an England.' We followed events in the desert with great interest. I remember reading in *Il-Berqa* that Bardia had fallen and asking mother what this really meant. The fall of Bardia, she said, meant that the Allies were advancing into Italian Libya. The desert war had a ping-pong effect. By this time we, children, were not only getting accustomed to the war, but we were actually enjoying it. When the air-raid warning sounded, we rarely took cover. Instead, we used to run up to the roof to watch the air attacks or battles. We kept doing this until the *Luftwaffe*'s fierce attack on the aircraft carrier *Illustrious* in harbour, when we learned what war really meant.

I remember seeing the evening before a big, grey plane flying very low. It had a particular drone. Its low flying was very ominous and threatening. When, the following afternoon, the siren announced another air raid, I saw with my own eyes the horror of war. The Stukas, swarms of them, were diving on the *Illustrious* with a horrific, frightening wail. The anti-aircraft guns fired a heavy barrage. A German plane came flying low over our house, so low that I could almost see the pilot's face. Bombs were dropped in Strada Zecca and our house missed a direct hit by just a few seconds. Several people were killed. Now Valletta and the Three Cities were being heavily bombed.

In the first months of 1941 the raids were constant, each lasting hours. On coming out of shelters, we would usually be struck by the extent of the damage – buildings reduced to heaps of rubble and others badly damaged. Yet, we stayed in Valletta, and we used to take shelter just across the road. The shelter under the law courts covered the whole quadrangle formed by Strada Reale, Strada San Giovanni, Strada Stretta, and Strada Santa Lucia. By now street names had been changed to English and Maltese. Although some of my generation still refer to the streets of Valletta by their Italian name, given when the city was founded in 1566, in these memoirs I shall now be using the English names. Only very recently did the Maltese names become the only official names of the streets.

The shelter was very big, looking in shape very much like a big bell with connecting corridors and having exits in Strait Street, Kingsway, and St Lucy Street. I said earlier the air raids were only meant to hit military targets. Not just – the enemy also wanted to break the fighting spirit of the population. We stayed in Valletta throughout the first months of 1941. The night raids were now causing death and ruin. I remember seeing HMS *Terror*, berthed at Marsamxett harbour; it put up quite a stiff anti-aircraft barrage. So did the artillery. In time, we learned to distinguish between the normal anti-aircraft gun and the Bofors. At my father's shop, soldiers, sailors, and airmen had replaced lawyers and court people as clients. The airmen were very popular. Then, suddenly, graffiti 'Bomb Rome' started appearing on walls of buildings, something that revolted me. For sure, Rome was '*caput mundi*', the seat of the Catholic Church; Rome was the Coliseum, the Pantheon, and St Peter's Basilica. Yet, in spite of this sense of revolt in me, I could understand the anger of the people at the destruction of their homes and of the island's palaces.

Life in the shelters created a camaraderie spirit among the people and, sometimes, friction too. Being woken up in the dead of night was a regular ordeal. Each had to carry a folding stool. Mother used to carry a handbag in which she kept the little jewellery she had, which she so cherished. When our financial position got worse, she had pledged the jewellery at the

Monte di Pietà. In fact, she had always considered her trinkets as an insurance if matters got worse.

On March 16, 1941, my great uncle, Zio Kelin died. He had gone to live in Balzan, close to San Anton Palace, at the outbreak of war. We all went to his funeral. Zio Kelin left my sister and I as his heirs and the usufruct to my father. Our financial situation changed for the better, although in times of war one could hardly say how long immovable property would remain intact. The air raids increased in intensity. I remember the sensation of feeling the shelter shake as the explosions were taking place outside. On one particular night in April 1941, we heard one really big explosion. It was a direct hit on the law courts building, the Auberge of the Knights of Auvergne. Suddenly we heard the people scream; others huddled together and prayed fervently. For a few seconds, the shelter shook violently and we were thrown about. We thought our end had come. It was a most frightening experience. The air in the shelter was thick with dust. Then they started bringing in the wounded. The sight and smell of blood brought fear and tears in our eyes. There remained only one shelter exit open, that in Strait Street, close to our house. The others were blocked by debris.

As we emerged from the shelter, we were shocked at the scene of devastation that hit our eyes. That part of Valletta lay in ruins. But our house still stood. Or so we thought. It must have been between 5 and 6 a.m. when father unlocked the door of our house, 17, Strait Street. The door opened on its hinges all right but it led into ruins. Most of the staircase had collapsed. We tried to save as many things as possible, but there was not much that could be saved. We then hurried to father's shop at the end of the block between Strait Street and St Lucy Street, taking with us the bird we had kept and which, luckily, had survived the raid. The shop sign, 'Haven Bar', was still intact, and what a haven the shop proved to be, at least for some time. When the air-raid warning sounded again, we rushed to a shelter under the church of St Paul Shipwrecked. What a shelter! It was packed to capacity and the foul smell emanating from the mass of people in the restricted, air-less quarters of the shelter was simply nauseating. Worse were the drops of water constantly falling from the rock ceiling over our heads. To protect us from the water, Carmen and I were made to wear a kind of scarf that made us look like little monks.

The bombing was horrible and continuous. It was now getting far too close to us. When the air raid ended at dawn, we thought we could get some real sleep at the Haven Bar. But the Haven Bar was no longer there. All that had remained standing of the bar was one solitary wall. Believe it or not, we managed to recover the bird. It seemed that, like cats, it had more than one life. And so, once again we had to move out of Valletta. It was a *Via Crucis* for us, as indeed it had been for so many other people. The law courts and other buildings were completely destroyed and many others damaged. Even St John's co-cathedral was damaged. What a sight we must have looked, mother still holding on to her handbag, and Carmen and I holding the bird in its cage in turns. We managed to get our folding stools, too. Leaving Valletta, the city where I was born, where I lived my happy childhood, and which the war was now turning into ruins, just broke my heart. We moved to a flat in Blata l-Bajda, which father had just inherited from Zio Kelin, and which, luckily, was now vacant. The caretaker kindly let us have a spare mattress which we laid on the floor. And so, cruelly evicted from Valletta by the *Luftwaffe*, we were back in Hamrun. With his shop now reduced to a heap of rubble, father was now looking for a job again.

5

School days during the war

Life in Hamrun was rather unsettling for me. Mother insisted I had to continue to go to school in spite of the heavy air raids. I used to go to Valletta by bus. My friends at the time were Charles Boffa, Lino D. Abela, and Tancred Fleri Soler. When we were about to break up for the summer holidays, I was given a drawing of airplanes attacking Malta! If I remember rightly the 'artist' was Charles Boffa. Charles is a collector of Melitensia and has published studies of Malta at war.

My mother had become a good friend of a woman who lived nearby. Her son attended St Aloysius College and it was this woman who persuaded my mother that I should continue my secondary education at St Aloysius. For some time during air raids, we used to go to her private shelter. Her son had become a doctor and later joined the Society of Jesus. A cousin of his stayed most of the time with his aunt; of all the names, his was Napoleon. He, too, had become a medical doctor. Both of them were my seniors by three years, and I used to go to college with them.

Before I was admitted, I had to do an oral examination in Maltese, English, and Italian. It seems I made a good impression on the prefect of studies because he patted me on the back and said, 'You will do well at college. On my first day, in October 1941, I felt a sense of pride when I saw the pictures on the walls of so many students who had studied there since the beginning of the twentieth century. I got along well with my new school friends. Mother was not amused at all when, on returning home from school that day, I repeated a stupid phrase I had heard from other boys about the prefect of studies, Fr Busuttil, whose nickname was '*Il-Bużaq*'. '*Id-Divina Providenza,*' I said, '*Il-Bużaq qabad ma' Wenza.*' I loved the college. It has influenced my thinking ever since. There could have been no better Jesuit to run the college than Fr Ġużè Delia. He was erudite, sensitive, and had a sense of humour, too, but he was never sarcastic. He

27

was a poet of no mean stature and his legends in verse have not lost any of their appeal.

We had some of the best teachers, some of them Jesuits, others lay priests and laymen. I remember with affection Fr Bernard (*Il-Bunny*); Fr Naudi; Fr Divine; Canon George Sciriha, whose enthusiasm for the Italian language was infectious; Canon Aquilina; and Mr Zammit who were good teachers of mathematics, the Gozitan priests, Dun Franġisk and Dun Anġ, not brilliant but very kind; and, later, as the war was coming to a close, Fr Bartolomew Vella, who was responsible for discipline, and whom we used to call, very unkindly, 'the beast of Belsen'; Fr Pace, who resembled *Il Duce*, Fr Savona, a holy Jesuit and an excellent teacher of mathematics and science, later rector and then provincial; Father Darmanin, affectionately known as *Il-Karrozzin*; and Fr Copeland and Fr Firth, who launched the Debating Society. I enjoyed taking part in the events of the Debating Society and I often found myself alternating in the role of prime minister and leader of the opposition.

During air raids, some of the lessons were given in the shelter. The college theatre was turned into a hospital. In our school breaks, we used to play in the college grounds, just as boys do today. The game I loved most was called *ħarba*. I also took part in activities of the Sodality of Our Lady, and simply loved scouting. I started off as a Wolf cub and still remember the day when I was promoted *sixer* at our Għadira camp on September 8, 1943. I remember the date so well because Italy surrendered on that day. The Jesuit Fathers have a knack for targeting students who in their view could make good and intelligent Jesuits. I never felt particularly inclined to join the Society of Jesus, although I have always felt admiration for the virtues and qualities of St Ignatius of Loyola. As for St Aloysius Gonzaga, I thought he was too saintly. At times I did feel a calling for missionary work. In fact, it still does appeal to me. It's in my heart. Both at the college and at the university, I used take an active part in the activities of the Students' Missionary League.

Studying at St Aloysius College was very stimulating. I found the study of Latin a good discipline of the mind. The way the declensions are formed and the syntax make of this language an exercise in logic. I remember mother quickly testing me orally in the declensions before I left for school in the morning. Although she had never studied Latin, she did her best to ensure that I studied them properly. Canon Sciriha, a good teacher of Italian, made us study the language through its literature, and introduced us to Leopardi's 'Sabato del Villaggio' and Manzoni's *I Promessi Sposi*. He was also a poet. The one I remember most of his poems is 'Pasqua di Sangue', which deals with Easter during the war. To be honest, I was not the best of students in mathematics. Fr Divine taught us English language and literature. He was joined later by Fr Copeland and Fr Firth. They imbued me with a great love for English literature: Shakespeare and Wordsworth, Keats and Byron. But Shelley was and remains my favourite English poet. I can still quote with relish 'Ode to a Skylark'. I share with Shelley a sense of studied revolt. This reminds me of the time I wrote an essay on the MacDonald Constitution which had re-introduced a measure of self-government in 1939. It was an expression of resentment at the thought that Malta's right to having or not having a constitution depended on Whitehall's decision. Self-government, I argued, belonged to our people as of right. Fr Firth thought the revolutionary character of my essay 'almost worthy of Shelley himself'. Of the many books I read at the time, *The Meditation of Marcus Aurelius* had a strong impact on me. When I was promoted to the fifth form, mother gave me as a present *The Complete Works of Shakespeare*. I managed to go through them all, including the sonnets, that summer.

There were several students who abandoned their studies during the war. I remember once a woman telling me while I was on my way to school, 'How does your mother send you to school when we are having so many raids?' When I told mother about this, she just hugged me. She did not say a word. But I know that all she wanted to do was to help me build a future for myself. But it was difficult, and sometimes dangerous, going to school. Once we are back on the war, let me recall first the July 1941 E-boat attack on Grand Harbour. From Blata l-Bajda, we used to hear the advance warning of an air raid. Immediately we heard it, we would rush to the shelter father had dug up under our apartment. One day, after an air raid lasting all night, we heard a different kind of explosion. It was a most daring attempt by Italian E-boats to penetrate the boom defence in Grand Harbour. Their aim was to make the place accessible for an invasion. But the E-boats were spotted by radar and brave Maltese gunners under Colonel Ferro did the rest. It was the first and last attempt by the Italians to force the surrender of Malta by sea.

The situation on the island was now worsening by the day. Warships protecting convoys were met with strong naval and air attacks by the Axis. With food shortages now making an impact on the lives of the people, rations were introduced. Our flat in Blata l-Bajda was badly damaged in heavy bombing; once again we found ourselves homeless, refugees. For a few days, we stayed at the house of a distant relative in Balzan; then we moved to Lija, where we were put up at a place called Is-Salvatur, where we had no running water and toilet facilities. Fortunately, we then moved to a lovely palazzo, today called Casa Sant Cassia. We were given the largest room on the roof.

When we first moved to Blata l-Bajda, my father had started work as a salesman with a candle-making factory. Candles were, of course, very much in demand because of the very restricted use of electricity and a shortage of kerosene. But the job lasted for only a short time as business dwindled. So, father was out of work again. Eventually, he found a job as a messenger in the protection office for the three villages of Lija, Attard, and Balzan. The office was close to the statue of St Joseph at the corner of the Percius Garage in Lija. Though Lija was considered as a relatively safe area, it was not all that safe as it was close to Ta' Qali where we used to watch aerial dogfights with almost professional interest. The Messerschmitts were very adaptable fighters and the Hurricanes were no match for their fire power. When, finally, the Spitfires came, the fight was more balanced. RAF pilots were highly popular.

By now, food was becoming scarcer by the day and we had to queue for meals at the so-called Victory Kitchens. The food was almost unbearable to eat. Lack of food and long hours spent in humid badly-ventilated shelters were having their toll on the health of the people, and scabies, a skin infection, became rampant. At the height of the siege, in April, 1942, news spread that King George VI was awarding Malta the George Cross. At college and at home, we considered the award with pride, but there was a feeling Malta was on the brink of surrendering. However, almost overnight the situation began to change. Rommel's advance into Egypt was halted, mainly because of lack of supplies.

Malta played a key role in this through the submarine flotilla based here. Submarines used to leave harbour during the night and torpedo Italian convoy ships carrying supplies to the Africa and Italian armies. The irony is that Rommel must have been well aware of the fact that, while he could not keep up his advance with his Panzer divisions because he had no petrol supplies, Libya had great oil reserves! As Field Marshal Montgomery pushed the Axis forces back from Libya through a carefully-planned counter-attack, American forces under General Dwight Eisenhower landed in North Africa, locking the Axis forces between the two allied armies. When Tripoli fell into British hands, the siege of Malta was lifted. What a relief to return to normality!

When the Santa Marija convoy reached Grand Harbour, with the tanker *Ohio* bringing in fresh supplies of oil, so essential for continued resistance, we realised that the worst part of the war must be over. Malta, battered by Axis bombs and struggling to survive, went on to play an even more important part when, in 1943, it was used as a launching pad for the invasion of Sicily. We then began seeing invasion barges in harbour and Basuto soldiers camped close to the cemetery in Lija. I remember following a detachment of these soldiers marching for Church service. Events were happening fast now. We learned from the radio news that Mussolini had been removed from power following a vote of no-confidence by the Fascist Grand Council. He was replaced by Field Marshal Badoglio, who on the radio stated *La guerra continua a fianco dell'alleato Tedesco*. But Badoglio was working for his country's peace with the Allies, and in fact Italy surrendered on September 8, 1943.

Victory over the Axis forces in the Mediterranean was in part due to the heroism shown by the Maltese people whose sense of resistance and defiance remained indomitable. In its historical context, the heroism was even more remarkable when considering that for years Malta had been denied the right to self-government, that the leaders of the Nationalist Party were first interned and later illegally exiled to Uganda, and that the colonial government had forced its policies against Malta's Latin culture. Even so, we all felt during the worst days of the war that Malta's future stood with the democratic world. Indeed, we fought for democracy when we were being denied democracy. At least Britain as a nation, and the Allies, believed in democracy, while the Axis, apart from the cruelty they inflicted by their actions as occupying forces, stood for the denial of democracy and had dictatorship as part of their ideology. Never were the Maltese so close to the British as during the war years. When King George VI paid a lightning visit to Malta in June 1943, I was there on the harbour bastions with so many other Maltese to greet the King, crying with happiness and shouting 'God save the King'.

6

Peace and its aftermath

After the war, father at first thought of moving to Valletta again but then decided to rebuild his Blata l-Bajda flats through War Damage Commission funds. He kept his job with the government and, when the protection office closed down, he was transferred to the education department and started working at the Lyceum in Valletta and later, at the Lyceum in Ħamrun, which he considered as the best school in the island. He was regarded as a fatherly figure by the students. I could never follow him in his simplicity. My sister Carmen continued her schooling at St Joseph's High School, and the family environment was once again serene as before the war.

I had become an avid reader and my debating skills were improving. In my essays, I was not so good in description but I could keep up an argument with vigour and conviction. I loved languages and I felt at ease writing in English, Italian, and Latin. I started loving Maltese, not so much at St Aloysius College, but through *Il-Moviment tal-Malti għat-Tfal*. It must have been 1944/45 when I started attending *Moviment* talks on Maltese literature at St Gaetano Band in Ħamrun. The founder of the *Moviment* was Kelinu Vella Haber. We had some good lecturers not only in literature but also in civics. Fr Frans Camilleri, who taught me Maltese at St Aloysius, had good ties with St Gaetano Band Club and with the *Moviment tal-Malti*. He was a very approachable person, had a kind smile and a particular style which I liked. *Moviment* members were given the opportunity of broadcasting works over the radio cable network Rediffusion, which at that time had its studios on a ground floor flat in Vincenti Buildings, Valletta. My first broadcast was an essay on 'Arthur Mee, l-akbar ħabib tat-tfal'. Arthur Mee was an English writer who summarised Shakespeare's plays for children. We later had a play on the life of St Cajetan, and we read poems, too. I have continued to love the language since. I was fortunate in having Prof. Ġużè Aquilina, an expert in the language, as my lecturer at university.

VE day was a day of great celebration. We all went to Valletta and gathered at the Palace Square. The fireworks were fantastic, and the streets were all decorated. Bernard Zammit, who had a beautiful house in High Street, Hamrun, close to where we lived, decorated his balcony with red, white, and blue badges, and full-size statues of King George VI and Queen Elizabeth. When the band taking part in the celebration reached Bernard Zammit's house, Mr Zammit offered the bandsmen refreshments and a memento to the band club.

But the war against Japan was still on. In April 1945, we learnt on the radio that Mussolini had been captured by the partisans, shot, and taken to Piazzale Loreto in Milan where he was hanged by the feet at a petrol station, together with his mistress Clara Petacci, and several other leaders of the Fascist Repubblica Sociale Italiana which he had set up in northern Italy. Even though I was still 13, I found the shooting and hanging by the feet of a person who had received so much adulation in his life, a profound lesson in the moving sands of politics. Hitler's suicide was in style with the man. The cruelties of the Nazi regime and the mass killings and gassing in the concentration camps were revolting. The images of the corpses of the millions who ended their life in the gas chambers showed the bitterness of war and the hatred it can unleash. A regime is indeed evil when it manages to make its country's citizens take part in such massive cruelty and genocide, when being a Jew meant a warrant for deportation and murder in the gas chambers, and when it kills innocent people for an ideology. We later got to know of the mass murders committed by the Stalin regime, and of the mass murders at Katim of hundreds of Polish officers by the Soviet authorities.

Before VE day, Churchill and Roosevelt visited Malta on their way to Yalta. I remember seeing Roosevelt at Castille Place, looking frail, sitting in a Husky 'Jeep'. The Yalta meeting was fundamental to a future in which Malta later had a measure of involvement. At Yalta, the United Nations was born as an organisation with high ideals. But it had its limitations from the start. In the light of the fact that the cold war ended in Malta, Churchill was prophetic when he wrote 'From Malta to Yalta and back to Malta'. For the Yalta meeting was in fact the pre-cold war between the Allied nations. Roosevelt was weak in Yalta, giving way to Stalin's demands. Churchill sensed the negative consequences of the Soviet advance into Central and Eastern Europe. His anti-Bolshevist stand put him under no illusion as to what Soviet occupation would mean for these countries that had been the immediate cause of Britain's and France's declaring war against Nazi Germany. Poland and Czechoslovkia as well as the Baltic states were to end up behind the iron curtain, as Churchill so well described it. When my mother saw the red flag of the Soviet Union being carried in outdoor celebrations, she told me, with some foresight, that Bolshevism was as bad as Nazism.

Little did I imagine then that the cold war that started in Yalta would end in Malta, when Bush met Gorbachev in December 1989. This is confirmed by Edward Shevardnadze in his book *The Future is for Freedom*, when he says: 'In Malta, in the midst of a Mediterranean storm, we buried the cold war.' But, of course, no one could see so far ahead at the time. To me as a schoolboy, the end of the war also meant a return to normality. It was a relief seeing shops reopening and goods appearing on the shelves again. Over time, food rations became a substitute for food subsidy.

Roosevelt died at Warm Springs less than a month before VE Day. I had grown to believe in the United States' positive contribution to world freedom. My reading led me to understand Roosevelt's opposition to Churchill's colonialist approach to Britain's possessions and empire. On Roosevelt's death, several students at the college, including myself, wore a black tie. Roosevelt was succeeded by Harry S. Truman, whose first summit with Stalin and Churchill took place in Potsdam. It was to be Churchill's last summit as the British electorate had then voted Labour into power, ushering in Clement Attlee's reforming government.

It was amazing how the electorate, in recognising Churchill's unique contribution to victory and his outstanding leadership when Britain stood alone, saw its future in a Labour administration, which went on to introduce a new concept of the welfare state. Attlee took Churchill's place in Potsdam: of the original trio, only Stalin remained. And he made full use of this fact. When Truman decided to drop the atom bomb on Hiroshima and Nagasaki, we all realised that the face of world warfare had suddenly changed. Nuclear warfare had the effect of putting us all under a suspended death sentence. But, above all, it brought about a greater realisation of the consequences of war. Japan's surrender in August 1945 brought the war to an end.

I did quite well in my GCE examinations, but I found the matriculation exam by far superior. The sixth form, or as it was better known at the time, the matriculation class, was an exercise in school leadership. I had started my studies at St Aloysius at 10 and was now leaving college at 16, ready to go to university. At that time university courses started every three years and I had a standing year. I had enough qualifications to take up work as an emergency teacher, but my parents were against it as they thought – and probably I did too – that, if I started earning a salary, this could tempt me to give up university education. So, even though we lived on my father's small salary and the meagre rents we had from property inherited from my grand uncle, I was discouraged from taking up the job. Instead, I attended university as an 'occasional student'. This meant that I would be allowed to attend lectures, in a selected course, without being entitled to sit for examinations. I opted to take the arts course.

At 16, I was still wearing short trousers. So was another 'occasional student' by the name of Ugo Mifsud Bonnici. At the time boys started wearing long trousers at 18. In no time, we were called to the rector's office. The rector was a quiet gentleman with a political background linked to Strickland and his Constitutional Party. He said he knew we were still young but added with a smile, 'But don't you think that coming to university in short trousers gives the impression of being in a secondary school?' Ugo told him that his long trousers and a new suit would be ready in time for the feast of the Immaculate Conception in Cospicua on December 8, and I was having mine by Christmas. A tailor living close to us, Debono Ross, promised mother he would deliver by Christmas, and she had also somehow managed to modify one of my father's suits to fit me. So I turned up for my 'second' term at the university properly attired, as requested by the rector.

The third year of the arts course had students from both the law and theology courses. The reason for this was simple. The first two years made up a preparatory course. Students who did well in the preparatory course could then follow the arts course up to a BA degree, besides taking the law or theology lectures. Among the students in the third year were Natolino Mizzi; Eddie Borg Olivier, half-brother to George Borg Olivier, then deputy leader of the Nationalist Party; Wallace Gulia; George DeGaetano; Guido Saliba; and George Cassar.

I put my time in my standing year at the university to good use, deepening my knowledge of the classics, reading Russian literature, and dabbling in Thomistic philosophy. The university, then at its old and original seat in St Paul Street in Valletta, was small in terms of number of students but rich in student societies. The Virgil Society was practically in the hands of the Mifsud Montanaro brothers. It was rare to meet students of such intellectual capabilities. The Classical Society was Carmelo Muscat's domain. His knowledge of Greek and Latin was superb. In my view, the *Classical Journal* remains one of the best student publications ever. Albert and Joe M. Ganado, and Hugh Harding before my time, were the leading lights of the Law Society. Their lectures, notes, and in particular the *Law*

Journal showed their commitment to a professional approach to the study of law. The society still functions with a measure of success. Then there was the Literary and Debating Society and the University Sports Club, both the domain of Prof. Fogarty. I followed the activities of the Għaqda tal-Malti (Università) with keen interest.

My time as an 'occasional student' helped me mature in my academic approach to studies as I began to enjoy learning for its own sake. It was also at that time that I made up my mind to become a lawyer. In a way, it was Sir Arturo Mercieca, one of Malta's best chief justices, who indirectly helped me confirm my decision as he made me realise, through his memoirs, *Le mie vicende*, that, through law and the legal profession, I could also contribute to the constitutional and political development of Malta.

As I did not have the money to buy the book – it cost 9s.6d. – I had to read it at the Public Library. As chief justice, Sir Arturo made a name for himself and gave stature to the court of appeal through his very important constitutional judgments in defence of the right of the people to govern themselves. When war broke out, the colonial government forced his resignation and later interned and exiled him to Uganda together with leading members of the Nationalist Party. On his return from Uganda, he started writing articles under the pen-name 'Cato' in the evening English language newspaper *The Bulletin*. He also published a book of poems, *Canti dell'Esilio*. Well, as I said, it was his work that made me decide to take up law.

7

University life

When, on October 1, 1948, we students walked from the university to the Jesuits' church in Valletta for the inauguration of the academic year, life, in Malta was picking up steadily after the devastation of war. The building industry was in full swing, mainly through funds made available by the War Damage Commission for reconstruction. Valletta and the Three Cities had become huge building sites. Although work at the dockyard was in decline following the reduced presence of the Royal Navy in the Mediterranean, there was still a lot of activity by the British forces. The General Workers' Union, which, under Reggie Miller, gave the dockyard workers a political and economic platform, had only been in existence for some five years.

Malta was experiencing a second attempt at self-government, with a diarchic system – an elected government to run internal affairs and an imperial government responsible for reserved matters, which included defence, foreign affairs, immigration, and a long list of reserved powers. In the 1947 elections, the Labour Party won an absolute majority and Dr (later Sir) Paul Boffa became prime minister. Prominent in the cabinet were Arturo Colombo, who was appointed minister of finance, and Dom Mintoff, minister of works and reconstruction. Mintoff and George Borg Olivier were to dominate Maltese politics for several decades.

The Nationalist Party did well in the elections, despite the humiliation it suffered and all the pressure to which it had been subjected by the colonial government and the smear campaign of the Strickland press. It won the second largest number of seats and votes and Nerik Mizzi, just back from exile in Uganda, became leader of the opposition. He had a number of relatively young men in his team – George Borg Olivier, Giuseppe Maria Camilleri, Jackie Frendo Azzopardi, and Alexander Cachia Zammit. Most prominent in the Democratic Action Party (DAP), which represented the 'conservative' element in the country, were Prof. A. Hyzler and Dr Giuseppe Pace. The Constitutional Party was led by Prof. Galea, former university rector, with Mabel Strickland financing it. The Gozo Party and the Jones Party took all the Gozo seats.

The Nationalist Party had somehow managed to survive the war and, in my view, it could have expanded even further at the time if only it had sought to evolve a national social and economic policy while still upholding its national aspirations. In other words, it had to update itself to face the new realities. Sometimes I used to attend sittings of the legislative assembly and I would wonder when I, too, would take my place there as an elected member. Time was on my side. I began following three courses, all linked to each other – the academic course of law leading to the LL.D. degree, that leading to the diploma of legal procurator, and the BA course. I needed the LP diploma to put my first foot, as it were, in the law courts and start building my clientele before graduating as a lawyer. The LP course brought me in contact with a very intelligent lecturer, Maurice Caruana Curran. In the arts course, the lecturers who stood out most were Fr Gerald Seaston, a superb lecturer in Latin literature and the Classics; Prof. Coleiro, who was very knowledgeable and took pride in his lectures; and Prof. Ġużè Aquilina whose thinking of the language was free of the prejudice of colonial manipulation and political strife. He correctly analysed the two currents that made up the language – the Semitic base, the backbone of our language, and the Romance element that provided us with the alphabet and vocabulary and which made the language rich in words and concepts.

Prof. Aquilina renounced in no uncertain terms the concept of *Malti safi* and held that culturally we belonged to the Latin south. This may sound all so obvious today, but stating the obvious a few years after the war and in the wake of colonial propaganda that made the 700-year presence of Italian culture in Malta an act of treason, required a strong sense of scholarship that defied political pressures. I admired the deep learning of Prof. Aquilina as shown in his *Il-Polz ta' Malta*, a series of essays on subjects ranging from literary criticism to comparative philosophy. Above all, Prof. Aquilina gave the study of Maltese a wider cultural dimension.

Our lecturer in Italian and literature, Giovanni Curmi, made us almost live the times of Dante, Petrarch, and Boccaccio, ensuring that our voyage into the literary sea of Italian literature moved through Foscolo, Leopardi, and Manzoni, into Moravia and the Futuristi. I will always treasure his memory. His *Storia della Letteratura Italiana*, although brief and succinct, is a learned one and remains most helpful. In his time, we resurrected the *Società Universitaria di Letteratura Italiana*.

The study of Latin was taken very seriously in my days. I personally found in Latin and its culture an encounter with the history of Europe and the Mediterranean. Through the study of Latin, and its Roman belongingness, one can well understand what *Mare Nostrum* meant. Latin literature and culture bridge Rome from Classical times to the Christian era. How right Dante is in his Canto XXXI of the Purgatorio, '*Roma onde Cristo è Romano*'. I still read Catullus, my favourite Roman poet, and find in Lucretius a genius of eminence. Cicero has also shaped my thinking and my style of writing.

The study of Roman history was a constant reminder of the mandate given to Rome, so well expressed by Virgil when he wrote in *The Aeneid*, '*Tu regere imperio populos, Romane, memento (hae tibi erunt artes), pacisque imponere morem, parcere subiectis et debellare superbos.*' It was with a particular sense of history in mind when, on the eve of the end of my mandate as president of Malta, I inaugurated a monument called *Enea*, by Ugo Attardi at the Lower Barrakka gardens in Valletta.

Ċensu Gatt, a lecturer in political economy, had a lasting effect on my political studies. He was not profound as an economist, but he was sensible, down-to-earth and had a social conscience that inspired his students. He taught us not to resort to condemnation unless first we understood the causes giving rise to a particular situation. This is why I have always been inclined to the so-called left. I found in Alcide de Gasperi's definition of Democrazia Cristiana, '*un partito di centro che guarda a sinistra*', the realisation of my political and economic philosophy. It has stood me well in my political experience.

After I received my legal procurator diploma, I worked for a year with a law firm, mainly with Prof. J. H. Xuereb, whose offices were at Vincenti Buildings in Valletta. I was 20 then. Most lawyers, including Vincent Scerri and Joseph Flores, who were the leading criminal lawyers at the time, had an exceptional workload before the magistrates' courts. It was not easy starting a legal practice from scratch and since none in my family had a legal background, I had no one to fall on for advice and help. But I had the will to make it. I still vividly remember the first case I handled. It was about a dog whose owner complained that it had been stolen by someone living down Strait Street. When he asked for the dog back, the man said it was his and anyway my client could not prove it was his. But my client could indeed prove it was his; he knew it had spots on its genitals, while the man who stole it did not!

I did well in my studies for my BA General in my three chosen subjects, philosophy, Italian, and economics. I did a lot of philosophy reading and was impressed by Thomistic philosophy, mainly through the works of Jacques Maritain. I feel that my basic knowledge of philosophy and in particular my study of logic gave me a disciplined approach to argumentation. It was for me an achievement to have managed to follow three courses without ever having to sit for a supplementary examination. Lectures used to last till six in the evening and sometimes even later, but this did not keep me back from taking part in student activities, or in following the sentimental callings of the heart. My girlfriend did not miss attending at my graduation in arts, or the evening ball. Wearing a splendid evening gown, she was, in my eyes, the most beautiful girl around.

8

Violet - the girl of my dreams

Like other young students, I was on the look-out for the girl of my dreams. After a hesitant start in dating, and looking around at the few 'lady students' available, none of whom was particularly to my liking, it dawned on me that I was making a fairly good hit with the girls. Being a university student was then considered a positive introduction in life and my limited financial means were not an obstacle. In a way, a *studente povero*, as immortalised in *Addio Giovinezza* of Giacosa, was an attraction. Jokingly, I used to say at the time that I wanted to have seven different girlfriends a year, which, had I been successful, would have brought the number to forty-nine at the end of it all. It would also have meant that I would have had to marry the fiftieth.

I was in my second year in the Faculty of Arts. I had met Violet before, some years back at a wedding. I thought she had the most beautiful eyes I had ever seen. She was sister to Guido Saliba, a law student three years ahead of me in the course. He was very much involved in drama and particularly in the Fergħa Drammatika, Għaqda tal-Malti Università. He and Ines Soler, whom he later married, were the moving spirit in the student drama movement. Then I lost sight of her, only to see her again in Strada Reale, where she told me she was sitting for her matriculation exam. I remember trying to look for her at the examination hall, on the ground floor, in St Christopher Street in Valletta. But I missed seeing her at the end of the exam.

As Christmas approached, I was thinking of inviting her for the so-called Crib Party which the lady students were organising. But, as it happened, the prime minister, Enrico Mizzi, died on December 20, 1950 and the party had to be put off to a date in early January. Luckily for me, Violet was there. She had probably been invited by her brother, Guido. I found her on the dance floor. I went up to her to take the next dance with her but she said she was waiting for her partner who had gone to get her a drink. I insisted on

43

having the next dance and promised to hand her back to her partner the moment the dance was over. She accepted. Violet looked radiant. But we did not fix a date to meet, and only exchanged pleasantries. She told me, for instance, that she liked the profession of a lawyer, but later confessed she only said that because she thought it would please me no end, which in fact it did.

I saw Violet again when Prof. Fogarty died, on February 5, 1951. Prof. Fogarty, an institution at the university – he ruled over the Literary and Debating Society – died as he was going down the stairs at the Westminster Hotel in Kingsway, opposite La Vallette Band Club. At the news of his death, the university immediately suspended its activities. I was near the Wembley Store when I saw Violet coming into Valletta. She said she was going to the university to see if the matriculation results were out. I told her not to bother as the university was closed. As she lived in Pietà, I suggested we walk to her home. It was when we were on our way that I proposed to her in what my children consider to be a most original way. I told her: '*Tixtieq tkun tiegħi?*'. (Do you want to be mine?). I took her smile to be 'Yes.' And we have lived happily ever after.

9

University and my first interest in politics

I was elected to the Student Representative Council in my first year at the university. As I had been an 'occasional student' the year before, I already had an insight into student life. The SRC, formerly CPU (Comitato Permanente Universitario) and now KSU (Kunsill Studenti Universitarji) has always had an important role in student life. Students in Malta started organising themselves at the turn of the twentieth century, following the trend in neighbouring Italian universities. The first president was Arturo Mercieca. Because of my connection with the council in my student life, I greatly appreciated taking part, as president of Malta, in the centenary celebrations of the university students' first representative council. The council was then taking a leading role in national affairs. The Sette Giugno (1919) had also been a student revolt. The CPU provided the first political leaders when self-government was introduced in 1921. In the years when the colonial government was following a policy of repression against the use of the Italian language, contrary to the democratic will of the Maltese people, the university students became very actively engaged in political manifestations.

In his book *Dal Mio Taccuino Universitario*, Edoardo Magri, later Judge Magri, recounts the role of the students in the thirties. Similarly, Herbert Ganado who, like Arturo Mercieca and Edoardo Magri, was president of the CPU, recounts student life and activities of his time in his *Rajt Malta Tinbidel*. George Borg Olivier, later to become prime minister and the main architect of Malta's independence, was the last president of the CPU and the first president of SRC, thus ensuring a continuity that the colonial government could not succeed in interrupting. Eric Sammut, Wallace Gulia, and Eddie Borg Olivier were presidents of the SRC during my first years at university. I served in the council in all roles, except that of treasurer. I never did really like handling accounts. Josie Camilleri, a medical student, was president before I took over. I remember when we supported prime minister Borg Olivier who was against the British government's decision to use the 'colonial flag' of Malta (a blue background, with the Union Jack superimposed on the flag, and a small Maltese coat of arms in the corner) in the coronation cortege, to which he was going to be invited. Borg Olivier declined the invitation unless Malta's proper flag was used. It was only a last-minute intervention by the new Queen that ensured the prime minister's participation, but Borg Olivier had his way.

When the university authorities raised its fees for tuition, we decided to strike. I had wanted to see the participation of the theology students and went to see the rector of the seminary, Mgr Albert Pantalleresco, or *Pantalla*, as he was commonly referred to, about it, but he was against the idea. Pantalleresco, a man of culture who had also been interned and later exiled to Uganda by the British, put it to me this way: '*Non voglio fare dei miei seminaristi dei futuri Mannarini*', obviously referring to Don Gaetano Mannarino, who was regarded as the leader of the 'insurgents' in the so-called rising of the priests against Grand Master Ximenes in 1775 and was imprisoned at Fort St Elmo. He was only released by Napoleon Bonaparte when he occupied Malta in 1798.

I believed the student body had to give its contribution to constructive thinking. It is for this reason that I organised the first National Congress of Students. I remember, for instance, one committee discussing the problem of graduate employment. It was the first time ever the problem was treated in a scientific manner. Before I got married, I once raised the prospect with Violet of joining the Colonial Legal Service but the Mau Mau in Kenya made such prospect anything but attractive. But, to get back to the congress, the general conference was of a high standard. Dr Albert Ganado's contribution on 'The student and the state' was a studied one, as were those of Dr (later Mr Justice) J. Flores and Mgr Prof. E. Coleiro.

One outstanding contribution was that by Dom Mintoff, then leader of the opposition, very fiery and effective, whose lecture was on 'The student and the worker'. I remember, as president of the SRC, phoning him up at his office in Blata l-Bajda, not far from my parents' home. He grasped the invitation. He knew the university was, in the main, Nationalist in political orientation and he turned the lecture into a clarion call for students to identify themselves with the cause of the workers.

I would like to think that my term as president of the SRC had an important national bearing. As was the custom in those years, the Great Siege commemoration on September 8 was a rallying point for students to express their solidarity with the country's political ambitions. Instead of the usual morning address at the Great Siege Monument in Valletta, I introduced a spectacular 'torchlight' evening procession. At the traditional ceremony, I addressed the students and all those present, affirming the right of the Maltese people to be sovereign in their own country. I still remember a particular phrase I used – '*f'din is-siegha ta' glorja nazzjonali, meta l-qalb tifrah li hija Maltija*', (in this hour of national glory when the heart rejoices in being Maltese). In the evening, we walked in procession, torchlight in hand and still in our gowns, to the Auberge d'Aragon, at that time the official residence of the prime minister. Our aim was to affirm our faith in Malta's future, and in the prime minister, who then was the highest Maltese authority.

Borg Olivier greeted us on the steps of the auberge. Moved by the sight of so many students, torches alight, Borg Olivier first reminded us of how students had always been at the forefront of the nation's aspirations and then, in his deep voice, he said he wanted us to be the first to know of an important development. The Maltese government, he said, had requested the British government that responsibility for Malta be moved from the Colonial Office to the Commonwealth and Foreign Relations Office, making it clear that this was not so much a change of address as a change of status; in other words, a transition from a colony to an independent country within the Commonwealth. In fact Borg Olivier was restating, as it were, what a previous Nationalist government had asked for in 1932: dominion status, in terms of the Statute of Westminster. Borg Olivier's declaration was of great importance. It meant that Malta had once again taken the road to independence. What had yet to come was Mintoff's alternative. In league with Lord Mountbatten, then Commander in Chief, Headquarters Allied Forces, Mediterranean, he proposed that Malta be integrated with Britain. We, Nationalists, strongly rejected the proposal as it would have stopped Malta's ambition to become an independent nation and our absorption in the United Kingdom would have stultified our nationalism.

It was right at this time that I started taking a more active interest in politics. I decided to set up a Committee of Nationalist Students at the university. I thought that, if Nationalist students were to actively engage themselves in politics and start studying the history of the Nationalist movement and, also, contribute, through new ideas, to social and economic development, the political aspirations of the Nationalist Party would acquire greater support and importance. At that time it was prohibited to have any form of party political activity at the university. So I thought I should see the prime minister about it. He was quite clear in his reaction. Didn't I know that such activities were prohibited by the university's statute and that I could easily find myself in trouble? I said I did but felt the restriction was an anachronism. He looked at me and said with a smile, 'All right, carry on. Keep me informed.'

Borg Olivier knew me for my Nationalist feelings. On the first anniversary of Nerik Mizzi's death, I organised a commemoration at the Manoel Theatre and for the first time ever had a film made of his life, which included his address to the nation on accepting to form a minority government a few weeks before his death.

The KUN (Kunsill Universitarju Nazzjonalista) used to meet at the home of Vanni Bonello, who was to become a judge at the European Court of Human Rights, in Old Bakery Street in Valletta. Also on the council with me were Albert and Frank Camilleri, Albert Manchè, and Vanni Bonello himself. Vanni's father, Chev. Vincenzo Bonello, who had also been interned and exiled during the war, was a man of great culture and artistic ability. He had started the Fine Arts Museum, only to be removed some years later by the British colonial government for being considered 'not loyal'. He used to speak to us about the presence of Latin culture in Malta, its importance to our civilization, and, also, about Maltese personalities who, through their intellectual abilities, contributed so much to the cultural life of the country.

I absorbed all this but felt the need for the Nationalist Party to be more pro-active on two important issues. The first was the Maltese language, a determining factor of our culture, not a substitute to Malta's Latin culture. The language gave us a national identity. I also felt the party had to be stronger in its social message. I had studied the great encyclicals *Rerum Novarum* and *Quadragesimo Annum* and felt the Nationalist Party had to be close to the workers rather than to the professional middle class if it wanted to interpret the future. It was not enough to criticise socialism and consider it as a pale imitation of communism. It was very important to understand the social changes taking place in Malta and elsewhere, and that unless there is a true sense of social justice, there is no purpose to serve in politics. These were essentially the changes that were affecting my political reflections in those years of my political formation.

It was clear I was leaning to the left in so far as social policies and justice were concerned. As the island's population was increasing, emigration was

considered by all the political parties as the 'natural safety valve'. But I used to feel bad seeing Maltese leave their land in their thousands to settle abroad. I could never stand this. Although I thought the Nationalist Party was strong as ever in national aspirations, I also believed at that time that it had a social justice deficit in its thinking and political message. As my years at university were coming to an end, I felt my calling was that of a lawyer and of a politician set to change the party's social justice image.

I graduated as doctor of laws in November 1955. It was a great day for me, possibly an even greater one for my parents. Mother had great ambitions for her children, but father was quite different; he held his pride in silence. He had a quiet dignity but I am sure that graduation day must have been one of most beautiful days of his life. Every night before I go to sleep, I still find myself kissing their photo and say to them: 'Thank you.' I owe them so much. I feel they still look after me and pray for me and my family every day. They are so close to me, not in a morbid way, but in very loving way.

10

My first murder case

Since I had been practising at the law courts for two years when I graduated, I had already managed to get a few clients by then. They were mainly from Ħamrun. In no time I opened an office in Rabat. I remember once, when I was studying with Joe Fenech at home for my final exams, when someone came over to tell me that Ġużè Darmanin, known as *Iż-Żuż*, had been killed in a bar nearby. *Iż-Żuż* was known in Ħamrun for his violent character and many were scared stiff of him. I had first come into contact with him through one of my first clients, Giuseppe Tonna, to whom *Iż-Żuż* owed £100. Tonna had wanted to take action against him but had found no one prepared to take the brief. I accepted and immediately sent for him. *Iż-Żuż* was a big man. He came over and I remember him ringing the door of my parents' flat where I had my 'office'. As I opened the door, he almost stuck the letter I had sent him to my face and in a challenging tone said, 'Did you send me this?' Assuming an air of a superiority, I told him: 'Don't you think it would be better to step inside if you have anything to say?' I told him to sit down and he did. At least, we were then equal in height – more or less. Once inside, he began to change his tone. I said he had better propose how he planned to pay Tonna the money he owed him as we meant business. He calmed down and said he would pay in instalments. I accepted so long as he was prepared to meet his obligations. To my knowledge, he did.

Iż-Żuż was killed only some time after my brief encounter with him. Anyway, when he was killed, the man who stabbed him came rushing over to our house seeking my advice. As it happened, he was another client of mine, Manwel Mercieca, known as *Ix-Xabaj*, a cane-worker. He had been in a bar/coffee shop at the end of Schembri Street, corner with Mile-End, when *Iż-Żuż* called, apparently asking him for money. When Mercieca refused, *Iż-Żuż* got hold of him and lifted him up violently. Mercieca, fearing the worst, pulled out a knife that he used in his work and hit him in his breast. *Iż-Żuż* was struck down by a single blow. The knife penetrated his heart with almost surgical precision. I was only 23 and the first murder case had landed on my lap! I told Mercieca to go and report the matter directly to the police. The stabbing caused quite a stir. People sympathised with Mercieca, and I advised his family that it would be best to have Dr J. Flores involved in his defence. I was doing my *practicum* with Flores in so far as criminal work was concerned.

I never did like autopsies but I had to be present in the autopsy of *Iż-Żuż*. Flores told me to check the exact direction in which the man had been stabbed. The knife wound would show this. If it was from below upwards, normally that was considered a vindictive hit; if it was from up downwards, a defensive blow. The autopsy established that the blow was one from up downwards. What really impressed me most was the volume of beer removed from the stomach. I could not stand the smell of beer and the experience put me off beer for a good number of years. Flores entrusted me with the compilation of evidence almost exclusively. When the case was appointed for hearing, I had not yet sat for the warrant exam but I assisted the defence. My 'first' murder case was Flores's last case as he was appointed a judge a short time afterwards.

Flores wanted to have a long list of witnesses to give evidence on the character of the victim. It was important to recreate in evidence the situation that had confronted the accused when *Iż-Żuż*, in a drunken state, accosted him. Our line of defence was legitimate self-defence. If the issue of excess in self-defence was raised, then the proviso established by law that, if the accused, in exceeding legitimate self-defence, did so because he was taken unawares, or owing to fear or fright, then no punishment would be applied. When I explain this provision of the law to university students, I invariably refer to this case as I feel it illustrates the point well. Then Flores did one of his dramatic acts. He renounced to the calling of all the witnesses for the defence. Instead, he took the conduct sheet of *Iż-Żuż* and, in a courtroom so silent that one could hear a pin drop, started reading out the list of *Iż-Żuż*'s convictions . It was getting dark and, as the hall was in the upper floor of the Auberge d'Italie (today the ministry of tourism), a reddish light streamed beautifully into the hall. Flores had a commanding figure, a Roman head, and a resounding voice. His gown was always falling backwards. He started reciting, brawl after brawl, crime after crime. When he reached the end, he just looked at the jury with piercing eyes. His message was clear: 'What would you have done had you been faced with such an avalanche of crimes overpowering you?' The verdict of the jury was that of excess in legitimate self-defence. It was not an ordinary verdict. Even though Flores had been expecting, as I did, the application of the proviso under which the accused would have been exempt from punishment for having been taken unawares, or owing to fear, he still considered the verdict a fair and a correct one. The accused was jailed for six years; on his release, he emigrated to Australia with his family.

From then onwards I specialised in this line of court work, taking up a record number of cases involving trials by jury. Some were very important as they determined points of law; others were sensational. The death penalty was still on the statute book up to 1972. Although it had not been applied for quite some time, it was always there, sending shivers down the spine of defence counsel at the end of trials, lest a unanimous verdict would force the court to condemn the accused to death by hanging. As part of our studies in criminal law, we were once taken to see the gallows, and we all put the noose on, in turn, 'just for good luck'. I only realised how good my luck was when one student jokingly pressed the button and the trap-door opened. I was only a couple of feet away!

When I was first elected to Parliament in 1966, I tried to convince the prime minister, George Borg Olivier, to remove capital punishment from the statute book but he argued it was best to keep it as a deterrent. Later on, it was agreed that Parliament appoint a committee to examine the Criminal Code, with a view to proposing amendments. I sat on that committee and I suggested that we take up some issues that required immediate attention and amendment, such as the death penalty, adultery as an offence at law, and other matters. Ugo Mifsud Bonnici, who also sat on this committee, insisted that we start examining the code section by section in numerical order. His view prevailed. I understood then that there was no political will to move on. It was left to a Labour government, under Mintoff after the 1971 election, to abolish capital punishment.

11

I got to the church on time!

Violet and I were looking forward to the day of our marriage almost from the time we started going out together. Like other young couples, we used to dream of having our own home, but my earnings as a legal procurator during my student days were meagre. Gradually my financial prospects started to get brighter and we became engaged in September 1955, just four weeks before I graduated. I do not think my parents were all that keen seeing their son getting married so soon after his graduation, but they soon realised that Violet and I loved each other. Violet's mother had died in 1939 when she was six. Her two brothers were 12 and nine years respectively and her younger sister, one. Her father had remarried some years later and had a son from his second marriage. Relations between the children of the first marriage and their stepmother were not so good and for some years Violet and her younger sister were looked after by their aunt. Then she went to live again with her father. Owing to the strained relations with her family, Violet learned, the hard way, to look after her elder brothers and do some cooking. She also did very well in her studies. This ability to look after the family, much ahead of her time, gave her a greater sense of maturity. My parents liked her. To me, she was simply adorable.

We leased a house in Blata l-Bajda and reached agreement with the women who lived in it to take a vacant ground-floor flat next to my parents' house. Our first home was 786, High Street, Hamrun. My father lost no time in buying a nameplate, 'Violet', for it. The house still carries the same name even though we stopped living there in 1972. Violet ordered the furniture from a very good carpenter in Żabbar, but two months before the wedding he had only delivered a few pieces, despite the substantial deposit she had made on the purchase. More of such 'pleasures' were yet to come. One day, as Violet and her father were at the carpenter's to see how he was getting on with our order, a couple at the showroom were having a close look at the furniture we thought was ours. To all intents and purposes, they were acting as if it were theirs. In short, we found out that we were being deceived by the carpenter. It was obvious that we had to look elsewhere. The problem was getting the deposit back, but we did get it. In the meantime, we went to Arcidiacono, a friend of the family for years, and he very kindly accepted to provide us with the bedroom at least. The rest was to follow as soon as possible. Apart from the kitchen, the living room, and bedroom, we had no other furniture at our home on our wedding day.

We got married on December 30, 1956. Violet looked radiant as she entered the church of Sta Caterina d'Italia. The witnesses to our wedding were Mr Justice Flores and Prof. J.H. Xuereb. They were both known for not being punctual, and I was already getting a similar reputation. On that day, however, I was in church five minutes before the appointed time. So were the witnesses. The wedding Mass had to start at 9.30 a.m. We were all there… except for the bride. My mother used to say that '*la sposa si deve fare aspettare*'. At 9.45, my best man, Ronnie Conti, looked at me, smiled and said: '*Rega bdielha*' (She must have had second thoughts). When it was five minutes to ten and the bride had still not turned up, the words '*rega bdielha*' started assuming a sinister meaning.

Violet, who had always made it a point of being on time, arrived at 10 with a mischievous smile on her face. It was all the fault of the photographer who had gone away to fetch a piece of equipment he had left behind. The delay created a small problem. The sacristan took the law into his hands, as it were, and said we had to do away with the sermon as otherwise the 11 a.m. Mass would not be said on time. But I did not like the idea and had my way.

The celebrant was my close friend Fortunato Mizzi, who in his sermon openly urged me to take up politics and encouraged Violet not to stand in my way. My parents, father in particular, did not like politics. Father was a very peace-loving person, who considered politics and politicians as a disturbance of peace. I never felt my father ever having been so close to stopping a priest from continuing with his sermon! Our wedding reception was held at the Hotel Phoenicia Ballroom. Most of my memories of the occasion consist of the hassle we were put through by the photographer who kept taking pictures of us in different places of the hotel. I left for our 'going away' – always a very moving affair for families – *sans* one shoe: the other was tied to the mudguard of the car waiting for us at the gate, all supposedly done for good luck.

The following day, our families came to see us off at the airport before we flew off for our honeymoon. Violet's father was wearing a corset as he had started suffering from a serious backache. The problem for him was far more serious than we thought.

12

Rebel with a cause

We had very little money to spend on our honeymoon. I had just over £100 in bank deposits. Of this sum, which I withdrew, we had to pay for the air ticket to Rome and train tickets to Florence, Como, and Lugano. In Rome we went to the opera. Violet was wearing a lovely light blue coat and a white fur hat. We left our *pensione* by taxi and the taxi driver, seeing us dressed so elegantly, took us straight to the main door where we made a grand entrance, only to be told we had to go in from a side door as our seats were high up in the gallery. When you are young and on your honeymoon, you can laugh off such knocks and enjoy yourself. We had a public audience with Pope Pius XII. He had a unique personality; when he imparted his blessing, one felt the presence of the Vicar of Christ, a regal Christ, and a *Cristo Re*.

I have had audiences, both official and private, with all succeeding popes, except Pope John Paul I, Papa Luciani: his reign was far too short. Each pope has made a different impression on me. Pope John XXIII, as the world learned so well, was a people's pope. I can never forget the night before the inauguration of the Vatican Council II. Violet and I were watching the ceremony on television with little Giannella by our side. The pope looked at the moon and said: 'Even the moon wants to be happy on this occasion,' adding, 'if your children are next to you, caress them. Tell them that it is the pope who is caressing them.' We had tears in our eyes as we caressed Giannella, telling her that it was the Holy Father who was caressing her. Pope Paul VI had to handle the forces of change unleashed by his predecessor. In a way, I feel he suffered an inner conflict. He was all for change, but he felt he had to reconcile change with tradition, reforms with continuity. When I was a member of the cultural affairs committee of the Council of Europe, I once proposed a discussion of the encyclical *Populorum Progressio*. The pope's brother, senatore Montini, who belonged to the Italian

59

parliamentary delegation and was a Christian Democrat, greatly appreciated the gesture. Pope Luciani's sudden death gave rise to imaginary plots, giving the impression that the Vatican had returned to the Borgia days. His successor was John Paul II. And what a great pope he turned out to be! I met him several times, including in private audiences. His name will live on in history for his courage to bring the Church close to the millions who hold on to the faith of Christ. His thinking was, in a way, a contradiction – he lived the future and yet held on to the past.

But January 1957 was still very far away from Pope John Paul II's pontificate. We were living the cold war, Europe was divided in two blocs, and the Treaty of Rome had yet to be signed. Adenauer was building Christian Democracy in Germany and Schumann was dominating Christian Democracy in French politics. De Gasperi, whom I greatly admired as a politician, had died a few years before but his ideas were being brought forward by Amintore Fanfani, Aldo Moro, and Giulio Andreotti. Europe was on the move, but not Malta. Or, rather, the island was on the move but in a different direction, a negative one at that, for Mintoff had won the elections, mainly on his proposal for integration with Britain. It was 'integration now or never'.

I got immersed in my legal practice. Giannella was born in October 1957, a moment of great happiness. Violet says it was the happiest moment of her life. But her father had not lived to see his first grandchild. He had gone to England for a diagnosis of his back pain and was told he had cancer. He died in April 1957. I liked Violet's father a lot. He was a thoughtful man, always correct in his manners. His past political allegiance was to Strickland's party but with the passage of time he realised that the Nationalist Party was the party of the future. He distrusted Mintoff and felt it was only through the Nationalist Party that Malta could have a secure future.

Mintoff's integration proposal appealed to the Malta Labour Party and to those who considered themselves pro-British. Mabel Strickland stood out among those resisting the integration proposal, realising, perhaps, that in Mintoff's plan there would not have been any place for her. At that time I was in the Nationalist Youth Movement and had become editor of *Encounter*. I think the magazine was the Nationalist Party's reply to the *Knight*, edited by Mintoff himself; we started putting politics at a higher intellectual level. It was a great humiliation to me as a Nationalist to see so many thousands of people rallying at Mintoff meetings, carrying the Union Jack, and demonstrating for Malta to become part of the United Kingdom. How could have Mintoff, who had been and remains to this day a nationalist at heart, albeit a strange and difficult one, advocated Malta's integration with Britain? Some thought he might well have felt that, since his political future in Malta would have always been very limited for him, a seat for the island in the House of Commons would have given him a wider political dimension and standing. With a Labour government in Britain, and some close friends on Labour's left, this must have surely indirectly appealed to him. But in my view, although he might have considered all this, the determining factor behind his proposal was to get a better deal for the worker.

I remember taking an active part in the anti-integration campaign. The government made available schools where we could address meetings. I remember going to one of these meetings in Qormi. The hall was packed with hecklers, shouting their heads off. I could not even hear my own voice when I spoke. Out of desperation, I asked party supporters to join me in singing the PN's hymn and other popular songs suitably adapted for electoral purposes. This impromptu defiance worked well. The irony is that while the British empire had by then become a relic of the past and the colonies were fast winning their independence, Malta wanted to move in the direction of integration.

Meanwhile, we of the Nationalist Party were being regarded as upstarts and rebels. When the party tried to rally support against integration in the United Nations, and in countries such as Ireland, Mintoff thought that we planned to ask the Irish Republican Army for support in a bid to stop the integration process through violence and terrorism! His interpretation of our move was preposterous, but this did not stop him for saying that he intended arming his supporters against us!

Through an American organisation, CARE, Mintoff managed to get supplies of butter and cheese from the United States to be distributed free to the people. This was a great move on Mintoff's part. Borg Olivier decided to boycott the referendum, considering it a charade. The archbishop, Mgr Michael Gonzi, opposed integration too as he held that if Malta were to form part of the UK, the Catholic character of the island could be endangered as British laws would be made part of Maltese law.

The result of the referendum could be interpreted in different ways. It was certainly not the walkover the Malta Labour Party and the British government had expected. Nor could anyone consider the result as fair. But, whatever the people's will was, the integration proposal ultimately failed because the British government intended going ahead with the rundown of

HM's Dockyard, believing as it did that in the context of its new Mediterranean strategy there was no place for the thousands employed in the yard. The MLP's strength depended very much on its support from the dockyard workforce. Indeed, with Britain's plan to scale down the labour force at the dockyard, the first to realise that integration was not the solution to Malta's unemployment problem were the dockyard workers. In his irascible manner, Mintoff put an end to his integration proposal and started a campaign of violent protests against the British government. Governor Sir Robert Laycock, who had come to Malta thinking he would be assisting to the integration process, soon found that Mintoff had turned all his previous charm into anger and that his party was now standing for independence. The crowds were mobilised and violence was used to drive this point home. Borg Olivier exploited the situation and in December 1957 his support was instrumental to having the legislative assembly unanimously approve the so-called 'break with Britain resolution'. This could have well led to a moment of national unity, but Nationalist feeling could not tolerate Mintoff whose style of government was so disconcerting and so inimical to democracy.

When Mintoff resigned, the governor sent for Borg Olivier and asked him to form a government. Borg Olivier declined to accept unless he was assured that, if he failed, Parliament would be dissolved and general elections called. The British government could not guarantee this and, when faced with the prospect of further violence and the realisation that both parties were now clamouring for independence, the governor advised the Colonial Office to suspend the constitution.

Once again we had violence in the streets, and when Rediffusion refused to comply with one of Mintoff's requests, its poles were pulled down. The situation reached breaking point when the police were told not to keep order. It was in this political situation that the Colonial Office suspended the constitution. The governor took over the administration of the country and once again the people lost the right to govern themselves. This led to further division in the country, with one side considering the other as enemies rather than political opponents. I considered the British government's presence in Malta as humiliating. With his courage and intelligence, Mintoff could have done much for the people, but he chose to be divisive and dictatorial. Borg Olivier was the answer to my political aspirations although he did not come close to my belief in social justice. I was a rebel with a cause. There was a sense of dissatisfaction within the Nationalist Party. Few could understand Borg Olivier's style of quiet resistance to Mintoff. Borg Olivier realised he was facing an impossible situation. He held the British government responsible for delaying Malta's political evolution and was of the opinion that the integration proposal had been a plot hatched by Lord Mountbatten and Mintoff. He wanted to exploit the rift between Mintoff and the British government. He had very lay views on the functions of the archbishop's curia, yet he watched with interest the pending major quarrel between Gonzi and Mintoff. He understood Mintoff could well be defeated through his own tactic of fighting the British government, the curia, and the Nationalist Party at the same time. He let Mintoff fight his own battles and get exhausted in the process. The Nationalist Party had to keep its distance both from the British government, whom Borg Olivier considered to be the source of all problems, and from the Church. He felt any backing to the Church could only weaken Gonzi's stand rather than strengthen it.

Borg Olivier was right, but he became sullen and he failed to interpret the mood of his supporters. Nor did he provide the leadership many were looking for. He took the right policy decisions but then failed to put them across well to the people. Herbert Ganado was perhaps Malta's best journalist and political commentator at the time. His Nationalist credentials were impeccable. He had been the editor of the Church's newspaper *Leħen is-Sewwa* before the war, and he had also been interned and later exiled to Uganda. He was very alert to the needs of the working class, though ultimately he failed to deliver. I used to meet Herbert in court. He always impressed me by his deep culture, his narrative ability, and his gentlemanly character. Those who have read his *Rajt Malta Tinbidel* can easily understand Herbert Ganado's captivating personality

At about this time, I had begun taking part in committees, or study groups, set up to draw up fresh policies for the Nationalist Party. A driving force behind this work was the Nationalist Youth Movement, then presided by Albert Ganado, a cousin of Herbert's. Borg Olivier took this as a challenge to his leadership and, acting swiftly through his executive committee, expelled Albert Ganado from the party. This was done through a breach in the party's disciplinary regulations. Ganado took the executive committee to court, and asked a group of lawyers, including myself, to sign a writ of summons against the party, declaring that his expulsion was *ultra vires*. This led to a rift and I found myself with the Democratic Nationalist Party, which believed in nationalism with a strong social conscience. It provided what at the time appeared to be a fighting force to Mintoff's party, galvanising nationalist feeling in a new pro-active attitude. Herbert

Ganado's strong social approach was stimulating. Yet, I could well see certain hesitancy in his work, dictated by the fear of Mintoff towards Malta's constitutional ambitions. I tried to remedy the situation by making it clear in my speeches that we stood for independence, and the less the leadership mentioned independence, the more adamant I had become in this course of action.

Meanwhile, the Blood Commission, named after Sir Hilary Blood who chaired the commission, started hearing evidence in work that had to lead to a return to self-government. The Malta Labour Party, too, was facing a rift. Its general secretary, Toni Pellegrini, broke away over the party's quarrel with the Church, which had been provoked by Mintoff. Gonzi was not prepared to take such provocation lightly. Mintoff started flirting with communist front organisations, later joining AAPSO (Afro-Asian Peoples' Solidarity Organisation). We are now in the early sixties. Mintoff was fighting the British government and the Church at the same time, constantly defying Gonzi, whom he referred to as Sir Michael to project him as subservient to the colonial government. Mintoff may forget, but not forgive, and I think he was out to pay Gonzi back for his opposition to the integration plan, by showing that he would have to bear worse with independence. Gonzi replied in style, interdicting the Malta Labour Party executive committee.

We lived through unnecessarily difficult times and we were in a sense playing into the hands of the British government. The Church managed to unite all anti-Mintoff forces, and Borg Olivier, showing calm detachment and clarity of purpose, exploited the situation in favour of his party. As the elections were approaching, I felt it was time for the Nationalist parties to forget their divisions and unite again and, towards this end, I involved myself in shuttle diplomacy between them. But the two parties thought differently and would rather wait until the elections were over when they would be able to negotiate their future on the basis of their respective strength. To be honest, I could not understand this logic, although I admit I should have been craftier in this political game.

The Nationalist Party used my mediation to weaken the Democratic Nationalist Party and, on their part, Herbert Ganado and his supporters thought the division in fact strengthened their stand. I disagreed, insisting there was still time to reunite and face the common danger – Mintoff's iconoclastic approach to politics and to Church-state relations.

In the 1962 elections, the Nationalist Party obtained the highest number of votes, winning 25 of the 50 seats. This was enough for it to govern without the need of forming a coalition with any other party. The Malta Labour Party won 16 seats; the Christian Workers' Party, under Toni Pellegrini, four; the Democratic Nationalist Party, four; and the PCP (Mabel Strickland's party), one. Borg Olivier was again in government, much wiser as a result of his experience in opposition and this time with a clear sense of direction, aware that the British government saw in him the only person with whom the future of Malta and its relations with the United Kingdom could be negotiated. Britain was also moving towards Europe. In the end, Mintoff's 'break with Britain resolution' only helped raise expectations for independence in the hearts of the majority of the people.

13

My interlude with Herbert Ganado's party

The march towards independence was now picking up but there was still a substantial number of people who thought sovereignty might not be in the island's interests, even though, in theory, they believed in independence. The Church might have looked at the prospect of Mintoff getting elected in an independent Malta with a degree of suspicion, in the sense that he would have jeopardised the 'subtle guarantee' that the British presence provided.

In this context, Herbert Ganado was in favour of Malta becoming independent, but not at that stage. I realised his hesitancy during the election campaign when I purposely used to affirm publicly that, in so far as the future constitutional status of Malta was concerned, the Democratic Nationalist Party's stand did not differ in any way from that of the Nationalist Party. Indeed, even the name of the party, Democratic Nationalist Party, was the same as that which Enrico Mizzi had given to his party, Partito Democratico Nazionalista, before its fusion, in 1926, with the Unione Politica Maltese, creating the Partito Nazionale, or, as it later came to be called, Partit Nazzjonalista. The fusion brought together the two factions of the Nationalist movement.

By now I was also sensing that Herbert Ganado was showing a degree of ambivalence towards me. He got elected from two districts, the first and the seventh, but he decided to hold on to the first, from which I would most probably have been elected in a by-election. He left the seventh to an elderly doctor. Anyway, the situation in so far as I was concerned was unfavourable but tolerable. When Borg Olivier refused a financial offer from Britain, saying, 'I have not come to London to make a silver collection', and formally made Malta's request for independence, Ganado intensified his stand against independence. I openly disagreed with him, contested his decision, and declared that he was reneging on his political commitment. Albert Ganado had a negative political influence on Herbert. How could Nationalist voters be asked to renounce what was a sacred tenet of nationalism, the independence of their country? Yet, the two Ganados did not appear to realise this.

Nor could a party compromise its own conscience by scaring the people of the consequences of having Mintoff in power. I tried to persuade Ganado that, if Borg Olivier would not obtain independence for the island at that stage, sooner or later Mintoff would, and this would have prejudiced the interests of the Nationalist Party. But Ganado persisted in his approach both in Malta and, also, during the Round Table Conference at Marlborough House, as did Toni Pellegrini, of the Christian Workers' Party and Mabel Strickland although, in fairness to her, her opposition was more modest. I wrote to Herbert saying his stand was neither democratic nor nationalist. The majority of the people, Nationalist and Labour, were in favour of independence, and surely no nationalist could accept that his country remained a colony. I regretted having eventually to end my connection with Herbert Ganado, whom I sincerely liked and respected. He was a gentleman in politics and in his relations with other people. He was a good Catholic, and no bigot. But I felt his stand was politically unwise and morally wrong. Despite the fact that I had then resigned from his party, we kept on good terms – our relations were based on mutual respect and sincere friendship. Perhaps I was then too young to win him over, but I certainly felt I was right. And events proved me so.

My resignation from the Democratic Nationalist Party was raised in Parliament by Dr G.M. Camilleri. Borg Olivier was indeed pleased to see me taking active part in the referendum campaign for independence. I addressed meetings and conferences in such places as Marsa, St Paul's Bay, and Hamrun. In no time I was back on my stride forward in politics and my law practice was expanding. I had my second murder case in 1961. It involved a Chinese sailor, Ng Kwan Hung, who had killed another Chinese sailor on a ship, *Empire Fulmar*, on July 16. Ng was being given a hard time by Shan Zuk. One evening Ng had drunk more than his fair share and on his return to the ship he was welcomed none too kindly by Shan Zuk. Ng took out a penknife he used in his job as a saloon boy and struck the other sailor with it. Oliver Gulia (later Mr Justice), for the prosecution, said it was a wilful homicide in terms of law. According to our law, wilful homicide is when someone, maliciously and with intent to kill or to put the life of a person in manifest jeopardy, causes the death of another person. In my submissions, I observed to the jury that both the accused and the victim were non-Maltese and that the murder occurred on a foreign-registered ship. Yet, correctly, our legal system was applicable to the case in question, bringing into play the very important principle governing a fair trial according to law. These principles were based on the presumption of innocence of the accused and that the prosecution had to prove guilt beyond reasonable doubt. This presumption of innocence was equally relevant to the facts at issue as well as to the intentional element. In a murder case, the law requires the *animus necandi*, the intention to kill. This intention can be positive direct (the direct intention to kill) or the intention to put the life of a person in manifest jeopardy (positive indirect intent). In this context, the intentional element has to be proven beyond reasonable doubt.

According to our Criminal Code, intoxication shall be taken into account for the purpose of determining whether a person had intent, specific or otherwise, in the absence of which he shall not be guilty of that offence. I had proof from the forensic expert, Prof. Philip Farrugia, that my client had drunk heavily before the incident. I submitted that the prosecution did not prove beyond reasonable doubt that Ng Kwan Hung had the specific intent to kill or to put the life of Shan Zuk in manifest jeopardy, but had only the generic intent to cause harm, the *animus necandi*. I felt the jury could only find my client guilty of causing a grievous bodily harm from which death resulted. In cases for which the punishment, on conviction, involved a sentence of 12 years imprisonment or more, the criminal court used to consist of three judges, presided over by the chief justice, in this case, Sir Anthony Mamo, who accepted as correct my legal argument as to the consequence of intoxication affecting a specific intent required by law. By a verdict of seven against two, my client was found not guilty of wilful homicide but guilty of having caused a grievous bodily harm followed by death. He was jailed for 16 years. My client was grateful indeed. He wrote to me from prison expressing his appreciation for all I had done for him and praised the legal system under which he was tried.

When he was released after having been given some remissions, he came to see me at the Crown Advocate General's office, where by then I was working, thanking me once again. By the time the jury was over, the crew of the *Empire Fulmar* had become very friendly towards me. A few days before Christmas, a sailor who had acted as the court's interpreter, Zang Hu Sheu, came to my office and brought me presents. He gave me two small boxes containing a set of identical imitation jewellery, a necklace, earrings, and bracelet – 'one for your wife, one for your girlfriend!' Violet was not amused at this transfer of Chinese tradition to my household! The trial was held at the time when the Chamber of Advocates had called a strike over an order requiring lawyers appearing before the superior courts to wear striped trousers and black jacket, black waistcoat, and a white shirt and white bow tie. To defend Ng Kwan Hung, I had to appear before the criminal court 'suitably attired', as shown by a picture of myself carried in the *Times of Malta* and in *Il-Berqa*.

The plea of drunkenness did not fare so well in a subsequent case heard before the criminal court. An RAF man was accused of killing his wife when he threw her down the stairs. Prof. J.M. Ganado was appearing for the accused and he tried using the same line of defence I had raised. This time the court appeared more prepared to deal with this 'drunkenness' issue. In fact, the case 'Regina vs Broadhurst' (1964) A.C. 441 made legal history. The court, through Chief Justice Sir Anthony Mamo, basing himself on the British case DPP vs Beard (1920) directed the jury to consider that 'evidence of drunkenness, which rendered the accused person incapable of forming the specific intent essential to initiate the crime, must be taken into consideration with the other facts proved in order to determine whether or not he had an intent. But evidence of drunkenness falling short of this and merely establishing that the mind of the accused person was affected by drink, so that he more readily gave way to some violent passion, does not rebut the presumption that a man intends that natural consequence of his acts.' On the basis of this direction, the jury found Broadhurst guilty of murder. The defence appealed to the Privy Council. The Privy Council submitted that DPP vs Beard should not be treated as laying down the law with regard to the burden of proof regarding drunkenness. It is not for the defendant to prove incapacity affecting intent and if there is material suggesting intoxication – as I had maintained in Regina vs Ng Kwan Hung – the jury should be directed to take it into account and to determine whether this is weighty enough to leave them with a reasonable doubt about the defendant's intent. Today, the position at law is that as defined in the Broadhurst case at the Privy Council.

I made full use of this case in other cases in which drunkenness affected intent.

14

Independence

Borg Olivier was a skilful negotiator. He was strongest when others were weak. He could keep himself steady with a glass of whisky till the early hours of the morning. He was not an early riser, and when others were already at their office, he would still be asleep in bed. He was very urbane, never in a hurry or in panic; he would wait for his adversary to tire out and then he would pounce on him. But Borg Olivier did not just have tactics, he was a strategist, too. He had convinced himself that the moment had come for Malta to become independent. This was his encounter with destiny, or, rather, it was Malta's hour of destiny, and that he was to be the leader, the Nationalist leader to make this dream a reality.

At Marlborough House, Borg Olivier had everyone against him. Everyone, that is, except history. Duncan Sandys had no rush to see his country leave Malta, indeed the Services chiefs were revising Malta's strategic role and rethinking their previous 'lack of interest' in Malta. They were seeing the shifting sands in Libya, in spite of friendly King Idris being on the throne, and realising that the Soviet Union was re-establishing the Mediterranean region as a sphere of influence mainly through Egypt and the Maghreb. While in theory Mintoff was demanding independence too, he was all the time trying to undermine Borg Olivier's position by trying to make him look as weak and spineless. The small political parties were urging the British government to deny independence to Malta, insisting on the holding of fresh elections first. On its part, the Church was asking for the impossible. It wanted its position in the new constitution to be safeguarded to the extent that no action or pronouncement emanating from it could be considered a violation of fundamental human rights.

Yet, despite all opposition, Borg Olivier prevailed. He was steadfast and resolute in his aim. Borg Olivier may have had his shortcomings, as we all have, but in his quest for independence, he was a formidable negotiator, a diplomat, and a great leader. Malta, and generations of Maltese, owe a lot to this gentleman of politics.

On Independence Day proper, September 21, 1964, Borg Olivier could well sense that he had the majority of the people behind him, not just those who had voted for independence in the referendum. He had even managed to win over the difficult and demanding voters, those who are always critical of political parties and believe they know better than seasoned politicians. He made them feel it was in the country's real interest for all people to pull together and make a success of the island's new status.

On the night of September 20/21, Violet and I, together with my cousin Italo and his wife Josephine, went to Ix-Xagħra tal-Floriana to witness the country's appointment with destiny. To me and to thousands of Maltese who were there, that night remains unforgettable. Generations of Maltese had dreamt of the day, but were denied the happiness of experiencing it. The moment brought to mind prominent names in Malta's political and constitutional development, Giorgio Mitrovich, Camillo Sceberras, Fortunato Mizzi, Sir Ugo Mifsud, who died for a principle, defending the rights of the Maltese not to be exiled from their country, Mgr Enrico Dandria, and Enrico Mizzi, a statesman who lived and died for his dream of seeing Malta free from foreign domination. At the Xagħra that night, I remember seeing Sir Arturo Mercieca, heavy with years, but with a beaming smile on his face, taking his place.

On the stroke of midnight, I recalled what Pandit Nehru had said when India became independent: 'At the strike of the midnight hour, when the world sleeps, India will wake to life and freedom. A moment comes, which comes but rarely in history, when we step out from an old to the new, when an age ends and when the soul of a nation, long suppressed finds utterance.' I felt I was living such a moment. Then, as the British flag was lowered and the Maltese flag took pride of place, I burst out shouting, 'Malta, Malta'. I was so personally engrossed in the historical moment that for a fleeting moment I felt as if I were alone at the Xagħra. We had tears in our eyes. The people's enthusiasm and joy were indescribable. Never have I lived such happiness, not even when Malta joined the European Union on May 1, 2004, an event to which I believe I had contributed so much. The closest to it was perhaps when we won the 1987 elections, when we felt we had won freedom back. The only jarring note was when, at some distance from the Xagħra, now called Independence Arena, Anton Buttigieg, deputy leader of the Malta Labour Party, and a group of his supporters were demonstrating against the celebration. What a pity and how petty it all was!

They behaved so miserably. In later years, when Labour were in office, we would at times be beaten up by Malta Labour Party supporters, aided and abetted by a police force acting criminally, when we celebrated independence day anniversaries.

But on the night of September 20/21, the spirit of nationhood gripped us all. We felt the new Malta belonged to us, depended on us. Wordsworth's words on the French Revolution come to mind: 'Bliss was it in that dawn to be alive, but to be young was very heaven!'

15

When I first made it to Parliament

By now we had two lovely daughters, Giannella and Fiorella. When we called the second daughter Fiorella, friends of ours asked, tongue in cheek, how many more girls we planned to have with names ending in 'ella'. We called our first-born Gianella after Violet's mother and my mother, who were both called Giovanna. Besides, some time before Giannella was born, a young girl prodigy by the name of Giannella de Marco had conducted an orchestral concert. We liked the name. Fiorella also stood for 'Flos Carmeli', as Our Lady of Mount Carmel is referred to, and as we were devotees of Our Lady, the name fitted well.

Following an incident we had had on a plane travelling to Rome, Violet was now having a difficult time health-wise. One day we were flying on a BEA flight, on a circular trip, when, on approaching Rome, the plane plunged into what looked like a free-fall, throwing passengers out of their seats. Many passengers were injured, some seriously. We were later told the free-fall was a manoeuvre meant to avoid a mid-air collision with another plane. The plane landed safely, but there were dozens of fire-engines on stand-by at the airport as they first thought the plane might have had to crash-land.

At Ciampino airport, we were advised to go to hospital to recover from shock, but as we were eager to get into our holiday spirit, we declined the offer. My uncle Gian and his wife Elena were waiting for us at the airport, so we went straight to Rome. We had booked to go to Milan, Paris, Brussels, London, and Nice, but Violet was now scared of flying. I felt the only way to overcome her fear of flying was to continue the holiday as planned. This suited my holiday mood and my style of doing things, but with hindsight I think the decision to keep on flying at that point in time was wrong. Apparently, Violet was pregnant and, some time after our return home, she had what is called a missed abortion. The shock had severe effects on her health. She had gone through two other missed abortions, but she still wanted to have a boy. I used to tell her I was happy with a family of four. We went to Lourdes and Violet prayed to have a baby boy, promising that if she were to have a boy, she would call him Mario, for Our Lady.

Meanwhile, the post of crown counsel at the crown advocate general's office had become vacant. At the time the post carried great prestige; it was considered as a positive step in the *cursus honorum*, both within the crown advocate general's office and the judiciary, but the salary was inadequate. My family considered that the post would take me out of the political arena. I was appointed crown counsel in November 1964, the first to get the post since Malta became independent. The post gave me experience in the administrative side of the government. I found myself involved in drafting legislation; amending laws, to bring them in line with Malta's independent status; drafting advice for cabinet; and taking part in negotiations leading to the putting into use of the deep-water quay at Marsa. The post also helped me gain experience in negotiating with trade unions, shipping companies, and other companies involved in the workings of the harbour. I usually finished up siding with the cause of the port workers and genuinely believed the General Workers' Union could negotiate the best terms for workers, within the national perspective, whenever it was free of political motivation.

When Mario was born at the King George V hospital (today Sir Paul Boffa Hospital), on October 18, 1965, I was having talks with the GWU over some pending matters. As I did not wish to interrupt the talks, I remember holding one session at the hospital. My relations with the GWU have been positive ever since, in spite of the very difficult years that followed during the Mintoff years. Mario was a most welcome addition to the family and Violet was so happy. Mario's bond with his mother is very strong, even though both of them are not very demonstrative by nature. After Mario's birth, Violet's health problems persisted but she ultimately managed to overcome all difficulties. She remained to us all in the family a pillar of strength. The family, down to the grandchildren, revolves around her. We see in her not just love but stability too. She is always there for anyone, especially when help is needed.

Violet has never liked politics. When the 1966 elections were fast approaching, she felt safe as I was a crown counsel. She did not realise how open I was to temptation. A certain Giuseppe Zahra, who had supported me in the 1962 election, and who had a grocery store close to our house in Blata l-Bajda, urged me to contest. Borg Olivier added to the pressure. My problem was that, in order to contest the election, I had to resign my post as crown counsel. In a sense it was a leap in the dark. But I could not resist the challenge to be a candidate for the Nationalist Party. I have always liked law as a profession but my passion for politics is greater. It was difficult telling Violet that I had tendered my resignation, but I did not tell my father, who was suffering from mild heart attacks. My mother used to keep away from him newspapers carrying any mention of my name. I used to go and see my parents every day during the 1 p.m. break. It was a treasured appointment to them, and it helped me keep as close as possible to them. During my election campaign, I would normally stop my corner meetings or any other activity close to mid-day, purposely to go and see my parents before one o'clock. On my way I used to drive around at my district in order to be seen, even though at that time of day most people would be either at work or at home. It did not take long for father to know that I was going to contest the elections. 'Guido, why didn't you tell me that you were contesting the elections? Mr Schiavone came over to see me the other day and said he was going to give you the No. 1 vote.' On election day, when he was at the barber's, he canvassed for me and he had even hung a picture of me on the balcony of his flat.

I enjoyed the election campaign. In terms of popularity, I felt I could compare myself favourably with the other candidates in my district, even though some were of long-standing. Indeed, I was pleased in being considered as one of the party's 'young lions'. On the morning of March 29, my father and I went to the Knightshall (today the Mediterranean Conference Centre) to watch the counting of votes. In the afternoon, when I was about to have a rest, the phone rang. It was my father. 'I just heard the results of the first district (Valletta). You did fairly well, but if this is an indication of how things look right now, I would say you'll do much better in Hamrun.' I had another call immediately afterwards, from Tony Parnis, who is married to my cousin Marion. He worked at the Department of Information at the time and was phoning me up from the counting hall. 'Guido, come down here, the votes of the Hamrun district are being counted right now… it looks you have enough votes to be elected.' When I said I was just about going to have my afternoon rest, he said: 'I see, you want to play the part of Alexander the Great, sleeping before the battle, right?' Then my mother rang up: 'Guido, Guido come over quickly, papà is dying.' I told Violet about the call, rushed down the stairs, and ran home. I found him slumped in his armchair, breathing his last. I fell on my knees, hugging him and calling him over and over again. Then some people who had gathered in the house carried me away to another room. Father was dead. He died listening to the news about the votes I had won in the election.

I will never know what exactly caused his death, and whether the excitement of the moment had contributed to it. Whatever it was, I still bear a sense of responsibility, sometimes bordering on guilt, for his death. He may have thought the strain of having his son an MP would be too hard to take. This, and the responsibilities a politician carry along his career, confirm my belief that politics is a mission.

16

My early years in Parliament

Parliament used to meet on Mondays, Wednesdays and Fridays, from 6 p.m., onwards in the Tapestry Chamber at the Palace in Valletta. It is hard finding a place more beautiful than this for a House of Parliament. The Gobelin tapestries, the gift of Grand Master Ramon Perellos, are simply unique in their beauty. They show wild animals and exotic plants in striking colours from the Indies and Africa.

Others taking their seats with me in the chamber for the first time were Ugo Mifsud Bonnici; Albert Borg Olivier de Puget, whom I had known since I was at St Aloysius College; and the youngest of us all, Josie Muscat. At 21, the qualifying age to vote, Josie was the youngest MP ever elected. He was a student of medicine and took politics very seriously. He was a dedicated MP and had both courage and flair. I doubted his political judgement but not his dedication to his constituents. The other MPs on the Nationalist Party's side had been in politics for quite some years. To my mind, one outstanding member was Giovanni Felice. He was a man of culture, always very well prepared and good debater, too. He was respected for his integrity and correctness by both sides of the House.

Alexander Cachia Zammit, very popular in his constituency of Żejtun, had a promising career. A new addition to Parliament was Ċensu Tabone. Although he was in the same age group as Borg Olivier and Mintoff, he displayed energy and vitality. Carmelo Caruana was a party stalwart and it was mainly through his initiative and work that the party managed to build its headquarters and a modern printing press. Had it not been for his foresight, I wonder how the party could have resisted Mintoff. The Borg Olivier cabinet was held to be an experienced group of ministers, but intellectually, with the exception of Giovanni Felice, it had certain limitations. Borg Olivier's standing was at its peak. His leadership was strong, but not pervasive. He gave the new members a lot of leeway, but

79

little or no power. He saw to it that we learned along the way and he created the right opportunities for us to do so, sometimes at our own expense. Borg Olivier had an inbuilt reluctance to change anything and, although he must have realised that the ministerial team he had was at times tired and lacking in ideas, he failed to reshuffle the cabinet. He put more trust in the past than in the future. In doing so, he indirectly saved the new generation of politicians from being associated with the political defeat of 1971. But this defeat was some years off yet. In 1966, I contented myself with being myself, learning the ropes of political life in Parliament.

Mintoff was a tremendous force of energy and diatribe. He could be an excellent orator, an outstanding debater, and a villain all in one. He could massacre a person's reputation with no apparent feeling of guilt; he could reach heights of creative thinking and at the same time stoop to vulgarity. He remains a phenomenon in Maltese politics. Mintoff may be Marxist-inspired, but he was not a Marxist. He was anti-British, but very English in his culture. I believe he was a Fabian with a totalitarian inclination. He was, and remains, a democrat by persuasion, a dictator by inclination. I admired Mintoff mostly for his ability to improvise options. He had striven for integration with Britain, but added a rider to his proposal – unless Britain accepted integration on his terms, he would opt for independence. His was always a politics of vanishing posts. The moment you thought you reached an agreement with him, he would create more conditions, and when finally you thought you had reached an understanding, you realise he would have something else up his sleeve. His tactics worked at times, but they often created a stalemate and lack of trust. My knowledge of Mintoff and his techniques stood me in good stead when I had to negotiate with him the constitutional amendments of 1987.

Another interesting personality on the opposition side was Mintoff's deputy leader, Anton Buttigieg. Anton was a living contradiction. He was a poet, a very genuine and sensitive person. Yet, he could be harsh and unfair in his reactions. I think he sometimes purposely exceeded the limits so as not to be considered weak. When he started his political life, Anton was very close to Strickland's party. He later shifted to Mintoff's orbit and tried to copy Mintoff's style and even his rhetoric. When in opposition, he was very active at the Council of Europe. He could be very convincing in his work within the Socialist group. In fact, when he chose to adopt moderate views, he was very considerate and reliable. When he chose to be what he was not, he sounded hollow. Another strong Labour politician was Ġuże Cassar, a gentleman in most of his actions, very subtle as a lawyer and, later, as a minister. He had learnt how to handle Mintoff through intelligent manoeuvring, not direct opposition.

I had some good friends among the Labour MPs. One was Joseph Micallef Stafrace, whom I had known since my student days. Three years younger than me, he had later become a friend for all seasons. Micallef Stafrace was editor of the Labour Party organ during the difficult years of the colonial administration. When the paper published a caricature of Governor Laycock drinking from a bottle of whisky, giving the impression that he was drunk, he was sentenced to imprisonment and the sentence was confirmed on appeal. As he was being taken to the Black Maria, he asked me to ring up his girlfriend, today his wife, to tell her of the outcome. She used to work at the main office of the GWU in Mayfair House in Old Bakery Street.

When he graduated as a lawyer, he asked me if he could have his legal *practicum* at my office. Patrick Holland did the same. I accepted but I remember being told by certain prominent lawyers that I should have turned them down as they had been involved in cases in which criminal action had been taken against them. They felt I should not have been the one to give them the certificate attesting that they had carried out the one-year practice as required by law. But I made it clear that both were of good conduct, independently of their political activities that had landed them in trouble in colonial days and that indeed I could vouch for their character, perhaps more than for others because politically we were in opposite camps. I have always considered Micallef Stafrace as a gentleman, both in politics and as a lawyer. With Patrick Holland, events unfolded in a different way, during the time he was a minister under Mintoff, but I will be referring to this later.

I began taking a keen interest in legal affairs. Soon after I started taking part in debates of a legal-political nature, I was fortunate to be chosen by my colleagues to lead Malta's delegation to a Commonwealth Parliamentary Association meeting in Canada on September 8, 1966. The other two were Carmelo Refalo from Gozo, and Vincent Moran, for the MLP. What a great and beautiful country Canada is. We travelled from coast to coast. I formed part of a group that visited Newfoundland. I wanted to see Cabot's tower from where Marconi had sent his first wireless message. It was quite an experience. Newfoundland had opted to relinquish its dominion status and join Canada. We later visited Prince Edward Island, Winnipeg, Edmonton, Vancouver and Victoria Island. I remember writing to my wife telling her that, if we were ever to leave Malta, I would like to see my family settled in Victoria Island. Our trip took us to Montreal, Quebec, and Toronto. We held our sittings at the House of Commons in Ottawa. I found myself leading an interesting role, recommending changes to the constitution of the Commonwealth Parliamentary Association.

I was appointed a member of a working party that had to draw up amendments to the CPA charter. The working party eventually met in Malta, laying the foundations for the modernisation of the association's structure. The CPA gave me greater exposure in foreign affairs. The Commonwealth is a unique institution created with the Statute of Westminster of 1931, when a number of countries agreed to be independent in status, in no way subordinate to one another, and yet work together, through governmental, parliamentary, and other levels. The CPA is an excellent forum for the young politician wanting to be initiated in world politics and to understand the forces of history and live the problems of non-discrimination as to colour, race, or creed. We could live with the old countries of the Commonwealth but equally understand the new countries, some as large as India, others as small as the islands in the Pacific. The CPA reconfirmed my faith in the values of the Commonwealth. The political impact the Commonwealth can make on world affairs today may be limited, but the relationships it forges are of a long-lasting nature.

At the time of the Ottawa conference, world affairs were influenced by the situation in Rhodesia. I could well see the conflict Britain was facing. The African members of the Commonwealth were insisting on the use of force to bring down the Smith regime. The British government did not want to uphold Smith and his supporters who had taken over through a unilateral declaration of independence (UDI), but it was against sending in the army to bring the regime down. Instead, it opted for the imposition of sanctions. I was particularly struck by the arguments put forward by Nigel Fisher, a Conservative MP who had liberal views. He explained the grave implications involved in the use of force and said, 'I hope that the pressure will not be incurred too much by our Commonwealth partners. We too are independent and still a great nation. We do not care to be threatened with walkouts and withdrawals, and with the dissolution of the Commonwealth. There is indeed certain disenchantment with the Commonwealth among certain sections of the British people. I do not agree with it. Indeed, I deplore it, but it exists. Britain's enthusiasm for the Commonwealth should no longer be taken absolutely for granted.' These were strong words, coming from an MP convinced in the value of the Commonwealth. Nigel Fisher was a friend of Borg Olivier and of Malta. When the talks on Malta's independence were concluded, Borg Olivier celebrated the event at Nigel Fisher's place in Lord North Street, London.

Although Fisher was in opposition and Arthur Bottomley, a former secretary of state for colonial affairs, was head of the British delegation, both Labour and Conservative MPs took the same line where British interests were concerned. I kept up my link with the CPA throughout the years. The motivating force behind the CPA were three long-standing officials: Sir Robin Vanderfelt, Jack Fisher, and Betty May, a wonderful trio later helped by Ian Grey, an intellectual. From their small offices, they made every Commonwealth MP feel he was an important part of the association. They were tireless, inspiring, and dedicated.

Vincent Moran and I invited the working party to meet in Malta. Peter Hansen, from Australia, an RAF ace who had seen service during the war in the Mediterranean, was its chairman. The members were W. Kaleme, from Uganda, who became chairman of the CPA in 1967, and who was at the time his country's foreign minister, under Milton Obote; N.P Pereira, from Sri Lanka, a prominent Marxist who was greatly respected for his integrity; Senator John Connelly, from Canada; Bernard Braine, from Britain; and Roy McNeil, from Jamaica. McNeil was also minister of the interior in his country. When he was in Malta, he lost a ring which was of sentimental value to him. After all these years, I still remember the inscription he said he had on the ring: 'I love you today more than yesterday, but less than tomorrow.' Another member was Ronald Ngala who, together with Tom Mboya, two leading lights of a new Kenya, died in tragic circumstances.

The working party met in Malta from May 22 to 26, 1967 and the report that changed the course of the association in the following 15 years contained some important statements. It said, among other things, that 'one of the gravest threats today is the trend towards alignment of nations by race and levels of economic development. The Commonwealth, and at its core, the CPA, both multi-racial and multinational in character, play an important part in bringing together peoples of every race, nationality, religion, and culture on a basis of mutual understanding and respect. There is a purpose which an association, with its long and successful experience of multi-racial relationship, is uniquely equipped to promote. But to maintain its dynamism the association must keep its activities under constant review and seek new means of reaching its objectives'.

I then attended the 13th Commonwealth Parliamentary Conference in Uganda. It was inaugurated by Milton Obote, president of Uganda. He took a strong view on the Rhodesia issue, stating that 'once one man one vote was not observed, the answer should be one man one gun'. When I rose to address the conference, I reminded my fellow parliamentarians that during the Second World War, the leaders of the Nationalist Party in Malta had been exiled by the British to Uganda. Countries could forgive and forget and that the solution did not lay in 'one man one gun, but one man one book', implying that the solution lay in educating the people in the importance and value of sovereignty and independence rather than in strife.

George Thomson, then secretary for colonial affairs, led the UK delegation. He was a capable speaker and a politician of a certain calibre. He said no British government would have the support of the British people for a military invasion of Rhodesia but he affirmed his government's determination to ensure majority rule in that country. During my stay in Uganda, I got to know Idi Amin, then commander of the Ugandan Army. Together with Idi Amin and some parliamentarians, we went to a night club in Entebbe a day before the conference opened. We returned to our hotel in Kampala in the early hours of the morning, but Idi Amin stayed behind. We barely had enough time to snatch a couple of hours of sleep before we had to attend the inauguration ceremony. Guess who took the salute at the guard of honour? Yes, Idi Amin. I am sure he had had no rest but he did not show any signs of fatigue. His animal spirits were to be fully revealed over the following years.

When we returned home, we had the first visit to Malta of Queen Elizabeth as Queen of Malta. Borg Olivier had a sense of perfection and the royal visit went on smoothly. He also had a special liking for the Royal family as we were to realise later in the seventies when the issue of Malta becoming a republic was raised. Through my association with the CPA and the conferences I attended, I had an opportunity of meeting leading politicians from the Commonwealth and seeing beautiful countries that I would otherwise have not seen in my life. But more than the places I have been to, what mattered most were the people, the experiences I shared with others. Through such visits, I was also able to see with my own eyes the difficulties the new democracies were experiencing and could well admire those who in difficult circumstances had the courage to stand up and be counted. When Idi Amin took over and made himself president of Uganda, he ordered the chief justice, Benedicto Kabimu Mugumba Kiwanuka, whom I had also met during my visit to that country, to issue warrants of arrest against certain individuals. When the chief justice queried the legality of the order as it had not been backed with facts justifying the issue of such warrants, he was told to sign the warrants as otherwise the crocodiles would have plenty of food to eat. Kiwanuka chose to remain servant of the law, not of a dictator. In no time he simply disappeared from the face of the earth. I often find myself recalling the memory of this African chief justice who chose death rather than making a mockery of justice and turning law into an instrument of oppression.

There is another institution to which I am greatly indebted, the Council of Europe. I was first nomiated to the Council of Europe in 1967 and I kept my links with the council throughout all my parliamentary life. When I was first appointed as a substitute in Malta's delegation, I had as colleagues from the Nationalist Party Joseph Cassar Galea, Paolo Pace, and Albert Borg Olivier de Puget. The opposition was represented by Anton Buttigieg and Patrick Holland.

On the Nationalist side, Borg Olivier de Puget was very promising. He had a most cultured mind and could analyse a political situation with great objectivity. Above all, he had an elegant approach to most issues. He was deeply-read and well-informed too. But his main shortcoming was his inertia. Paolo Pace and Joe Cassar Galea were strong in their Nationalist beliefs, but I do not think that Strasbourg was really their forum. On the opposition side, Anton Buttigieg used to dedicate himself very effectively to the workings in the committees, especially in the committee for legal affairs; he tried to exploit Strasbourg to bring up real or imaginary grievances against the Nationalist government. I followed him keenly as he mastered the ropes in Strasbourg. In the process, I found I was learning a lot myself. There were two burning issues in Strasbourg: the takeover of the Greek government by the colonels, and the student revolt, which, from the United States, had moved to countries throughout Europe.

On the Greek issue, I found myself in disagreement with Borg Olivier de Puget and with many from the European Peoples' Party who were not in favour of expelling Greece from the council. I believed the council had as its primary belief democracy in Europe and the observance of human rights. In my view, the council had to sever its links with a state that renounced the organisation's basic principles and tenets as otherwise this would make a mockery of its belief. When the resolution came to the vote, I voted for the removal of Greece as represented by the colonels; Borg Olivier de Puget voted for its retention. In fact the colonels withdrew from the Council of Europe before the resolution was put into effect.

Meanwhile, a new dawn was appearing on the horizon of Spain and Portugal as dictatorship was dissolved in both countries of the Iberian peninsula. It was at that time that I got to know Mario Soares and Adelino de Costa, who was to die in tragic circumstances some years later. Portugal's encounter with democracy was not an easy one. The temptation for the country to slide into a dictatorship of the left had been very real at the time. My good friend Diogo Freitas do Amaral had to sleep in a different place each night as he feared for his life. Soares was a great democrat who ensured Portugal's firm stand for democracy, renouncing to dictatorship of either the right or of the left. In Spain, two factors contributed to the transition to democracy: the personality of the young king and the political skills of Prime Minister Adolfo Suarez. Though difficult, the process towards democracy was administered with great skill. The debate in Strasbourg over these matters was most interesting. All countries in Western Europe were now democratic but the iron curtain was still in place. We used to be invited regularly to Berlin to see the Berlin Wall and sometimes we even ventured into East Berlin. The experience of a divided city was a lesson to those who wanted to understand the difference between the two political systems.

I never felt so committed to democracy and to Western ideals as when I visited Berlin. Indeed, I felt 'I was a Berliner', which made it even more difficult for me at first to understand the student revolt of 1968 as well as later events. The revolt by students and young people caught on like wildfire in a number of European countries. It was very much a bourgeois revolt, leftist in nature. It was at its strongest at the Free University of Berlin, when I would have thought that West Berlin would be the least left-inclined. In some Western European countries, the slogan 'Better red than dead' was catching up steadily. I thought this was so insulting to those who, in defying dictatorship in Eastern Europe, had kept alive the will to be free. I was then a member of the cultural affairs committee of the Council of Europe. The committee's bureau had entrusted a certain French professor to explain to us the events of 1968 in a political and philosophical context. All this helped me read the political events of the time through a proper understanding of under-currents affecting society, rather than through clichés.

We learned about Rudy Dutschke and his thesis on authoritarianism, and about his analysis that the challenge to the established order of capitalist civilisation originated in two marked sectors of the world population, the under-class of the coloured people, including American Blacks, and the middle-class youth of the modern countries. The influence on political thinking of German-born philosopher and sociologist Herbert Marcuse and his *One-dimensional Man* was very pronounced at that time. Lenin and the communist parties were considered obsolete, and Daniel Cohn-Bendit and his team spoke of the left-wing alternative. In his book *Obsolete Communism: The Left-Wing Alternative*, which he co-authored with his brother Gabriel, Cohn-Bendit wrote 'the premature Revolution of 1968 has introduced an entirely new factor into the revolutionary process; the entry into the struggle of youth, often privileged, but in any case disgusted with present society and thus acting as rallying points for the toiling masses. The crisis of the culture, the break-up of all-time values, and the crushing of individuality will continue for as long as capitalism and its basic contradictions are deemed to persist.'

The Appeal from the Sorbonne of June 13–14, 1968 consisted of 30 theses. Some of them were confused notions; others may have appeared to be contradictory, but they were certainly revolutionary. Thesis 29 had an interesting proposition: 'The bourgeois revolution was judicial; the proletariat revolution was economic. Ours will be social and cultural so that man can become himself.' Ernesto 'Che' Guevara became the icon of the new left; his motto 'revolution is the best education for honourable men', became a tenet. The new left put communist parties in crisis. On the one hand, communism lost the support of the revolutionary wing, giving rise in Italy in particular, to the *Brigate Rosse*. On the other hand, intelligent leaders like Enrico Berlinguer and Santiago Carrillo opted for a Euro-Communism that renounced dictatorship of the proletariat. It ended up with the fall of the Berlin Wall and the dismantling of the Soviet Union and of the Warsaw Pact. The cause and consequences of the student revolt of 1968 have still to be studied. The Greens were an offshoot of a revolution that never was, but which produced soul-searching in a society that in its affluence was losing its ideals and forgetting its principles.

We at the Council of Europe did indeed study the future. The council made me live the European ideal. It made me aware of the European Convention of Human Rights and the workings of the European Court of Human Rights and made me study the decisions given both by the commission and by the court. My legal studies assumed another dimension. I saw the law not only as an instrument of public order and as a system of regulating relations between citizens, but also a political document to uphold democracy in a court of law. I understood as never before what Cicero had written two millennia before, '*Legum servi sumus ut liberi esse possimus*' (We are slaves of the law in order that we may be free).

When I first became part of the Maltese delegation to the Council of Europe in 1967, little did I think that I would retain my link with it for

20 years. I owe a lot of my political formation to this oldest of European institutions. I found in the Council of Europe a platform for the defence of human rights in my country when these were being threatened. As a young politician, only 35 at the time, I dreamt of seeing a united Europe in the space of a decade. But dreams are far removed from reality. Even so, it is wonderful to have such dreams. And Strasbourg cathedral, with its fine spire, gives the place a touch of eternity.

17

Twilight years for the Borg Olivier government

The Nationalist government of 1966-71 faced a number of problems. To begin with, it had problems with the British government over a financial agreement that had yet to be renegotiated before the lapse of its first five years. The situation at the dockyard was getting worse as relations with Baileys, the British firm to whom the colonial government had transferred the naval dockyard, were unsatisfactory. Besides, the Services' rundown was in full swing, raising the jobless figure. The Borg Olivier government may have lacked vigour but it was creative.

An industrial development agency, the Malta Development Corporation, was set up as part of an industrialisation drive. The guiding spirit behind it was Giovanni Felice, who was again instrumental in the setting up of the Central Bank. One day we were called with urgency to approve legislation for the takeover of the dockyard from Baileys and for the setting up of the Malta Dockyard Corporation. The move showed the government's commitment to save the dockyard. Another important parliamentary session was that called over the devaluation of the Malta pound following the devaluation of sterling. Again, Felice steered the ship of state with foresight and wisdom. I remember seeing the other ministers at work but was not much impressed by their performance, probably because when one is young and inexperienced one looks for action. At the time the government worked hard to attract foreigners to settle in Malta, and for this purpose it offered very generous income tax and fiscal advantages.

The crisis in Rhodesia and difficulties in the UK made a number of those looking for a new place where to settle to pick Malta. Mintoff derisively described them as the 'six-penny settlers'. But it was thanks to this move, which revived the building industry and, of course, to important developments in industry and tourism that the country started getting to grips with the impact of the rundown of the British Services. Land changed hands quickly and substantial profits were made. Quite rightly, some viewed such land transfers and the issue of some building permits with suspicion. We were treading very dangerous ground here, but I am sure that much of the negative criticism we received at the time reflected the envy of those who did not make it. It was clear by now that the country's economy was moving forward. Indeed, the situation had become a far cry from the time when thousands had to emigrate in search of jobs. Yet, despite the fact that we had full employment, there were still those who preached doom and gloom, and this had its damaging effect.

Meanwhile, in Parliament I was absorbing not only Erskine May and standing orders, but also studying debating skills. As I may have said before, Borg Olivier was at his best in difficult situations. He never lost his cool and knew precisely when to react or to simply choose not to react at all. But these were not the best of years in his personal domestic affairs. Although Borg Olivier was accessible and forthcoming in politics, he was personally a closed book. With Mintoff he had a unique relationship. They respected each other at a distance. They could understand each other without the need of talking to each other. At certain moments I could see that a simple nod of the head from both was enough for some complicated parliamentary argument to be settled. Mintoff was careful not to bring Borg Olivier's domestic problem out into the public, but I am sure he could, indeed should, have done much more after the elections of 1971 to stop his supporters' abuse and insolence against him. Mintoff was possibly at his best as leader of the opposition. His performance in a budget debate used to be superb from both an economic aspect and even more so politically. But in my view he ruined most of his arguments by resorting to vulgar populism, which, he believed, endeared him to his supporters.

These were also the years when tourism began to take root. The Hilton and the Sheraton were among the first hotels to come to Malta. Ta' Ċenċ set the standards in Gozo. Richard England was making a name for himself in hotel architecture with, among others, the design for the Ramla Bay Hotel and the Salina Bay Hotel. Mġarr Harbour was turned into an all-weather harbour and new industrial estates were built. With some delay and following some very negative propaganda, the government started tackling the housing problem by building housing estates. In the fifties the Labour government had also contributed to the building of housing units in Santa Lucija but the Nationalist administration had then carried out some extensive building projects in that locality as well as in San Ġwann, Msida, and Hamrun.

The university moved from Valletta to Msida. To those who belong to the generation of students that had studied in Valletta, there was a touch of nostalgia in the move. I still believe the university ought to have continued making use of the building by keeping some faculties there. It could also have been used by the university council. But the move to Tal-Qroqq was an important milestone. In my days, the number of students was under 500, today it is over 9,000. In a way, this was a cultural revolution. I feel I have directly contributed towards this development when I proposed that tertiary education be free of charge for all. In fact I argued in party circles that our education system should be free of charge at all levels, from kindergarten to doctorate level.

In an article I had once written for the *Times of Malta*, 'Blueprint for the university', I wrote that we should abolish the means test, describing it as a mean test. I well remember the time when my family had to do without certain basic commodities to pay my university fees. I had managed to convince Borg Olivier and his brother Pawlu, who at the time was minister of education, of the importance of my proposal for education in Malta. Ugo Mifsud Bonnici backed me throughout the campaign. The principle was introduced in the budget for 1971. For reasons that I still do not understand, the then Student Representative Council was not in favour of the move. Free university education at all levels is today part of the national *acquis*. The move boosted tertiary education, although most of the credit for expansion is due to the Nationalist administration of 1987.

The government's record of achievements by then was certainly impressive but the public did not appreciate the progress made and an Oliver Twist's mood of 'wanting more' set in. Borg Olivier did not even attempt to explain the progress that had been done. Rightly or wrongly, many believed that Borg Olivier had too many tired faces in his cabinet, and when Giovanni Felice resigned as minister, there was a popular demand for a cabinet reshuffle. When the parliamentary group insisted on Borg Olivier to take action, he simply said, *à la* de Gaulle, 'I understand.' But he would not do anything to change the situation.

I was not happy at the fact that the governor general was not a Maltese citizen. I had no problem personally with Sir Maurice Dorman, who was a likeable person and had strongly come out supporting the Maltese government during the crisis with the British government on the financial agreement. Those who lived the time remember him most for his open declaration: 'I stand foursquare with the people of Malta.' However, despite this, I felt the transition period following independence was now over and that it was time to have a Maltese as governor general. Besides, I also felt it was time too for Malta to have a republican system of government, with a Maltese head of state.

Towards the end of the legislature, the General Workers' Union called an overtime ban at the dockyard, bringing the enterprise close to bankruptcy. Lorry Sant, a young Labour MP, a dockyard worker and secretary of the union's metal workers' section, was turning the dockyard into a major political asset to rock the Nationalist government. Sant was an intelligent, energetic man, with little scruples in his political objectives. Joe Attard Kingswell, the union's general secretary, tried to help out during the rundown of the British Services and had actively collaborated with Borg Olivier to help find the right solutions to the problems but the GWU was by now becoming a willing tool to a Labour victory. The union's overtime ban at the dockyard was seen by most as having been politically motivated, so much so that when Mintoff was returned to power in June 1971 the ban was called off immediately.

Through the services of Mgr Emanuel Gerada, then bishop-in-waiting, Mintoff and Gonzi reached a measure of understanding. The interdict, which, in my view, should have never been imposed, was lifted. The interdict was an over-reaction on the part of the Church authorities to Mintoff's strategy to belittle the Church and its institutions in the eyes of the people. As the 1971 elections approached, the wind of change was blowing strong, not in the right direction in so far as the Nationalist Party was concerned.

In the time of the Borg Olivier government, the people felt generally relaxed as politics did not dominate daily life and the style of administration was far from overbearing. All this should have been a great political asset for the party. It proved to be otherwise, for many were by then taking progress and the stride forward the country had made since independence under Borg Olivier's guidance for granted.

The party's parliamentary group sensed that things were not moving in the right direction. 'Our' group – Ugo Mifsud Bonnici, Albert Borg Olivier de Puget, and myself – now had a welcome addition, Eddie Fenech Adami. He had not been elected in the 1966 general elections and he certainly felt sore about it. I had proposed Eddie for co-option when George Caruana, who had been elected in a by-election, died. I thought Eddie would make a good MP, a good investment for the future. But I found some reluctance at first to his acceptance for co-option, especially in the Borg Olivier family, possibly because Pawlu Borg Olivier, who was elected from Birkirkara, considered him a competitor for the Nationalist vote in that district. George Caruana had represented the district of Paola, with which Eddie had absolutely no connection. I therefore suggested that, if the party executive were to choose Eddie, he would have to bind himself to look after the interests of the Paola district, apart from contesting the Birkirkara constituency. The majority accepted the suggestion. On his part, Eddie accepted the condition but as events turned out, he did not pay much attention to the Paola district, though he most certainly served Malta well.

In the meantime, my legal practice was doing well. I had an interesting murder case. This time an 18-year-old from Marsa was accused of having killed his father when he hit him on the head with an iron bar. The man was found dead with rosary beads in his hand. At that time, murder carried the death penalty. After studying the facts of the case, I pleaded that the accused was mentally insane at the time he killed his father. The procedure followed in such cases is interesting. The court appoints experts to examine the accused and if these certify that he is insane the court, subject to certain other procedures, sends him to a mental hospital, to be kept there indefinitely. In this case, however, the experts decided that the accused was sane. The procedure allows the defence to contest the experts' opinion, and the case was brought before a trial by jury to determine the fact at issue, namely, whether the accused was insane or not at the time of the crime.

I submitted to the jury that the experts' conclusion was unacceptable and I supported the plea with arguments that touched upon his character, attitude, and reactions as well as family history. The trial was presided over by Mr Justice Flores. The jury's verdict was that my client was insane at the time of the commission of the offence. The case is a classic one in so far as the issue of insanity is concerned in that the jury did not accept the experts' opinion but relied on the evidence produced. There was an interesting aftermath to the case. One day the man climbed to the roof of Mount Carmel Hospital and threatened to jump off unless a petition he had made for his release from hospital was accepted. He found it difficult to understand how the psychiatrists insisted that he should be kept in hospital when they had found him sane. The jury had found him insane *at the time* of the offence. Anyway, he was eventually released, got married, and had children.

18

Labour's victory at the polls

In the first six months of 1971, Malta was gearing up fast for the general elections. Labour was organising itself in a big way. The Nationalist Party was relying on its track record. It had won independence for Malta, helped, through its policies, to bring about an economic boom, despite all the prophesies of doom, and above all established democracy. Tourism was expanding and the quarrel between the Church and the Malta Labour Party was dying out. Malta then began opening its first embassies abroad. An exceptional civil servant, Frederick Amato Gauci, set about building up the foreign office from scratch and he did so with flying colours. We had some very good people in the diplomatic corps, a number of whom gave an excellent account of themselves in the years that followed. Malta was punching beyond its size when at the United Nations Arvid Pardo launched the Law of the Sea debate, the seminal idea of the common heritage of mankind.

But the Nationalist Party had no proper organisation at the time. To begin with, it had few section committees and too few clubs. The party's newspaper, *In-Nazzjon Tagħna*, was launched in 1970. Ċensu Tabone was energetic both as general secretary of the party and, also, as a minister, but he had his mind set on the deputy leadership of the party. The electoral programme had been kept secret from most of us, myself included. In fact I had first learned of what the party was proposing in that election at a party congress called to approve the programme. To my astonishment, the main thrust of the programme was a proposal for the abolition of income tax. Since the electorate had not been taken in when the Christian Workers' Party made the same proposal in the previous election, I wondered why the party was suggesting the idea. The abolition of income tax could well help create jobs and attract new investment but it would also remove the correctional effect on newly-acquired wealth, which social justice required.

95

Speaking at mass meetings helped me improve my political image and build greater confidence in myself as a politician. Suddenly, violence started raising its ugly head. I remember once when as I was about to drive away from a meeting some people started banging on my car. I had Violet and the children with me. Then someone threw a floor tile at the car. The children were petrified. I first took them home and then went back, on my own, to the place where the incident happened, next to a bar in Balbi Street in Marsa. I just wanted to show them that they were very well mistaken if they thought they had scared me. When they saw me coming down the street, I could well see they felt bad about it. They did not boo me this time. Some looked sullen. Others just nodded their head. Some were my own clients. I kept going regularly to that bar in my years of campaigning to talk to constituents there, irrespective of their political persuasion.

I felt I was doing well with the electorate but I had a feeling the party was not. Were we heading towards defeat? Most likely, I thought. When, after the voting, the boxes containing the votes were being taken to the Mediterranean Conference Centre, I was at Elia Borg Bonaci Café in Ħamrun when I was told that I had an urgent telephone call – the prime minister wanted to see me at the Auberge d'Aragon. When I arrived at his office, I found Ugo there, too. He had received the same message. Borg Olivier was very calm. Without looking at us directly, he talked about the fact that we had not been fully utilised during the campaign, particularly in talks on television. But then, as if to justify the party's shortcoming on this, he said such talks were limited in number. Then, in a very disconnected way, he said we could not take victory for granted, and did not exclude defeat. Ugo and I did not understand why we were called. Before we could even enter into any sort of conversation with him, the unsolicited meeting was over. It was Borg Olivier's last time at the Auberge d'Aragon as prime minister.

Political tension was high in Żebbuġ where, just by a handful of votes, Labour won three of the five seats, inverting the majority held by the Nationalists in the previous election. We also lost the fourth seat in Gozo. Labour had won the general elections by a slim majority. This was bad, but worse was the violence that broke out immediately afterwards. Thousands took to the streets of Valletta, singing obscenities, threatening and beating up opponents, and breaking up shops. A neighbour of mine had a coffin put up on his balcony, just in front of my house, and the front door of our house was daubed with red paint. We had decided to move to a small place we had in Buġibba until the euphoria died out and when we returned to Ħamrun, we found the glass panes of our balcony shattered. We were told our house had come under attack because we had made rude gestures with our hands when a MLP demonstration was passing down the road. But we were not even at home at the time! So, Labour had come to power with a bang, one that was to last for 16 years. In many of those years of Labour's 'democracy', we suffered all imaginable humiliation. Labour excelled in intimidation. There were people whom I knew well who, on seeing me on my way to court, would cross the road lest they be seen saying 'hello' or 'good morning' to me.

At one time, I received a phone call from someone asking me to go to a house in Mdina because the police were carrying out a search at the house of Lawrence Cachia Zammit, the minister's brother. At that same time, Alexander Cachia Zammit was being arrested for, according to the police, 'stealing' government documents. This marked the beginning of the Cachia Zammit saga.

19

The Cachia Zammit trial

I was 39 when the Nationalist Party found itself in opposition, and 55 when it was returned to power. But it was not the length of time we stayed in opposition that put us and the country on edge, but the fight we had to put up to ensure the survival of democracy. However, the Labour government, first under Mintoff, until 1983, and under Karmenu Mifsud Bonnici, until 1987, can be credited with some positive and commendable improvements. It is important to write the story with a sense of history and I think Labour did well in setting up Air Malta and Sea Malta.

On the social front, the introduction of family allowances helped bring about a better quality of life to many. An important constitutional development was the change in the island's status to a republic. But in the years 1971 to 1987 abuse of power was made a system of governance. Violence became a tool in the hands of the party in government. Many Nationalist Party clubs were ransacked and some even set on fire. One club in particular, that in Floriana, opposite the Lion Fountain, was broken into no fewer than 21 times. When I took over as party general secretary in 1974 and started organising the party, requisition orders were issued on places that we had planned to turn into party clubs. The transfer of workers from one department to another in the government service became an instrument of political vindictiveness.

As I said, violence became the order of the day at public meetings and demonstrations. We even saw violence in Parliament. Pro-government demonstrations served as a means of intimidation. The law courts had been made part of this general abuse of power. After the Cachia Zammit trial, a violent crowd attacked the home of the presiding judge, Maurice Caruana Curran, overturned my car, which was parked next to my office in Old Bakery Street, and then went on the rampage, threatening people and using foul language.

Judges were moved from one court to another whenever a court gave a decision or decree unfavourable to the government. It was a farce of the first order. The General Workers' Union was harnessed to follow government policies. The Union Ħaddiema Magħqudin and the other unions came to be known collectively as the 'free trade unions', and their members were victimised. In some places workers who followed a union directive were suspended from work and left without pay for months. It was a recurrence of what had happened in Italy at the start of Fascism, as well as in Germany in the first days of Nazism. Some who did not live those years may find all this a somewhat exaggerated description of the times. It is not. It was thanks to two fundamental factors that events in Malta did not take the turn other countries had experienced in similar circumstances. These were the people's resistance inspired by the spirit of defiance shown by the Nationalist Party leadership, and the links Malta had with a free Europe, which helped expose the excesses of the Labour government.

I found myself experiencing the violence from the very first days Labour was returned to power. It was particularly evident at the inauguration of Parliament in August 1971. When we left St John's co-cathedral after hearing the Mass of the Holy Spirit, I found myself surrounded by a crowd of Labour supporters. They started calling me names and pushing me about. I tried to go for my car but I could not find it. Nor could I see my colleagues. I was being shuffled here and there, with people spitting at me. At one moment, just as I was about to be punched by someone, a certain Paul Aquilina, from Marsa, jumped to my defence. That saved the situation in so far as I was concerned, and I started walking to the Palace as best as I could. By this time, Inspectors Willie Moran and Paul Mamo had come to my assistance and they walked with me, giving me a measure of protection. But I was still being followed by a menacing crowd.

As I was about to reach the law courts, opposite the Great Siege Monument, someone threw a shoe at me. On seeing me go through the crowd, head held high, Herbert Ganado, shouted 'Bravo Guido'. The gesture showed his goodness.

When I reached the Palace, the crowd surged on me again. Some who had been watching the scene from the Palace balcony told me later they thought I would not make it to the door. I think I only made it through the protection I had received from the police inspectors. I had put on a new suit that day. It was all covered in spit by the time I made it to the Palace. I never wore it again. When I raised the matter at the first parliamentary sitting we had, I received no word of apology from the government's side, though I could feel that some of the Labour MPs with whom I had good personal relations had a sense of shame at what had been done to me. Borg Olivier hugged me. It was a bad experience, one that I had to face again at other times.

The Cachia Zammit case provided a backdrop to the atmosphere of intimidation that had developed in the Mintoff's years. When the first voting results appeared to go against the Nationalist government, some friends of Cachia Zammit had gone to the ministry to withdraw papers, files, and other objects belonging to him. Normally, a minister removes all his personal papers and objects close to the date of a general election. It is always wise to do so. Cachia Zammit must have thought otherwise.

His men removed the minister's files from his office and took them to his brother's house in Mdina. They were followed by Labour supporters. Later, the police swooped on the house and took away the files, which contained letters from persons who had written to the minister asking for favours – a job, a transfer within the public service, or some kind of medical assistance. They also took away cabinet papers, consisting of memoranda and minutes of meetings. The search was given great publicity, and Police Commissioner Effie Bencini, a showman *par excellence*, turned the event into a *cause célèbre* of a minister stealing government documents. He called a press conference and dished out pictures of the search. Cachia Zammit and his brother were arrested and kept at police headquarters. The political tension rose again. At Żejtun, a Labour stronghold, Cachia Zammit was projected as a criminal. Indeed, this was the image that was projected of him in the press and on television. At that time there was only one television station and soon after Labour's election it was turned into a tool in the party's hands, churning out dramatic accounts of the 'scandals' under the former Nationalist administration.

When I was asked by the Cachia Zammit family to take up the case, I went to police headquarters to speak to Effie Bencini, whom I had known for years. The police officers were hostile, but Bencini was courteous. It was clear Labour were out to make political capital of the case and to scare former Nationalist ministers. Labour newspapers showed Cachia Zammit in the blackest of terms, speculating with relish on the years he would have to spend behind bars if he were found guilty. Eddie Fenech Adami was asked to defend Lawrence Cachia Zammit. I thought it best to separate the defence as Lawrence's case could be dealt with less difficulty as he had only been accused of providing the place where the files were taken. Regretfully, when I sought the assistance of other lawyers who were more renowned and certainly more experienced than I was, I found no response. They could not, or would not, be available to defend Cachia Zammit. In a way, it was better they did not offer their services because, in shouldering all the responsibility of taking up the defence myself, I could decide on my own as to what line to take.

No major problems arose in the compilation of evidence. I did not want to reveal my line of defence at that stage. The prosecution was led by Dr Oliver Gulia, an experienced prosecuting counsel who was invariably correct in his attitude. He tried to get a conviction without resorting to excesses, which could easily happen in trials of a political character. We were fortunate in having one of Malta's foremost judges, Maurice Caruana Curran, as the presiding judge. The jury empanelled was, so far as I was aware of, a good political mix. My concern was that, at the initial stage, the judge seemed inclined to accept the thesis of guilt as submitted by counsel for the prosecution. I had to go into the minutiae of many of the items exhibited to show the 'personal character' of most of the files exhibited. I cross-examined with effect Alfred Wirth, who was the head of the civil service. Wirth confirmed it was common for ministers to take files away with them so that they could work at home after office hours. He also mentioned the case of Sir Paul Boffa, a former prime minister and a minister in Borg Olivier's coalition government of the fifties, who had returned office files he had kept at home months after he was no longer in office. He also confirmed that letters from constituents and others belonging to the minister personally had nothing to do with government files.

At one stage the prosecution shifted its attention to the possession of cabinet papers, rather than the minister's personal material. I consulted British constitutional authorities and I found that ministers were entitled to keep cabinet papers. Cabinet papers remain confidential documents of the administration to which they belong and a new government has no access to them. I therefore argued on these lines in my defence and held that, unless specifically regulated, a minister was entitled to keep such documents, even after the termination of office.

Labour supporters believed Cachia Zammit was going to be found guilty and were keenly waiting for the verdict in order to start celebrating their 'victory'. Inspector Willie Moran suggested to me that perhaps it would be better if I were to start moving in and out of court through the back door in Strait Street to avoid the crowds. I told him I appreciated his advice but I had always used the front door and that I had planned to continue doing so. For the duration of the trial, Cachia Zammit was allowed to stay at the

Excelsior Hotel, at his expense, provided he also paid the expenses for the court marshal who was to stay there to keep an eye on him.

Cachia Zammit was very good on the witness stand. His sincerity was quite evident though, to be frank, I did not like one comment he made, that sometimes he used to do crossword puzzles during cabinet meetings. I think I defended Cachia Zammit objectively, basing the case on constitutional arguments. In this way, what was obviously meant as a political trial was turned into a dispassionate examination of facts, strictly within a context of law. The address to the jury by Mr Justice Caruana Curran was correct from the legal angle, and he did contribute to further depoliticise the case. When the jury retired to deliberate, there was great tension, both inside and outside the law courts.

Cachia Zammit remained very calm, at least outwardly, but his brother had become a bit nervous. The crowd outside the law courts was divided in two groups, kept at a distance away from each other by the police. When the jury concluded their deliberations, we all trooped in. My daughter Giannella, then only 15, was there. She had followed the trial with interest. Dr J.J. Vella, who was doing his legal *practicum* at my office, was there too. The courtroom and the balcony were packed with Cachia Zammit's family members and supporters. But there were also some thugs sent in by Labour to watch the proceedings and to report to their quarters. When the jurors took their places, there was absolute silence; a silence begotten by tension is louder than sound. The eight-day trial came to an end on November 15, 1972 when the jury found Alexander Cachia Zammit unanimously not guilty. The same verdict was returned for his brother Lawrence. Tension changed into great relief and the Nationalist crowd outside burst into cheers and unforgettable shouts of joy 'Liberat! Liberat!' (He has been acquitted! He has been acquitted!) Eddie Fenech Adami, not very demonstrative by nature, shook my hand over and over again. Alexander Cachia Zammit could hardly suppress his emotions. The verdict was given at 2.45 a.m.

As we left the law courts, we were garlanded with flowers and lifted shoulder high by supporters. As from that moment, the Nationalists were back in the streets, showing to one and all that they were truly Nationalists and no longer afraid of Labour. We passed through very difficult times, times of shame, violence, and humiliation, but as from that night onwards the Nationalists stood up again and wanted to be counted. We never turned back.

20

The making and unmaking of a regime

When Mintoff took over, he did so with zest and energy. He started off by kicking out Nato headquarters. Malta had hosted Nato headquarters, Allied Forces Mediterranean since the early fifties, when the island was still a self-governing colony. Admiral Mountbatten was Commander, H.A.F.Med. Borg Olivier had not been on the best of terms with Mountbatten, who expected the Malta government to bow to his requests. He had the effrontery once to demand that police force horses be put at his disposal for the playing of polo at Marsa. He had also been involved in efforts to make a member of Boffa's party defect from the coalition government, which led to Borg Olivier's defeat and to Mintoff being elected on his 'integration with Britain' proposal. When Malta became independent, the status of H.A.F.Med in Malta had to be negotiated. Borg Olivier had sent out feelers that he was interested in having Nato's reaction to the possibility of Malta becoming a member of the alliance. Borg Olivier was never explicit on this and it appears that Nato did not react favourably to the idea. Nor did they accept to have an agreement with Malta under which their stay would be 'regulated' and compensation paid for the time they stayed on the island. In the end, they had settled on an arrangement under which Nato's presence in Malta was only 'regulated' and certain legal provisions were made.

At a time when the world was divided in two blocs, and Nato's presence in Europe was a determining factor in defending the Western world from communism and from the Soviet Union, Borg Olivier preferred to suffer Nato's rebuff in silence. He did so lest he would endanger the values of the Nato alliance and, also, the image of reliability that independent Malta, still in the process of moving out of its fortress mould with difficulties, was building for itself. His stand reflected his sense of maturity.

When I visited Nato headquarters as a member of the North Atlantic Association, which had a branch in Malta, soon after France had moved out of the combined command, I realised, through my talks there, the proper nature of Malta's 'arrangement'. I remember being somewhat struck by the emphasis they had made that it was not an agreement. Towards the end of Borg Olivier's government, Admiral Gino Birindelli had made a tentative proposal for a financial offer to be made to Malta, linked to the negotiation of some sort of agreement, but Borg Olivier told him that, had Nato really been concerned about Malta, it should have helped the island when it first sought its assistance. He felt it had not been proper to negotiate an agreement with Nato in the last months of a government in office. Borg Olivier's stand was confirmed to me by Nato sources some years later.

So, to get back to Mintoff, when, on his return to power, he kicked Nato out of the country, I did not feel all that bad about the move, even though it hit the interests of the Western Alliance, of which Malta had still formed part. Nato had taken the island for granted for far too long. Having removed Nato from Malta with great ease, Mintoff set about tackling the British government on the financial agreement that Borg Olivier had negotiated with it with so much difficulty.

Mintoff wanted more. He put the island's defence treaty in abeyance and started negotiating a new one under which Malta would rent a military base to Britain. I disagreed with the notion of renting one's country to a foreign state. It was one thing having a defence treaty, quite another renting part of your territory in a mercenary approach. To my mind, this reduced the country's sovereignty. The Nationalist Party took up this line of action.

When, on March 26, 1972, he reached an agreement under which defence facilities were rented out to Britain for seven years, up to 1979, for the payment, in conjunction with Nato, of £14 million annually, the mercenary element involved in the deal was ignored and Mintoff was regarded as a saviour, '*Is-Salvatur*', for having successfully concluded an agreement with the UK for a much higher amount than that which had been negotiated with Borg Olivier. Lord Carrington had found Mintoff's bargaining skills better than he had imagined but he did not expect that he would fly off to China the moment the agreement with Britain was signed. Mintoff's trip to China, arranged through the good offices of Nicolae Caucescu, Romania's notorious president, was made at a time when that country was establishing itself as a country standing up to what it described as American hegemony, and seeking a presence in the Mediterranean, which it had succeeded to get for some time through Albania.

At the time that negotiations with Britain were taking place, Mintoff had also exploited to the maximum the good relations he had built up with

Muammar Gaddafi of Libya. Besides financial help, he had also managed to make arrangements for Libyan personnel to man the airport's control tower. Mintoff had also started using the Conference for Security and Co-operation in Europe, which had begun in Helsinki in 1972, to his full advantage. He put forward the theory that there could be no security in the Mediterranean without security in Europe, and that there could be no security in Europe without security in the Mediterranean. He found opposition to his stand from both the United States and the Soviet Union. But he persisted and was not afraid of using the veto to stall proceedings. In fact, his veto kept the CSCE in a stalemate, something that earned us the wrath of several members. Mintoff ultimately managed to have the so-called 'Mediterranean basket' approved by the conference, but the political tactics he used in Helsinki were not forgotten, as I were to find out for myself at the time of my meetings abroad in later years, particularly during the negotiations for Malta to join the European Union.

Malta's Mediterranean policy was one of the first outward manifestations of independence. Borg Olivier's first official visits abroad after independence were to Libya and Italy. He had also gone to France and I recall Borg Olivier recounting to me the call he had made on President Charles de Gaulle. But I think it was Mintoff who made the need of ensuring Mediterranean security a cornerstone of our foreign policy. He had, of course, wanted to exploit Malta's geographical position. After he had at first established close relations with Israel, mainly through the Socialist International, he swerved completely to the Palestinian and Arab side.

At home, Mintoff presented a real challenge to democracy. He started off by wanting to scrap the constitution as he argued that it had been imposed by the British, completely forgetting that it had been approved in a referendum. He stepped up his threats by failing to set up the constitutional court. He did this through a very simple method, the non-appointment of the vice-president of the court. When Sir Anthony Mamo, the chief justice, was appointed governor general to take the place of Sir Maurice Dorman, the then vice-president, Professor John J. Cremona, was appointed chief justice and president of the constitutional court. Mr Justice Flores, very deservingly, was appointed vice-president. When Flores retired in 1972, no vice-president was appointed. The constitutional court could not function without a vice-president but Mintoff refused to appoint anyone to the post. This was an unacceptable situation that persisted for three years, from 1972 to 1974.

Acts of violence against individuals and at Nationalist Party meetings raised political tension in the country to a new level. Independence Day was removed from the national calendar of public holidays, a move seen by most Nationalists as an attempt by Mintoff to play down the significance of the event. Ardent Labour supporters considered the Independence Day anniversary as one of shame. On the day of the first anniversary under a Labour administration, when the pubic holiday was still on the statute book, the Nationalists felt that, one way or another, they still had to mark the anniversary, so they first went to the church of St Paul Shipwrecked in Valletta to hear Mass said for the occasion. When a spontaneous demonstration was held afterwards in Merchants Street, the police stepped in. That marked the beginning of the time when Labour began to go all out to start instilling fear in Nationalist Party supporters. People of excellent conduct were arrested on the grounds that they had taken part in an unlawful demonstration and causing public disturbance when they shouted 'Viva Malta Indipendenti'. I defended several of them in court. Clearly, the aim was to stop the Nationalists from celebrating Malta's greatest day in its history. This showed the extent to which Mintoff's regime could go in its pettiness. We faced worse violence from Labour thugs a year later, when the police not only failed to protect us, but they actually joined forces with the thugs. They were terrible days. But again, the way ahead was stiffer still.

In the meantime, the Nationalist Party was undergoing a process of change. At long last Borg Olivier was persuaded that the party had to have a deputy leader. I was considered a likely candidate for the post, but I realised I could be 'used' as a pawn so that no candidate would get the number of votes required. What those in my circle wanted to see was a radical change in the party's leadership, not a change of leader. We agreed that Censu Tabone be nominated as candidate for deputy leadership, myself for the post of general secretary, Eddie Fenech Adami for the chairmanship of the administrative council, and Ugo Mifsud Bonnici for the presidency of the general council. A shadow cabinet was appointed and all this, together with changes made to the statute, injected new life into the party.

Life began to get a bit more difficult as Labour started resorting to abuse of power. We had obtained a police permit to hold a demonstration in Valletta as part of our activities marking the 1973 Independence Day anniversary. When, a day before, we held a mass meeting and Labour supporters began throwing stones in our direction and threatening us, I spoke strongly against this and began using the slogan 'no to abuse of power'. In the evening of that same day, my mother was simply terrorised by Labour supporters when they passed by her house during a demonstration in St Joseph High Street, Hamrun. I was at home, L'Orangerie, in Blata l-Bajda at the time. We had moved there in December 1972. The telephone rang and my heart sunk when I heard mother crying hysterically. She was petrified when supporters began breaking the glass windows and shouting all sorts of abuse at her.

She had had some heart problems and had in fact been at St Luke's Hospital for some time. I did not think for one moment it was wise of her to continue living on her own, but she used to say *'non voglio essere di peso a nessuno'*. After the incident I managed to convince her it was better for her to stay at Apap Institute in Santa Venera, which was run by the Dominican nuns. She had a room to herself there and could move about. On the feast of Our Lady of Mount Carmel in Valletta, she insisted on going to the church to hear Mass and see her beloved Madonna. *Patri* Avertan made her day by keeping a special place for her in the church. She felt so happy singing the *Salve Regina, mater misercordiae*, and that beautiful anthem *Fjur tal-Karmnu*. Soon, however, her health started to get worse.

Independence Day 1974 was similar to that of 1973, marked by violence. When the party's demonstration was over, I rushed to Apap Institute to be with my mother. She died three days later. We all love our mothers, and I simply adored mine. Someone wrote to me in one of the letters of condolence I received in the days after her death: 'You need not pray for your mother, she will pray for you.' I have missed my mother every day since.

September 21, 1975 was a horrible day, one I would have wished my mother not to know anything about had she been alive. Again, as the party's general secretary, I had made the usual arrangements for the celebration of that year's Independence Day anniversary and had obtained all the necessary police permits . As the demonstration reached the Malta Labour Party club in Republic Street, Valletta, we were attacked by Labour thugs who had been allowed to assemble there by the police. Hard objects rained on us from the terrace of the Bank of Valletta as the thugs surged on us like lions on their prey. At one time, the police joined the thugs, beating us with their batons. A number of Nationalists were injured. I remember seeing Notary Joe Cachia, a quiet and unassuming person, being manhandled and beaten up. The float taking Borg Olivier and others steered in the direction of Old Bakery Street and I tried to keep our supporters together, urging them to resist, as passively as they could, to this bout of violence against freedom of expression.

It was dreadful seeing Maltese turn against other Maltese with such vehemence. In the eyes of the regime, celebrating our country's independence was a crime. Some of the policemen had clubs larger in size than they usually used. Suddenly, a policeman whom I knew, broke away from the rest and made straight to me, hitting me on the temple with his club. Blood streamed down my face and I fell to the ground. I was taken to the Casino Maltese, where a number of our supporters were taking shelter. Violet was there too. I remember her telling me that I was setting a good example to others. It was not over yet. Police then started running after Gianella and her friends, running after them like wolves. The wound required nine sutures and Ċensu Tabone said I was lucky I was not killed on the spot by the blow. One of my supporters, Mrs Busuttil, expressed horror at seeing me in that state, covered in blood. She had not been made aware yet that her son Dennis had been hit on the head and was in a critical condition. Back at party headquarters, I found Borg Olivier waiting for me. He told me 'Aħna kburin bik' (we are proud of you). I still treasure a picture I have showing Borg Olivier with his arms around me.

The irony is that this happened to me at a time when I was involved in talks aimed at finding solutions to constitutional problems. Mintoff had wanted to make Malta a republic and he advanced a logical argument. I did not think it would have been very difficult to come to an agreement over this but, following the bouts of violence, the situation had become so bad that the lines of communication between government and opposition had been cut. One day, Dr John Mamo, son of the governor general, Sir Anthony Mamo, told me his father wanted to see me in private. Sir Anthony told me when I went to see him at San Anton that he was prepared to mediate over the constitutional issue if he were asked to do so. I consulted Borg Olivier and, at a meeting of the party's executive committee, I was authorised to tell Sir Anthony that we had been prepared to discuss constitutional changes in full observance of the constitution. Sir Anthony attended the first meetings, but we then started meeting at the ministry of justice. Among those taking part were Anton Buttigieg and Ġużè Cassar, for the government, and Borg Olivier, Ugo Mifsud Bonnici, Eddie Fenech Adami, Ċensu Tabone, and myself for the opposition. Despite the lengthy talks we had, we did not make any progress. Borg Olivier preferred shelving the issue over Malta becoming a republic till after the forthcoming general elections.

Mintoff refused and wanted to thrash such pending matters as the issue over burial at the cemetery of those who were at odds with the Church and expropriation of land. At one time, he also proposed removing the George

Cross from Malta's flag. Very important for Mintoff was the reference to the Roman Catholic religion in the constitution. Some of the proposals he made involved important issues of values; I felt that, had the political situation in the country not been so tense, we might have been able to make progress in solving other matters that had been brought up in the talks. At any rate, the situation deteriorated because at the time we were involved in these talks, Labour were holding public demonstrations at which we were openly being threatened with physical violence.

Eddie and I tried to distinguish between core constitutional matters and others that could be dealt with through amendments to other laws. I had insisted all along that any changes agreed upon had to be made in accordance with the provisions of the constitution but a subsequent meeting at Castille with Mintoff cancelled out all the efforts I had made in this direction. Ugo could not take part in this meeting as he had to act as witness at the marriage of a lawyer who worked at his office. When the preliminaries were over, Borg Olivier told Mintoff, to our complete astonishment, that he was prepared to accept that the necessary changes be made to the constitution without the need to hold a referendum, in cases where referendum was required, provided that the issue over the change from a monarchy to a republic be shelved till after the elections and provided also that a referendum be held on this proposal. We could not understand what had made Borg Olivier do this. We remained dumbfounded. Mintoff immediately sensed that Borg Olivier had put himself and us in a corner. He insisted he had legal advice that Article 6 of the constitution was not in itself subject to change by a qualified majority. Borg Olivier's proposal had nullified our stand. Mintoff now had the upper hand as he could well tell his people that the Nationalists were prepared to risk constitutional chaos just to keep the Queen as head of state.

When we returned to party headquarters, I tendered my resignation as secretary to the parliamentary group and asked that it be kept secret for the time being so as not to hurt the morale of Nationalist supporters. Borg Olivier held on to his stand. The parliamentary group was strongly divided. We pleaded with Borg Olivier to remove his objection to Malta becoming a republic so that we could concentrate on the other issues being discussed. At one point Ugo, in a very theatrical gesture, kneeled down before Borg Olivier and implored him to change his mind. But Borg Olivier would not budge. The only thing he did concede was that the opposition members be given a free vote in Parliament over the issue, to be declared by him as leader of the opposition.

Anyway, we were not prepared to see Mintoff simply scrapping the Independence constitution. In the end most of the amendments agreed upon were the result of a compromise. But Mintoff still objected to the holding of a referendum over the proposed changes, even when I told him that we could do so on a common platform. But, either because he felt we could never carry Borg Olivier with us, or because he considered holding a referendum an unnecessary risk to his government, he stood his ground and no referendum was held. And we had to acquiesce to legal advice given by the Crown Advocate General, Dr Edgar Mizzi, that the amendments could 'legally' be made without the need of calling a referendum. The party wanted to have further constitutional advice on the matter from Britain and Eddie was sent to London together with Victor Ragonesi to seek a second opinion from constitutional jurists. We were told we could contest the issue in our constitutional court, but this was not very helpful since the constitutional court had not been reconstituted yet. And even if it had been reconstituted, jurists doubted if the Privy Council would interpret Article 6 of the Constitution as a 'super norma constituzionale'.

When the proposed amendments were tabled in Parliament, the Nationalist opposition split up, with seven, including Borg Olivier, voting against, and the rest of us, voting with the government. As it had been agreed beforehand with Borg Olivier, the members had been given a free vote. It was a most painful debate, one that has remained vividly in my mind. The date was December 13, 1974. Malta was declared a republic and, as had also been agreed upon in the two-party talks, Sir Anthony Mamo was voted by the House as Malta's first president.

I felt better that we had managed to deal with constitutional issues separately from matters of a political nature. But the Nationalist Party was at its lowest ebb in December 1974. I then managed to have the party executive and parliamentary group approve a unanimous declaration of policy, thus leaving behind us moments of agonising debate and division. Personally I felt very bad finding myself holding different views from those of Borg Olivier whom I held in great respect, but I loathed seeing further division in the country on an issue over which I felt we should have all been united, that of turning Malta into a republic. Had the party not been divided over the issue, we could have possibly been able to delineate a better role for the president. We had to leave the evolution of the president's role to the character of the individual holding the office and, also, to the circumstances of history.

Settling the constitutional issue did not make Mintoff a democrat in his behaviour, so much so that Independence Day was abolished as a national feast. September 8, celebrating Malta's victory in the 1565 siege, was made a national day. This was then replaced by Republic Day, December 13 and, as if this were not enough, this was in turn replaced by March 31, marking the closure of the British base at the termination of Mintoff's own rent agreement with Britain. It required a change of government for a measure of consensus to be reached. The agreement was for the country to have five national feasts: September 8, September 21, December 13, *Sette Giugno*, and March 31. Too many, I agree, but at least we managed to agree on the choice of dates!

As the political violence increased with the approach of the general elections, the government was concurrently seeking to find a more subtle way of beating us at the polls. It did this through changes to the electoral districts that were seen to have been skilfully calculated to give advantage to the Malta Labour Party. In fact, in the 1971 general elections, Labour won a majority of one seat, which was increased by an additional one when Alfred Baldacchino crossed the floor. Baldacchino had been elected in a by-election following the death of Dr Thomas Caruana Demajo. Just before Baldacchino made the announcement in the House, both Borg Olivier and I somehow sensed that he was going to cross the floor. Hardly had Baldacchino opened his mouth when Borg Olivier whispered to me, '*Dan ser iħallina*' (He's going to leave us). When we started booing Baldacchino, one Labour MP ran over to our side, jumped on one desk, and started punching our members. I felt really angry at Baldacchino as I thought he was betraying us at a moment when Nationalists were risking their jobs and their future. I remember going straight to the opposition room in parliament and writing an article about him for *In-Nazzjon Tagħna*. It was called '*Miskin Baldacchino*' (Poor Baldacchino).

In spite of all that Labour had done to us – ransacking of our clubs, beating up of our supporters, and outright victimisation – we fought the 1976 general elections with great courage and determination. We had come to know what life under the Mintoff regime really meant. The elections were timed in such a way for the results to become known on September 21. We lost the elections, but we kept our electoral support base intact. Mintoff, of course, thought that we were going to be destroyed, but we were not. In that hour of defeat, most of our party clubs were set on fire. I had written the editorial of that day's *In-Nazzjon Tagħna*: it was called '*Illum kellu jisbaħ jum isbaħ*' (A better day had to dawn today). But never as in this bleak moment

113

did I feel more confident that once the Nationalist Party had survived five horrible years since 1971, the future would be ours. For out of its suffering and in the face of adversity, the Nationalist Party was being born again, stronger than ever, ready to keep up its fight for social justice and against abuse of power.

21

Changes at the top

The 1976 elections led to a definite turn in the Nationalist Party's affairs. Many of those who had run the Nationalist government from 1962 to 1971 had been found wanting in the new circumstances that had arisen following Mintoff's return to power. Mind you, they had served their party and the country well but they had not read the signs of the times. Many also believed that Borg Olivier had served his time and purpose. He was now identified with two successive election defeats and his performance did not measure up to what had been required to meet Mintoff's belligerency.

At one point I was asked by some party movers if I would be interested in standing for the leadership if Borg Olivier were to be removed. I said no as I felt the solution lay in changing the leadership style, not the leader, whose name had symbolised the island's quest for independence. I thought it was wise to build on this 'asset' and at the same time allow our generation of politicians to take over the running of the party. But others did not agree with this approach and thought Borg Olivier had to be removed. Three of these were Eddie Fenech Adami, Ugo Mifsud Bonnici, and Ċensu Tabone. John Camilleri, the party's administrative secretary, put all his weight behind the party sections that worked for the removal of Borg Olivier. In the drive to renew the party, we first started with updating and amending the statute. This required the election of the party leader to be made not through the party congress, at which all party members were entitled to vote, but through a general council, which was representative of the party's sections. Borg Olivier realised this was an indirect move to remove him, for he knew only too well that, though he still had great support within the party, people active in the party machine were not so supportive.

I agreed we could no longer hold on to outdated leadership election methods if we wanted to prepare ourselves well for future general elections. I had spoken about this at the party congress and I felt that my words had a determining effect on the outcome. Immediately afterwards, the pressure to remove Borg Olivier intensified. I felt that removing Borg Olivier was damaging both to the party and to himself since his health was deteriorating. Those who were for the removal of Borg Olivier as leader were organising themselves in section committees and in the Nationalist Youth and Women's movements. An important meeting was held at my home, when all factions managed to agree to a solution, that of appointing a leader-designate. In theory, the exercise involved keeping Borg Olivier as a leader.

Having solved this issue, the party found itself in the midst of a *de facto* leadership election. There were three candidates: Ċensu Tabone, deputy leader; Eddie Fenech Adami, president of the administrative council; and myself, general secretary. In the campaign, John Camilleri supported Eddie to the hilt. Indeed, he organised the election campaign for him. This gave Eddie an edge over the other contestants. I had strong support at grass-root level since party supporters had become well aware of my involvement in party work. More than that, they knew I was taking up most of the political court cases, particularly of those who were being unlawfully arrested. Those who had worked hard for the removal of Borg Olivier backed either Eddie or Ċensu. They had been doing their homework for quite some months.

The party's general council met on January 2, 1977. Ċensu Tabone was eliminated in the first round, having come third with 48 votes; Eddie polled 274 votes and I got 213 votes. In terms of the statute, a candidate had to win two-thirds of the votes to get elected leader. In the second round, held on the following Sunday, January 9, Eddie won 315 votes and I received 228 votes. As Eddie lacked the majority required by statute for election, I realised I had to choose between continuing to contest the post or declare my support for Eddie. Choosing the first might have created acrimony, something I thought would have defeated the purpose of the reforms we were introducing and give Labour an advantage, that of a divided opposition. My major concern was that of seeing the party facing up to its responsibilities in defence of democracy; when the general council met again I declared I was casting my vote for Eddie, who was therefore elected leader-designate. Ċensu Tabone resigned from the post of deputy leader, having failed on the first vote to qualify for the leadership. I was then proposed for the deputy leadership post and was elected uncontested.

My place as general secretary was taken by Louis Galea, then a young promising lawyer and politician, while Ugo Mifsud Bonnici took over as president of the general council. All this time Borg Olivier was suffering in silence. Eddie then started pressing for Borg Olivier's resignation so that he could take over the leadership. Borg Olivier resigned on April 11, 1977.

Though outwardly complying with the wish for him to step down, Borg Olivier refused any place of honour at party meetings or even in Parliament. He felt hurt and let down. I had great sympathy for Borg Olivier but I felt the party had to move on. I felt we could not move forward by looking backwards. When I saw him getting weaker and weaker by the day, finding it difficult to go up the stairs of the Palace for meetings of the House, I recalled what he had said to me once: 'Leaders of the Nationalist Party died as leaders'. He naturally had Ugo Mifsud and Enrico Mizzi in mind.

The new leader, Fenech Adami, had just left for a visit to Australia when we celebrated Independence Day in 1977 with a demonstration and a public meeting in Sliema. As acting leader of the party, I had to conclude the meeting myself. When I finished, I asked Borg Olivier to give a message. Independence Day was certainly his day and I was very moved when, in a plea from the heart to Mintoff and to his supporters, Borg Olivier said that independence had been won for all, not just for the Nationalists, and that it had been won not just for the people of his time, but for the Maltese people of all times, for generations to come. It was the last time he addressed supporters at a public meeting. It also marked his exit from politics. Shortly afterwards, he had to go for medical treatment abroad.

In his last speech in Parliament, Borg Olivier had spoken in favour of the police force, even though he and his party had been suffering a great deal at the hands of the politicised elements of the force, those who thought they were in the force at the service of the MLP rather than the country. He called on the force to hold the country's interests high and on the people to show their respect to it. It is rare for a country to produce such people. Borg Olivier died on October 29, 1980. I was among those who carried his coffin most of the way down Republic Street. Borg Olivier was, and remains till this day, an inspiration to many of us. I was close to him when he was feeling down, and I take some comfort in the knowledge that I did not fail him in my political life.

22

When the Socialists showed their might

The children were now growing up fast. Giannella and Fiorella first studied at St Dorothy's School in Mdina and had now begun their university studies. Giannella used a standing year to study economics before taking up law. Owing to a last-minute change in the statute of the university, Fiorella could not start law and took up arts. She did very well. Both Giannella and Fiorella studied hard and would usually step up the tempo before examinations. When I first learned they were going out with boyfriends, I got the sensation that I was moving on in years. Mario did well at St Joseph School in Rabat, even though he did not like the school. He did very well at St Aloysius College too, showing dedication to his work. Of the three, Mario resembled me most in so far as his studies were concerned, although he knew how to enjoy his free time better than I ever did.

Violet kept the home and also helped me in my legal practice. She had a no-nonsense approach to life. I was now also heavily engaged in defending clients in trials by jury. Trials are very demanding, usually requiring specialised studies in one line or another, such as ballistics and medicine, for instance. It also involved looking up authorities, local and foreign. I used to study in great detail the evidence given by witnesses during the compilation of evidence. I would often ask Violet for her opinion of witnesses and she would find herself discussing with me the best way to deal with the defence. If I failed to persuade her in an argument, I would find, usually to my cost, that a jury would not be persuaded either.

Violet was also keen on antiques, and had an eye for bargains. Thanks to her, we managed to buy some pieces of furniture and paintings at a good price. Almost single-handedly, she was responsible for the building of our home in Blata l-Bajda. She had inherited the land together with her brothers and sister from her father and, on her insistence, the property had been divided. She had to take care of all the work that had to be done to build a house from the very foundations. She was also wise in buying and selling. We bought a small flat in Buġibba, which she converted into a lovely place. She then sold it at some profit and bought another summer place. We also bought a flat at Islets Court in St Paul's Bay. Since our means were limited, I always had cold feet in buying property. Not so Violet. She realised that what would appear to be a heavy price today could turn into a profitable acquisition tomorrow. It is thanks to her that I first bought a house in San Pawl tat-Tarġa and a flat in Sliema. She later sold the place at San Pawl tat-Tarġa and bought land, also at San Pawl tat-Tarġa, where we built the new house, 'Violetta'. She had also sold part of the garden at L'Orangerie so as to be able eventually to buy a small villa at Ta' Ċenċ in Gozo, which we like so much. I am mentioning all this to show that, while I was heavily engaged in my legal and political work, Violet not only looked after the family, but in her inimitable way she also looked after the 'financial' side, giving us all a measure of comfort in security.

Did she approve of my political life? Well, she just tolerated it. But to her credit I can say this about her: although she never did like politics and considered that politics was taking me away from the family, she did understand that the situation required people like me who were prepared to take risks and dedicate time and work in an effort to bring about change. The country was still passing through very difficult times, with people being arrested by the police for 'political' reasons. People would be rounded up and arrested by the police on the eve of some demonstration for no reason whatsoever. They were usually held for longer than the 48-hour preventive custody prescribed by law and by the constitution. And very often persons held under arrest used to be beaten up as well. In fact, I used to tell clients to go and see a medical doctor to certify they had no injuries before going to police headquarters for interrogation.

This brings to mind the case of Nardu Debono. It appears that Debono and another person had been suspected of having placed an explosive at the door of Police Commissioner Lawrence Pullicino. Fortunately, the explosive did not go off. I can well understand how bad the commissioner must have felt about this, but I had no reason to believe there was any political motivation behind the placing of the explosive. Debono was arrested as a suspect. I knew the Debono family and I was asked by a brother of his to look after his interests. Some days later, as I was leaving court, Magistrate (now Mr Justice) J.D. Camilleri told me on the steps outside the law courts that he had just been to a place in Marsa where the body of Nardu Debono had been found under a bridge. I found that very strange since Nardu was still supposed to be under arrest. When the autopsy was about to be held, I was asked by the family to attend to determine the cause of death.

The magistrate acceded to my request to follow the autopsy. Debono had no serious visible injuries; his death was due to a blow on the lower abdomen which burst his spleen. According to a police report, Debono had run away from police headquarters. Again, I found this strange to believe and, also, very difficult to happen. I received information that an Englishman who had been locked up at police headquarters at the time had heard Debono moaning. I learned later that a burst spleen causes great agony. The matter was also raised in Parliament. It was abundantly clear to me that the story that Debono had run away from police headquarters was completely false and that he had died as a result of police beatings at headquarters. But I could only learn the details of this most foul event when I became a minister responsible for the police force. I will have more to say about this story later.

My law practice was doing very well and I was personally taking up the defence in most murder trials, some of which had an important bearing on legal issues. My law firm had lodged the first appeal ever in a case before the criminal court of appeal following a trial by jury, Regina vs Falzon. I had also been defence counsel in the first retrial granted under a new procedure establishing the court of criminal appeal. In one particular case, that against Lepre, the judge, Mr Justice Scerri, had dissolved the jury when he was making his summing-up and had ordered a retrial. In my view the presiding judge had been influenced by the prosecution. I interrupted the judge when in his summing-up he failed to mention the argument for the defence. This led to a strong exchange of words between the defence and the prosecution. Mr Justice Scerri decided to dissolve the jury and this gave Lepre a second trial in which he fared well.

In one double-murder trial in Gozo, the accused was charged with having murdered a brother and a sister. All the evidence, including a 'confession' and a palm print, had at first suggested he was the murderer but he was found not guilty by the jury. I considered this as being almost a Houdini case. I realised that the force of the evidence against my client was strong if considered as a whole, so in my defence I broke up the evidence produced, finding its faults and, on the basis of a thorough analysis, making every part of it subject to doubt. In these circumstances, the jury rejected the evidence of the prosecution.

I am often asked what is my reaction to a trial in which the defence is particularly successful in its outcome when evidence might have suggested otherwise. With just one exception, I can honestly say that the verdicts in the cases I took up were fair and just. Armchair critics who follow trials superficially from newspaper reports often cast aspersions on the accused and his defence counsel when the verdict is not to their liking. Obviously they are entitled to their opinion, but I do not believe they should pontificate, especially when they are not fully aware of all the legal issues involved or have not gone into scientific and ballistic points that require study with an eye for detail. At the time I was also taking up legal cases of a political nature, or dealing with infringements of fundamental human rights, besides defending government employees before disciplinary boards of the Public Service Commission. I defended a journalist working for *The Daily Telegraph* as well as the editor and deputy editor of *The Times* (of Malta), and journalists from *In... Taghna.*

Together with Dr (now Mr Justice) Joe Galea Debono, I appeared in a case against Emanuele Cachia, who had been accused of slandering a minister in Mintoff's cabinet. The case was over an allegation of bribery for the procurement of a government import licence. When Cachia was persistently asked by Mintoff to mention just one case of bribery, Cachia blurted out the name of a minister and gave details of the case. Action was taken against Cachia who was expected to prove his allegations. It was a sad case for me since I had known the minister since childhood. In my view, Cachia's version of events was truthful and forceful. The court held that '*reus in excipiendo fit actor*' and, therefore, in pleading the truth of what he had alleged, Cachia was put in the role of an accuser. He was found guilty and jailed for 16 days. But the general feeling in the country was that Cachia's accusation had been well-founded. Indeed, the licensing system that had been introduced by the Socialist government had turned out to be a source of serious abuse and contributed in no small measure to the government's loss of credibility.

Most of the human rights cases I took up were about abuses by the Housing Authority. It is difficult to understand today what requisition orders meant in the period between 1971 and 1987. A property owner could be dispossessed of his property and see it being allocated to persons whose only claim to it would simply be their association with a Labour MP or candidate. One case stands out, that of a hawker selling fruit and vegetables directly from a van. One fine day, he received a requisition order on his house, which he had taken on lease. It was passed over to a newly-married couple. So, the hawker and his family found themselves out on the street; with nowhere else to go to, they had to sleep in the van parked just outside their 'former' house. On behalf of the hawker, I claimed an infringement of the family's fundamental human right, the right to privacy of one's own house. But the court ruled that once a requisition order had dispossessed the owner of the property, he could not plead denial of his own home because, through I what believe is perverse legal logic, his house was no longer his. In the end the hawker had to abandon 'his' house to the newly-married couple and accept an alternative place that was offered to him.

The government then enacted a law that was generally considered as *ad hominem*. It precluded lawyer MPs from acting as defence counsel in cases against the government dealing with a long list of offences covered by the Criminal Code. Clearly, the law would have stifled my work in the criminal court and, also, in cases over the infringement of human rights. We contested the law and the court found it was unconstitutional, but there was a snag – the court only decided the issue some time after the Nationalists were returned to power! This and so many other cases showed that the Socialists were in a confrontational mode all the time. Take, for instance, its long-running dispute with doctors in government hospitals. When the doctors took limited industrial action over a relatively minor issue, the government locked them out.

Most of our excellent doctors had to find work in Britain, Saudi Arabia, Kuwait, and other countries. Medical students had to go to Britain for their studies, imposing added financial strains to their families. The British Medical Association was of considerable help in finding places for our students in teaching hospitals and universities. Only a few of the Maltese doctors had declined to follow the doctors' union's directives. To make up for the exodus of Maltese doctors, several of whom, particularly specialists, had been discharged from the government service, Mintoff started importing doctors, mainly from Eastern European countries. However competent these doctors might have been, most had one big problem: they could not communicate with their patients since they obviously did not know any Maltese and only a few had a smattering of English. In most cases, this was not enough to make themselves understood. The government expected total submission from the doctors, but the doctors were in no way prepared to give up their rights. I greatly admired their will and courage in the face of such ruthless action. Many of them had eventually found top posts abroad, indicating the high standard of our medical school. Even so, leaving Malta and the practice they had taken years to build involved great personal sacrifice.

The people were realising now to what extent the Socialists government was prepared to go to crush opposition, using the maximum force against the minimum of resistance. The expulsion, in December 1981, of the much-loved Blue Sisters (Sisters of the Little Company of Mary), which led to the closure of their hospital, was yet another example of the government's dictatorial approach. The hospital, a bequest by Emilia Zammit Clapp and her sister Mary Zammit, was one of only two private hospitals on the island. When the nuns turned down a request for a number of beds to be made available at the disposal of the government, they were ordered out of the country. They took their case to court, which decided in their favour but, despite this, they were expelled and the archbishop had hardly time to see them before they flew out of the country. Eddie and I went to the airport to see them off in what must have been to us one of the saddest farewells. The Blue Sisters' case had been brilliantly taken up by one of our foremost human rights lawyers, Giovanni Bonello. This was by far the most unwise action taken by the Socialist government up till then.

Then the government opened a full-scale war against free trade unions belonging to the Confederation of Malta Trade Unions, suspending from work Telemalta Corporation workers for following directives given by their union, the Malta Government Employees' Union, in a dispute with the corporation. The MGEU subsequently opened its doors to all classes of workers and changed its name to Union Ħaddiema Magħqudin. Bank employees supporting Telemalta workers were also suspended. It was one of the saddest chapters in the history of trade unionism in the country. At this time, in the summer of 1977, the GWU had not yet been statutorily fused with the party in government, but its newspapers came down hard on the free trade unions. The GWU had always been pro-Labour in its policies, but its fusion with the party, signed and sealed in May 1978, was possibly its most serious mistake since its foundation. Just when Polish workers, through Solidarnosc, were struggling to free themselves from the shackles of the communist regime in their country, in Malta the GWU willingly accepted to be fused with the MLP, which even gave it a seat in the cabinet, supposedly to take part in decisions affecting the interests of the workers. But this made them willing tools in the hands of the Socialist party. As the GWU allied itself with the party in government, the UHM kept its independent stance and managed to attract an increasing number of workers who would otherwise have found themselves unprotected. I admired the courage and resistance that the workers belonging to the free trade unions showed. The free unions had their heroes, too. Two of them were Salvinu Spiteri and

Maurice Agius. Still I believe that over time Malta's trade unions will move towards closer cooperation with one another and possibly towards fusion.

The height of Socialist violence was reached on October 15, 1979, a date that has come to be known in Maltese political history as Black Monday. The starting point was an incident at the office of the prime minister at Castille in the morning when a Mintoffian supporter by the name of Karmenu Grima was reported to have made an attempt on the life of the prime minister. The man, feeling cheated over a building permit, had been overpowered by the staff. I was later asked by his family to defend him in the criminal action taken by the police against him. It was a case of temporary mental derangement.

The incident gave Socialist supporters another opportunity to vent their anger in violence and they did so in a manner that exceeded all limits. That same evening, a group of supporters broke away from a demonstration that was being held in Valletta and went on the rampage. Their first target was a bust of Enrico Mizzi in St John's Square, opposite the co-cathedral. They then ransacked a Nationalist Party club in Republic Square; broke into the offices of the Church newspaper *Il-Hajja* in Archbishop Street; and then headed straight towards the printing press of Allied Newspapers in St Paul Street. There, they terrorised the workers and set the building on fire. Their orgy of violence was not over yet. They then raced to the house of the opposition leader, Eddie Fenech Adami, in Birkirkara. His elderly mother and his children ran to the roof and sought shelter at their neighbours' houses. Eddie's wife, Mary, was attacked by Socialist thugs as she was about to get into her house, literally a few metres away from a police station. They then ransacked the ground floor of the house.

As Progress Press was burning down and thugs were ransacking Fenech Adami's house, the state broadcasting station, Xandir Malta, announced in its news bulletin that the Malta Labour Party club in Birkirkara had been attacked! This was a crude perversion of what was really happening. I was at my office in Blata l-Bajda when news reached me of what was happening. I rushed to Parliament and Eddie and I made it clear to Mintoff at his office there that we held him responsible for all that was happening. Mintoff acted as if nothing that had happened justified our alarm. He had his adviser, Edgar Mizzi, with him. Police Commissioner John Cachia was immediately called to report about the incidents and he told us the crowd had become very rowdy indeed but that he had a contingent of his men guarding Enrico Mizzi's bust. Mizzi promptly observed that it would have been better for the police 'to protect the living than the dead'.

We were getting very concerned and Eddie and I told Mintoff in no uncertain terms that there would be serious consequences if the PN headquarters and printing press were attacked. Mintoff instructed the police commissioner to ensure that the headquarters and press were adequately protected. We were then told to go to Fenech Adami's house and we did so in a police car. Along the way we could hear on the police radio that those ransacking Eddie's house were actually telling the police what they were doing!

In the meantime, I got in touch with Charles Grech Orr, editor of *The Times*. He told me the printing press was gutted but that fortunately none of the workers had been injured in the fire. When I asked him what he planned to do about the morrow's issue of the newspaper, he said, 'Forget it'. I remember telling him that since not even the Luftwaffe had managed to silence the newspaper in the war, no one was going to stop it now. I made arrangements for the newspaper to be printed at our printing press in Pietà. But Grech Orr was very sceptical about the idea, telling me that 'by the time we go to the Nationalist printing press, it will also be destroyed'. I said, 'We will see to that when it happens, in the meantime see that you go.' Grech Orr and a small team of editorial people rose bravely to the occasion and *The Times* was out on the streets the following day, later than usual and reduced in size, but it kept its tradition of never missing an issue.

We then held a mass meeting close to Eddie's house to protest against the violent acts of October 15. It was the first of a series of mammoth meetings the party held to reaffirm its supporters' determination not to let the Socialist party intimidate them through violence. October 15 raised Eddie's stature as a leader. He had become an effective politician, a true leader, a man whom the people learned to trust in the battles that had yet to come.

Let me now pass on to a killing that had greatly disturbed me, that of Karin Grech. We were at an executive committee meeting at the AZAD offices in Sliema when we first learned about it. We had held the meeting there to avoid the interruptions we usually faced at headquarters. The girl was killed when she opened a small package, addressed to her father, containing an explosive device which exploded in her hands. I knew her father, Edwin, well. We were in the same class at St Aloysius College. We matriculated together. We were also at university together. He took up medicine and I took up law but we kept our friendship over the years. Edwin later worked in Uganda, looking after the family of President Milton Obote. When I visited Kampala for a Commonwealth Parliamentary Association meeting in 1967, I remember being met at the airport by Edwin and his family as well as by Dr Richard Manchè and others. Karin was with her father, a sweet girl waving a Maltese flag. I was therefore shocked when I learned of the killing. I knew, of course, that Edwin had come back to Malta to work in the government service and as such was regarded as a strike-breaker by the medical profession. I went to see him at his sister's house. Karin's killing was a cruel act.

When, in 1987, I took over as minister of the interior and justice, I gave specific instructions to the police to further investigate the cases of Karin Grech, Raymond Caruana, Wilfrid Cardona, and Lino Cauchi. In the Karin Grech case, I told the police and the Forensic Laboratory to look into a possible Australian link. I entrusted this investigation to Superintendent (later commissioner) Alfred Calleja, then considered to be the best investigator in the police force. I still feel bad that we did not manage to trace the killer. I feel worse over the fact that a girl died as a result of a climate of violence that was breaking up the country.

23

A perverse election result

I was now going through what was perhaps one of the busiest periods of my life. In the morning I was usually in and out of different halls at the law courts every day. Then in the afternoon I had to find time to see my clients, while in the evening my time would generally be taken up by political work, either at party headquarters or in Parliament, taking part in debates and shadowing bills on major issues dealing with the law courts and the judiciary. The party sought to exploit its contacts abroad, particularly those with Christian Democratic parties. It had an excellent rapport with the Italian Christian Democratic Party. We had to explain to our Italian friends that the political support Italy was giving to Mintoff was having a negative impact on our struggle to keep a measure of democracy in Malta. I had written an editorial for the party paper headed '*O tempora, o Moro*', taking the cue from Cicero's diatribe '*O tempora, o mores*'. When, in November 1977, a party delegation visited the leadership of the DC in Rome, we called on Aldo Moro, then president of the party. I treasure the memory of that meeting. Moro shared our concern and told us: 'Our support to Mintoff is intended to stop him from taking extreme measures, which could ultimately have very negative effects on you and on the Maltese people as a whole. If, owing to our influence, Mintoff is stopped from taking extreme measures, you will be able to fight another day, and through what is left of democracy you would be able to make a comeback, with the backing of public support.' Wise words indeed.

It was the time – called '*gli anni di piombo*' – when the Red Brigades were waging war against state institutions. Together with Enrico Berlinguer, Moro was advocating the so-called *compromesso storico*. Moro, one of Italy's longest-serving post-war prime ministers, was kidnapped on March 16, 1978 by the Red Brigades and killed after 54 days in captivity. I still keep in my study a picture of Aldo Moro greeting me when we called to see him over our concern about Italy's support to Mintoff. To my mind, Moro, Andreotti, and Fanfani, all three Christian Democrat prime ministers, were *cavalli di razza*; in different ways, the three influenced my thinking.

Besides my interests in justice and home affairs, I also found myself involved in foreign affairs. Mintoff was now showing a steady inclination to take Malta closer to Libya, at the time considered a country holding extremist views on most issues. Mintoff's Libyan overtures irritated the West, which had now become increasingly aware of his poor respect for democratic institutions and the rule of law. When Mintoff came up with a proposal for the island's neutrality to be guaranteed by Italy and France, from the European mainland, and Libya and Tunisia, from North Africa, I remember arguing that the alternative, membership of the European Economic Community, was a better proposal for Malta. The need to ensure the island's security had by now become an added concern and I was very careful not to prejudice the Mediterranean policy that Mintoff was advocating. Indeed, I tried to interface his policy with our long-term aim of making Malta part of the European Economic Community, as it was then called. This was the spirit behind a resolution which Fenech Adami moved, and which I seconded, in February 1979 for the party's executive committee to start looking at membership of the European Economic Community, as a political objective. As the general elections were drawing closer, I could well sense the upsurge in national support for the Nationalist Party. I sensed too, as others no doubt did as well, that the way the electoral districts were being redrawn, we could well end up with the party winning a majority of votes but not of seats.

The 1981 election campaign was tense, hectic, and highly charged. The Nationalist Party was very well prepared and the supporters' enthusiasm for the party and will to win was very strong. Thousands upon thousands were turning up for our meetings. We had even managed to attract many who traditionally stayed away. Those who only up to a few months before would not even buy a party newspaper lest they be identified as PN supporters were now expressing their views openly, even though they knew they could well be victimised at their place of work, particularly if they worked in the government service. Support grew to such an extent that we started holding our meetings on the Granaries in Floriana. Mintoff must have certainly been astonished at the way we were building up support for a new way of life, a new style of government.

A will to resist had taken over. Up till then people had been generally afraid of being arrested or beaten up, but our supporters were now holding their heads high. Our campaign came to an end with a grand meeting in Ta' Qali. It was a manifestation of faith in the party and in the future of our country. The party leadership, Eddie, Ugo, Louis Galea, George Bonello du Puis, and myself, had worked hard as one team throughout the campaign. Although some within the party structure were gradually introducing the *Fuhrer prinzip* style of leadership, that is, giving the leader the role of a *generalissmo*, we who worked so closely with Eddie did not feel this at all. We worked together and had trust in one another.

The counting hall at Ħal-Far looked like a concentration camp. The policemen posted there were all in riot gear and carried machine-guns. Fenech Adami remained at party headquarters and I went up to the counting hall to take care of our interests and be with our candidates and agents. At one point, as I moved from one counter to another, I felt a machine-gun sticking at my back. It was a horrible experience. We were doing very well in terms of votes cast in our favour, but we soon began to see the effect of the surgical way in which the districts had been redrawn. In short, we had won the absolute majority of votes but Labour had won a three-seat majority.

We were faced with a dilemma, either react very strongly with all the risks involved or accept the result as if we had not won the election at all and live a sham democracy. One thing was certain, we did not intend carrying on business as usual. We first called on the president of the republic, Anton Buttigieg, whose mandate was now nearing its end. Eddie and I explained the abnormality of the situation. For a party to get over 50 per cent of the popular vote and not be able to govern was in itself a negation of democracy. The situation had to be seen in the context of the structural and studied changes made in the electoral districts and, also, against the background of all the violence and discrimination our supporters had suffered since Mintoff's return to power in 1971. Buttigieg listened to us very carefully, indeed sympathetically, although both sides were well aware of the fact that he had a very limited say.

Even so, the party felt it was important to give our stand a constitutional basis. We drew up a list of four requests we felt were moderate in nature but important nonetheless. These were that the new president of the republic be appointed on the basis of consensus; the speaker of the House be appointed by consensus; the electoral districts be reformed to ensure fair and equitable results; and that an election be held as soon as agreement is reached on these points.

Mintoff had pledged before the election that he would not govern unless he had majority support. Mindful of this commitment, we felt that Mintoff too was finding the situation uncomfortable. At the same time, we had realised only too well by then that his cabinet ministers were not prepared to loosen their grip on power. In his new cabinet, Mintoff gave up two important ministries – foreign affairs, which he passed over to Alex Sceberras Trigona, and the interior, to Lorry Sant. We considered the allocation of the interior ministry to Lorry Sant as a direct challenge to us. We felt convinced that under his control the police would harden their attitude against the Nationalist supporters. At a massive candle-light meeting on the Granaries, I pledged, on behalf of the party's parliamentary group, that we would not take up our seats in Parliament unless the substance of our demands was adhered to. I can never forget the sight of so many thousands of people in a sea of shimmering light.

Agatha Barbara was made president of the republic and Kalcidon Agius, the same man who had written a letter in *l-orizzont* headed '*Tuna l-armi, Perit*', ('Give us the weapons, Perit'), presumably for them to use against the Nationalists, was elected speaker. We felt the situation was now getting out of hand but we kept up the momentum by holding a mass meeting practically every Sunday. Our supporters were solidly behind us in our stand. I had never felt such a close association between the party and its supporters as at that most difficult period for democracy on the island. Some time later we were unseated and by-elections were called, a move that meant we were on the brink of dictatorship. Mintoff soon found out that we were not bluffing and in fact not one single Nationalist candidate put forward his or her name to contest by-elections. They were testing times indeed. Had we overstepped our mark, the whole democratic structure would have collapsed.

Then one day I was asked to go and see Agatha Barbara with whom I have always had a good working relationship. She was a talkative person and would normally take two hours to say what could easily be said in thirty minutes. She said she was prepared to mediate to make the two parties settle their differences. Since she was very close to Mintoff, I realised that she must have had his blessing in the approach she had made. The first problem, of course, was over our representation in Parliament. In spite of what was happening, I am sure Mintoff did not wish to go down in the island's history as the man who had destroyed democracy. On our part, we had to be careful not to play into his hands and give his party some justification for introducing a one-party system of government. We had reason to believe that the temptation on the part of some belonging to the extreme left wing of the Malta Labour Party to work towards this end must have been strong indeed.

So, while in public we kept firmly to our stand, I was trying, through my contacts with President Barbara, to find a way how we could take our seats back under the best possible terms. I was, of course, in constant consultation with Eddie and our parliamentary group during the crisis. Agatha and I started exchanging draft correspondence in a bid to find a solution without unnecessary delay. One thing was uppermost in our mind: at all costs, we should not have a repeat of the 1981 result.

The worsening political situation weighed heavily on the people's mind. Politics dominated practically every aspect of life in the country, creating a tense atmosphere. Ironically, at this time I was found guilty of a charge of making slanderous statements about the situation in Malta. I was actually charged with the malicious spreading of false news. The case was decided by Magistrate Dennis Montebello on May 28, 1982. After taking into consideration 'all the circumstances of the case', including my 'clean conduct and the fact that the speech was made impromptu in a pre-election atmosphere', the court held that a 'fine was more appropriate than the penalty of imprisonment contemplated by law'. The fine was of Lm300.

Needless to say, I was simply disgusted at this decision. In my view, the court had neglected taking consideration of the violence perpetrated against Nationalist Party clubs, Nationalist members of Parliament, and newspaper offices. It had apparently not taken consideration also of the moral violence resorted to by the state broadcasting station, the interference in the administration of justice, the attacks against the press and the arrest of journalists by the police, and the enactment of legislation limiting judicial control in the case of abuse of power. Did not all this raise doubts as to the future of democracy in the country? Yet, I was found guilty of expressing such concern and, out of the goodness of its heart, the court did not send me to prison, mainly because of my clean conduct sheet! The case reflected the seriousness of the political situation in the country.

Needless to say too, I appealed. In doing so, I thought of putting on record, for posterity, an account of what the country was going through, bringing up first all the violence Nationalists MPs had been subjected to, at times even in Parliament, and on occasions outside Parliament in collusion with the police. Then I referred to the violence resorted to by Socialist supporters at Nationalist Party meetings. At one meeting in Kalkara on April 21, 1975, a man known to the police, Totò, drove his car dangerously into the crowd of our supporters. Instead of arresting the man, the police beat up Nationalist Party supporters! A Nationalist MP for Gozo, Anton Tabone, had been badly injured at a Nationalist Party meeting celebrating the 10th anniversary of independence and had to undergo surgery. Six other Nationalists had been injured at the same meeting. Albert Borg Olivier de Puget had been beaten up by the police. I mentioned my case and that of Notary Cachia as well as the many incidents in which many supporters were injured, one critically, and naturally all the October 15, 1979 incidents. Did not all this represent a threat to freedom and democracy in the country? This was the question I put in my submissions. But the magistrate thought differently. He felt that once Mintoff had said that his government was democratic, I could not say that the political situation gave rise to great concern!

Indeed, believe it or not, the court did not seem perturbed by the government's interference in the administration of justice. The constitutional court, for instance, had been suspended for three whole years. Nor had it been perturbed by the attack on the house of the trial judge following the acquittal of Alexander Cachia Zammit, or by the suspension of all judges in January, 1981, thus depriving the country of its courts for over a month and establishing the concept that the courts exist if, when, and how government wants. Again, in the opinion of the magistrate, all this did not give rise to serious concern about the political situation in the country and did not represent a threat to the people's freedom. I did not stop there. I also referred to the arrest of journalists who did not follow the government's line. I remember coming out in defence of the free press at a meeting in Qormi, arguing that journalists would not be intimidated by arrests.

The court of appeal reaffirmed my right to comment freely on events and found me not guilty of the charges brought against me. The judge, Lino Agius, gave a well-studied judgment. My only criticism in his regard is that it was given *after* the 1987 general election. Fenech Adami had gone on record saying, when referring to the case at a meeting in Mosta on May 30, 1988, that the Nationalists had been prepared to go to jail to defend their right to freedom of speech.

Six months after the 1981 election that had produced the perverse election result, that is, on June 11, 1982, we held on the Granaries what I still regard as one of the greatest political manifestations in the island's political history, both in terms of attendance and political significance. In an impassioned speech, Fenech Adami warned that, if the government persisted on the road of confrontation and continued to refuse to reach a decent agreement on the political crisis, the Nationalist Party would embark on a campaign of passive resistance and civil disobedience. The moment of truth had come, and he appealed to the Socialists to renounce violence. We did not believe in violence, but in the fight for a solution to the political crisis, we were prepared to go to prison for disobeying the government.

I then read out a resolution, drawn up in the form of an oath meant to be taken by the Maltese to their country. In it the people reaffirmed 'their love, faith, and loyalty towards the country and the republic' and pledged that they wanted to live 'in genuine unity in a truly democratic environment' and to work 'to ensure that freedom, justice, and peace would once more reign among us'. The absolute majority of voters had voted for a change of government, and in no circumstances should the people's will be ignored. A government that lost the people's confidence would no longer be in a position to ensure justice and good governance. Such a situation would represent a threat to employment, social life, and economic activity. In addition, the quality of life, built on respect for human and moral values, would be diminished. A government that found itself in power through gerrymandering the electoral districts was not considered legitimate in a democracy. 'Therefore, we do not feel bound to regard it as a government elected democratically by us.' The people wanted the restoration of true democracy in the shortest possible time so that together, Labourites and Nationalists, 'we would embark on national reconciliation' that ensure a future to which the people could look forward with confidence and in security and happiness. 'This is a right that belongs to every Maltese. We are prepared to strive for all this till the end.'

The resolution reaffirmed a good number of democratic values, such as belief in justice and in the holding of free and fair elections, and in the running of a clean administration, free of corruption, lies, and deceit. It called for free broadcasting and for a fight against what it described as 'today's Fascism', which had turned Malta into a country where a small group appeared to have the power to control workers, Nationalists and Labourites. The people were prepared 'to shed blood so that we and our children would not live under a dictatorship' that had the cheek to camouflage the perverse election result by the law.

Reading the original text of the resolution today, one is immediately struck by its rhetorical vein. It is highly emotional too, and maybe a bit too long as well. But we meant every word we said. Taken in the context of the political environment in which we were living at the time, it encapsulated all our concerns and as well as our belief in the country's future.

24

Passive resistance

I have been an admirer of Mahatma Gandhi ever since I was young. Having lived the tragedies of World War II and seen the process of decolonisation, I am all in favour of passive resistance in struggles for autonomy or democratic rule. Comparing events in Ireland and in India, I feel the best way to overcome a powerful enemy is not through violence, but through the moral force that passive resistance can bear on an oppressor. In our particular political situation, I was convinced it was best to fight on two parallel lines, passive resistance and massive political activity, including calling the masses out in the streets in protest manifestations. At the same time, however, it was important not to let go of the possibility of establishing dialogue that might lead to solving the impasse. This was the manner in which the Nationalist Party planned to lead in its struggle to ensure that the democratic will of the people would prevail.

Besides holding more public meetings, we then made a bold move – at least for that time it did seem somewhat bold. As Xandir Malta was totally biased in favour of the Socialists, churning out endless Goebbels-style propaganda, we began broadcasting from Sicily. Taking up the microphone across the channel on behalf of the Nationalist Party was Richard Muscat, who was made to suffer dearly for his daring venture. At first, it seemed almost an impossible task for us to broadcast from Marina di Ragusa but the risk we had taken paid off as most Nationalist supporters started to follow the transmissions. Mintoff did his best to close the station down; when he realised that there was no way of stopping us, he brought in the experts to jam the transmissions. The end result was that this made the broadcasts even more popular.

Our passive resistance was working well. We contested the government's monopoly in broadcasting in court but by the time the case was decided in our favour, the political impact had been lost. Our campaign of passive

137

resistance and civil disobedience brings to mind our stand over the feast of St Peter and St Paul, *l-Imnarja*, celebrated on June 29. The government had removed the feast from the calendar of public holidays, but that year the Nationalist Party had issued a directive calling on the people to regard the day as a public holiday. Before doing this, the party had discussed its plan with the retailers' union as well as with trade unions, the Federation of Industry, Chamber of Commerce, Malta Hotels and Restaurants Association, and private schools. I was in Catania that day as Gianella had decided to give birth there because of the doctors' strike in Malta. Had she decided to go to a local hospital, the Socialists would have made political capital out of it, so she wisely opted to go to Catania. My second grandson, Gianluca, was born on June 24, 1982.

Even so, while I was there, on the eve of *l-Imnarja*, I was asked by the party to make an appeal over our 'broadcasting station', Studio Master, in Marina di Ragusa for the people to follow our directive. I remember it was one of the hottest days in Sicily ever. I was driven from the place I was staying to the 'station' by Joe Caruana Curran. I knew we had a makeshift place for a station but I did not imagine it was just a small room, probably the washroom, in a small house. Very primitive indeed. The equipment we had was somewhat primitive, too. In fact, I had to repeat the broadcast three times as the first two were unsuccessful. We made it on the third count only when the technician banged on some of the equipment and used some very colourful and foul language. Very few in Malta knew the kind of 'station' we were running in Marina di Ragusa, not to mention the level of skill of our technician!

Our *Mnarja* stand was supported by thousands. The government, seeing red at the success of our move, reacted harshly. Government and parastatal employees who did not report for work were suspended from work, and shopkeepers who had followed the directive were told they would pay dearly for their defiance. As Mintoff was on a tour of the Far East at the time, it was the acting prime minister, Ġużè Cassar, otherwise a very correct politician, who had ordered the mass suspension of workers from work. To add fuel to the fire, Lorry Sant, then minister of the interior, issued a press release to the effect that the government 'would be prepared to consider recommending, if necessary, the expropriation of business establishments, if legitimate orders by the police were retaliated against'.

The following day the police called on shopkeepers ordering them not to open their businesses and those who did were taken to court. Workers who had absented themselves for one day on *l-Imnarja* were called before the

Public Service Commission and dismissed from their employment. This was the way the government wanted to impose its will on the majority. Then on August 8, 1982, the government worked out a way of pardoning the workers, making it look like an act of munificence. It was prepared, it said, to pardon the workers who had followed the directive so long as they declared that they had not been aware of the consequences and, also, that they would not follow any directives 'intended to bring down the democratically elected government'. Our directives had not been intended to bring down the government but to make it accept the fact that the election result was perverse and to force it to enter into consultations with us so as to ensure that the people's will would be respected.

There is one man in particular who comes straight to mind every time the *Mnarja* incidents are recalled – Furtu Selvatico. He suffered great humiliation when, on returning to the dockyard after our *Mnarja* protest, he was physically assaulted and prevented from returning to his place of work. I will never forget his pleading eyes when he came to see me at my legal office in Blata l-Bajda, asking me for advice. But there was no way one could guarantee him protection from his 'fellow workers' at the yard. He never went back to the yard and he must have certainly felt a sense of defeat in not being able to do so. Instead, he dedicated himself to the party's workers' secretariat and did sterling work. Furtu was well loved and every time I see his grave, which is next to our family's at the Addolorata cemetery, I pay a silent tribute in my heart to one of the many workers who suffered so much for the cause of freedom.

Meanwhile, the government was doing its best to make things difficult for us to voice our stand abroad. It was painful raising the problem abroad but we felt we would have failed in our duty as parliamentarians had we not had the moral courage to raise the erosion of democracy in Malta in the Council of Europe. We had to make the council aware that a perverse election result, one that we had foreseen when the electoral boundaries had been redrawn, had denied the party that had won the absolute majority of votes the democratic right to govern. We felt the Council of Europe had to be informed of what had been happening since.

With this in mind, and in view of the fact that the political affairs committee had on its agenda a motion 'on the grave political situation in Malta', I wrote to Tom Urwin, a British Labour MP and president of the council's political committee, giving him an overview of the situation. The motion had been tabled in April 1982. I told him that the situation had since worsened and that the government had no moral authority to govern and was clinging to power against the will of the absolute majority of the people. It was making up for its lack of moral authority by becoming daily more repressive. The one-party Parliament, as it then stood, had, on August 31, approved the Foreign Interference Act, making it illegal for a foreign journalist to report from Malta unless he first obtained the permission of the minister of foreign affairs. It was also made illegal for a foreign churchman to carry out any religious activity on the island without first obtaining the consent of the minister. The Church of England had to apply for permission to be able to continue holding its religious services on the island! A foreign lecturer could not give a conference on the French Revolution or on the glory that was Rome without first getting permission from the minister of foreign affairs! And any Maltese cooperating in the holding of such 'foreign activities' would be considered an accomplice in crime and likewise punished. This meant that if I gave an interview to a foreign journalist in Malta, we would both have been guilty of an offence.

When the government threatened to throw out the Italian military mission in Malta, our TV 'station' in Marina di Ragusa was closed down on the basis of a law judged unconstitutional by Italy's constitutional court. And anyway, the Foreign Interference Act made broadcasting from abroad illegal. All this meant that the majority of the people were being reduced to third-class citizens in their own country. We had a government of the minority, by the minority, for the minority. Having said all this and more to Mr Urwin, I asked to be given an opportunity of speaking at the council to explain further the situation. If Mintoff's representative had a right to put his point of view, I said it was only proper that the representative of the majority of the Maltese people should likewise be heard.

As we moved from one crisis to another, I kept up my contacts with Agatha Barbara. Her manners might not have been all that polished, but she certainly had political integrity. Our meetings had become more frequent and meaningful. I used to remain at San Anton till late at night engaged in endless talks on how to ensure the return of the Nationalist MPs to Parliament under acceptable conditions. Agatha was, of course, reporting the outcome of each and every meeting to Mintoff, and at one point Edgar Mizzi began taking part in the talks as well. Edgar was a brilliant lawyer. Through his service as commissioner of land and, later, as deputy attorney general, he had gained Borg Olivier's trust. When Maurice Caruana Curran was appointed judge, Edgar was appointed deputy crown advocate general, as the post was then known. It was the

140

time when I spent some 14 months as crown counsel. So, we worked at the same legal office and had learned to trust each other. On the retirement of Dr Michael Tufigno, Edgar was appointed crown advocate general and became Borg Olivier's right-hand man. Edgar's grandfather was Fortunato Mizzi, founder of the Nationalist Party, and Enrico Mizzi was, therefore, his uncle.

Mintoff had no particular liking for Edgar Mizzi when he was leader of the opposition. In fact, he thought Mizzi often held Borg Olivier back from making deals. But, some time after he was returned to power in 1971, Mintoff changed his mind about Mizzi who, over time, became a strong influence on him. I need to qualify this a bit, for Mintoff is no man's man. Mintoff is a man who acts on his own initiative but he is intelligent enough to exploit good advice. And it was here where Mizzi usually came in. Given that he was in the right mood, Mintoff knew how to listen, but he would not let himself be used as a tool in anyone's hands. Mintoff could also flirt with people and with governments but he always kept his own sense of direction. He wanted us back in Parliament because I believe he felt he could get on better with a Parliament with us in it rather that with a Parliament made up of only 'his' people. This may appear contradictory when Mintoff was the prime mover in all that had been happening since the election. But Mintoff is a man of contradictions.

I drafted a letter to Mintoff, obviously reflecting, in substance and detail, Fenech Adami's thinking as well. Before passing it on to Agatha Barbara for onward transmission, I submitted it to the party's leadership for consultation. It was not easy agreeing on a common stand and, as can well be imagined, my role as negotiator in this constitutional crisis was most difficult. Some thought I was being too chummy with Mintoff or that we were giving up the fight. But, of course, I was not being chummy. Nor were we giving up the struggle. We were laying the ground for the party to win the next elections, which was after all what really mattered. To my letter, Mintoff replied to President Barbara on February 18, 1983. The letter is being reproduced *in toto* as it underlines the spirit behind the long and tortuous discussions.

'On Tuesday, February 15, at about 1 p.m. you kindly left with my secretary the second draft of a letter which Dr Guido de Marco gave you after his talks with you and after the meeting which you had with me where I gave you may reply to the first draft. It is proper that what I told you on that day I repeat to you in writing so that definitely nobody can misunderstand me.

141

I have told you and I repeat, that on my own personal responsibility – despite the fact that I am committed with my Cabinet colleagues and the other members of the Malta Labour Party and of the General Workers' Union, not to move from my last public declaration that there would be no agreement on anything with the Nationalist Party – I promise to do my utmost so that before another election, after talks held in all matters which the two sides would like to change, new amendments are introduced in the 1974 Constitution according to what is agreed between them. I am doing this on my personal responsibility because I want to show all Maltese and the foreigner that I, both as Prime Minister and as leader of the Socialist movement, and also as an individual, have done everything possible to save democracy in the country.

If this declaration of mine is acceptable as an answer to the two drafts presented to you by Dr Guido de Marco, the leader of the Nationalist Party only has to inform me in writing that he has seen this letter, of which he has a copy from you, and that therefore the former Nationalist Deputies wish to take the oath of office in Parliament. I would then take the necessary action.'

Fenech Adami replied on March 7: 'Her Excellency Agatha Barbara, President of the Republic, passed on to me a copy of your letter to her of February 18, 1983, after meetings she had with Dr Guido de Marco.

The Nationalist Deputies returned in the election of December 12, 1981, considered your letter carefully and decided to take the oath of office in Parliament.'

Following the 'co-option' procedure, we, the representatives of the majority of the people, took our oath of allegiance. As from that moment, we moved on to the most important, but perhaps more painful and patient, task of negotiating with our opposite side, and I can say straightaway that, were it not for Mintoff's involvement, we would not have budged an inch from Labour's entrenched position. We had now managed to slip back into dialogue, but the way ahead was still very rough, and the people had to face greater suffering in the long wait to the next general elections.

25

'Wied id-Dies' and other court cases

During this period I was putting in twelve to thirteen hours a day. I could keep to this punishing schedule for weeks on end. My secret lay in having a rest in the afternoon. I used to resist going to the so-called business lunches and made it a point to have lunch at home with the family. I am still in the habit of taking an afternoon nap, usually of not more than half an hour, after lunch. It helps break the day into two working days, as it were. In my days, I could read whole documents very fast and I did a lot of studying late in the day.

Although Malta had never been as politically divided as during that period, my clients came from both political camps. Naturally, as I said before, I handled a number of hot political cases, but I have defended many Labourites in criminal cases as well. I have often been asked how can a lawyer defend a person whom he thinks has committed a serious criminal offence. The answer is clear and simple. Lawyers are there to defend a person accused in terms of the law. We are not defending the crime, we are defending the person who is entitled to the best possible defence according to law. We do not choose our clients. Our clients choose us. And, in the criminal field, we have no right to pick and choose. Indeed, with certain few and grave exceptions, no lawyer can refuse defending a client, provided that the client compensates the lawyer for his services. Certainly lawyers cannot become accomplices in a crime by, for instance, bringing false witnesses into a case. Any accused person has a fundamental human right of having a defence counsel. A lawyer has to be loyal to the court in that in his defence he has to produce arguments that are relevant to the case and reflect legal authorities without any alterations, for a lawyer is an officer of the court.

I have already referred to some of the cases I handled early in my career, but now that I am back discussing my legal work, I can recall the case of a young man who was accused of causing the death of a Sudanese tourist.

The tourist had bought some bottles of beer and cigarettes from a bar in Gzira and had asked for a bag. When told that the bar did not have any, he smashed two bottles of beer, one after another, and attempted to attack the sister of the accused who was serving at the bar. The accused, my client, arrived at the bar a moment later and, on learning of the incident, followed the Sudanese outside and punched him. The tourist fell to the ground and suffered a brain haemorrhage. It later transpired that he had a rare condition, a thin skull. Our law does not recognise antecedent accidental cause as an element of defence. The court did point out, however, that there was no proportion between the act of the accused and the Sudanese man's ensuing death. I think that even the prosecution had understood this. In any case, the jury held that the Sudanese had died as a result of infections that had developed later and were accidental, not consequential, to his being pushed by the accused. My client was sentenced to ten months' imprisonment.

Another interesting case, one that I am sure is remembered by many, was that of two young men who had broken into the house of a woman in Żurrieq to steal from her and had gagged her to prevent her from screaming. The woman had respiratory problems and died in her struggle to free herself. In my submissions I pleaded that there had been no specific intent on the part of the accused to kill or to put the life of the woman in manifest jeopardy. The accused were found guilty of theft aggravated by time and place, but the jury concluded that the death of the victim was caused involuntarily. The two young men were jailed for three years.

When medical issues arise in criminal cases involving violence, as is often the case, a lawyer has to consult medical practitioners. I had an interesting case of a man from Żurrieq who was charged with the wilful murder of his wife. They were both in their thirties and their marriage was on the rocks. I think the husband had been too lenient as regards his wife's behaviour. In fact, I think it would have been wiser on his part to seek separation proceedings. Anyway, both parties had drifted apart, but they still lived under the same roof. They did so probably because of the children. One night, the wife started being provocative in language and behaviour. She stepped out of the house and he followed her. When he tried to stop her in the garage, he dealt her a single blow in the neck and she died instantly. Her husband then took her to a building site, where he worked, and buried her there. He later reported her absence to the police. But he soon broke down and confessed to the killing of his wife. The prosecution accused him of wilful murder. I realised from the start that the case hinged on the cause of death and the violence inflicted. The doctors who carried out the autopsy were inclined to suggest that the poor woman had died strangulated. However, as a result of my cross-examination, they reached the conclusion that the probable cause of death was the result of a single blow on the neck causing what is known in medical terminology as vasco-vagal inhibition.

A court expert testified that a blow on the neck could cause the blood pressure to fall suddenly, leading to loss of consciousness (vasco-vagal inhibition or collapse). Apart from stopping blood circulation, a strong blow could also cause instant death. As it happened, the victim had had her thyroid gland removed only a short time before the incident. Had she not done so, the gland could have reduced the crushing impact on the neck. The man was found not guilty of wilful homicide, but guilty of causing a grievous bodily harm leading to his wife's death and was jailed for 14 years. In my view, the verdict was correct, although I felt consideration should have been given to what is known in law as mental excitement and sudden passion in consequence of which he could not measure the effects of his action.

A case that caused a great stir was that of Wied id-Dies, in which three were accused of the murder of Duminku Zammit, of Għargħur. The prosecution said Zammit had quarrelled with the three on the evening of September 10, 1979 at the Għargħur police station where he had threatened to reveal something unpleasant about them. According to the prosecution, later that night Zammit accepted an invitation by the accused to go out for a drink with them in Paceville. Driving back from Paceville, the accused were said to have driven their van off the road just before reaching Wied id-Dies and pushed Zammit out of the van and into the valley. Then, according to the prosecution, they beat the man to death, rolled him down further into the valley, and buried him under a pile of stones.

The prosecution based its case on the evidence given by an 'accompanying witness'. But his evidence was a mass of contradictions, laid bare by the change from summer to winter time, as shown by a church clock. The sacristan had changed the hour in the evening, ahead of the time at which winter time began so as not to wake up at that ungodly hour. This upset the whole time-frame as presented by the prosecution witness. One of the accused was known to be a simpleton and his counsel agreed with me and with the other colleagues in the defence team that he would make a very bad witness were he to be called to give evidence. We were aware that the jury might draw negative conclusions were he to be the only one not to give evidence, but we felt that our case was strong enough to justify taking the risk. But in taking this line of action, we had not foreseen the judge's reaction. In his summing-up, he said it was bad, very bad indeed (*huwa fatt ikraħ u ikraħ ħafna*) that the accused had not taken up the witness stand. An accused in a criminal trial is a competent but not a compellable witness; indeed, his right to silence is considered a fundamental human right in terms of the constitution. So, one can imagine how frustrated we felt at the remark passed by the judge at a time when the defence could not make further submissions. The three were found guilty and sentenced to long terms of imprisonment.

In the light of the mistaken direction given by the trial judge in his summing-up, a criminal appeal court ordered a retrial. This time we did not take any risks and called all the three witnesses to the stand to give evidence. I had learned a lesson, which is that, in defending a client who is a co-accused, I had only to consider his interests, even if this could cause collateral damage to the others. From the legal angle, the case was a triumph at law, but a Pyrrhic victory in that the accused had spent long years in preventive detention.

A difficult case, possibly the most difficult I have defended, was that of a Gozitan man who was accused of killing two brothers in Qala. The charge was that he had broken into a house in order to steal and shot dead the two brothers who had woken up at the noise. The shooting had taken place in the presence of their sister. When he was being interrogated, the accused had taken a number of pills, possibly to commit suicide. When he was in that state of mind, he made a statement confessing his responsibility for the killing of the two brothers. According to the police, a palm print of the accused had been found at the home of the victims. And, to complete the picture, the gun was found in the home of the accused. But I argued in defence that the statement made by the accused had to be rejected because of his state of mind at the time. Serious doubts were raised as to whether or not the palm print was of the accused, while the fact that the gun had been found at the home of the accused was no fool-proof evidence that he had killed the two brothers. The accused was found not guilty and walked out of the court a free man. It is not for defence counsel to fulfil the function of judge and jury, still less of the role of the prosecutor.

I have pleaded before quite a number of distinguished judges. Those that readily come to mind are Anthony Mamo, Anthony Montanaro Gauci, William Harding, Maurice Caruana Curran, and, perhaps the most outstanding of them all, Joseph Flores. Others are Carmelo Schembri, Oliver Gulia, Vincent Scerri, Wallace Gulia, and Lino Agius. They all contributed, at different levels and in different ways, to keeping high the standard of justice at our courts. I had learnt a lot from prosecution counsel, particularly from Caruana Curran, who was a master in the art of cross-examination, and from Victor Borg Costanzi, who studied every case deeply. He was a formidable opponent in court and our clashes were frequent and tough. Yet, we held each other in high esteem at all times.

Just as my legal career was at its zenith, the 1987 general elections were drawing fast. It was a time when, unless a solution to the political problem was found, the country could have well plunged into civil strife. The island's political future was beckoning.

Enrico Mizzi

George Borg Olivier waving the constitutional instruments granting Malta's independence. Also in the picture are Chief Justice Sir Anthony Mamo, Minister Giovanni Felice, and Minister Joe Spiteri.

Sir Arturo Mercieca, Chief Justice, author of "La Mie Vicende".

Sir Anthony Mamo, Chief Justice, who later became the island's first president.
He was a role model for me.

Dr (later Mr Justice) Joseph Flores, the great defender.

Mr Justice Maurice Caruana Curran – master of cross-examination.

Newly-engaged at a family wedding at the Hotel Phoenicia in Floriana in 1955.

On our wedding day.

Herbert Ganado

Mabel Strickland meeting Margaret Thatcher when she was Britain's prime minister.

Queen Elizabeth II, as queen of Malta, and the Duke of Edninburgh with members of parliament at the Palace in Valletta in 1967.
Five have occupied the post of president of Malta – Anton Buttigieg, Agatha Barbara, Ċensu Tabone, Ugo Mifsud Bonnici and myself.

Violet being introduced to Archbishop Makarios, president of Cyprus,
by Sir Anthony and Lady Mamo.

On Gianella's graduation, 1981: With Violet, Gianella, Fiorella and Mario at our home in Hamrun.

A family picture with Pope John Paul II in February 1991. The children are Angelica, Joe, Matthias and Gianluca.

Christmas, 2005: The family at my home, 'Violetta', in San Pawl Tat-Tarġa.

My family at home in San Pawl tat-Tarġa in 1998.

With Mario and Andrea.

With 'my boy' Gianluca.

With my son Mario after I was elected deputy leader of the PN in 1977.

With my four 'boys', Matthias, Gianluca, Joe, and Mario.

A proud moment: Presenting my son Mario with the warrant to practise as lawyer.

At San Anton Gardens with Gianella, Violet and Mario.

At the congress of the European Union of Christian Democrats (EUCD), Venice, in September 1968, with Albert Borg Olivier de Puget and Eddie Fenech Adami.

With members of the parliamentary delegation to the Council of Europe: Maurice Vella Gregory, Clerk to the House of Representatives, Anton Buttigieg, Albert Borg Olivier de Puget and Patrick Holland.

Giovanni Felice, whom I greatly admired for his wisdom and statesmanship.

Alexander Cachia Zammit triumphant.

Leaving the law courts at the end of the eight-day trial of Alexander Cachia Zammit on November 15, 1972. With me are Gianella and Eddie Fenech Adami, who was counsel to Lawrence Cachia Zammit.

George Borg Olivier embracing me when I was beaten up and injured in an Independence Day anniversary celebration in Valletta.

Carried shoulder high in an Independence Day celebration in Valletta.

With Joe Tonna (right) and David Casa.

Paul Spiteri, one of my long-serving political canvassers.

The scene outside Allied Newspapers Limited in St Paul Street, Valletta after Socialist thugs set the building on fire on October 15, 1979.

Allied Newspapers Limited workers clearing a room after the October 15, 1979 fire.

Being received by Aldo Moro at the headquarters of Democrazia Cristiana in Piazza del Gesù in Rome.

Agatha Barbara

The chapel at the archbishop's curia when it was ransacked by the "aristocracy of the workers".

Karmenu Mifsud Bonnici in step with Dom Mintoff.

An innocent victim of political violence, Raymond Caruana. Eddie, Ugo and I at the Gudja PN Club shortly after Caruana was murdered. 'The horror of this moment will remain in mind for as long as I live.'

Funeral Mass for Raymond Caruana at Gudja's parish church.

Edgar Mizzi

26

Moment of truth

Soon after we had taken our seats in Parliament, we began having regular meetings on changes that needed to be made to the constitution and to the electoral system to ensure that the democratic will of the people prevailed. This was in accordance with the agreement that had been reached between the two sides. Our first meetings were held with President Agatha Barbara at San Anton, with Ġużè Cassar leading the government's side. Eddie, Ugo Mifsud Bonnici, and myself represented the Nationalist Party. As we used to meet on Saturdays, the meetings earned the name of a popular television programme running at the time, *Sibtijiet Flimkien*. Round about mid-day, Cassar would turn to Barbara and tell her, '*Agatha, è l'ora dello spirito*', indicating it was time for a drink. The atmosphere was cordial and conducive to reaching agreement. We made it a point of proposing solutions without being either too aggressive or too demanding. The real problem, as we saw it, was that despite the fact that we could have well reached agreement within a reasonable time, it appeared that the government's intention was to cling to power up to the time allowed by law.

A bomb placed at the door of Albert Mizzi, chairman of Air Malta, was used by the government as a pretext to suspend the talks. A short time before, a man at our club in St Julian's, close to Albert Mizzi's house, had avoided a tragedy when he removed a bomb from the club where a social function was being held at the time. He tossed it out onto the rocks right across the street from the club where it exploded. To our amazement, the policemen who came over to investigate the case arrested the man – Paul Cremona – whose act of courage had saved the lives of several people at the club, instead of trying to find the culprit. Needless to say, I was indignant at their action and protested in no uncertain terms.

It was in this state of political limbo when a new avenue for headway in the talks appeared to be opening. One day in Parliament Mintoff sent

149

me a note telling me he was having Guido Carli, an Italian politician and economist of international repute, at his home, *L-Għarix*. Would I be interested in meeting him? Eddie agreed with me that it was an occasion not to be missed. Mintoff can be most charming when he wants to. He told me that, besides the official meetings between the two parties, it would be best if we were to start exchanging views between us directly in an effort to sort out difficulties that may arise in the talks. So, we started meeting regularly. At one point, he asked Edgar Mizzi to take part in our meetings so that he could draw up draft changes to the constitution and to the electoral law.

Of course, we had different ideas. Mintoff's main concern was to ensure that Malta remained neutral and that it would not be used as a military base again by any foreign country. He also wanted to enshrine Malta's neutral status in the constitution. Our main concern was that of having free and fair elections and that there would be no gerrymandering of the electoral districts to avoid having another perverse result. We sought convergence through these parallel lines. I agreed that in the cold-war post-Helsinki situation, there was no need for Malta to be used as a military base by anyone, including Nato. I could never forget the time when Nato had ignored Borg Olivier's soundings for Malta to join the organisation. In the late 1960s, when the cold war was at its worst, Nato considered its 'arrangement' with Malta sufficient for its needs. So, I thought that as an independent country, Malta should not now prejudice its future by joining Nato. I was therefore personally inclined to accept Malta's neutral and non-aligned status. However, I disagreed with Mintoff that this should be incorporated in the constitution as international circumstances could change and what might appear justifiable at one moment might not be so in a different political climate. Besides, neutrality was a status in international law, whereas non-alignment was a political choice.

Mintoff agreed that we had to ensure that the party winning the absolute majority of votes had to get a majority of seats. Edgar Mizzi had already drawn up draft legislation to this effect. In the talks with Mintoff, I raised the issue of broadcasting as I strongly believed that, for an election to be fair and free, it was important for the country to have an impartial broadcasting station. We both thought the president of the republic should be given a greater role, provided he was elected either by a two-thirds vote in the House or, if the House failed to elect one in this manner after taking a number of votes, by popular vote. A president elected in this manner could, for instance, break a deadlock in the appointment of persons to particular institutions by making the appointments himself. We thought the president could also be nominated as commander in chief of the Armed Forces. At no time had Mintoff proposed to make a final agreement conditional to his being nominated president of the republic.

Fenech Adami was sceptical, at least at first, as to the possible outcome of the meetings. I believe his thinking was that, if anything good were to come out of them, the party would gain; if not, I would be held to blame. I know it now sounds somewhat Machiavellian but it was quite understandable in the circumstances. My political colleagues believed Mintoff would eventually trick me into agreeing to some arrangement that would not be in the country's interests. Make no mistake about it, I was aware that any failure on my part would have rebounded on my political career, but I carried on regardless. In any case, I felt at ease dealing with Mintoff and, considering the deteriorating political situation in the country, I argued there was nothing to lose. As it turned out, our talks eventually led to a solution.

Political confrontation in the country had not eased in any way, even during my talks with Mintoff. One burning issue, that over a government claim for Church-run schools to be made free of charge, had not been settled yet. It was clear then that the government's aim was to have control of all institutions as well as of the educational and social services in the country. In a *Malta Soċjalista*, trade unions had to be considered as part of the administration; imports had already been made subject to strict licensing and essential commodities were bought in bulk; the banks had been taken over; and, when unemployment rose to new heights, the government set up para-military labour corps. As to the dispute over Church-run schools, Pope John Paul II had made the Church's stand clear in no uncertain terms when he received Mintoff in an audience at the Vatican on November 11, 1981, just two days after the dissolution of Parliament before the general elections held on December 12, 1981. This is what the pope had told Mintoff: 'The Church offers a highly precious contribution to the life of civil society, as attested by the various institutions in education, social assistance and charities, as well as the inestimable wealth of the value of the family. It was in order to be able to provide this that the Church demands the freedom to which it is entitled in view of the task – and therefore the right and duty – to preach the Gospel. This is the work which is being carried out, meritoriously, by the bishops who are entrusted with the pastoral care of the people of Malta.'

The pope had put the discussion on a proper course but, despite the fact that the Socialists had lost majority support in the 1981 elections, they stepped up their confrontation over the Church-run schools and, also, over its property. New regulations laid down that 'no school could charge fees higher than those payable in 1982 and that any remuneration or other consideration and any donation or contribution given or provided, by or on behalf of a person liable to school fees, shall be taken into account in establishing the amount charged or received by way of school fees'. The *'jew b'xejn, jew xejn'* campaign was now in the hands of Karmenu Mifsud Bonnici, who had been co-opted to Parliament on May 2, 1983. He was first made minister of labour, and later appointed minister of education. Mintoff had corresponded directly with the Vatican and had done so in his usual aggressive style. He had found Archbishop Mercieca's way of resisting him difficult to accept. In one letter to the Vatican secretary of state, Cardinal Casaroli, dated November 26, 1980, Mintoff described Mercieca as 'a man with a weak and indecisive character, desirous of pleasing rather than guiding with firmness'. He told Casaroli that Mercieca 'was misleading the people quoting from documents of the Vatican Council'. The parting shot was: 'We have reached such a point that, as long as Mgr Mercieca remains Bishop of Malta, we shall be prepared to discuss the problems concerning the Church in Malta solely and directly with Rome.' Mintoff had acted in a similar manner with Archbishop Gonzi, but Mercieca was very careful to avoid open confrontation even in the face of great provocation. It was not in Mintoff's style to accept a kind of Byzantine (or, as some would describe it, Gozitan) reaction as that which Mercieca was offering.

In June 1983, a government white paper proposing legislation for Church property – land, buildings, and rights thereon – which the Church had acquired by prescription, that is, by the mere act of having possessed it for more than 30 years, to devolve to the government, sparked a fresh dispute with the Church. On its part, the Church took the dispute to the courts but this did not deter the government from threatening 'to take over Church schools and use all legal means to do that'. The minister of education informed private schoolteachers of the government's intention and asked them if they were prepared to continue to teach in the schools should it become necessary for the government to run them itself if their administrations objected to provide free education. The dispute over Church-run schools stirred great emotions and in August 1984 the curia made it clear it intended reopening its schools in the forthcoming scholastic year 'to safeguard their autonomy, identity, and character'. The Church expected the full support of all parents 'in this moment of trial so that the rights of parents and of the Church will remain intact'. The parents backed the Church to the hilt, as shown by the thousands that used to attend public rallies supporting the schools.

When negotiations between the Vatican and the government reached a stalemate, Karmenu Mifsud Bonnici informed the Vatican on March 28, 1984 that, as from the following September, all secondary schools in Malta had be free to all students. The government tabled amendments to Education Act under which private schools required a 'new' licence to operate, renewable every scholastic year. One licence condition was that the schools could not charge fees; nor could a school receive donations from the parents. The archbishop and the Federation of Parent-Teacher Associations reacted strongly to the government's moves. In the meantime, the government had made its own arrangements. For example, girls from St Dorothy, St Joseph's, and Sacred Heart were to attend at Sandhurst School, Pembroke, St Patrick's; students from St Aloysius at the Lyceum in Hamrun; and students from Stella Maris College at Marsa Secondary School. But the government's policy misfired. Of the 3,000 students who attended the Church-run schools, only some 300 opted for the allotted schools.

As the dispute over the Church-run schools simmered, Mata had yet to see more violence. On September 28, 1984, hundreds of dockyard workers taking part in a carcade headed by Karmenu Mifsud Bonnici attacked first the law courts building and then turned their attention towards the archbishop's curia in Floriana, just across the street from police headquarters. At the curia, they broke into a chapel, bringing down holy effigies and whatever came to hand. To Mifsud Bonnici, these were the 'aristocracy of the workers'. As he had done to Mabel Strickland when Socialist thugs burned down the *The Times* building, Mintoff expressed his regret to the archbishop.

Two days later the archbishop decided not to open the schools 'to avoid further tension' but secret arrangements were made for students to get their schooling in the private homes of teachers who chose to defy the government's action rather than give in to its threats. Parents used to pick up students from various points and take them to the appointed places. The Nationalist Party stood foursquare with the parents; in Parliament we voiced our opposition to the proposed amendments to the Education Act.

When the Church's court case came up for hearing, judge after judge abstained on grounds that they had relatives attending Church schools.

Mr Justice Carmelo Scicluna was prepared to continue to hear the case, even though he declared he too had relatives attending Church schools. Both parties to the case did not object to Mr Justice Scicluna hearing the case, but when he gave a decree that was not to the government's liking, the government appealed before the constitutional court. Even here, the court faced a series of abstentions. There remained only three judges left, apart from Mr Justice Scicluna, who could sit in the constitutional court. When an issue about a court decree dealing with the admission of evidence was decided against the government, the case went back to Mr Justice Scicluna. Now the government chose to challenge Mr Justice Scicluna from continuing to hear the case. But Mr Justice Scicluna said the parties to the case had already given their consent to his hearing the case and, moreover, he had to stay on as otherwise there would be no judge to hear it.

When the archbishop said in court that the Church made no distinction between children admitted to its schools, someone present in court hotly protested that this was not so. Mr Justice Scicluna said he himself was a worker's son and had attended a Church-run school. The government took exception to this comment but instead of just filing a note of protest it brought a motion in Parliament, on November 13, 1984, strongly censuring Mr Justice Scicluna. I am reproducing the motion here because I feel it is important to recall in this context the kind of aggressive, threatening climate that state institutions were facing.

'This House, while realising it is difficult, if not impossible, for the constitution to be amended, or be implemented as it stands in order to remove a judge from his post in cases of party political controversy;

Nevertheless feels that its majority, according to the same constitution, should express itself on what is going on in our courts, when abuses by judges take place, as in fact happened in the past, and recently in a very clear and clamorous way when Judge Carmelo Scicluna, in the case instituted by the archbishop against the government on the reforms of free education for all;

(a) decided to continue hearing the case when three judges and the president of the court himself had decided to abstain from hearing the same case for reasons similar to those for which Judge Scicluna was recused, namely that they had relatives attending at one of the Church's schools, and

(b) when the archbishop was interrupted when he said that the church did not make a distinction between the social class of the children admitted to its schools, he showed that he agreed with this allegation – an untruth and something which the Socialist government is striving to change – by exclaiming that he was the son of a worker and that he had been educated in a Church school, and thus showed that he was prejudiced in his judgment and not impartial as required by the same constitution;

Therefore this House recommends that the president of the court draw the attention of Judge Scicluna to this serious failing on his part and, in the light of the principle of the impartiality of judges, to how great his responsibility would be if he continues to hear to the above-mentioned case;

At the same time this House resolves that, in the event that the above-mentioned judge decides to continue hearing the case, the minister of justice should take the necessary steps, according to law, so that this same judge would be unable to do this;

And besides, the House urges the minister of justice that, if similar abuses recur in future he, after seeing whether it would be less harmful to the people that a judge continue to be paid while being relieved of his functions than be allowed to decide certain cases according to his passions, will move a resolution in this House so that that judge is relieved of his functions although he would continue to receive his salary.'

I pointed out in the House that the motion was irregular. Parliament had the authority to dismiss a judge in accordance with the approved provisions of the constitution, but it should not put pressure on a judge on the eve of the day he was to decide whether to continue hearing a case or not. The motion, I argued, was an abuse of power. The minister of justice was proposing to 'remove' a judge presiding over a case in which the government was the defendant. The motion would imply, if it were to be carried, that, whenever a government was not happy with a judge hearing a case in which it was involved, it could simply put him in cold storage until the matter was disposed of.

In any case, the motion had now been overtaken by events because, while the judge had that morning repeated that he could not recuse himself, he said later that in view of the circumstances known to all, he would refrain from taking further cognisance of the case. The arrogance of power had triumphed over what one believed to be right. The case was a very serious one indeed, involving an alleged breach of fundamental human rights. Such arrogance of power could also affect the ordinary man in the street, for example, someone who sued the government after being evicted from his home.

The country was passing through a time when it was being denied the government that the majority of the people had elected. The rule of law was breaking down and we were seeing clear interference in the judiciary; the government was locked in a fierce dispute with the Church over its schools; the state-owned broadcasting station had been practically taken over by the party in government; and the police were in many instances failing to keep public order. In the face of this situation, the Nationalist Party and the people had the stamina and political courage to stand up to the Socialist government.

27

Police raid at PN headquarters

One day in November, 1983, I was returning home with Violet from a party at Luqa, which at that time was part of my constituency when, close to our house, we were stopped by a military patrol. The soldiers looked at me and said, 'All right, you may proceed.' I turned into Mile End and said something to the effect that they were so very nice in allowing us to get home! Just a few minutes after we arrived, the telephone rang and someone on the line told me, very excitedly, that the police were all over our headquarters in Pietà. I rushed to Pietà and found the whole place surrounded by the police and Gejtu Cuschieri, the man in charge of security, sitting on the steps of a side door. He had been called from home to open doors to headquarters for the police. Superintendent Carmelo Bonello, the senior police officer at the scene, told me they were there to see if we had any portable telephones! There must have been some 100 policemen taking part in the raid and they were breaking down doors, drawers, wardrobes, safes, and even soffits. Their aggressiveness was absolutely horrendous. The party's general secretary, Louis Galea who, had he been asked, could have given the police the keys to all the doors in the building, had not been allowed in. Then, suddenly, we heard shouts of '*Sibnihom, sibnihom!*' (We have found them, we have found them!).

The police said they found four dismantled shotguns and some helmets. Eddie and I had no idea where the shotguns had come from. They had possibly been kept there for self-defence in the wake of all the threats the party had been receiving. Or they could have been purposely planted at headquarters to give the police grounds for a search. In his book *Malta in the Making*, Edgar Mizzi said the instigator for the search was a former Nationalist supporter who had switched his political allegiance to Labour after he had been dismissed from his job at headquarters for having been involved in a theft. At one point during the search, someone found a Malta

Labour Party emblem, probably used as a prop in a political broadcast, and put it up in one of the windows, as if to show that the PN headquarters had been taken over by the Malta Labour Party. One policeman even spat on a bust of Borg Olivier, a vile act that reflected the dreadful spirit in which they were carrying out the search. Naturally, we had lodged strong protests over the search and a civil court eventually found Superintendent Bonello and Inspector Paul Bond, who were both responsible for carrying out the search, guilty of causing wilful damage to the party's property and fined.

There was a sequel to the story. Some time afterwards, a search was carried out at the Vella brothers' stores where some 'arms' were found. The Vella brothers, known Nationalist Party supporters, were in the transport business. I was at their home when they were released from police custody. They had been beaten up badly by the police and one had his arm dislocated. A civil court had found Superintendent Bonello, Inspectors Noel Schembri, David Stubbings, and Joseph Pico, and P.S. Mario Cassar responsible for the torture of the Vella brothers while they were under arrest and during interrogation. They were ordered to pay Lm18,000 to the Vella brothers. Following the finding by the police of these 'weapons', the government once again suspended the talks between the two parties that were meant to find a solution to the constitutional impasse.

28

Mintoff resigns as prime minister

Dom Mintoff stepped down as prime minister on December 22, 1984, passing the leadership of the government and of the party to his anointed man, Karmenu Mifsud Bonnici. Mifsud Bonnici remains a living contradiction. He is a man of great personal integrity but had no political scruples when he dealt with matters that concerned workers. He comes from a very Catholic family background and yet, in one speech he had given at the headquarters of the General Workers' Union, he had described the Church as 'one of the biggest and the worst multinationals in the world', adding 'that so long as the Church does not go back to the teaching of Christ, there shall be no peace with the workers' movement'. This was in September 1984, when Pope John Paul II was revitalising the world, as it were, through his commitment to human rights and freedom, leading to momentous events in Poland and Western Europe and to the fall of the Berlin Wall in 1989.

Before the 1987 general elections, jobs had been found in the government service or with parastatal bodies for no fewer than 8,000 people. 2,222 were employed in the last week alone. Mifsud Bonnici is a man of very simple tastes, a man of law with a great sense of correctness in his behaviour. Even so, he failed to show solidarity with me, a fellow lawyer, when, after the 1976 general election, I used to be insulted by Labour supporters as I entered or left the law courts when I, on my own behalf and on behalf of Nationalist candidates in my district, moved before the appeal court proceedings for the annulment of the election in my district for corrupt practice. When I protested, he had the audacity to tell the court that the crowd had a right to show their anger (*il-qilla tagħhom*) against me for starting proceedings over corrupt practices. Mifsud Bonnici's entire family was Nationalist both by tradition and conviction, but he was a Socialist. The problem was that his brand of socialism was more extreme and certainly more doctrinaire than Mintoff's.

Free of his responsibilities as prime minister and leader of the party, Mintoff now felt freer to negotiate than when he was still in the saddle, but his hold on the Labour parliamentary group had weakened. Ugo and I were meeting with the government side in a select committee of the House set up in 1985, but these talks were held on an on-and-off basis. Sometimes, we used to spend hours waiting for the committee to start its meetings; when we eventually met, very little progress was made. But, in the meantime, I was still having my regular meetings with Mintoff. When, at one time during these talks, Eddie had to go to London for some medical treatment, Mintoff sent him a letter, through Edgar Mizzi, establishing the basis for further official talks between the two parties. Eddie sensed that Mintoff did not have as yet Karmenu Mifsud Bonnici's support, still less of the Labour parliamentary group and therefore felt it was not wise to accept a proposal that was not yet endorsed by the Labour Party.

In the select committee of the House, matters were not moving well at all. On November 26, 1986, Ġużè Cassar tabled in the House a report of the committee. It essentially carried two conclusions, the government's and the opposition's. The government said it was prepared 'to propose that if the representatives of the Nationalist Party accept the proposal of the Socialist Party concerning the status of neutrality of Malta, based on the principles of non-alignment, the representatives of the political parties will bind themselves before the forthcoming elections that, if the result will be the same as that of 1981, these parties will start negotiations to find the measures necessary to seek solution'. We thought this was an insult to the people. In fact, the report convinced Eddie and the rest of the PN leadership that my meetings with Mintoff were the only means for an acceptable solution. But now events had taken an irreversible course.

29

Tal-Barrani

Today's generation may find it hard to understand the implications involved in a decision taken by the Nationalist Party to hold a public meeting in Żejtun on November 30, 1986. Żejtun was a Labour stronghold where the Nationalists were considered outcasts. Any Nationalist presence within its confines could not possibly blend with the Socialist takeover of that locality and of most of the areas of the south of Malta for that matter. Nationalist supporters had been reduced to pariahs in their own home town, often harassed and insulted.

The PN felt it had the right to have its voice heard and its presence felt in Żejtun. The message was well understood by the Malta Labour Party, and its club in the locality mobilised its forces to stop the meeting from taking place. Karmenu Mifsud Bonnici decided to forbid the party from holding the meeting and we took the matter to court, which decided in our favour as it held that the government's decision was in breach of the constitution and of our fundamental human rights. The government appealed, but the constitutional court upheld the decision.

So, all was set for the meeting to be held as planned. We realised the situation required both physical and moral courage but we argued that no sacrifice was big enough in the fight to win back freedom. The people backed us to the hilt and thousands made their way to Żejtun to share the responsibility that the leadership of the party had taken. Echoing the highly emotional words from the party's hymn, '*Demna inċarċru għall-libertà*', we were indeed prepared to shed our blood for freedom's sake. Whole families had made it a point to stand up and be counted as they enthusiastically responded to the PN's rallying call. It looked very much like the Israelites leaving Egypt towards the promised land, with the difference that in our case the Pharaohs were ahead of us, waiting in ambush, not following us. Violet, Giannella, and Mario were there. Fiorella would also have been there had she not been abroad as her husband was working as an architect in Saudi Arabia.

As we were approaching Bir-id-Deheb at Tal-Barrani, we were pelted with stones, but the Nationalists kept moving on. Eddie, Ċensu Tabone and I were on an open truck following another truck that was leading the carcade into Żejtun. At one point Labour supporters gave the impression they were withdrawing but this was just a ruse to make the Nationalists move further in and become more exposed to attack. Then the worst happened. We were again pelted with stones. Shots were fired and the police used tear gas to disperse our supporters. Despite this attack against us, Eddie and I started off the meeting. We wanted to keep the people together. It was a terrible experience. As the tear gas reached us, we could hardly speak. Eddie and I were taking the microphone in turns. I felt as if my chest were splitting in two. It was difficult to breathe. We had to put handkerchiefs soaked in water to our mouth. Suddenly the driver of our truck reversed and the meeting broke up.

Twenty-three people were injured, four with gunshot wounds, and about 16 cars were set on fire and destroyed. As against other times in the island's history when Maltese fought against the foreigner, this time the Maltese turned against their fellow Maltese and the fight was over the restoration of full democracy. I saw women being beaten up most savagely, others running across fields to escape the attack. One woman had part of her nose bitten off. The Socialists thought we were 'barranin f'artna' (foreigners in our own country), but we were not going to give in to their arrogance. How ironic that the locality where the attack took place is called Tal-Barrani!

In Parliament the following day, Fenech Adami denounced the barbarity of the action taken by the government, by its supporters, and by the police in no uncertain terms. At one point Colonel John Cachia, who was present in the House, standing behind the speaker's chair, with other government advisers, felt irritated at the criticism that was being levelled at him by the leader of the opposition and made a move in Eddie's direction. He was stopped in his tracks. But the scene remained impressed in the minds of many. It reflected the depth to which the Socialists had sunk in their reaction to our protests.

30

Raymond Caruana: Murder most foul

Political violence reached its peak when a young Nationalist Party supporter was gunned down at a party club in Gudja. The killing sent shivers down the spine of the people, putting the country on edge and, at the same time, stirring further political divisions. It happened on the night of December 5/6, 1986 when a car driven at some speed suddenly stopped in front of the club and a passenger or passengers in it riddled the club entrance with bullets, killing Raymond Caruana.

At the time of the killing, I was at José Herrera's graduation party at the Sliema house of his father, Mr Justice Joseph Herrera. Immediately I was told of the incident, I rushed to the club. I thought I would find the place choked with people, but there was no one around, not a soul. I could feel broken glass under my feet as I walked to the club. Inside, a young man was lying in a pool of blood, face downwards. A few men were around him, astonished and in a state of shock.

When I arrived there was only one policeman and he was acting more like an onlooker than an investigating officer. Then a number of high-ranking officers started arriving. I had almost to shout at them to ensure that precaution be taken for the street to be closed to traffic and to ensure that no evidence be tampered with. Eddie, Louis Galea, and Ugo Mifsud Bonnici were there, too. We were all shocked. We had been expecting something really bad to happen, but we still hoped it would not come to this. Raymond Caruana had stayed behind with some friends after a social activity at the club for a quiet drink before returning home that night. Caruana, still in the prime of life, had been planning to get married. Louis Galea turned Caruana's face upwards – he was covered in blood.

I later got to know Caruana's family well – his parents, brothers, and sisters. But even in that moment of sadness and tragedy, I was trying to figure out what had happened exactly. The shooting in Gudja was a replica of another that had happened at our Tarxien club four days earlier following a Labour demonstration. I insisted with the police that an intensive search take place for the bullets and for any suspects to be rounded up immediately so that they could be examined for any gunpowder residue on their body. We had also given the police the names of people we thought could have been involved in the killing but some of the officers did not appear very enthusiastic in their investigations.

Thousands turned up for the funeral. At one moment there was a bit of a commotion when the crowd saw Dr Joe Brincat, then a government minister, attending the funeral together with his young daughter. I could well understand their feeling of resentment but I thought his presence there was a positive move.

Raymond Caruana's killing jolted the country's to its senses, creating a greater sense of revulsion against violence. In a way it also served as a catalyst for progress in talks over the proposed changes to the constitution which Mintoff and I had been working on for months. For a moment, as we were carrying Caruana's coffin I thought we had reached the nadir of man-made tragedy. But events proved me wrong.

Eddie and I on our way to Tal-Barrani.

Addressing the crowd at Tal-Barrani.

My son Mario and Adrian Hillman giving a helping hand to a woman injured in the Tal-Barrani incidents.

Taking my first oath as minister.

*Receiving US President George Bush at my office at the United Nations
when I was president of the General Assembly.*

Greeting Mikhail Gorbachev on his arrival in Malta for his summit meeting with US President George Bush. Also in the picture are Speaker of the House of Representatives Lawrence Gonzi, Chief Justice Hugh Harding and President of Malta, Ċensu Tabone.

MINISTERU
TA' L-AFFARIJIET BARRANIN
U GUSTIZZJA

MALTA

MINISTRY
OF FOREIGN AFFAIRS
AND JUSTICE

Il-Viċi Prim Ministru

The Deputy Prime Minister

16th July, 1990.

H.E. Gianni De Michelis
President of the Council of
the European Communities
Brussels,

Sir,

On behalf of the Government of Malta, I have the honour to
submit Malta's application for membership of the European
Economic Community in pursuance of Article 237 of the Treaty
establishing the European Economic Community.

Please accept, Sir, the assurance of my highest,
consideration.

Guido de Marco
Deputy Prime Minister
and Minister of Foreign Affairs
and Justice.

*My letter to Gianni De Michelis when Malta submitted its application for
membership of the European Economic Community.*

MINISTERU
TA' L-AFFARIJIET BARRANIN

MINISTRY
OF FOREIGN AFFAIRS

MALTA

Il-Vi͜c͜ Prim Ministru

The Deputy Prime Minister

10ᵗʰ September 1998

H.E. Wolfgang Schüssel
President of the Council
of the European Union
Ministry of Foreign Affairs
Republic of Austria

I have the honour to inform you that the newly elected Government of Malta wishes to reactivate Malta's application for membership of the European Union.

Malta's application was submitted in July 1990. The European Commission in June 1993 delivered a positive Avis. In June 1994 the Corfu European Council declared that "the next phase of enlargement of the Union will involve Malta". The Essen European Council confirmed this declaration in December 1994.

In April 1995 the General Affairs Council decided that accession negotiations with Malta would start six months after the conclusion of the then ongoing Intergovernmental Conference which was scheduled to conclude in early 1997. The Cannes. Madrid and Florence European Councils reiterated this decision in June 1995, December 1995 and June 1996 respectively. A pre-accession strategy in preparation for the eventual negotiation, including the initiation of a structured dialogue, was also mapped out by the General Affairs Council in 1995 and started being implemented in early 1996.

In October 1996. the Government notified the General Affairs Council that it intended to suspend Malta's membership application.

Following the elections of the 5ᵗʰ September, the Government of Malta. in line with its electoral mandate, and in full consideration of the decisions regarding Malta's pre-accession process already taken, wishes to reactivate its application to join the European Union.

Please accept, Sir. the assurance of my highest consideration.

Guido de Marco
Deputy Prime Minister and
Minister of Foreign Affairs

My letter to Wolfgang Schussel, president of the Council of the European Union, reactivating Malta's application for membership to the EU.

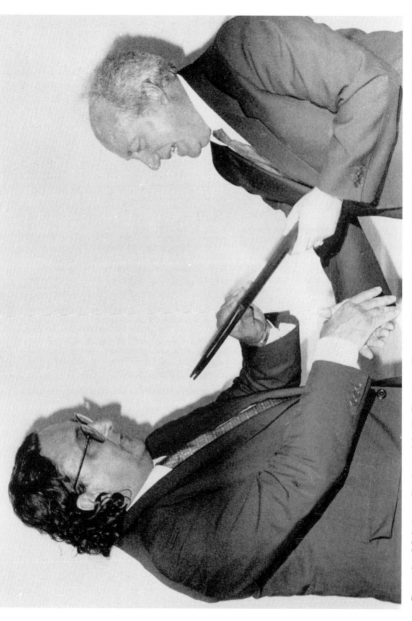

Presenting Malta's application to join the European Economic Community to Gianni de Michelis in Brussels on July 16, 1990.

'Star Quality' – Malta applies to join the European Economic Community.
(The Sunday Times, July 22, 1990)

With Malta Labour Party leader Alfred Sant and Libyan Ambassador to Malta, Hind Siala.

With French President François Mitterand at the United Nations.

With Lawrence Gonzi during the 1998 election campaign.

UN secretary general Javier Perez de Cuellar handing me the speaker's hammer as president of the UN General Assembly in September 1990.

With Kofi Annan, secretary general of the United Nations, at UN headquarters in New York.

Speaking at the opening meeting of the 45ᵗʰ regular session of the UN General Assembly. On left, secretary general Javier Perez de Cuellar; and, right, Ronald I. Spiers, under-secretary general for political and general assembly affairs and secretariat services.

US President George Bush speaking at the 45th session of the UN General Assembly.

Meeting children at the Teferi Ber refugee camp.

Being brought up to date on the tasks carried out by UNICOM Peace-Keeping Forces (the Blue Berets) at the demilitarised zone between Kuwait and Iraq.

With Alexander Dubcek, who led his country during the Prague Spring in 1968.

With President Kim Il Sung and his foreign minister during my visit to North Korea as President of the UN General Assembly. Also in the picture are Violet, three ambassadors, Walter Balzan, Alfred Zarb, and Joseph Cassar, and Olaf Terribile.

Lockerbie: The Pan Am jumbo jet that exploded in mid-air on December 21, 1988, killing 270 people, including 11 on the ground.

Omar Mohammed Ali Rezaq being escorted down EgyptAir plane hijacked to Malta on November 23, 1985. It was one of the worst hijackings in the history of aviation.

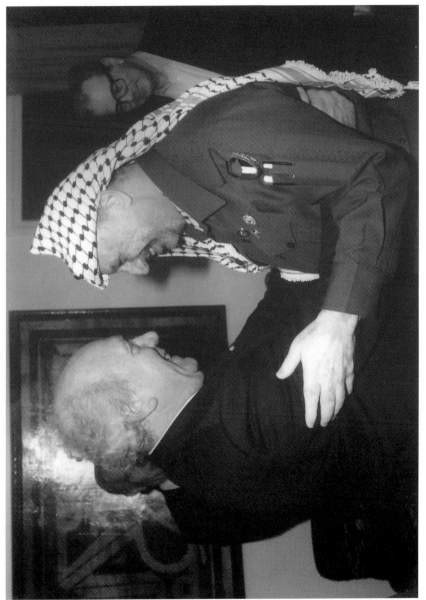

With Yasser Arafat, a man of principle, a man of courage.

With Shimon Peres, a statesman for Israel, a statesman for peace.

With Amr Moussa, secretary general of the Arab League.

Taking the oath of office as President of Malta.

'When Malta forged a-head (or two) – to coin a phrase!' (The Sunday Times, September 30, 1990).

With my family at San Anton on the day of my inauguration as President.

Prime Minister and Mrs Eddie Fenech Adami calling on new President and Mrs de Marco at San Anton Palace.

As President of Malta (second from left, front row), next to European Union president Romano Prodi after the signing of the European Union Treaty of Accession in Athens, Greece, April 16, 2003. Dr Eddie Fenech Adami stands sixth from right.

At Buckingham Palace receiving the Honorary Grand Cross of the Order of St Michael and St George from Queen Elizabeth II.

At Rila Monastery, 117 kilometres out of Sofia. The monastery, one of the most popular tourist attractions in Bulgaria, is believed to have been founded by a hermit, John of Rila, in the 10th century, during the reign of the Bulgarian Tzar Peter (927-968).

With Fra Andrew Bertie, grandmaster of the Sovereign Military Hospitaller Order of Jerusalem, of Rhodes and of Malta, after being conferred with the Collare dell'Ordine al Merito Melitense on January 16, 2000.

With the president of the Federal Republic of Germany and Mrs Johannes Rau at Schloss Bellevue, Berlin, during a state visit on November 8, 2001.

Brush with death: Two of the cars in my presidential motorcade after the accident on our way to Sofia following our visit to Rila Monastery in the mountains. A trailer had first hit our car, spinning it out of control, and then crashed into other cars carrying members of my delegation.

To His Excellency
Guido de Marco
President of Malta

As Your Excellency knows, I have had the joy of fulfilling my heartfelt desire to mark the Two Thousandth Anniversary of the birth of our Saviour by making a religious pilgrimage to places connected with his life and work. After Sinai and the Holy Land, my intention has always been to complete this spiritual journey at the places linked to the evangelizing mission of Saint Paul and the first expansion of the faith as described in the Acts of the Apostles. It is for this reason that I am especially grateful to you and to the Maltese Government for making it possible for me to revisit Malta, and I am looking forward very much to that meeting with you and your fellow citizens, as I follow the path which Revelation itself has taken.

Please be assured, Your Excellency, of my goodwill and affection for the Maltese people, and accept the assurance of my prayers to Almighty God for the well-being and harmony of the nation.

From the Vatican, 27 March 2001

Joannes Paulus II

Pope John Paul II's letter of March 27, 2001 informing me of his plan to visit Malta on his pilgrimage to places "linked to the evangelising mission of Saint Paul".

With Pope John Paul II on the Palace balcony in Valletta.

A moment of intense happiness.

With Vaclav Havel at an informal meeting at Verdala Palace.

Under the tree of love at the Royal Palace in Beijing, China.

With Chinese President Jiang Zemin in Beijing during my state visit to China.

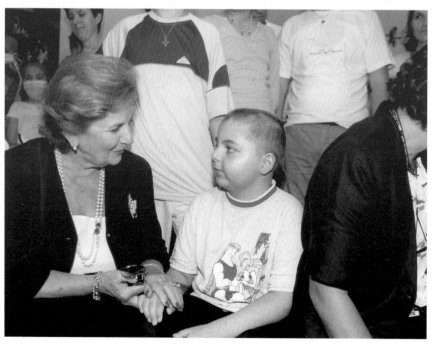

Violet at a house for children with serious illnesses during my state visit to Greece.

Being received at the Quirinale by President Carlo Azelio Ciampi and Donna Franca.

Libyan leader Muammar Gaddafi seeing me off after a state visit in February 2004.

Violet with Muammar Gaddafi's wife and daughter Aisha (left) and Isabelle Borg.

With the Emir of Kuwait on my state visit.

Being welcomed by King Juan Carlos at the opening of the Euro-Med Conference in 1995.

As chairman of the Commonwealth Foundation, visiting tsunami victims in Sri Lanka.

Visiting a village in Sri Lanka weeks after the tsunami in December 2004.

Time to say farewell at San Anton Palace at the end of my term as president.

Receiving Gustav Stresemann medal shortly after the end of my term as President of Malta.

On our fiftieth wedding anniversary on December 30, 2006. On right is our daughter, Gianella.

Gianella (centre) with Fiorella and her daughter Angelica.

With Violet, Mario, Gianella and Fiorella.

Holding Luca, our latest addition, born on July 5, 2007.

31

Pietru Pawl Busuttil: The frame-up

We now come to an account that has cast one of the darkest shadows on the island's police force: the frame-up of Pietru Pawl Busuttil. In the early hours of one December day, I received a phone call from a woman who said her husband, Pietru Pawl, had been arrested by the police in the dead of night and taken to his farmhouse where a search was being carried out. Although I was somewhat used to getting early calls, this was earlier than usual and in the light of the political circumstances of the time, rather ominous.

I learned later that some police officers were in a triumphant mood following the search at Busuttil's farmhouse. Indeed, there were rumours that the police had made a find that was linked to Raymond Caruana's murder. Then in the evening of December 13, 1986, I was informed that Pietru Pawl Busuttil was to be taken to court. To my astonishment, I was given to understand that he was going to be charged with Caruana's murder and that the machine-gun that was used to kill Caruana had been found in Busuttil's farmhouse. Pietru Pawl was a quiet man, a Nationalist, and not given to resorting to violence at all. I was also given to understand that the machine-gun used to kill Caruana was the same that had been fired at the PN club in Tarxien. Now surely, I thought, since Busuttil was a Nationalist, he could hardly have been in the carcade in Tarxien or in the car from which machine-gun fire had killed Caruana. So, how did the machine-gun end up in Busuttil's farmhouse? Two searches had been made at the farmhouse. The machine-gun had been found in a sack in the second search, wrapped in copies of *In... Taghna*. Police Commissioner Lawrence Pullicino told Busuttil: 'You're sitting on a volcano. Your life is finished.'

Busuttil was charged with Caruana's murder, firing a machine-gun at the Nationalist Party club in Tarxien, possessing and using the machine-gun, and, also, possession of drugs. What was particularly strange from the outset was that a police photographer had been asked to be at police headquarters before the CID received the 'anonymous' call that there was a machine-gun hidden in Busuttil's farmhouse. Very ominous, too, was the presence of Inspector Joe Pico, of the security branch, a branch answerable directly to the police commissioner. Pico denied any connection with the case and having been present when the farmhouse was searched. It was only after cross-examination, and when Pico was actually identified in a picture taken at the farmhouse, that he had finally admitted his presence at Busuttil's farmhouse.

Anyway, to go back to the time he was taken to court, as the evening turned to night, the tension at the court hall was unbearable. I heard shouting in the corridor. It was Pietru Pawl Busuttil, crying his heart out; he was in a hysterical state. 'They are accusing me of having killed Raymond Caruana... that I killed Raymond Caruana.' His cry pierced the heart of the people around him. As I tried to calm him down, he passed out in my arms. I felt as bad as when I was at the Gudja party club looking at the lifeless body of Raymond Caruana on the floor.

Busuttil was taken to hospital and kept there under constant watch by the Special Mobile Unit. When evidence started pointing towards the uncovering of a frame-up, I was given to understand that the man's life could well be in danger. Someone might think of the idea of throwing him out of the window, making it appear as if it were a suicide. So I decided to go and warn him. An SMU policeman wanted to be with me in the room when I talked to him, but I refused and I had to physically shove him out. In fact that very night some policemen entered his room and, in an effort to scare them away, he started shouting 'What are you here for, what are you here for?' If their intention was to make him commit a forced 'suicide', it failed.

I said at the beginning of this chapter that the case had cast a shadow over the police force. It did, but in all fairness, there were also a few officers whose behaviour was impeccable and were loyal to the oath of office. They had in fact helped in the efforts to expose the frame-up. In doing so, they risked their career, and maybe their life, too, and I pay tribute to them. I have great admiration, too, for two magistrates, Gino Camilleri and Geoffrey Valenzia, who had had the courage to proceed with the inquiry into the case, seriously questioning the charges drawn up by the police. But I had to write a formal letter to the Attorney General's office in order to get a copy of the *proces-verbal*. The MLP came out of the whole frame-up affair in the worst possible light, with its president, Alfred Sant, sneering at Pietru Pawl Busuttil's supposed ailment and claiming that this was taken advantage of by the Nationalist Party.

Busuttil was eventually charged with having been in possession of an explosive substance under suspicious circumstances as well as a sub-machine-gun and ammunition and the plant cannabis. In my defence of Busuttil, I tore apart the evidence brought against him but by the time the case came up for judgment, the political scenario had changed. I had become deputy prime minister and minister of the interior and justice. Busuttil was found not guilty of all the charges brought against him. It was one of the worst frame-ups ever concocted.

32

Election victory

December 1986 was a most turbulent month. It was possibly also the most decisive month for the Labour government. In that month we had Raymond Caruana's murder, the frame-up of Pietru Pawl Busuttil, and a speech by Mintoff on the 'moment of truth'. One morning I received a message while I was in court that Mintoff wished to speak to me. By this time my contacts with him had become frequent. On the phone Mintoff told me in the clearest of terms that he was prepared to speak in Parliament that evening and have the whole issue settled. He only asked that I renounce speaking on the budget, as had been planned, and instead allow him to say what he had in mind. He told me that, before announcing his proposals, he had first planned to make a strong attack on the opposition as he thought this would have a favourable effect on the mood of the Labour MPs.

In a nutshell, his proposed solution was the acceptance by the Nationalist Party of Malta's neutrality status and a commitment on the PN's part not to allow the island to be used as a military base, and the drawing up of arrangements under which the party winning an absolute majority of votes and a minority of seats would be allotted additional seats to reflect the majority. I think Eddie was at first taken aback by Mintoff's proposal to take up our time but he then realised it could lead to a breakthrough. The House Select Committee was driving us down a dead alley, and we realised that, unless corrective measures were taken to ensure majority rule, we might easily have another perverse election result similar to that we had had in 1981. We were well aware, too, that our supporters' patience was wearing thin and they were expecting concrete developments.

Eddie (whom I personally call Dwardu) agreed with Mintoff's proposal that we allow him to take up our time in Parliament. True to his word, Mintoff made a violent attack on us, something we had to take with clenched teeth. The Socialist MPs just loved it. As they invariably did whenever Mintoff made important speeches, they applauded him and banged on their desks in approval. Then, at the very moment he felt sure he had them all on his side, he announced the proposed amendments that had been discussed at our meetings and which had been drawn up by Edgar Mizzi. Mintoff challenged Fenech Adami to accept the proposal. The government believed that some of our MPs were not prepared to accept the compromise. I thought that, when the country had gone through so many difficulties and violence, the proposed 'neutrality and non-alignment' clauses were not such a high price to pay if their acceptance meant the avoidance of civil strife and a return to majority rule. After all, neutrality and non-alignment had been found useful to certain countries, such as Austria and Finland, which turned them to their national advantage in the service of peace to them and to the international community. When Mintoff finished his speech, I remember going over to the government side to compliment him. He had finally done a decent gesture in a difficult moment in history.

From that moment onwards, my meetings with Mintoff had become even more effective and conclusive. It was a great relief to the country when, in January 1987, Parliament unanimously approved the proposed constitutional amendments. As I said before, I think I had taken great risks in going on for so long with my talks with Mintoff for, although I had enjoyed considerable trust from my colleagues, many felt the talks were doomed to failure. As I was to discover later, Mintoff had gone through some rough time himself, too, with his colleagues over these proposed amendments. To be fair with Mintoff, while he was to blame for much of what had happened since 1971, through the way he had governed the country and through the violence that had caused so much division and so many political scars, it was through his work that a solution was finally found.

However, in spite of this important development, we were still having bouts of violence. In Rabat, policemen from the Special Mobile Unit had even shot at Nationalist Party supporters, injuring a couple critically, and our club was set on fire. When I went personally to the district police to enquire about the incidents, the policemen simply sneered at me. Clearly, their shooting was the act of desperate men who were sensing that the day of reckoning was fast approaching. When I addressed a mass meeting a few days later, I held the police officers personally responsible for the shooting and told our people they should not be drawn into a position where they could get shot at. Karmenu Mifsud Bonnici sought to gain all the time constitutionally available to him before the holding of general elections and, in a desperate move to win votes, employed thousands at the shipyard and with government service and its agencies.

Just a few days before the election, I had come to know of plans for the disruption of the counting of votes if at any time it appeared likely that we were set to win the election. According to the reports we received, a number Labour supporters were to force their way into counting hall compound and cause havoc, disrupting the counting process. We felt it was counter-productive informing the police commissioner about the reports. Instead, we reported the matter to Mifsud Bonnici, who seemed genuinely concerned. He gave us his word that no such thing would happen.

As expected, the political atmosphere in the country on election day was tense indeed. We had some incidents in Żejtun, where some Socialist thugs prevented some of our supporters from voting, but on the whole the elections went smoothly. The party was well organised at every level. Polling booths were well 'guarded' and street leaders worked wonders. Party headquarters was very busy, with expectations running high. Eddie remained at headquarters and I spent most of the time at the counting hall to have an overall view of what was happening.

There were moments of great tension in the counting hall and I hoped to God there would be no incidents. My mind raced to the Rabat incidents when members of the Special Mobile Unit shot at our supporters. Mercifully, the SMU was kept away from the counting hall. I saw Lorry Sant and Wistin Abela talking together, not a good omen, I thought, since Sant had acquired a reputation as a bully. But I was reassured by the fact that our observers and candidates were all there, keeping a sharp eye on the counting of votes. Slowly but surely, the results from the districts were showing that we had won an absolute majority of votes but, had it not been for the amendments made to the constitution, we would have had a repeat performance of 1981.

As I was leaving the counting hall, several policemen, who only up to a few hours earlier had shown disdain at my presence there, stood to attention, obviously sensing that I was going to be their minister. I headed towards the Special Mobile Unit room where the men still posted there looked quite dejected at the outcome of the elections. Then I headed straight to Safi to share our first moments of victory with Pietru Pawl Busuttil who had been so shamelessly framed. From there, I went to party headquarters to meet Eddie and to celebrate our victory with the party people. My only worry at that time was that some of our supporters might show excessive enthusiasm in their celebrations and resort to vengeance, something that would have gone against all we had stood for over the years. But, except for some isolated incidents, the celebrations that night went well. I remember seeing Joseph Frendo Azzopardi, one of my staunchest supporters, in Republic Street in Valletta. He was overjoyed but his joy did not last long as he had a heart attack and died a few hours later. The election victory brought an incredible sense of relief in the country.

When I returned home late that night, I hugged Violet and the children – it was a great day, possibly one of the happiest in my life. In effect, it also marked the end of my life as a lawyer. A new life was dawning, that of a government minister.

33

Pastures new

Late in the evening of the election victory, the acting president, Paul Xuereb, phoned up Eddie Fenech Adami asking him to be sworn in as prime minister. He wished to have the swearing-in take place that night as Karmenu Mifsud Bonnici had already tendered his resignation and he did not wish to have a power vacuum. But the party's inner circle thought it would be advisable to hold the swearing-in the following morning in order not to give an impression that there had been any sort of emergency. We also wanted to give the people an opportunity of celebrating the event.

Eddie Fenech Adami was sworn in as prime minister the following day, May 12, 1987. Xuereb received us with great courtesy and the ceremony was over in no time. We then appeared on the Palace balcony where in the square below a jubilant crowd gave us a tremendous welcome. Exuberant supporters enjoyed every minute of their party's moment of triumph as they crammed every available space in that historic square. The crowd followed us to Castille, from where Eddie told the crowd that the time had come to put the country back on the road to prosperity in a truly democratic environment.

The crowd dispersed and we stayed behind discussing cabinet appointments. Apart from Eddie and myself, there were Ugo Mifsud Bonnici, Louis Galea, and Ċensu Tabone, as well as John Camilleri, Eddie's private secretary. I was given the designation of deputy prime minister, leader of the House, and minister of the interior and justice. There were some doubts at first as to whether interior and justice should be joined in one ministry. Apart from a short spell when Lorry Sant had been minister of the interior, the police had been the responsibility of the prime minister. However, we thought that in the prevailing circumstances, it was best to have a separate ministry responsible for the police force, and in any case the prime minister was expected to have his hands full running a new administration. Ugo was the obvious choice as minister of education. Apart from his personal cultural background and interest in education, he had been shadowing the education ministry during our time in opposition. Censu Tabone got foreign affairs, again a ministry which he had been shadowing for years, and his experience both in Strasbourg and in international meetings of the Christian Democratic movement gave him the right credentials. He was, in fact, the only cabinet minister who had previous ministerial experience, having been a minister in Borg Olivier's last government, that of 1966-71.

Louis Galea was given the health and social services ministry. I was personally against having such a big ministry, but the thinking was to have parliamentary secretaries to assist him. Another obvious choice was that of George Bonello du Puis as minister of finance. I think George gave an excellent account of himself in the five years that followed. It was not so easy making other appointments. The appointment of ministers and parliamentary secretaries is the prerogative of the prime minister, but in May 1987 Eddie preferred sharing the exercise with us. Manwel Bonnici was made responsible for parastatal bodies, and Lawrence Gatt for agriculture and industry. I think Gatt was very well prepared for agriculture but had to rely very much on his parliamentary secretary where industry was concerned. John Dalli was chosen as parliamentary secretary for industry. John's strong personality and intelligence made it difficult for him to work in a role subordinate to a minister.

Michael Falzon was an obvious candidate for a ministry that included public works and the environment. Michael is a very intelligent person, moody at times, but he can grasp things quickly. As to who was going to take responsibility for Gozitan affairs, one idea was that the work be entrusted to a parliamentary secretary at the office of the prime minister but I disagreed since we had specifically promised a Gozo ministry. Ultimately, there was general agreement about this and, as expected, the post was given to Anton Tabone, who succeeded to make people think of Gozo not just as a constituency but as a region, with its own special needs that had to be tackled at national level. George Hyzler, who had been shadowing health for a number of years, must have been somewhat disappointed when he was made parliamentary secretary responsible for health. John Rizzo Naudi was appointed parliamentary secretary with responsibility for the elderly. We had no idea he would make such a success in the post, taking the sector to the forefront of the government's social development programme. As parliamentary secretary to Manwel Bonnici, taking responsibility for maritime affairs, Joe Fenech brought new vigour to the maritime sector, particularly in work connected with the new yacht marina, maritime legislation, and the setting up of the International Maritime Law Institute.

I am not in favour of having parliamentary secretaries in the government set-up. In any case, I would have preferred the designation junior minister to parliamentary secretary. Often enough, parliamentary secretaries consider themselves ministers-in-waiting and do not keep the right kind of relationship with their ministry, more so when they operate from a different building. I believe a smaller cabinet is better to the proper governance of the country. I do understand, however, that a prime minister has to take other matters into consideration in the appointment to cabinet posts, such as, for instance, the sterling service given by members of Parliament and constituency interests.

We were alone at Castille when we formed the cabinet and I had to call for my secretary at my legal office, Vera Lungaro Mifsud, to type the cabinet list for us. Somehow, Castille was an eerie place that night. We were later summoned to San Anton Palace where we were sworn in. As I left the palace, I realised the magnitude of the new responsibilities I would be shouldering but I was raring to go. Remembering John Milton, I said to myself, 'Tomorrow to fresh woods and pastures new.'

34

Winds of change

My office was on the ground floor of the Palace, just opposite the entrance to that of the attorney general. It consisted of a large vaulted room in what is probably the oldest part of the palace with some small adjoining rooms for the secretariat. One serious drawback was that the general office door led directly to the minister's office. On the other hand, the area allocated to the ministry of justice had some beautiful state rooms used by clerical staff. After some months, I moved my office to a small beautiful room that Borg Olivier had once used as his parliamentary office. It had a door leading to the Perellos Hall, which was useful for receptions and meetings, and an ante-room opening into the Palace's dining hall.

I had three different roles. As minister of justice, I was responsible for the justice department, the lands department, and the prisons, and as minister of the interior, for law and order and for the police force. As leader of the House of Representatives, I had to keep parliamentary schedules and ensure a proper balancing of rights and duties of the government and the opposition. One has to keep in mind that we only had a majority of one seat.

I had no major problems when I came to set up my secretariat. Joe Tonna, who had worked at my legal office since 1966 and whom I had known before at the crown advocate general's office, was my personal secretary. Joe had a quiet efficiency, a person that got on well with everybody. His loyalty was outstanding. Michael Vella, a government clerk who had previously worked at the social services department, was a very good and dedicated civil servant. I had lost a true friend when he died three years later. Walter Balzan, now serving as an ambassador, joined my secretariat some time later. Walter is very intelligent and has a likeable personality. His art of gentle persuasion is an important part of his character.

One of my first jobs was to underline the independence of the judiciary and the importance of the rule of law for a true democracy. I made it clear to the judiciary that the days when judges were suspended from their court duties and were made to play musical chairs at the government's whim were over. I had known all the judges and magistrates personally and naturally I was fully aware of the tough time they had gone through, time that had brought out their strengths and weaknesses. I had made it clear that the people were expecting greater efficiency in the administration of justice, underlining the legal maxim that delay was a denial of justice. I know this sounds as if I am stating the obvious but, in doing so, I felt I was laying out our political programme which was inspired by judicial democracy.

The most difficult part of my ministry was the police, which consisted of over 1,000 men. Not more than 100 had Nationalist Party sympathies and, after 16 years of Socialist administration, most had lost the will to stand their ground in their duties. One group of officers could hardly be called heroes in their defence of law and order and indeed a number of them had given in to the bad influence of their superiors. I felt these could be turned into loyal policemen again if they were given the chance to do so. There were others who were simply criminals in uniform. This may sound a harsh statement, but it was true.

Just a few days after my appointment, I addressed the police force for the first time. I had full trust in Deputy Police Commissioner Anthony Mifsud Tommasi; he had given me good advice and I appointed him acting police commissioner. Police Commissioner Lawrence Pullicino had gone on sick leave immediately after the election. Pullicino was eventually tried in 1993 before a jury and convicted of being an accomplice to causing grievous bodily harm resulting in the death of Nardu Debono. He was sentenced to 15 years' imprisonment and the judgment was confirmed on appeal. The Court of Human Rights in Strasbourg rejected his application to have the judgment reversed.

In my address to the police force at police headquarters, I again made certain comments that may appear all too obvious today. They were not at the time. The police, I said, were not there to serve any political party but to serve the nation, without fear or favour. And in the light of the behaviour that had been shown by some of the policemen in the years of Socialist administration, I made it clear that I would not stand for any brutality or use of force unless this was done within the limits strictly permissible by law. I said I had planned to start going to headquarters regularly and to have an office there to monitor developments in the force. I had regular meetings with the officers and began going through daily reports of registered infringements of the law and of the follow-up actions taken.

On my first official tour of police headquarters, Inspector Charles Cassar took me to the room where the police kept their arms. Strangely enough, the room did not fall under the responsibility of the armourer but of the Special Mobile Unit which reported directly to the police commissioner. We still needed the SMU, but the attitude and behaviour many of them had shown during the time Labour were in power were simply unacceptable in a democracy. I tried to salvage what I could from the unit. Two of the commanding officers were prepared to help in the planned reform. I had to draw a distinction between those who, in spite of their past bad behaviour, were now ready to give of their best and those who only intended to disrupt the reform.

A few weeks after taking over the ministry, it was decided that criminal action be taken against Labour supporters who had threatened and injured people when they were voting in Żejtun during the election. The accused were persons who had long been involved in political violence. Eddie had brought the matter up before the party's executive committee as he felt the matter had a great bearing on people who had suffered at the hands of those who were to be charged. When I was asked what measures were being taken by the police to ensure that the due process of law be observed, I said we had a complement of some 200. One member of the executive, a former police officer, thought this was a substantial deployment of force. My stand was that, in so far as law and order were concerned, the action planned to be taken against the men was premature. The force, as it was still composed at the time, was unreliable and few were prepared to face a hostile and violent Labour crowd. My view was that, before taking action against those who had threatened voters in Żejtun, it was advisable to build up the force to be able to control a hostile crowd, if the need for such control arose. But the executive committee did not take my advice as it felt it was important not to give the impression that we were giving in. They did not realise that, in certain circumstances, discretion is the better part of valour.

Events proved me right. When the accused were arraigned, a violent crowd gathered outside the law courts. The accused had no jacket on when they appeared in court and the magistrate lost no time in warning them that they had to go to court hearings properly dressed, that is, wearing a jacket. To ridicule the courts, the following day the accused turned up in morning coats. On their way to the law courts, they were accompanied by a crowd of supporters, who soon started getting rowdy and violent and breaking up shop windows. They later even attacked the court building and set halls on fire. It was no ordinary attack. There was a calculated method in their violence, so much so that documents relating to evidence given in some important criminal cases and kept in safe-keeping in court offices, were stolen. Of the 200 policemen on duty outside the building, very few offered any resistance. One who did and whose name comes readily to mind was Inspector Charles Cassar, of the SMU. Most of the rest did not lift a finger, not even to protect the magistrate who, ironically, had to be escorted out of the building by Lorry Sant, who was with the crowd at the law courts.

Part of the building was gutted by fire. At one moment, soldiers on a truck parked next to the Palace, close to my office, showed their political colour openly by singing Labour Party hymns. They must have thought the Nationalists' days in government were numbered as they would soon give in to street violence. Eddie called an urgent cabinet meeting that evening. I had been right in my foreboding and I realised more than ever how important it was to speak clearly in politics. I told the cabinet that, unless the police force employed a substantial number of new entrants, we would not be able to keep law and order. This time my warning was heeded and action taken to enrol new men.

The acting police commissioner was a sorry sight when we sent for him over the matter. 'My men let me down,' he said. In the circumstances, we thought of appointing a new man to lead the force and he agreed. Colonel John Spiteri was prepared to take over but he wished to have some Army officers to assist him in his work. His request was readily acceded to. Col. Spiteri's appointment created an excellent relationship between the police and my ministry. Mifsud Tommasi was a gentleman throughout. He realised he could not lead the force but I must say that his contribution had been most positive, both in terms of the sound advice he had given on matters relating to the correct functioning of the force as an executive organ of the courts and, later, in the setting up of a police academy. Spiteri brought order and discipline in the force and gradually the country started feeling the winds of change.

Hundreds applied to join the force when the call for applications was made. The new recruits received proper training under military NCOs at Ta' Kandja. These were the first batch that was to help renew the force. I saw to it that some former police officers who had left the force for some reason or other be allowed to join at the rank to which they would have been promoted had their service not been interrupted. Alfred Calleja rejoined the force at superintendent rank. He was certainly an asset both in his investigative qualities and in leadership style. I set my mind on having a force trained in crowd control and in checking street violence. For this reason the SMU was replaced by a Special Action Group whose men were trained by Italian officers from the Italian military mission. SAG men proved themselves competent and effective. I used to go and see them at Ta' Kandja frequently for moral support.

When the compilation of evidence against those who had been charged with the incidents in Żejtun continued, Col. Spiteri managed to contain all new attempts at street violence, even though the precautions he had taken might have given the impression that there was a state of emergency in Republic Street. A further attempt, this time by a sizeable crowd, at street violence was stopped by the SAG. All this showed the usefulness of the group.

The next step was to set up a proper security service. The one we had when we took over had been used mainly to monitor Nationalist Party meetings and to keep tabs on those perceived as hostile to the Socialist administration. The men were known in the force as 'nimrods'. I enlisted the help of the Italian security service and got to know Admiral Martini, who had been responsible for it for a long time. I also had the help of the British security service. Eventually, close cooperation was established between our security service and those of several other countries, including Germany and the United States. I had always made it clear that our security service had to stand on its own, lest we might be used by others in their interest. Today, the necessary legislation is in place to regulate their activities and society in general has appreciated the important role it is playing in state security work and in the fight against drugs and international criminal activities.

I also wanted to see a greater police presence in the towns and villages. In my view, a police force has to be close to the people and has to be seen to be such, particularly through the police stations which ought to act as a guarantor of order in the locality. Much depends on the quality of the police. I started making surprise visits to police stations to check how the citizen was faring. On some of my visits at night, I found the police officer on duty either asleep inside or not there at all! Every Sunday I used to hear Mass at police headquarters and later have coffee with the officers. Through regular meetings, I managed to win the trust of a substantial number of officers, independently of their political persuasion and, indeed, of their past in the force. It was certainly not an easy task, nor was it always successful. But the police force had been put on the right track, ready to meet open challenges to law and order, and was now winning the support of the people in general. From a force that had earned notoriety for political discrimination and abuse of power, it was now turning into a new professional organisation. A few police officers who had erred were disciplined and removed from the force. Others were given a chance to prove themselves, even though they did not have an unblemished record. Most managed to do so and served well.

It was also important for a modern police force to have a well-equipped forensic laboratory. My aim was to make the laboratory a national institution, close to but independent of police investigation. Dr Anthony Abela Medici was an accomplished scientist with a mind for research. With his help and cooperation, we acquired some indispensable modern equipment, particularly that needed for a quick examination of fingerprints. Arrangements were also made for Abela Medici to travel abroad in connection with police investigations. Alfred Calleja, whom I had put in charge of special investigations, was asked to look into some specific murder cases – those of Karin Grech, Lino Cauchi, and Raymond Caruana. None of these cases was solved. When it was thought that there might be some evidence to be tapped in Australia in connection with the murder of Karin Grech, we sent out Maltese investigators to that country, including Abela Medici, to follow up any leads there. But, despite all this and the fact that I had put Alfred Calleja, the best investigator we had in charge of the investigations, the outcome was regrettably a failure. To be fair, years had passed since the murder had taken place. In the case of the Raymond Caruana murder, though, very important evidence that could have been lifted from gunpowder residue on suspect persons was not taken with the urgency that such cases required.

In spite of the great changes that were taking place in the police force, I had long been realising that the force did not have an institution that looked after the formation of its members. While army officers used to be sent to Sandhurst and other military academies for instruction in leadership and army affairs, police officers, of whatever rank, did not receive such specialised training. To get an insight into police training, I visited Bramhill, the police college for staff officers in the United Kingdom and also consulted some Italian experts. I suggested to the cabinet the setting up of a police academy at Upper St Elmo. Both Upper and Lower St Elmo had been abandoned when the British forces left Malta. This very historical fortress was in a very bad state. Parts of it had been illegally taken over and used for all sorts of activity, including the storage of carnival floats and the keeping of dogs. In a matter of months, Major Cutajar (*Il-Ġemel*) turned Upper St Elmo into a place fit for the academy. Anthony Mifsud Tommasi, who had reached pensionable age by now, was appointed commandant of the academy. Dr Guido Saliba took in hand the running of the academic studies of the cadets, and Col. Kenneth Valenzia was entrusted with training and discipline. A number of lecturers, including judges and experts in different fields, were appointed. It was a great day for me and for the police force when we inaugurated the academy on July 12, 1988. Hundreds of recruits have since been trained there, and I still look back with pride at that day. When, some time later, Michael Ellul, the architect who was responsible for the restoration works of the fort, published a book about the history of the fort and asked me to write the preface, I did so with a sense of history. Like practically every other institution, the academy has had its good and not-so-good times. I hope the minister responsible for the police and the police commissioner will continue to dedicate some of their attention to the academy.

35

Race against time

Police affairs were taking up a considerable part of my time as a government minister. But I had to give great attention, too, to my other responsibilities. As leader of the House, I had to ensure that we worked well in Parliament, particularly since, as I said earlier, we had a majority of only one seat. We were drawing up a considerable legislative programme and, as expected, Labour were far from being co-operative. Since we wanted to ensure that the observance of human rights be made the hallmark of the new Malta, the first act that Parliament enacted was Act XIV of 1987, which integrated the European Convention for the Protection of Human Rights and Fundamental Freedoms into the Maltese legal system. In the drafting of the law, we sought out the help of Dr Vanni Bonello, whose dedication as a lawyer in defence of human rights was well known. We aimed at giving maximum protection to the citizen.

Another important law I piloted that required a lot of background and study was that setting up a Permanent Commission against Corruption. The government wanted to ensure that corruption be properly investigated by an independent body, chaired by a judge or by a person having the same qualifications of a judge. The first person appointed to chair the commission was Mr Justice Victor Borg Costanzi, who made good use of his probing intelligence. Past cases of corruption were properly investigated but, more importantly than dealing with past cases, the commission acted as a deterrent. Corruption is the worst enemy of any administration and it was therefore important to have the right machinery to deal with it. An equally important bill I piloted was Act of 1987 for the investigation of injustices. Immediately after we were elected, we were inundated with requests to rectify injustices that many had suffered under the Socialist administration. We set up an independent commission to look into the hundreds of claims that were made and eventually we had to have more than one commission to speed up work. A remedy was given to those whose claims were upheld.

I gave a lot of personal attention to the law courts. The judiciary was a major victim of the Socialist administration. Some judges and magistrates remained passive to the arrogance of the executive and others had not bothered to stand up to defend their independence, but some others did a good job. As I have said before, I had been found guilty by a magistrates' court of having maliciously spread false news for having said that democracy was being endangered by the behaviour of the Socialist administration in making the judges play musical chairs, in suspending the constitutional court and all courts of first instance for a time, and for repeatedly threatening the judiciary in its work. The sentence was reversed by a court of appeal. Some members of the judiciary, like Don Abbondio in Alessandro Manzoni's *I Promessi Sposi*, 'non erano nati con un cuore di leone' (had not born with the heart of a lion). Notwithstanding this, some judgments and decisions had done honour to the judiciary. One such judgment was that which upheld the Nationalist Party's right to hold the meeting in Żejtun. Special mention must also be made of the magistrates involved in the Pietru Pawl Busuttil case.

I have only mentioned the more outstanding cases. There were other instances when the judiciary had defended freedom and lived up to its best traditions. When I met the judiciary, I expressed the need for their independence not only to be proclaimed but also for the people to believe in it. I did my best to deal with the problem of delays in the hearing of court cases. I doubled the number of judges dealing with cases in courts of first instance; set up another criminal court to hear trials by jury; ensured better terms and conditions for the judiciary; and saw to the building of new court rooms and to an extension of the building. I gave the go-ahead for computerisation and for the setting up of a law library at the courts for the benefit of both the judiciary and lawyers. I also appointed a Permanent Law Revision Commission to keep the law under constant review. Unfortunately, however, this was dissolved some years later.

We planned to modernise the public registry, which was an efficient department. We started off by having a pilot project in computerising all wills registered between 1911 and 1983. The public registry, a repository of so many historical documents, reflects the life of a nation. We even opened an exhibition room, where we held exhibitions on the lives of important personalities, such as George Borg Olivier, Enrico Mizzi, Sir Paul Boffa, Lord Strickland, Sir Temi Zammit, and the Nanis. It is a pity that this initiative, which had proved so popular, was discontinued.

Another major initiative was a decision to amend the Marriage Act. Civil marriage had been introduced under the Labour administration. Up to this time, marriage in Malta was regulated by Canon Law in so far as Catholic marriages were concerned; nullity cases were determined by a curia tribunal, with a right of appeal to the Holy Rota in Rome. The Labour administration removed the jurisdiction of the Church tribunal in so far as the state's recognition is concerned, whilst recognising the jurisdiction of other countries to Maltese marriages when applicable. This had brought about an unfavourable reaction, not only in Church circles but, also, among the population. My thinking was that civil marriage had to be kept for those who did not wish to get married in Church and that the law applicable in these cases should be the Marriage Act, as amended by Parliament. On the other hand, those who chose to be married according to the rites of the Catholic Church would have their marriage governed by Canon Law and nullity cases to be dealt with by the curia tribunal. All this may appear simple to state now, but it was difficult to put into effect at the time. I was entrusted to look into the matter and discuss the issue with the apostolic nuncio and the Church authorities. I will be dealing with this matter later on.

Let me pass on now to something that preoccupied us a great deal then: airport security. With Malta having passed through the tragedy of the EgyptAir hijacking, in which no fewer than 58 of the 99 passengers had been killed in a raid by Egyptian troops, we were naturally anxious to beef up security and put the necessary arrangements in place to meet threats to civil aviation. It was a major challenge. There were times when I used to test ground security myself. An air commodore by the name of S. Langer was appointed to draw up a report on the state of security at the airport. Most of his recommendations were put into effect. When the Lockerbie crisis struck and our airport came under international scrutiny, we were not found wanting.

The prisons, too, fell under the responsibility of my ministry. Prison regulations dated back to 1931 and the staff consisted of an assortment of wardens, policemen, and soldiers. It was clear that policemen and soldiers had to be replaced by people trained in prison duties – prison wardens. On March 25, 1986 the Labour administration had appointed Mr Justice Caruana Curran to investigate allegations made in Parliament about inhuman treatment at the prisons. When I received his report confirming evidence of abuse and ill-treatment, I removed the director of prisons and the chief officer and appointed a new board of visitors, with Joseph Cassar Naudi, an experienced probation officer, as chairman, and Dr Lawrence Gonzi and Dr Maria Sciberras as members.

The first year of the legislature was busy indeed. We had no fewer than 202 sittings. Of the 38 bills tabled, 25 became laws. I just loved Parliament, its atmosphere, and the cut-and-thrust of debates. It was my preferred habitat, except, of course, when members hurled insults at each other or when a few had even resorted to physical aggression against other members and even the press. In my time in Parliament, both on government and opposition benches, I believe I managed to keep good working relations with all members. When the going was really tough, particularly in times when we felt threatened, some of my colleagues wondered how I could keep on speaking terms with opposition members.

I could well understand their feelings but I felt it was unwise to burn bridges. I was working very long hours, 12 hours a day, more often 14. It was always a race against time. We had been waiting in the wings for far too long and now the time had come for us to deliver what we had promised the electorate, and we were not going to let the people down. We worked as a team. I think the 1987 cabinet was one of the best I can remember in my time in Parliament.

36

Skin disorder

It was at this time, early in 1988, that I had first noticed a small pimple on my forehead. I did not think it was anything alarming. I had high blood pressure but I was generally in good health. Suddenly the pimple started to grow, and I was advised to have it removed. And so I did, but soon it turned into an oozing sore and, within a short time, I had more of them all over my head. To cut a long story short, I had pemphigus, a very painful skin disorder that causes blisters. The name is derived from the Greek word *pemphix*, 'bubble'.

I was seen by specialists, including Dr Joseph Pace and Dr Denis Soler, who tried their best to cure me. I was advised to go to London to see a Harley Street specialist. He was a gentle and clever doctor, but his diagnosis was not different from that made by my Maltese doctors. I was given steroids as treatment. When I returned to Malta, the disorder spread to my chest and shoulders. I could not even sleep on a bed. The only way I could rest was to sit upright on a chair, resting my chin – the only part of my face not affected – on a support. I still continued going to the ministry and tried to carry on business as usual, until one evening the pemphigus started affecting my eyes as well. Eddie was very concerned over my health and implored me to take a rest. By this time the steroids were altering my face; it started taking what the doctors called a moonish shape. My hands trembled and I could hardly make a signature.

The Harley Street specialist I had gone to see in London was brought over for consultation and I was given the impression that, unless the disorder was controlled, it could be fatal. I did my best not to give up, even though it was painful to do such simple things as getting dressed. My shirt used to get stuck to the blisters. Still, I continued attending parliamentary sittings whenever I felt slightly better. And that – attending Parliament – was what actually led to a cure. One day John Rizzo Naudi, who was sitting next to me in the House, asked me what kind of pills I had been taking for my high blood pressure. When I gave him the name, he showed me an article in a medical journal that said that the kind of pills I had been taking could trigger pemphigus as a side effect. It had to be Rizzo Naudi who led me to the road of recovery. I immediately got hold of my doctors who contacted the firm making the pills for advice. I was told to stop taking them. Almost miraculously, the disorder started receding. I recovered well in time to be able to attend the inauguration of the Police Academy.

When, late that same summer, the disorder started reappearing, I was advised to go and see a Neapolitan doctor who was a specialist in the treatment of the condition. I had Dr Pace accompanying me to Naples and I remember we had a somewhat difficult flight from Rome to Naples as we headed straight into a big storm. The specialist who saw me gave me further treatment and said that he had been carrying research on the pill I had been taking for my high blood pressure and that he had also informed the makers of its side effects. The manufacturers had only given rash as a possible side effect. I claimed damages and as the firm did not pay up I started civil proceedings before the High Court of Justice in London. Eventually, the firm paid a modest sum in an out-of-court settlement. Thank God, the disorder did not make a re-appearance. I must say that throughout the time I had this pemphigus (what an ugly name!), I had great support from my secretariat at the ministry as well as from the police force. And I wonder what I would have done without the loving care and support of my wife and children. Naturally, I owe a lot, too, to the Maltese and foreign specialists who saw me and, particularly so, to John Rizzo Naudi who, as I said, identified the possible cause of the disorder and put me on the road to recovery. Thank you.

I was still convalescing when I went to speak at a mass meeting on the first anniversary of our 1987 electoral victory. Denis Soler stood next to me, looking worried lest I over-exerted myself. I will never forget the prolonged applause I received at that meeting. It was very moving.

37

Socialist challenge to law and order

The Socialists had not given up defying law and order in the country. When, on June 25, 1988, HMS *Ark Royal* and HMS *Edinburgh* called at Malta on a courtesy visit, a group of men commandeered a Greek tanker and other vessels and blockaded Grand Harbour. The tanker was towed to the place where the *Ark Royal* had planned to berth while barges blocked the fairway. But, as Labour supporters were taking this action in harbour, the Royal Navy ships headed towards St Paul's Bay, where they were cheered by thousands of people.

I remember another serious incident, that of July 14 in that same year. Malta Shipbuilding workers left their place of work, commandeered public transport, and went to Luqa to show their might in support of a strike at a Bank of Valletta branch. They went so far as to attack a police station where bank employees who had refused to take part in a strike had sought protection. But the SAG, showing great courage and efficiency, handled the situation well, thereby avoiding a serious escalation of the incident. There were a number of other incidents, such as those that happened at the March 31 regatta in Birgu and in the morning of that same day when, during the Freedom Day ceremony, the brigadier was pushed into the sea as he was inspecting a guard of honour.

I did not take the situation lying down. Having suffered so much in the time of the Socialists, we were not going to be bullied into submission. The police force had been reorganised by now and a new commissioner, Alfred Calleja, appointed. Col. Spiteri had done an excellent job but it was time for him to return to his proper army duties. Calleja had a sense of fairness and helped in building bridges in a force that was sharply divided by political sympathies. He shared my belief in the importance of keeping the SAG so long as there were still people around who could not accept the 1987 election result. I was fully aware of the risks SAG members had to take in their work and ensured that those injured in the course of duty received compensation. It was also agreed to give an *ex gratia* payment to those who had suffered bodily harm in a breakdown of law and order and to those who had suffered personal harm at the hands of the police. Cabinet had approved a memorandum I had submitted proposing an interim measure for compensation to victims of crime. The amount to be given had to be determined on the basis of the advice given by specialists who were to follow the norms used by the courts in awarding damages.

Eventually, the Socialists' challenge to law and order was curtailed in most of Malta, but not in Żejtun from where most of the violence stemmed. Nationalist supporters used to report regularly that they were being insulted and threatened by Socialist supporters, with the police in that locality and in other neighbouring areas not daring to move a finger against the culprits. I could well understand their fear but the situation was obviously unacceptable. We tried to have the right mix of constables and officers at the Żejtun police station in order to create a sense of trust, but it was to no avail.

Matters came to a head on June 2, 1989 at the wedding of Paul Abdilla's daughter. Abdilla, well known for his Nationalist sympathies, had remained loyal to the party despite political pressures in the years of the Labour administration. He had asked for Eddie and I to act as witnesses and we both accepted as we thought it would be a way of expressing appreciation for his political steadfastness. Little did we think that this would not go down well with the Socialists of Żejtun. They thought it was unacceptable for the prime minister and the interior minister to visit their 'territory'. Their thinking was that, although the country had a Nationalist government, it was they who ruled in Żejtun, which they considered as a sort of a Labour enclave.

Just before the wedding, someone had put up a placard on a lamp-post with a most provocative message: '*Żwieġ kampjun u Prim Ministru miġnun*'. A police inspector was ordered to remove it within 15 minutes, but he did not do so. Inspector Lawrence Cutajar and Assistant Commissioner Maurice Borg called a fire-engine to have it removed. A police Landrover soon made it to Żejtun but a commotion ensued and the vehicle was overturned by a crowd. Police reinforcements were called but the Socialist supporters were determined to ruin the wedding. As soon as the bride and her family arrived at the church, they pelted them with eggs and fruit. The Socialists' callousness had hit rock bottom.

Eddie and I both thought to leave our wives at home but we decided to go and do our duty as witnesses. We used my car, driven by Joe Debono.

As we approached the church, we were soon surrounded by hostile Labour supporters but we had somehow made it inside. While we were in the church we could hear sporadic bursts of gunfire, which, naturally, put us all on edge. To make matters worse, the celebrant felt completely unperturbed by the political tension outside the church and went on and on about the significance of the occasion for the couple getting married. I was counting the time by the second.

When it was over, and we stepped outside, a bullet shot whizzed by, seriously injuring a policeman. The Żejtun Socialists had burst into a wave of violent acts. Eddie was pelted with rabbit skins and other objects; a Landrover was set on fire; a car belonging to Dr Joe Psaila Savona, a Nationalist MP, was vandalised; and a driver from John's Garage, who had brought some guests for the wedding, was beaten up. Several policemen were fired upon and seriously injured. We came to know later that some of the thugs carried automatic weapons. The SAG, under the charge of Supt. Charles Cassar, took the brunt of this open defiance to law and order and had to use tear-gas to bring the situation under control.

The inquiry report by Mr Justice Godwin Muscat Azzopardi showed how close we were to organised violence. The shooting had come from the direction of the Malta Labour Party club, which was close to the church. It was clear that they had planned the attack for they had first shot at the lights in the street so that they could operate under cover of darkness. The SAG had not only managed to stop the violence but, in the following days, they practically took over Żejtun. We had to make it clear that Żejtun was part of Malta too and that law and order had to be restored in that locality. No citizen ought to be harassed, or feel threatened, for his political beliefs. This time the thugs of Żejtun had overplayed their hand. I gave the police officers who had suffered injuries in political violence a gold emblem in appreciation of their contribution to the defence of law and order.

As the police force was regaining its dignity and trust in itself, I felt it was time to give the force members better conditions. These were announced in the presence of the prime minister when I opened a new hall, Vilhena Hall, at police headquarters on the 175th anniversary of the foundation of the Malta Police Force. Besides an improved pay, they were to receive a basic overtime allowance of Lm10 a month, for seven hours of overtime work, whether worked or not, plus overtime payment for any time worked over and above the seven hours. But the most important improvement was that over their pension rights. Under a Boffa government, the police had become entitled to a pension after 25 years' service. In the time of the Mintoff administration, the pension entitlement had been suspended if the retired member undertook paid employment. At their retirement age, most officers would still have a family to look after. So when, as part of the new conditions, I told the force members that on their retirement they would remain entitled to their pension even if they undertook paid work, they greeted the removal of the restriction with thunderous applause. We also replaced their khaki summer uniform with a light blue one of a better material.

Meanwhile, we felt we had to have better police patrolling. The drug squad had to be reinforced and trained in new drug identification and investigation methods and the SAG trained in rescue recovery and scuba-diving. I also tried, not too successfully I admit, to introduce neighbourhood watches. On a completely different level, in close collaboration with John Rizzo Naudi, parliamentary secretary for the elderly, we introduced the 'life-line telephone' for the elderly.

An interesting episode with a dimension reflecting the Middle East problem was that involving a yacht that belonged to the Palestine Liberation Organisation, and which was berthed at Marsaxlokk harbour. PLO security men had found two limpet mines attached to the yacht, *Angel*. These were removed in time by the bomb disposal personnel and the police but had they exploded, they would have caused loss of lives and serious damage to the yacht and created a diplomatic incident. I have a feeling the yacht had been targeted by the Israeli secret services.

38

The Bush-Gorbachev summit

International events were moving fast. I had made an official visit to Hungary in September 1987 and could well see the new spirit taking over in that country. Although the Communist Party was still in power, it was in the process of dismantling structures that had helped it keep its hold over the country and was also introducing a measure of market economy. A wind of change was blowing across Europe. Soviet leader Mikhail Gorbachev was a catalyst in bringing about the change. Almost half a century of a Europe divided by an iron curtain, which had brought about an ideological confrontation under the threat of nuclear warfare, was gradually being brought to a close. Little did we imagine that the end of the cold war was to happen so suddenly, still less that the two world leaders were to end it in Malta.

In November 1989, the Berlin Wall, symbol of repression and division, was brought down by a surge of popular revolt. I had visited Berlin several times. My first visit was before the wall was raised. I had seen with my own eyes the destruction caused by the war. One day, I went to a restaurant for lunch in the eastern part of the city and the food I ordered took so long to arrive that a guide asked me if I had sought political refuge in the Soviet zone! On my visits to Berlin as part of a Council of Europe delegation, I could well assess developments in the two Berlins and compare the striking difference between the economic and social models adopted in the East and West. The way West Berlin managed to survive the embargo and remained for long an enclave of freedom within a communist-dominated territory made me understand, and, indeed, identify myself with President John F. Kennedy's famous words '*Ich bin ein Berliner*'. The fall of the Berlin Wall heralded the great political change that was about to happen.

I remember one day Eddie phoning me up very excitedly, which is not typical of him, telling me that he had had a phone call from US President

George Bush asking him if he could favourably consider hosting a meeting between him and Gorbachev in Malta. It was decided to hold the meeting on board a military vessel. Eddie told the emissaries of the two countries that Malta generally had good weather in winter but early December could be stormy. One could hardly foresee the kind of storm we actually had when the two leaders met in Malta. The Maltese joked at the time that the last time the island had such a bad storm was probably when St Paul had been shipwrecked on the island on his way to Rome.

The two presidents arrived separately by air on December 2, 1989. Gorbachev wrote in his memoirs: 'The Malta Summit – the first since the new American President and his administration had taken office – could be regarded as symbolic in many respects. We met at the junction of three continents, the crossroads of the world, and the meeting point of manifold interests. The talks were to take place on warships, symbols of the military might behind the Soviet and American leaders. The world was on the threshold of a new era.'

Bush and Gorbachev originally planned to hold their meetings alternately on the Soviet warship *Slava* and the USS *Belknap*. A Soviet tourist liner, *Maxim Gorky*, was to serve as a hotel for the Soviet presidential delegation. But, as Gorbachev said in his memoirs, 'natural elements introduced some radical corrections'. He wrote: 'The sea was stormy and the transfer by boat to the Soviet cruiser *Slava*, where we had initially planned to hold the first round of talks, proved difficult. Both our sailors and the Americans were against such an operation and it was suggested that we should organise the first meeting on board the *Maxim Gorky* moored in the port.'

During their meeting, I visited Marsaxlokk to ensure that everything was in place in so far as public order and safety were concerned. At one point I saw President Bush coming down the *Belknap* and boarding a boat when a huge wage engulfed the boat. For a moment I could not see the boat at all and my heart missed a beat. Much to my relief, it resurfaced and headed towards the *Maxim Gorky*. I recall President Bush recounting the incident when I called on him to invite him over to Malta for a commemoration of the tenth anniversary of the Malta Summit. He said he had never felt so close to drowning as on that day. I told him I had seen the incident from ashore and that my heart nearly stopped beating. 'So did mine', he said laughingly.

The Malta Summit is now part of history. In his book *The Future belongs to Freedom*, Soviet Foreign Minister Edward Shevardnadze said that in Malta 'in the midst of a Mediterranean storm, the cold war quietly came to an end'. Gorbachev confirmed in his memoirs: 'The Malta Summit had drawn the curtain on the cold war, although we still have to live with its difficult legacy.' The German unification problem was part of this difficult legacy. It required 10 more months to solve.

But how did Bush pick Malta for the summit meeting with Gorbachev? It appears the island was recommended to him by his brother who had come to Malta as guest of the Maltese government for the 25th anniversary of the island's independence.

The end of the cold war brought about a rethinking of the world situation. Without the iron curtain, what future lay for communist dictatorships in Eastern Europe? With his *glasnost* and *perestroika*, Gorbachev was revolutionising the Soviet system. Democracy was on the move. A new Europe, based on freedom and democratic principles, was shaping the new security architecture. German reunification was the key to the future of a post-cold war Europe. And the United Nations was about to embark on a process of renaissance. I certainly did not foresee that I was to play a part in this renaissance!

39

Insistent, persistent, consistent

When Censu Tabone was elected Malta's fourth president in 1989, Eddie Fenech Adami added foreign affairs to his portfolio. It appeared from the beginning that this was meant as a temporary arrangement. Although there were times when he enjoyed the foreign contacts he was making, I felt he was always more inclined to concentrate on domestic affairs. Then I gathered from political circles that I was being considered for the post of foreign minister. My name was being bandied about mainly because of my interest in foreign affairs and, also, in the light of my 20 years' experience in Council of Europe work and my strong involvement in the party's international relations, particularly the European Union of Christian Democrats (UEDC) as well as the Commonwealth Parliamentary Association.

As deputy prime minister, I had visited Algeria and Hungary a few months after taking office and in January 1990 I had led a delegation to the United Nations in New York for a special session of the General Assembly. It was at that session, called to discuss drugs, that I had first addressed the General Assembly. Several ambassadors asked me if I planned moving to the foreign ministry, but I felt I was still needed at the interior ministry. The police force was in a process of change; it had won back its role of maintaining law and order and was gradually shedding the name it had won for bad practices. Those within the force found guilty of crimes or of gross misbehaviour had been removed by legal means and I was at this time involved in bridging differences and healing wounds. When I eventually left the interior ministry to become foreign minister, I felt as if I were leaving part of myself behind. I believe that at the interior ministry I served my country at one of the most difficult and challenging times. That these times are today referred to as the 'past' is only attributable to the hard work that had been put to reorganise the police force and give it back its proper role.

At the foreign office I had to take some important decisions. The first was over the island's membership of the European Economic Community, as it was then known. A European directorate was set up with Dr Joe Borg as its head. Previous ministers had been advised that the conditions were not yet right for Malta to apply. I could well understand this but I felt we had to make up for the time lost. Malta had to compete with others in its membership application. Austria had sensed the future and applied in July 1989. Since Austria, too, was a neutral state, its application was important for Malta. I argued it was essential for the island to apply so that we would not find ourselves trailing behind others. Cyprus, too, had planned to apply. Cabinet decided that I should present Malta's membership application to the three organs of the European Community.

At first we thought the application should embody a statement of political belief in Europe but we opted for a more practical approach. Since Italy held the presidency of the Community at the time, I submitted the application to Italy's foreign minister, Gianni De Michelis, in Brussels on July 16, 1990. As I have said elsewhere, I am a devotee of Our Lady of Mount Carmel, whose feast is celebrated on July 16. In my heart I entrusted Our Lady with Malta's application and in the long years of expectation I had always prayed to Her to guide us to our future. As it happened, as president of Malta, I signed the bill for Malta's membership of the European Union, as approved by Parliament, on July 16, 2003, feast of Our Lady of Mount Carmel, 13 years to the hour I had submitted the application.

I recall with a sense of nostalgia and history the statement I made at the presentation of our membership application to De Michelis. I spoke of the emerging Europe, no longer static and split in two blocs, but a dynamic Europe progressing towards greater unity. In Malta's aspirations and vocation, we had always lived our European identity in a Mediterranean context. We wanted to focus more on the Mediterranean dimension of Europe. I said that as frontier people we are tied to our traditions but were also determined to live in friendship with our southern neighbours. De Michelis, with whom I had established a good working relationship, spoke about the importance of the Mediterranean in Malta's foreign policy and about the potential contribution that the island could make in this direction in the Community.

We had started our long journey to Europe. I was fully aware of the difficulties we were about to meet on the way, but as we found out for ourselves, awareness is different to actually having to tackle the difficulties. It was uphill going practically all the way. We needed a strong will to make it and stamina to deal with the hurdles. As I used to say so often, we were insistent, persistent, and consistent. In spite of the many problems we faced. I had no doubt that one day we would be in the European Union, as it later came to be known. The march towards Europe was irreversible.

40

New direction for foreign ministry

The foreign ministry was a challenge in every respect. During Mintoff's administration, the diplomatic corps had been practically dissolved after the strike of 1977, taken in solidarity with Telemalta Corporation workers who were engaged in a long-running dispute with the government. By and large ministry officials were employed on the basis of their Labour sympathies, and the few embassies that Malta had abroad were no more than an extension of the Malta Labour Party. However, there were some notable exceptions. Victor Gauci, Victor Camilleri, and Evarist Saliba were three of the diplomats who, in spite of the fact that they had different political leanings, had, to their credit, given a solid contribution. The Labour administration had lost the services of the much respected ambassador to the UN, Arvid Pardo, whose employment was terminated in a humiliating manner. Joe Attard Kingswell, a former General Workers' Union general secretary, took over and did his best to represent Malta with dignity and competence. However, Mintoff failed to grasp the importance of Malta's proposal to exploit the potential of the oceans and the concept of mankind's common heritage, initiatives that Pardo had pursued with vigour. Mintoff only realised his mistake when Jamaica was tipped to become the base for the Law of the Sea Authority. He then made a belated attempt for Malta to host the authority but it failed. In Mintoff's years, the foreign ministry was reduced to a little more than a government mouthpiece.

Mintoff's unique style of doing politics tended to dictate events. At times, however, he did have foresight. He used, and was used by, Muammar Gaddafi, and the relationship between them was one of extremes. For example, there were times when for Mintoff the Libyan people were our 'blood brothers', and other times when they were our 'worst enemies'. When it came to China, Mintoff was ahead of other contemporary leaders and established good relations with that country as far back as 1972. These relations have withstood the test of time and are still strong today. He had also established strong relations with Kim Il Sung, secretly signing a treaty in 1982 under which North Korea provided arms to Malta. Both Censu Tabone, when he was foreign minister, and Fenech Adami had succeeded in distancing the foreign ministry from the Mintoff and Sceberras Trigona era and, when I took over in 1998, I was determined to give Malta's foreign affairs a sense of direction, particularly in Mediterranean affairs. Key to that was a strong drive to take Malta into the European Economic Community.

Joining Europe was not just a strategy but a political ideal. I have been a convinced European since my student days and was strongly influenced by European federalism. I still believe in it, but I think the EU needs to develop further if its ideals are to be realised. I felt an intellectual and political affinity, based on the concept of Christian democracy, with the statesmen of Europe – Konrad Adenauer, Alcide de Gasperi, and Robert Schumann. This was the driving force behind my commitment to see Malta in Europe.

However, I realised from the outset that Malta's role in Europe could not be won merely on the basis of its size or history. That would have given us scant relevance. It needed to be linked to the part we had to play in the Mediterranean. Not everybody shared this view and I was criticised, both in party circles and sections of the press, for underlining the island's Mediterranean dimension. Yet I steadfastly made it part of the ministry's strategy to build strong bilateral ties with Mediterranean countries, taking an active interest in the Middle East problem and discussing with foreign ministers in the region new approaches to co-operation and security in the Mediterranean. I maintained strong links with Libya, even though it was difficult at times, sustained by my belief that bilateral relations were a vital precursor to security and trade opportunities. At a meeting of the Non-Aligned Movement in Algeirs, I proposed for the first time the setting up of a Council for the Mediterranean. In doing so, I was very much influenced by the Council of Europe's role and its sterling work in building our *maison commune*.

I believe in a Mediterranean policy for Malta and in the idea that the island can act as a bridge between the north and south of the region. I referred to, and adopted, the principle – if not the method – that Mintoff had put forward in Helsinki, namely that there is an indivisible link between security in Europe and security in the Mediterranean – the so-called Mediterranean basket. To those who criticised me, often behind my back, for attaching so much importance to the Mediterranean, I explained that our ties with Europe were inexorably linked to the region. The importance of such dual strategy, Europe and the Mediterranean, soon started being well understood both in Malta and abroad.

I strengthened our embassies in Rome, Tripoli, and Paris, and opened new ones in Cairo, Tunis, Athens, and Madrid. I tried to hold on to our small mission in Algiers until the situation there became too dangerous for our staff, and with very little success I attempted to revamp our office in Riyadh. Naturally I knew that our foreign office could only be successful in its work if it was properly set up. We had to have a diplomatic corps made up of professionally prepared diplomats with an *esprit de corps*. I realised our predicament in a crude manner only a few weeks after taking over as foreign minister. A party supporter who worked as a post office clerk came to see me at the foreign office in Palazzo Parisio and asked me to send him to Rome. I asked him why, and his straightforward, if unabashed, response was that he wanted to be one of the embassy staff. I tried to explain that, before being considered for such a posting, he would first need to become acquainted with the foreign ministry. But he was clearly not amused and said: 'You're changing the system!' He argued he was not prepared to go through all that. Party affiliation was going to play no part in the foreign ministry while I was in charge and I immediately took the matter up with the ministry's permanent secretary.

Eventually I did get some help from Victor Gauci, a seasoned diplomat whom I recalled from the Canberra High Commission to be secretary of the ministry. Together we drafted the necessary regulations to set up a diplomatic service and offered our staff the option to join at agreed grades, right through from second secretary to ambassador. We also decided that potential recruits would have to be graduates and that they had to sit for an examination. When the preparatory work was ready, I presented a memorandum to cabinet and, with their approval, we set about setting up a quality diplomatic corps. I did not like the fact that most of Malta's ambassadors were not civil servants but so-called political appointees and I am still uncomfortable with it today. But hopefully this will become less necessary in future as the diplomatic corps becomes stronger.

I made full use of the Mediterranean Academy of Diplomatic Studies, which the government, together with the Swiss government, had set up in 1990 with the collaboration of the University of Malta. Most of our young recruits have attended the academy. I also believed it was important for recruits to follow specialised courses at foreign universities and to gain experience in our embassies. To my astonishment I found that our foreign office had no library worthy of the name and I made it a point to obtain the periodicals and reference books that are indispensable to the ministry.

In collaboration with the academy, we also started publishing our own *Foreign Office Review*. This was an important contribution to our foreign policy. Another important innovation was the annual meeting of ambassadors, with the first being held between August 11 and 13, 1990. For the first time, our ambassadors abroad and the heads of division at the ministry met, under my chairmanship, to exchange views, study strategy, and report on the work of our embassies abroad. I wanted our embassies to adopt an organic approach to the challenges they were facing. In particular, I wanted to coordinate the efforts of our embassies in pushing forward our application for membership of the European Community. I wanted to brief our embassies and senior ministry officials on our Mediterranean policy and, as I was about to take over the presidency of the United Nations General Assembly, also to see how my new role could be effective in its own right as well as being an important instrument of our foreign policy.

41

If you can make it in New York...

When I became foreign minister on May 5, 1990, I was briefed about Malta's position with regard to the candidacy for the presidency of the United Nations General Assembly. Before I took over at Palazzo Parisio, I had heard rumours that our permanent representative at the UN, Dr Alexander Borg Olivier, was aspiring to this high office since Fenech Adami was doubling as foreign minister and would not have been able to be absent from Malta frequently. Most of the UN presidents had been foreign ministers or prominent personalities – a mark of respect to the concept of the UN. After consulting Eddie, I decided it was in the country's interest to have a high-profile candidate in this post, particularly since the opportunity rarely presents itself more than once every century. Unfortunately, our permanent representative in New York did not share the same view and reacted in an unacceptable manner. I took this quite badly, particularly since I had been close to his father, George. These things happen in politics.

I wanted to use the presidency to raise Malta's image internationally, and particularly to press for EC membership. It was not unusual to meet politicians who were unaware even of Malta's existence, but I remained undeterred. The political moment was certainly unique. The cold war had ended and there was a positive mood in New York. The security council was coming into its own, not as a motion-vetoing and confrontation venue but as a council which, for the first time since the promulgation of the UN Charter, was realising its relevance in the promotion of peace and world security.

The UN General Assembly over which I was about to preside was taking a fresh look at the emerging world. The Non-Aligned Movement was retreating from its political function of staying out of the power bloc confrontation and assuming a role as the voice of the developing world. In this context the invasion by Iraq of Kuwait on August 2, 1990 upset a world that was thinking anew, where democracy and the rule of law and a rediscovered value of human rights were creating a new security landscape in the world. When the tanks of Saddam Hussein rolled through the desert, abolishing the very existence of Kuwait, the die was cast. Hussein had to withdraw or the UN and all it stood for would be nullified.

It was against this backdrop that I had become president of the UN General Assembly. In view of my increased commitments, I had to have a strong and dedicated team in my secretariat. Joe Cassar, Victor Camilleri, and Michael Bartolo, who had already worked at the UN before, were in the core group together with Walter Balzan, from my secretariat at Palazzo Parisio. The UN provided me with Fred Echard, an excellent media relations man; Linda Smith, a competent secretary; and Sigmund Sigmunson, a giant of a man with the biggest of hearts, as my security official. Sigmund, called Siggy, was from Iceland.

Before I left for New York, supporters and well-wishers organised a party at the Upper Barrakka Gardens. There was great enthusiasm at the fact that a Maltese was about to take up what is probably the most senior post in international affairs since Malta gained independence. The days running up to my taking office were taken up with preparing my statement for the General Assembly, which I had written in my hotel room. I had then bounced it off my team, who all offered advice and suggestions.

On September 18, 1990, I was led to the podium, as demanded by protocol, and was greeted by Javier Perez de Quellar, the Peruvian secretary-general, and Ronald Spiers, the deputy secretary-general, as well as by the outgoing president, Joseph Narvel Garba, from Nigeria. I must confess I felt a measure of pride when I took the floor, and was glad the event was being televised live in Malta. I felt the presence of my deceased parents to whom I owe so much. But I also sensed a spirit of continuity with the leaders of Maltese nationalism, in particular Enrico Mizzi, Sir Ugo Mifsud, and George Borg Olivier. I realised I was living that moment as a result of their dedication, suffering, and determination to see Malta take its rightful place in the community of nations.

In many ways the feeling was surreal. Within a few months of taking charge of Malta's foreign ministry, I was occupying a leading role in the UN and I dedicated all my energy to the task. There was a saying on my office floor at the UN that the president was the first to arrive and the last to leave. But my overriding objective was to ensure my term would be a presidency with a purpose. I kept abreast of what was happening in Kuwait and had the privilege to be in direct contact with heads of state, prime ministers, and foreign affairs ministers, who regularly came to see me at my office. It was especially gratifying because their visits were not just courtesy calls, but meetings that demanded action and answers. I had excellent relations with de Quellar, a seasoned former diplomat. I particularly admired his quiet style of diplomacy and pursuit of peace. We used to have long discussions on what measures could be taken to try and ensure that Kuwait would be liberated through diplomatic means rather than by force. Together with certain foreign ministers and permanent representatives, we discussed the possibility of an Arab force peacefully taking Kuwait from Saddam Hussein, and then handing it over to the emir and people of Kuwait. This would have provided an 'Arab' solution to an 'Arab' issue. Indeed, through my ambassador in Rome, I ensured the proposal was passed on to the Iraqi embassy. But the Iraqi leader decided to ignore it, choosing instead to persist with his hostile occupation of Kuwait. In the process he linked his army's presence there with occupation of the Palestinian territory.

I was also in touch with the five permanent members and had a great deal of respect for US Secretary of State James Baker. His style was forceful and yet diplomatic, even as the inevitable was approaching. When de Quellar mooted the possibility of introducing a diplomatic move, he was stopped dead in his tracks. And when he was at last sent to Baghdad to convey a message from the security council, he was more of a postman than a diplomat. The Iraqi leader made things worse by his contemptuous attitude and he left the secretary general waiting outside his office for some time. De Quellar tried to impress on Hussein that, for all his bravado and propaganda, he would be defeated in a military conflict. 'Mr President,' he told him, 'you, as an army man, know the correctness of my statement.' To this Hussein replied, to the astonishment of the Peruvian: 'I am not a soldier; I am a lawyer by profession.'

I had a good working relationship with the permanent observer of the PLO in New York. As a veteran of the Palestinian cause, he was impressed by my explicit reference to the issue in my first presidential statement. I was concerned that the Palestinians, both in the occupied territories and in Kuwait, were siding with Saddam Hussein. Giorgio Giacomelli, an official from the UN's Relief and Work Agency for Palestinian Refugees (UNRWA), whom I received with urgency, spelt out in some detail the plight and the suffering of the Palestinians. He told me in no uncertain terms that the Palestinians, living under the humiliating cruelty of Israel's occupation, had lost all faith in the UN and its resolutions. I felt this was the right time to visit the Palestinian refugees, since I wanted to explain to them that they were siding with an aggressor who would be defeated. I also wanted to reassure them that the UN would stand by them as it had stood by the people of Kuwait.

The UN high commissioner for refugees, Madame Sakako Ogata, an accomplished and high-ranking Japanese diplomat, strongly supported my wish to visit the occupied territories at this difficult time. The secretariat was not overjoyed and washed its hands of the initiative, but it realised I was playing on home turf and that this was an innovative move. The US permanent representative, Tom Pickering, had a different opinion. He asked for an urgent meeting and came straight to the point: 'Do I understand you intend visiting the occupied territories?' he asked. When I said yes, he said, 'The State Department is against such a visit.' I told him I was prepared to listen; so he went on to explain that in the circumstances my going there could be interpreted as aiding and abetting the Palestinians, whose attitude to the occupation of Kuwait did not entitle them to any sympathy.

I asked him if he had more arguments and he added little. I told him in a measured tone that the Palestinians had long been humiliated and had lost all faith in the UN. They had been suffering occupation for decades and security council resolutions taken in their favour had not been enforced. The Palestinians therefore felt it was contradictory for the UN to sanction military action for the liberation of Kuwait and not do the same for the liberation of the occupied territories. They felt the reason for this was that they did not have oil. The aim of my visit was to assure them that the General Assembly would defend their rights in accordance with UN resolutions that had been approved by its members, which included the US. Pickering realised my decision was final and that it was motivated by the belief that the UN is the international instrument of peace and freedom. To be fair to Pickering – and I would meet him years later in different circumstances – he came to see me after my visit to the occupied territories and to congratulate me on its success.

During the Christmas holidays, I received frantic calls from permanent representatives asking me whether it was true that I intended to convene the General Assembly to counteract the resolution being passed by the security council. I suspect a Maltese diplomat in New York had given them this impression, which was completely untrue. The last thing I wanted was to pit two UN organs against each other. Such a move could only have benefited Saddam Hussein, who was refusing to comply with the resolution to move out of a sovereign country.

The pace at the UN was hectic. To complicate matters, my presence in Malta was required not just in connection with ministry work but also because since we only had a one-seat majority, I had to be in the House when a vote was required to be taken. I used to come to Malta almost every week and return to New York as quickly as possible, making full use of the six-hour time difference. I would leave Malta at 7.15 a.m., take the 11 a.m. Concorde flight from Heathrow, and be in New York by 9 a.m. local time. Then a helicopter would take me to the UN buildings, which meant I could be on the podium to preside over the general council within an hour. Of course, all this is not possible today since Concorde has regrettably been taken out of service.

A normal day at the UN would start at 8.30 a.m. I would go through the day's agenda and discuss pressing issues with Camilleri, Balzan, Cassar, Bartolo, and Eckard, before briefing the press. As I said before, Eckard was a first-class UN civil servant. When Kofi Annan became secretary general, he served as his press officer. He maintained excellent contact with permanent representatives as well as with NGOs and was a good go-between with the secretariat, which often felt that, through my pro-active approach, I was treading on their toes. However, my relations with Perez de Quellar, whom I held in high esteem, remained good throughout. We met and consulted each other regularly. Eckard excelled when he met the media and he treated all pressmen with respect. So did I in my regular meetings with them. My first was just two days after taking over the presidency and I recall being asked whether it was possible for the UN to play a mediating role. I said it could do more in this respect, especially when it came to conciliation proceedings, even if this increased the risk of mistakes being made. 'One can take one's mistakes in one's stride,' I told them, 'provided one does not lose the objectivity of one's actions and the integrity which the UN has always observed whenever it is involved. It is a question of mentality; it is a question of correctness which we at the UN have a great responsibility to shoulder.'

We were expecting a high-powered summit to receive the Convention of the Rights of the Child as the World Summit for Children was being held at the UN in New York between September 29 and October 1. I wrote a message for the *Diplomatic World Bulletin* to mark the occasion, stressing that this was an opportunity to express our 'belongingness to children so frail, so dependent on us, so much the fruit of our love... it is because we realise that the great love for children unfortunately does not always prevail in society and even more because famine and want hit at the frailness of the

40,000 children who die every day due to avoidable causes that this Convention of the Rights of the Child is being endorsed at this summit'.

On October 1, 1990, together with the secretary general, I received 71 heads of state or government. The meeting itself was an expression of political will to try and ensure that children's rights were respected the world over. But I also took the opportunity to remind those present of the precarious situation in Kuwait. 'We are caught up in a struggle,' I told them, 'to ensure the observance of the rule of law in international relations and the need to maintain peace. May we, through the authority which comes from this, the most representative of all organs of our organisation, the assembly of 160 nations, appeal to those who have the immediate responsibility in stopping the course of events and perhaps of history, that there is no loss of face in the search for a peaceful settlement of a dispute. Nothing is lost in perusing that goal. We owe it to our children not to add to the thousands who die every day from avoidable causes, the thousands who may die and the many who will suffer. We owe it to our children and to world peace. But it has to be a peace in freedom. This is our permanent plan of action as the collective responsibility of our assembly.' Reading this statement 16 years after the conference, I still feel the depth of suffering which so many children have been subjected to owing to war, strife, famine, and natural disasters. If we could only hear the collective heartbeat of the millions of children that have died due to avoidable causes, we would surely not be able to bear it for long.

In my capacities as president of the UN General Assembly and foreign minister, I attended the meeting of foreign ministers and heads of delegation of the Non-Aligned Movement. We all realised that the end of the bi-polar system, the *raison d'être* of the Non-Aligned Movement, would have a determining effect on the movement and I felt I should raise this point when I addressed them in October 1990. 'In the same way that the UN has emerged from its years of trial much better equipped to follow the principle of its creation, so also should the Non-Aligned Movement see to the dismantling of East-West confrontation an opportunity for it to return to evolve further its ideals.' The task ahead remained immense. 'True enough, the world no longer lives in the shadow of a possible Armageddon sparked by ideological competition. Yet poverty, suffering, and injustice still abound in frightening dimensions. Bloc confrontation can no longer be considered a pretext for the problems which now confront us. On the contrary, many will see in this problem the harbinger of risks that are concomitant with a most relaxed international commitment consequent upon the rapprochement between the superpowers.'

I also raised the issue of tension in the Mediterranean region. 'The countries of the Mediterranean, including the non-aligned members among them, have long been aware of the strains which the interplay on these various problems exert on the security of the region; in particular there is major concern at the fact that the security situation has so far prevented any extension to the region of the confidence and security building measures being adopted on mainland Europe as a result of the relaxation of international tensions.' I did my best as General Assembly president to raise awareness of the problems in the Mediterranean region. I also felt the duty to underline that democracy was the cornerstone of freedom.

I believe my interventions were having a positive effect. Speaking on the 30th anniversary of the declaration of the granting of independence to colonial countries and people, I reminded the assembly that 'the process of decolonisation has seen the emergence of 80 new states; vast territories have attained independence, thus forming the community of nations. Many of us here have lived through and contributed towards this process and hence cherish the memory of the day when our countries became sovereign states. Seven hundred million people were living under colonial rule in 1945. In 1990, only about two million lived in non self-governing territories.'

On October 10, I made the concluding remarks at the end of the general debate which was addressed by 27 heads of state and 15 prime ministers. The Gulf crisis inevitably dominated the debate. Two common themes flowed from the unanimous conviction that the invasion and annexation of Kuwait constituted a flagrant violation of the UN charter as well as being a serious threat to international peace and security. There was a firm demand, voiced by practically every speaker, for the restoration of the sovereignty and territorial integrity of Kuwait in full conformity with the relevant security council resolutions. At the same time there was the widely expressed opinion that efforts should continue to be made to achieve a peaceful outcome to the crisis on a collective basis, within the framework provided by the UN charter.

Participants in the debate also looked at the wider regional framework in which the crisis was unfolding. Here again two common themes emerged: There was an absolute rejection of any direct linkage between the invasion of Kuwait and other outstanding issues in the Middle East. At the same time, however, it was clearly acknowledged that the firm international reaction to the invasion was setting a new high moral standard of action that could be applied to other problems in the region, especially to bring about a fast and permanent solution to the question of Palestine. I suggested calling the long-awaited peace conference and in the concluding session I made reference to the dramatic thrust of Eastern Europe towards freedom and democracy leading to the unification of Germany, which would be a catalyst to unify Europe as well as to South Africa's continuing march towards justice and freedom. I concluded: 'Many have reflected upon the prospects which these positive developments open for renewed efforts for the resolution of these deeper and more fundamental problems, which still confront the international community – the poverty curtain, with the diseases and misery that still hold sway over a significant proportion of mankind and that threaten to perpetuate an unbridgeable gap between the haves and the have-nots of the world; the ever-increasing burden of debt, especially among the least developed countries; the scourge of drug trafficking; the dangers of a deteriorating physical environment; the plague of terrorism; the continued flouting of human rights; the plight of millions of refugees.' The comments on poverty seemed to make an impression, and I am happy to say that today almost every leader is talking about it. However, as with the other problems I had listed, there is much that remains to be done.

42

The Palestinian Cause

Of the several issues demanding my attention at the United Nations, disarmament was one issue to which I felt I could make a positive contribution, particularly since in the preceding 12 months international relations had undergone tremendous changes in several key areas. The global community had seen the end of the cold war and the emergence of superpower partnership. A new security system was imminent and we were all preparing for the November meeting of the Conference on Security and Cooperation in Europe (CSCE) which led to the setting up of the Organisation for Security and Cooperation in Europe (OSCE). I observed in one statement at the UN that 'just as we are heartened by the positive developments, we are faced with a new regional conflict that threatens to destabilise global security and jeopardise the life and well-being of millions of innocent people... bilateral arms-control negotiations must be complemented by multilateral and multi-factual efforts. In this respect, the UN has a pivotal role in all relevant areas, including confidence and security building, arms transfers and verification'.

I pointed out that the well-known dictum '*Si vis pacem, para bellum*' (if you want peace, prepare for war) should be modified in this day and age to read: '*Si vis pacem, para pacem*' (if you want peace, prepare for peace) and I told them: 'A step forward in disarmament is a step forward in the survival of mankind. But one should distinguish between pacifism and preparing for peace. Preparing for peace involves not only a *forma mentis* towards peace but also in some instance that peace itself should be defended.'

On December 10, 1990, Human Rights Day, I made a speech on a subject that has remained close to my heart, and it gave me the opportunity to speak about my personal experiences. One comment was: 'In my life, both as a politician and as a lawyer, I discovered that human rights have a value only if they become living realities in a society. Perhaps there is no more tiring hypocrisy than living with human rights proclaimed on paper and disregarded in practice.'

Apartheid had quite rightly figured prominently in debates and activities of the UN and we marked a day of solidarity with South African political prisoners. But, at least, the drive towards the removal of this unjust system were good. Nelson Mandela had been released only a few months earlier and had addressed the UN committee that was tackling apartheid. I appealed to the South African president, Frederik Willem de Klerk, who was contributing to the advancing dawn, to release all remaining political prisoners. When the English poet, Richard Lovelace, wrote 'stone walls do not a prison make, nor iron bars a cage,' he must have been thinking of dissidents imprisoned merely for holding a particular political or religious belief. The political prisoner is more often than not absorbed in the logic of his principles. Some require a symbol but, in the case of most political prisoners in South Africa, for example, their plight was caused by the colour of their skin.

However, the issue that received most of my attention at the time was Palestine. Through my contacts at the UN and international circles, I was realising how the Palestine issue was poisoning relations between the Middle East and the West. The Arab world was shedding the skin of its colonial past, but at the same time damaging this healing process by failing to help the Palestinian people realise their inalienable right to statehood. Malta had played an active part as *rapporteur* of the committee on the exercise of the inalienable rights of the Palestinian people and, when the UN marked the International Day of Solidarity with the Palestinian people, I remarked: 'The tragedy which we are all called to examine is that of a people who, in the turbulence of historical events, have been left totally dispossessed of the homeland to which all aspire – yet a people who, in the midst of a tragedy and injustice, have retained their sense of dignity and of nationhood and their collective determination to pursue their legitimate objective until it is finally achieved... our final commitment of solidarity with the Palestinian people is therefore not only a necessary political decision but also a personal expression of our one individual commitment against all forms of injustice. In this perspective there is particular relevance and urgency to the question of how the new sense of international morality is going to be applied to the Palestinian question. Just as peace is indivisible, so also must the commitment to principles be indivisible.'

While there was no link between the invasion of Kuwait and the Middle East issue, a golden thread bound them together; in both cases the sovereignty of a people was at stake. I was further perturbed by the negative stand taken by the Palestinians regarding the occupation of Kuwait. I did on occasions raise the issue with Yasser Arafat and spelt out the negative repercussions it was having on the Palestinian cause. Critics sarcastically were remarking that the Palestinians never missed an opportunity to miss an opportunity. But people are bound to lose their sense of direction when they are deprived of their land, see it made subject to military occupation, and when so many so many of their children end up in the prisons of their occupying rulers. My visit to the occupied territories was meant to bring new hope to these people. I wanted to show them that the General Assembly stood four-square by its resolutions and that, in recognising Israel's right to safe and secure frontiers, it was equally determined to uphold the right of the Palestinians to have a state of their own. Israeli settlements on Palestinian land were an abuse of international law and a defiance of UN resolutions.

My five-day visit to Palestinian refugees began in the occupied territories on January 2, 1991. I felt there was no better way to gain a better understanding of their plight. I explained that, far from trying to add fuel to the fire, I was there because the issue had been on the UN's agenda for decades. The United Nations Relief and Works Agency had provided tents, blankets, and food when about 1,000 families on the West Bank had lost their homes in the conflict. It ran 34 health centres, and 15 emergency health clinics were operating round the clock to treat casualties. Some schools were closed for almost three years. But most disturbing of all was the number of schoolchildren that had become casualties: Fifty-eight had been killed and almost 18,000 had been injured in nine years.

On the West Bank, conditions were just about bearable. In Gaza, however, the military occupation was total. The Palestinians were denied access to the sea, an important means of livelihood, and the place resembled a concentration camp. My statements at the time reflected what I was seeing with my own eyes. In December 1987, the Palestinians' frustration over their miserable living conditions, 20 years of Israeli occupation and the world's seeming indifference to their plight, erupted into an *intifada*. While the *intifada* had had some political success in attracting international attention to, and sympathy for, the Palestinian cause, the people living in the occupied territories paid a heavy price. In spite of several calls for aid, the daily toll of deaths and injuries continued. Despite moments of hope – the Oslo agreement and the award of the Nobel Peace Prize in 1994 to Arafat, Rabin, and Peres – the passage of time had only shown that the situation had deteriorated.

I held meetings with both Israeli and Palestinian administration officials. David Levi, Israel's foreign minister, was a moderate though it would be wrong to describe him as a dove among hawks. He was a Jew from Morocco and was therefore conversant with Arabic and French. He accepted my visit with good grace and was diplomatically very correct. One Israeli I did admire was the legendary mayor of Jerusalem, Theodor 'Teddy' Kollek, who was responsible for modernising the city and transforming it from an Arab city into a major Israeli centre. However, problems remained since the Palestinians in Jerusalem did not recognise Israel's presence. Nor did they accept to pay for water, which had prompted the Israeli municipal authorities to cut off their supply. When I raised this issue with Kollek in an attempt to reinstate the water supply, he resisted at first but, as I continued to press the case, he admitted: 'If I were a Palestinian, I would probably do the same.' I understand the issue was eventually resolved.

Some Israelis viewed my presence as a move to oppose their occupation of the Palestine territory. My visit was not without its hair-raising moments. At one time I got caught up in the stone-throwing and gunfire between the *intifada* youths and Israeli forces. On another occasion, as I was travelling from Bethlehem to Jerusalem, my car was surrounded by a considerable number of Israeli settlers who attempted to overturn it. The Israeli police just looked on, reminding me of the bad old days in Malta when I had been subjected to the same kind of treatment by a Labour Party mob. However, I must say I was surprised to see that even a UN president could be treated in this way by over-confident Israeli settlers. I felt the pungency of the occupation when I visited a small hospital in Gaza, manned by a group of Scandinavian doctors. I saw a young boy whose bowels had spilled out by gunshot wounds. He was terrified at the sight of TV cameras, since his family could be victimised by Israeli forces for his 'crime' – throwing stones at his country's occupiers.

The Palestinians kept their dignity in spite of difficult circumstances. While I was there, I met some interesting personalities. I was particularly struck, for instance, by Hannah Ashrawi, a highly intelligent woman with a nose for politics. She had proved to be an excellent spokeswoman for Arafat and later held a cabinet post when the first Palestinian administration was appointed with him as its head. A news conference I gave in Jerusalem, which was attended by the major media organisations, reflected the impact my visit had made and, for the moment at least, they were talking about the plight of the Palestinian people rather than the invasion of Kuwait.

In Jerusalem I also met the so-called consuls whose role is to defend the interests of their nationals as well as the historical and international character of Jerusalem. Italy was represented by a diplomat, Marino Fleri, whose Maltese mother had once lent me money to see me through when I was stranded in Rome. I had heard through the grapevine that Fleri was going to be the next Italian ambassador to Malta. We also talked about Palestinian issues. He knew a Christian woman who was close to Arafat and who had played a leading part in the resistance to Israeli occupation. She was the mother of Suha Taweel, who years later was to marry Arafat and whose brother later became Palestine's ambassador to Malta. It is indeed a small world!

Together with Giorgio Giacomelli, the high commissioner for UNRWA, I met Palestinian people both in Gaza and the West Bank. Giacomelli was highly respected among the refugees for his dedication and sincerity and it was thanks to him that this visit, considered a landmark for the presidency of the General Assembly, took place and assumed a political dimension at a unique moment in the history of the Middle East. The visit gave me a better understanding of the people; indeed, I could feel the humiliation to which they were subjected. On the other hand, I also realised that indelible marks of suffering had been left on the Israelis and how close they felt to a country that had ceased to be theirs. 'Next year in Jerusalem', they used to say in their prayers durng Passover, reflecting their strong sense of belonging. Their insensitivity to the plight of the Palestinians should also be seen in this historical context. To us, it's the Holy Land. To the people of Israel, however, it's the Promised Land.

I was the first person to be authorised to travel by air from Jerusalem to Amman – in a plane provided by the UN. My close aides and Giacomelli were with me. As we were flying over the occupied territory, the pilot flew low over the Israeli settlements, strategically located on the West Bank to impede the possible creation of a Palestinian state, so that I could get a good look at them. It is only relatively recently that Israel has accepted, albeit in a measured manner, a two-state solution. At that time the West Bank was referred to by Israel as Judea and Samaria, the biblical names. I realised there could be no solution unless the two states originally envisaged by the UN resolutions – the state of Israel and the state of Palestine – were in fact both set up. How right French President François Mitterrand was when, in his statement to the General Assembly, he asserted that the UN resolutions must be respected by all.

On arriving in Amman, I called on Prince Hassan of Jordan, who invited me to a round-table discussion on the economic and human effects of the crisis in the Gulf. A presentation was also made of the impact of the crisis on Palestinians in the occupied territories. I was made to realise that the excessive sanctions against Iraq were being felt mainly by the Iraqi people and neighbouring states – Jordan in particular, since it depended on trade with Iraq. Prince Hassan very kindly invited me to spend the evening at his home. The royal family was extremely cultured and there was a running argument between the prince and his wife, the princess, as to the merits of Oxford and Cambridge where they had respectively studied.

Amman was an oasis of peace in a desert of war and power struggle. Yet, thanks to the wisdom of its ruler and its governing class, it has succeeded in maintaining good relations with its neighbours and the West. The Palestinian refugees were well looked after, some reaching high posts in the Jordanian government service. At a reception held in my honour, I met Farouk Khaddoumi, head of the political department of the Palestine Liberation Organisation. I had met him some time before, together with Arafat, in Tunisia, and he had told me he was going to meet Saddam Hussein. But it was not, as I had hoped, to persuade him to withdraw from Kuwait. I told him how disappointed I was to have found support among Palestinians for a dictator who had arbitrarily taken away the independence of neighbouring Kuwait. I also told him that, as a Palestinian who was suffering the effects of occupation, he should have been the first to protest against occupation of another country. I do not think my words had any positive effect on him and I got to know later that he was in Baghdad when the first US air raids hit the city.

When I presented my report to the General Assembly, I said the visit was meant as a message that the UN was positively seeking to uphold the rights of the Palestinian people within the context of Security Council Resolutions 242 (1967) and 338 (1973) – no longer to occupy a backseat in the international scene. I tried to explain that the purpose of my visit was to send a message that the future of the Palestinian people lay in the observance of the UN charter. In my discussion with the Israeli government, I explained the General Assembly's resolution – based on the concept that living in peace with one's neighbours and in recognition of the right of the Palestinians will bring about an international commitment to secure and guaranteed frontiers of all states in the region – would safeguard their future. I then made a direct appeal to Israel. 'To those in Israel who believe that the international guarantees arising from a conference of peace in the Middle East do not offer the necessary security, the lesson of the Gulf, the commitment of so many nations in a coalition led by the United States of America, are certainly an eye-opener that if so much was done to free Kuwait, certainly not less will be done were Israel's survival to be threatened... I believe that the two peoples, victims of the adventures of history, required the solidarity and involvement of all who can help us mould events towards peace in the region. We at the United Nations have a responsibility towards the grandchildren of those who suffered in the concentration camps as well as to the children of the *intifada* of today. The visit was intended to pave the way for those who, conscious of their political responsibilities, can help in contributing towards lasting peace, which will give the people in the region man's most coveted gift: peace in freedom.'

As I said, the visit was a landmark in the history of the UN presidency and it certainly left a mark on my life.

43

A presidency with a purpose

The presidency of the UN General Assembly is what the holder decides to make of it. To those who are protocol-minded, the president is entrusted with ensuring that proceedings are observed according to standing orders. I have never been keen on protocol, though I have always observed it. To me, the president's role was to make the General Assembly more effective, to speak and act on its behalf, and make recommendations; the president not only presides over the General Assembly, but he also has the duty to represent its member states. I emphasised the need to revitalise the General Assembly at a time when its relevance in international affairs could be determining. I underlined that it was the only UN organ with permanent members across the board. It reflected a world parliament where states, irrespective of size, wealth or relevance, were equal in their sovereignty and had the same right to voice their views.

I believed that the UN General Assembly had to continue to support the security council in its approach towards Iraq, leading to the eventual use of force to ensure the liberation of Kuwait. I was in constant contact with the emir of Kuwait, Sheikh Jabir Al Sabah, and his government in exile. The emir was a soft-spoken but determined man who invited me to Kuwait just weeks after the liberation, since he wanted to express his nation's gratitude for the continued support which I, on behalf of the General Assembly, had extended to him and his people in the dark days of the occupation. In Kuwait I was received by the emir in a makeshift residence, since his palace had been destroyed by Iraqi forces who had made destruction a hallmark of the occupation. They had made the university, one of the finest in the region, and the laboratory, unusable, and killed members of the resistance and Kuwaiti citizens whom they suspected of supporting the emir. Their worst act, however, was reserved for Kuwait's life-blood – the oil wells – which were set on fire. I saw the wells on fire during a helicopter trip over the oilfields. At one point the heat from the burning wells was so intense that the pilot had to fly to a higher altitude. As I looked down, I could not help thinking of Dante's inferno – it looked so much like the mouth of hell. I visited the UNCAR peace-keeping forces in the demilitarised zone before my helicopter landed next to a hospital run by Scandinavian doctors in Basra in Iraq. Predictably this caused a great deal of commotion, though once they realised who I was, the Iraqi forces were courteous. Back in Kuwait, I met the family of a Kuwaiti officer who had been tortured by Hussein's forces before being executed. I also pleaded with the emir to take back the Palestinians who were working in Kuwait during the invasion and sympathised with Iraq, explaining to him that they too had been victims of aggression and foreign occupation. But the emir was clearly upset, and when he said, in Arabic, that the wound was still gaping, I required no translation and felt that, for the time being at least, I should not push it further.

On a trip to Washington on February 25, 1991, I had a long meeting with James Baker, one of the finest secretaries of state the US had during my time in politics. We talked about the Middle East problem, the emerging post-Gulf situation, security in the Mediterranean, and the rights of the Palestinian people. I explained in detail that financing Israeli settlements in occupied territories ran contrary to UN security council resolutions. I told him what I had seen in the West Bank and invited him to see for himself the strategically placed settlements that were intended to stop the possible emergence of a Palestinian state. I invited him to fly over the West Bank and see for himself. Eventually Baker did go and, together with President George H. Bush, took the decision to stop financing settlements in Gaza and the West Bank, which, of course, irritated Israel. The Bush administration also succeeded in starting the Madrid Peace Conference, which was a step in the right direction. But Bush was defeated in the 1992 election by a little-known governor, Bill Clinton, partly because he had lost the support of the Jewish lobby.

On February 28, 1991, I was granted an audience by Pope John Paul II and had the privilege of having my family with me. In our private meeting, we discussed at length the situation in Kuwait – on the day when the entire country was liberated – as well as the situation in the Middle East. His Holiness was well informed of the situation and expressed his desire for, and commitment to, peace in the region. The pope was aware I was visiting Albania on the morrow and filled me in on two important facts: first, Mother Teresa would most probably be on the same plane that was taking me to Tirana; and second, that the Vatican's secretary of state, Archbishop

Angelo Sodano (he had become a cardinal in June of that year), had something important to tell me. Then my family were shown in. First, Violet was introduced and later my children and grandchildren. The pope was friendly towards Angelica and, as she was surrounded by two naughty cousins, Joe and Gianluca as well as her younger brother Matthias, asked her in Italian if they had been treating her well. The pope was still in his prime at the time. I had the good fortune to meet him on a number of occasions over the years and had the honour of receiving him in Malta as president both when he was healthy and when he wasn't.

Mgr Sodano told me about a bishop, well into his 70s, who had been imprisoned by the Enver Hoxha administration for 30 years. Although the bishop was allowed to send letters to the Vatican, the Albanian authorities did not allow Church officials to visit him. I told Mgr Sodano that I would do my best to raise the issue. As I flew to Tirana on March 2, I expressed to Mother Teresa my great admiration for her work for the needy. I felt I was close to a saint and, in the course of a few days, had had the privilege to meet two people whose lives were dedicated to holiness. As our aircraft arrived in Tirana, a guard of honour stood to attention. There were a number of ambassadors too. I asked Mother Teresa to descend the steps before me, but she steadfastly refused. I felt so insignificant in the presence of a woman who had done so much to deliver Christ's message to the poor, the sick, and the dying, and I treasure that encounter.

Once there I met the foreign minister, Mohammed Kaplani. We had met previously and had got on well together but this time the atmosphere was tense. Just days before, there had been violent scenes in Tirana, Valona, and other cities. A massive statue of Enver Hoxha, who had ruled with an iron fist for so many decades, had been pulled down by the protesting crowd. There was unrest among army officers, since they sensed change was about to take place; and farmers who had obtained land expropriated from landowners were being told that it may be taken away from them. This gives an idea of the tension that gripped Albania at the time. Before dinner, I approached Kaplani privately and raised the issue of the imprisoned bishop. He reacted negatively, remarking sharply: 'Have you come here as UN president or as the pope's envoy?' I said: 'I am visiting Tirana at the express invitation of your president to see the democratic progress Albania has made. Do you think that locking up an old man, who happens to be a bishop, for over 30 years on a charge of having exercised his religion is a good way how to start a democratic process?' Taken aback, he said he would look into it.

One of the conditions I made when President Ramiz Alia asked me to visit Albania was that I be allowed to meet representatives of the opposition. He had hesitated for a moment but then acceded to my request. Neither of us had foreseen that my visit would coincide with the protests and, the following day, when I met the opposition, Sali Berisha was ushered in. He expressed thanks for my visit, adding immediately: 'It could not have come at a more opportune moment.' I imagined he said this because of the demonstrations in favour of democracy but I could not have been more wrong. He said: 'The army officers are planning a take-over unless you persuade President Alia to react strongly to this. By this evening we will all be arrested and in all probability executed.' I realised the seriousness of the situation and when I was received at the president's palace, Alia and I started conversing in Italian. After the usual formalities, I came to the point. Alia replied: 'Dr Berisha is right; the army officers are against reform and want me to halt the process. You notice that I am losing my voice. In the Albanian language, the term vocal "chord" stands both for "the chord of one's throat as well as for sword". I prefer to lose the chord of my voice than having to use my sword. But you can tell Dr Berisha that so long as you are here nothing will happen to him.' To this I countered: 'Are you suggesting that I camp in Tirana to ensure that nothing will happen to Dr Berisha?' We laughed it off, but both realised the gravity of the situation.

I doubt there were more than 100 cars in Albania at that time, all belonging to the political class. The airport area and the countryside were dotted with embedded defence posts, which, I was told, were meant to prevent paratroopers landing in the area. As I was about to board the flight to Rome, I was again approached by Kaplani, who told me he had news for me: first, that the president had overcome the crisis and that Berisha was no longer in danger. The second, he said, was that I could tell Mgr Sodano that he may send anyone to see the bishop in prison. I was pleased that my visit to Tirana had contributed to the nation taking another step on the road to democracy. As soon as I landed, I called Mgr Sodano who was elated at the news. Some weeks later, he told me his emissary had visited the bishop in prison and that he was subsequently released. He also told me that for the first time since 1939 diplomatic relations had been established between Albania and the Vatican.

The situation in China following the repression of the Tiananmen Square demonstration as well as the difficulties arising with the two Koreas were also receiving attention at the UN. Meanwhile, in the Soviet Union, Edward Shevardnadze had departed as foreign minister and Aleksandr

Bessmertnykh had taken his place. I was invited by the cabinet of ministers of the USSR to pay a working visit to Moscow and, with Bessmertnykh in particular, I discussed the revitalisation process of the UN; the need for political leadership to ensure good management; and the necessity to have right mechanism in place to guarantee the implementation of UN resolutions. The need to deal not only with political crises but also with ecological problems was also considered at length. As Malta's foreign minister, I had actively argued that the CSCE should be the regional organisation for peace-keeping in terms of chapter VIII of the UN charter.

In Moscow, as president of the UN General Assembly, I raised the importance of developing close links between regional organisations and the UN with particular reference to chapter VIII. I was very encouraged by the then under secretary for foreign affairs, Vladimir Petrovsky. A joint statement issued at the end of my visit mentioned the increased role of the General Assembly, its active participation in the settlement of regional conflicts and in the development of multilateral disarmament process, as well as the resolution of global problems. With Bessmertnykh, I also discussed the visits to China and the two Koreas, where I was going to after the Soviet Union. He argued that in the long run the isolation of China, would be in nobody's interest, and that the country could best be influenced by taking part in the international community. In so far as North Korea was concerned, his view was that China could have a measure of influence over its leader, Kim Il Sung, though he reiterated that South Korea would not be allowed to join the UN unless North Korea joined too.

My meeting with Russian Vice-President Gennady Yanayev stands out in particular. He was neither a diplomat nor a leading political personality but he had a strong background in the workers' union of the USSR. I was immediately struck by his openness in discussing the problems of the Soviet Union. He told me the economy was not performing well and he foresaw that, in the coming winter, unemployment would increase and that pensions and wages would not be adequate. He then told me quite frankly that something had to be done to resolve the problems. 'We will be taking certain measures,' he said, though not in a manner that de facto abandons glasnost and perestroika. Less than two months later, on the morning of August 19, 1991, I was listening to the BBC world service as usual and heard that a coup was in progress in Moscow against President Gorbachev. It was led by Yanayev. When he delivered a message on behalf of the coup organisers, he basically repeated almost word for word what he had told me in Moscow. His ultimate failure – the coup lasted just three days – gave Boris Yeltsin a spectacular opportunity to become president of the Russian Federation. Shevardnadze, although a determining figure in pronouncing himself against the insurgents, was highly critical of Gorbachev. I returned to Moscow that month for a human rights meeting and spoke to Yeltsin. I also met Gorbachev. Although he tried to put a brave face on it, it was clear that he was a defeated man. The coup had clearly taken its toll. The man who had been instrumental in ending the cold war and bringing down the iron curtain, the main player behind German reunification, much admired by the world for his vision and commitment to democracy, had lost the support of his own people. He was removed in quite a unique way. The Soviet Union was dissolved and the president therefore found himself unemployed!

To this day, Gorbachev is regarded negatively in the Russian Federation. Some criticise him for introducing reforms, which, according to his critics, led to the break-up of the Soviet Union. The day will come when the people of the Russian Federation will recognise Gorbachev's role in promoting the road to freedom and democracy for his fellow citizens. He showed that the greatness of Russia does not depend on its potency as a superpower, but rather on being a positive world player in maintaining peace and freedom.

I proceeded to Beijing where I was received by China's President Yang Shangkun, Prime Minister Li Peng, and Foreign Minister Qian Qichen. We talked about strengthening the role of the UN General Assembly and the new world order. They believed my impending visit to North and South Korea could prove useful. Although Qian made it clear to me that the North Koreans were very independent minded, he said my visit was a good move as it would show that the international community wanted to give political relevance to the Democratic People's Republic of Korea, which had always felt isolated.

Yang told me during a banquet held in my honour that, in spite of the events in Tiananmen in 1989, China had received one million tourists. Rather undiplomatically, I pointed out that in 1990 Malta had received 1.2 million, adding rather cheekily that this amounted to three times the island's population. Yang turned to me rather incredulously and asked, 'Is that true?' 'Yes,' I said. Yang, a former general, struck his forehead with his hand, and added: 'You know, if this were to happen in China, the rest of the world would be empty!' We burst out laughing.

When I arrived in Pyongyang, I was received by North Korean Foreign Minister Kim Yong Nam with whom we discussed international issues affecting the region. I emphasised the positive role that his country could play through membership of a revitalised UN. His main concern – and that of his president, Kim Il Sung – was the future of Korea. Kim was certainly a formidable personality. His ministers acted as if they were students in the presence of a Harvard professor; when they spoke it was to endorse their leader. Kim believed the partition of Korea had defied history and the oneness of the Korean people. He maintained that if the UN allowed North and South to join separately, it would only serve as confirmation of this historical mistake. He said he was prepared to consider UN membership provided the two Koreas applied as one country. I pointed out that in effect there were two Koreas in the international community and that both had their own specific foreign policy, yet he insisted they could share the UN chair, even if they alternated every six months. I pointed out this was not realistic and explained how in October 1990 the UN witnessed two German states – the Federal Republic of Germany and the Democratic People's Republic of Germany – merge into one. For decades they had been separate states, but through diplomatic efforts by the German people and through the co-operation of the international community, these two states had become one again. That, I told him, was the way forward for Korea. In New York the two delegations would have the opportunity to meet in back-room diplomacy which could eventually lead to real discussions that matured at the right political moment. I got the impression this argument was having a positive effect on Kim. He appreciated that I had travelled to Pyongyang on a mission of persuasion and said his country would join the UN. Mission accomplished.

North Korea is a beautiful country. We were taken to Mjonggang, which is one of the most picturesque places I have ever seen. Kim was only negative about one of my proposals – that I should go to Seoul by crossing the armistice line at Panmunjong – which he said would amount to recognition of the artificial frontier. Having achieved the real purpose of my visit, it was not wise to press the matter further. This meant that to get to Seoul I had to fly through China.

South Korea does not have the beautiful scenery of the north, but it certainly has a high standard of living coupled with industrial development comparable to that of advanced Western states. I could really see what being an 'Asian tiger' meant in the technological and industrial senses. I discussed UN membership of the two Koreas with Foreign Minister Lee Sang-Ock and even he expressed the hope that UN membership would help the two Koreas towards meaningful dialogue leading eventually to unification. However, I got the feeling that the Koreans were more interested in guaranteeing their sovereignty within a UN structure than unity. South

Korean President Roh Tae Woo believed the Republic of Korea could contribute towards peace once it obtained UN membership and he bestowed me with the Order of Diplomatic Merit. Since so little was – and still is – known about North Korea at the time, during my press conference I was asked whether Kim had plans for nuclear development. I maintained that UN membership would place a measure of control on the North. The subject matter is more relevant than ever today.

In June of that year I had the great privilege of being received by Czech President Vaclav Havel, a leading intellectual with a sense of history and a vision for Europe. He was tired, having spent the night in discussion on the future of the Czech and Slovak republics, and felt exasperated by what he termed as the non-logic of the debate over whether government gave power to the two republics or vice-versa. He clearly wanted to establish the powers each should have and, reading between the lines, I could sense that the two republics were heading for divorce.

In Prague I met another great personality, Alexander Dubcek. At that time, this Slovak was president of the Slovak Parliament but his great claim to international fame came from leading his country during the Prague Spring (a period of political liberalisation in Czechoslovakia which started on January 5, 1968, and ended on August 21 when the Soviet Union and its Warsaw Pact allies invaded the country). He had tried to introduce communism with a human face, only to see Soviet tanks bringing to an end an opportunity for freedom. I was struck by his sadness and the beauty of his deep blue eyes as we discussed the past, the present, and the future. He was being touted as the future president of a separate Slovak Republic, but unfortunately died prematurely in a car accident. It was so sad to see a man who had lived a communist ideal, only to see it turn into a monster of dictatorship, and the memory is as vivid today as it was then.

Following my successful visit to the Palestinian refugees in Gaza, the West Bank, and Jordan, I visited the refugee camps in Ethiopia. At the time CNN had broadcast an excellent programme, 'Famine in Africa', just as events in Ethiopia were taking a turn for the better. A few days before I arrived in Addis Ababa, the 14-year-long Haile Mariam Mengistu dictatorship was brought to an end. He was finally forced to leave Ethiopia, which he had ruled with an iron fist and so badly. The streets of the capital were deserted and patrolled by soldiers and young boys with Kalashnikov rifles firing at anything that moved. Arrangements were made for me and my delegation, made up of ambassador Joe Cassar, my personal adviser Michael Bartolo, and my private secretary Joe Tonna, to fly from Addis Ababa to the nearest place to my destination, Teferi Ber. The plane was an old Fokker, which had no seats. To make matters worse, next to us was a barrel filled with aviation fuel and I had to keep a watchful eye on Cassar – a chain-smoker – to ensure he did not even think about smoking lest that flight would be our last. If taking off was an experiment in flying, landing was even more dangerous as we came down hard in a field. Things did not get much better on solid ground. The jeeps we used for transport were acceptable, and the road – a remnant of Italian occupation – was relatively smooth, until we reached a point where there was no road at all, just a dusty track.

Thousands of refugees lived in Teferi Ber. People were dying of hunger every day and the sight of squalor everywhere was depressing. Refugees just lay on the ground, their eyes staring into blank space. At one point a woman came over to tell me she was starving. Suddenly she collapsed in front of me and died. I cannot describe how I felt at that moment but I was overcome with humiliation. CNN interviewed me and tried to place the blame on the UN. I reacted strongly, saying it was doing all it could; providing food and medicine in spite of the impossible situation. The UN, I said, was as strong as its members wanted it to be and criticism should be directed at the rich countries that were failing to contribute to ensure that the UN, through its agencies, could do more.

The only redeeming factor in Teferi Ber were the children. At least in their eyes there was still some hope and through their smile I could see the future. The UNHCR was doing an excellent job against great odds. The young people working with *Médecins Sans Frontières* and Oxfam were relentless in their efforts. In the evening I stayed in a compound not far from the camps and talked late into the night with UNHCR representatives and with young doctors working with the charitable organisations. I felt reinvigorated by their dedication to their mission. Before I left Ethiopia, I had a long meeting with ambassadors accredited to Addis Ababa, as well as with the president. They all underlined the famine and shortage of oil they were facing. The problem was not just shortage of supply but also one of distribution – ensuring that trucks loaded with goods actually reached the people they were intended for, since bandits often had other ideas. The best we could do was to provide armed protection.

From Addis Ababa I flew to Rome. Flying on the same plane was the daughter of the former Ethiopian Emperor Haile Selassie, who had died in suspicious circumstances in jail in 1975. The princess herself had just been released. On my arrival I was received by Italian Foreign Minister Gianni De Michelis, who immediately authorised supplies to be sent to Ethiopia. I took a particular interest in the plight of refugees, their legal status in international law, and in particular in issues of humanity. In 1991, more than 700 Albanians crossed to Malta on two ships seeking some assistance. The cabinet had no option but to ensure they returned to Albania. But, before sending them back, I saw to it that their safe return be guaranteed mainly through my contacts with the Albanian Foreign Minister Kaplani. We gave them humanitarian and medical assistance, and our police officers accompanied them on the plane home. They were not political refugees, but they were hungry.

I raised the issue both with the UN Secretary General Perez de Quellar and the UN High Commissioner for Refugees, Madame Ogata. I suggested that the necessary initiatives be taken so that the concept of 'refugee' be extended to cover those who were forced to leave a country because they were hungry – 'hunger refugees' as I called them – and that measures be considered to encourage further economic assistance both through bilateral as well as multilateral sources in these important circumstances. Madame Ogata said: 'You are absolutely correct in underlining the essential link between democratic observance of fundamental freedom and economic and social development. With its economy virtually paralysed and its population – especially its youth – in a state of despair the democratisation process in Albania is not only at risk, but so is the stability of the surrounding region as well.' However, she was not so encouraging about the concept of hunger refugees: 'This is a particularly complex and sensitive question at this juncture. The experience of my predecessor and my own would suggest prudence on the question of legal definition as it could put in jeopardy the internationally accepted norms of refugee law.'

The role of my UN presidency extended itself to the workings of the organisation. I set up an open-ended committee to discuss the revitalisation process of the UN with particular emphasis to the General Assembly and I had benefited positively from my discussions with diplomats and politicians at an important moment in the history of humanity. As the term was drawing to a close, I had the opportunity to spell out my thinking: 'I believe that the work of this assembly should constitute a blend of the political thrust and the diplomatic exercise. Over the years our assembly has lost its political edge by marginalising the ministerial role to that of welcome but short-staying honoured guests whose role is to deliver speeches before quickly departing. In my consultations I have explained the possibility of greater ministerial involvement in the work of the General Assembly and creating the opportunity for a more active role by parliamentarians in the work of the main committees, perhaps through a better staggering of assembly meetings throughout the year.' In my discussion on UN reform, I had the benefit of the advice of diplomats who had long been involved with the UN. And, together with Michael Bartolo, I saw to it that these ideas formed the subject of a book we jointly authored, *A Second Generation United Nations – For Peace and Freedom in the 21ˢᵗ Century*, which was published in 1997. Following an interesting conversation with Prof. David Attard, I stated in my concluding address to the General Assembly that, in addition to its role under the charter, the trusteeship council should hold in trust for humanity its common heritage and its common concerns: the environment; protection of the extra territorial zones and the resources of the sea and of the seabed; the climate; and the right of the future generations.

In her book *Ocean Governance in the United Nations*, Elizabeth Mann Borgese picked up on the proposal I had made and went on to comment that the trusteeship council should hold in sacred trust the principle of the common heritage of mankind and report any infringement to the General Assembly. She felt the trusteeship council should act as the conscience of the UN and the guardian of the future generations.

In my concluding address to the General Assembly I also spoke of the need for the assembly to go through a revitalisation process. 'During the tenure of my presidency I made it a primary objective to generate thinking on the revitalisation process of this assembly. This was done on the firm conviction that recent developments in the world order have created a unique opportunity to unleash the vast potential for deliberation and decision-making that has to a certain extent lain dormant in our assembly for over four decades. I believe in a second generation United Nations: a United Nations rooted in the principles and aspirations which went into its foundation 45 years ago, but taking nourishment from the breathtaking developments in international relations that have been occurring in recent years and have gathered even greater momentum over the last few months. The General Assembly should be at the heart of these developments.

'It is the only principal organ under the charter in which not only all members are equal, but in which all members are permanent members. It is the organ, which has both the authority and capacity to deliberate on all matters, which affect international relations. It is the unique forum, where issues can be considered in their inter-related aspects, where all parties to a problem can be consulted simultaneously and where the process of decision-making can be complemented by an opportune process of implementation. It is important that "a balanced constitutional relationship" be maintained with and between the principal organs of the organisations, including the General Assembly, the Security Council, and the secretariat.'

I found confirmation of this line of thought in the secretary general's report. He said this 'is not merely an issue of the internal working of the organisation, it bears on the guardianship of peace exercised by the United Nations'. In the foreword to the book *A Second Generation United Nations – For Peace and Freedom in the 21st Century*, Vladimir Petrovsky, UN under-secretary general and director general of the UN office in Geneva, wrote: 'In the United Nations and the OSCE one can trace the very specific diplomatic style of Malta. Professor (Guido) de Marco's presidency of the 45th Session of the United Nations General Assembly has become a landmark in the process of renewal of this unique body of multilateral diplomacy.'

44

The uphill journey to Europe

Enthusiasm is an important element in politics but perseverance is crucial. We embarked on our journey to Europe on July 16, 1990 and arrived at our destination on May 1, 2004. Ever-changing events and *dramatis personae* seemed to line the route every step of the way. From the outset I warned my staff that the road to Europe would be anything but smooth. As I remarked elsewhere, the government required three fundamental assets in its drawn-out discussions with the EU: insistence, persistence, and consistency. Some have argued that the government should have submitted the membership application a year earlier. In fairness to Ċensu Tabone, he had sometimes advocated that Malta should submit its application, but at that time Eddie felt Malta was not yet ready to take this step. In this regard, he had acted on the advice of two of his advisers on Europe, ambassador Joseph Licari in Brussels, and Dr Joe Borg, who in 1989 was entrusted with the setting up of the European Directorate.

As the cold war thawed, the thrust of the European ideal made its way to Sweden, Finland, and Norway. Although their application trailed behind ours, they were considered as instant contributors as they brought the Scandinavian dimension to the EU, which made a lot of sense, particularly in economic terms. Jacques Delors, European Commission president, said in an interview with *Liberation* in 1992: 'Let us not forget that in the year 2000, we shall be more than 12, maybe a little more than 20. There is a country one forgets, but which is very important as a symbol, Malta. We must not displace Europe too much to the north while forgetting the south, since we could risk losing our sensitivity to the Mediterranean world, which is our world but which at present has dangers for the future of all of us.'

This embodies the approach I had adopted in my meetings with commissioners and ministers of EU countries. I underlined Malta's positive contribution to international politics, mentioning in particular Malta's role in the UN, its positive contribution to the CSCE (later OSCE), and our continued presence in the Council of Europe in defence of democracy and human rights. In most countries, the attitude towards our application was neutral, and in some downright negative. Only one country backed us from start to finish: Italy. For quite some time Britain was sceptical, and the 'link' with Cyprus did not help. However, once British Foreign Secretary Douglas Hurd had become convinced of our case, he and his successors in subsequent UK governments supported us throughout. There were problems with France, Germany, and Spain, especially when certain ministers were in office.

One of the difficulties was Malta's size. When I told them the size of Malta's population, around 400,000, they would retort, 'So you are not even as large as a European city, say Catania or Liverpool', though I would counter that by pointing out that Luxembourg, one of the founders, was not larger either. Luxembourg was not too pleased with this as it feared it would work against them. When they asked if, on membership, we would demand a commissioner and the right to veto, conditions enjoyed by all the other member states, I argued that we were not prepared to accept 'second-class citizenship'. We were a sovereign state, like the rest. I also stressed the Mediterranean dimension, which required greater attention from the EU. My insistence on this with Commissioner Manuel Marin led to the Barcelona process of 1995. Here Malta's role in the Mediterranean was recognised and our determining contribution to the region upheld. Even so, there were some who argued that we could well abuse the right to veto as former Maltese governments had done before. My response to this was that Malta's insistence in Helsinki had led to the drawing up of the 'Mediterranean basket', which was universally recognised as an important element of the final agreement. Spain, Portugal, and Ireland were reluctant to commit themselves on our membership application and, although Greek Foreign Minister Michalis Papakostantinou told me, 'You are knocking at an open door,' his government's support clearly depended on Cyprus's entry. Belgium and the Netherlands were at best lukewarm in their attitude.

I observed in my publication *Malta's Foreign Policy in the Nineties*: 'In 1990, Malta's foreign policy reached a watershed when we formally submitted our application for membership of the European Community. For us membership of what since (the) Maastricht (Treaty of 1992) has become the European Union constitutes a culmination of the accelerated process of our national development. It provides a long-term anchor for our security, especially in terms of the safeguarding of those human, social, and civic values, which we deeply share with other European nations. At the same time our participation in the European experiment, open as this is to all other regions of the globe, also represents the means whereby we can consolidate and reinforce our commitment to the collective endeavour for stability and progress at both regional and wider levels.

'We have been working to join a dynamic European Union at a time that it is undergoing a major process of evolution and advancement in the face of a radically changed international environment. We ourselves have been directly exposed to the new forces of change in the way they have affected the ever-volatile Mediterranean region. This is strongly evident in the way events have unfolded and continue to unfold in the Middle East and in Bosnia. It is equally though less visibly present in the way in which socio-economic and other factors are affecting inter-Mediterranean relations in general.

'Present circumstances have rendered more complex the process of European enlargement in which Malta is a front runner. Even in the process leading to its accession, Malta has had the opportunity to gradually but consistently develop its role as a valid player in the Euro-Mediterranean partnership. It is in effect the area of Euro-Mediterranean relations that Malta will bring its most valid and original contribution as a member of the European Union.'

I have quoted this passage because it best explains my thinking and actions in the first five difficult but important years after Malta submitted its application. The report on Malta's preparedness for membership, known as the *avis*, took a long time to be published. I had a feeling that it was ready quite some time before it was issued on June 30, 1993, so there is a question mark hanging over what kept it in Jacques Delors's drawer. Some are of the opinion that, since it was positive, there must have been political difficulties in delaying Malta's entry. Austria, Sweden, Finland, and Norway had all applied after Malta and were scheduled to join in 1995. Some feared that our chances for membership were diminished because of the opposition to Cyprus's membership owing to the political division in that country. One commission report affirmed the candidacy of Austria, Sweden, Finland, and Norway and cautiously added 'and possibly Malta'.

The 1993 *avis* stated that Malta possessed the necessary credentials for accession since 'its culture and history reflect its long-standing links with Europe, which have over the centuries developed its European identity'. The *avis* also said that: 'Bearing in mind the country's democratic status and its consistent respect for human rights, Malta is entirely justified in asserting the vocation for membership of the European Union.' The commission, clearly intending to send a positive signal to the Maltese, formally announced 'that the Community is willing to open accession negotiations with Malta as soon as conditions allow'.

A debate was taking place at the time over whether a process of strengthening relations between the existing member states should take place before the EU embarked on enlargement. In the meantime, the list of countries waiting to join was growing. Apart from Austria, Finland, Sweden, and Norway (which eventually voted against membership in a referendum), the three Baltic republics of Estonia, Latvia, and Lithuania, as well as the Czech and Slovak republics (following their partition) and Slovenia, Hungary, and Poland were all in the queue. The Baltic republics had the strong backing of the Scandinavian countries. Germany backed them as well.

Notwithstanding the altered political scenario, we succeeded in keeping pole position. The European Conference decided in its 1994 Corfu Summit that 'the next phase of enlargement of the Union will involve Cyprus and Malta'. This was reaffirmed later in the year during the Essen Summit. Twice during 1995, at Cannes in June and in Madrid in December, the European Council reaffirmed the commitment to start accession negotiations with Malta six months after the conclusion of the 1996 Inter-Governmental Conference (IGC). We started also a pre-accession programme with the European Union consisting of a structural dialogue on foreign and security policy and home affairs, and held discussions about a possible package of agreements on specific subjects that would further consolidate Malta's links with the EU.

Five solid years of relentless and persistent diplomatic activity changed the issue from one of whether or not the island would be accepted to one of when it would become a member. The structural set-up at government level contributed considerably to what had been achieved. Our diplomatic corps was also rising to the occasion. In Brussels, I appointed Charles Vella to replace Joe Licari, who was posted to Paris, while John Vassallo took over as our ambassador to the EU when Vella retired. Vassallo was a diplomat with great sense for detail as well as being dedicated to the vision of Malta in Europe. Joe Borg was doing a splendid job at the European Directorate, preparing for eventual negotiations and the pre-accession programmes. At government level we had an inter-governmental committee to coordinate activities within the different ministries, a cabinet committee to discuss in detail European Union problems and issues as they evolved, and a Maltese-EU Parliamentary Committee which met regularly. All these contributed to creating awareness locally about the problems and issues connected with membership.

The real change in the attitude of member states came through persistent lobbying, particularly with ministers and the commission. I had my fair share of let-downs and disappointments. It was particularly frustrating when ministers would change because it meant the process of persuasion would have had to start all over again. Prior to my meetings with ministers and commissioners, I would acquaint myself with their curriculum vitae and background. Establishing a personal relationship was a vital means of gaining their support. I feel this approach contributed greatly to the progress made in our work over the application. By this time the scepticism had evaporated and, although the debate over enlargement continued, Malta was steadily moving along the road to membership. We were waiting for the IGC to get on with its work.

Of course, this situation did not diminish my disappointment at not seeing Malta join in the first enlargement along with Austria, Sweden, and Finland, even though I was well aware of the advantage these countries enjoyed in terms of political and economic clout. But I did not for a moment falter in my sense of direction. During one meeting, French Foreign Minister Alain Juppé concluded by paying me a compliment: 'You are a good advocate for your country', he said. I appreciated it, since throughout my political life I have tried my best to promote Malta's interests. I think the fact that Malta eventually joined is a lasting legacy which, in cooperation with others, we succeeded in passing on to future generations.

45

Two tragedies: EgyptAir and Lockerbie

By now I was the proud grandfather of four: Giannella's Joe and Gianluca and Fiorella's Angelica and Matthias. Violet was a dedicated grandmother, especially after the break-up of Giannella and Joe's marriage. Gianella's two boys would spend a lot of time at our home while Giannella was asserting herself as a leading lawyer in the criminal court. She works with a sense of determination and dedication, preparing her cases with diligence and attention to detail. She has also developed excellent cross-examination skills. Fiorella specialised in family law and succeeded in building a good practice without in any way neglecting her family.

As justice minister, I had the pleasure of issuing personally to my son Mario his warrant as a lawyer. He was a dedicated student, and after graduating in Malta, undertook post-graduate studies at Trinity Hall, Cambridge. One of his professors there told me they would have liked to have him as a lecturer. When he returned to Malta, he struck up a good working partnership with Joe Said Pullicino who, together with Gianella and Fiorella, kept the firm Guido de Marco and Associates on the move. On being appointed minister, I severed my links with my law firm but I retained my post of lecturer at the university. Lecturing always gave me a great deal of satisfaction. Even when I was taken up with ministerial work, I found time to meet my students. I treasure the link I still have with the university.

The university is the backbone of our intelligentsia; it provides us with politicians, lawyers, priests, physicians, architects, engineers, journalists, economists, teachers, and accountants. Although I have never been an education minister, I feel that, as a cabinet member, I have contributed to ensuring that tertiary education be made available to all with the aptitude to study, not just to the children of the rich and the elite. When the Nationalist Party came to power in 1987, we were burdened with the student-worker scheme and the requirement for undergraduates to find a sponsor prepared to pay for their studies at university. These absurdities have now been relegated to the past and, from about 700, the number of students is now more than 10,000. And, unlike the situation in many European countries, university education is still free of charge.

As justice minister, I was also responsible for the prisons. One prisoner we had there at the time was Omar Mohammed Ali Rezaq who, together with three Palestinians, had hijacked an EgyptAir plane to Malta on November 23, 1985 after it had taken off from Athens. Ali Rezaq had shot five passengers, killing two. American citizens were among the injured. Without warning, Egyptian special forces had stormed the plane, leading to the death of 56 of the 88 passengers on board, including two of the hijackers. Most of the passengers died as a result of the explosives used by the Egyptians.

For security reasons Ali Rezaq's trial was held at Fort St Elmo and he was sentenced to 25 years' imprisonment. However, for a variety of reasons – including amnesties which followed the constitutional amendments of 1987 and the first-ever visit by a pope to Malta in 1990 – Ali Rezaq, like all other prisoners, benefited from a reduction in sentence, and he was eligible for release after seven years. I was abroad at the time and Eddie had asked me to return immediately. He was concerned because the US ambassador, Sally Novetsky, was up in arms over his release. To make matters worse, Novetsky alleged that the attorney general had given her the impression that the release would not take place for some time. On my part, I wanted to ensure that the length of his sentence was in line with the regulations that governed such reductions.

A high-powered US government delegation had made a categorical demand: either we stop his release or, if we decide to release him, we should hand him over to them. I made it clear that as a minister I was not above the law; indeed I had the responsibility to see it was upheld. If Ali Rezaq spent one extra day in prison, I would be guilty of illegal arrest. I also told them that only the courts had the power to deliver him to them, after a request for extradition was made. However, I stressed that the double jeopardy rule applied in this case too. He could not be tried twice for the same offence. Without batting an eyelid, the delegation head told me: 'We want you to connive with us. You release Ali Rezaq, put him on a plane, and give him the impression he is going to a country of his choice, and we will seize him.' No one had ever proposed such a blatant illegal move to me before. I kept calm and explained that over the years I had striven to ensure, to the extent of being beaten up myself by police, that Malta was a country where the rule of law prevailed. Of course, I disapproved entirely of the terrorist act, irrespective of the terrorists' motives. But Ali Rezaq had served his sentence, and the reduction he benefited from had applied to all prisoners. I told the delegation: 'Conniving in an illegality is not part of my character.' Immediately I said this, I stood up to indicate that the discussion was over. Eventually Ali Rezaq was arrested in Lagos by the Nigerian authorities who handed him over to waiting FBI agents. Somebody in Nigeria had obviously connived to bring this about. Looking back on it, I think we were right in our stand, though with the benefit of hindsight we should have excluded certain offences from acts of clemency.

Another event that created diplomatic problems for us was the Lockerbie tragedy. A Pam Am jumbo jet, Flight 103, exploded over the Scottish village of Lockerbie on its way from London to New York on December 21, 1988, killing 270 people, including 11 on the ground. Terrorism was immediately suspected as the cause of the explosion. Police investigating the crash had recovered from the wreckage items of baby clothing bearing the label 'Yorkie'. They believed the garments, made by a company in Malta, had come from a suitcase that contained the bomb. When I was asked if Malta was prepared to collaborate with the British investigating team to look into any possible Malta connection, I immediately assented since I had always condemned international terrorism.

The investigators started working with our security service and I was regularly kept informed of the progress made. Attention was focused on an Arab who owned a bakery on the island. Eventually security services from other countries, including Germany, became involved in the investigations. I made it absolutely clear that investigations in Malta had to be carried out only through our security service. At one point I learned that the British secret service was tapping the telephones of people living in Malta without consulting the Maltese authorities. While I was all for cooperation, I felt no one should be allowed to treat Malta as if it were their own, and I immediately ordered the investigating team to stop any activity in Malta and for our security service to withdraw its cooperation. The British investigating authorities resented my stand but I made it clear that the sovereignty of our country had to be fully respected. The Scottish authorities were worried about this and the lord advocate of Scotland spoke to me of the importance of allowing the Scottish investigating team to return to the island for further investigations. I accepted, so long as they followed my instructions to the letter. The lord advocate agreed as he had obviously realised that any self-respecting country would impose the same conditions.

In the meantime investigations in Frankfurt were taking a new dimension. The investigators said the Pan Am plane had taken passengers and luggage from a feeder flight in Frankfurt. Months after the explosion, they were also investigating a claim that this feeder flight had received luggage carried on an Air Malta flight to the German city. I once again stressed that we were not objecting to any investigation and that we would face up to our responsibilities if we were to blame in any way. Still I was not at all convinced that the investigations carried out in Frankfurt were correct in so far as the involvement of the Air Malta flight was concerned. A German investigator who had come over to update me on the investigation said an Air Malta tag had been found on unaccompanied luggage which, according to a German source, was eventually put on the feeder plane to London, and following that, on the Pan Am flight from London to New York. I let him have his say but it was not credible. A Pakistani cleaner had apprently found the tag and brought it to the attention of the German investigating team. A book on the Pan Am bombing published some time after the incident had commented on how poorly the German official had responded to my questions.

After originally suspecting a Syrian-based group as masterminding the bombing, the investigators turned their attention to Libya, and Malta was once again placed on their map. Edgar Mizzi, who was Air Malta's legal adviser, told me that a UK television channel had alleged that a Samsonite suitcase containing explosives had been placed on an Air Malta flight to Frankfurt as unaccompanied luggage, put on the feeder flight to London, and from there loaded on the Pan Am flight. It seemed highly unrealistic to me that a timing device could have been put inside unaccompanied baggage that took such a complicated route to get on the plane, since there was so much room for error.

However, I still wanted a full investigation to be carried out, not only by the Maltese authorities but also by the foreign investigators operating in Malta. We had every interest in getting to the bottom of the issue and, if someone in Malta or from Malta, was responsible, we would deal with it. According to the investigating team, the 'Yorkie' clothing item belonged to a Libyan who had bought items from Mary's Store in Sliema on a rainy day. From my discussions with British Foreign Minister Douglas Hurd and other officials, no one was putting the blame on Malta. In fact, according to them, neither the airport authorities nor Air Malta were found wanting in their handling of the luggage in question. Indeed, I received a letter of thanks from Hurd for the help the Maltese authorities had extended to the British investigating team.

Two Libyan nationals were identified as the suspects responsible for placing the Samsonite case on the Air Malta flight to Frankfurt for subsequent transfer to London and the matter was brought before the UN Security Council. Some time before, the British under-secretary at the home office, Douglas Hogg, came to see me and explained that the security council would pass a resolution directing Libya to hand over the two suspects. I asked him if international law on terrorism permitted this, since I was under the impression that only the country concerned had jurisdiction to try the suspects under the principle of *aut dedere aut judicare*. Hogg said that, whatever the law stated, the security council would pass the resolution.

When the UN's intentions started to become clear to the international community, Libya's number two, Abdul Salam Jalloud, made a surprise visit to Malta. Eddie received him in my presence and he immediately came to the point. Jalloud said Libya was prepared to hand over the two suspects to Malta as they trusted the Maltese courts. He did not think there was a chance for the men to have a fair trial in Scotland or the United States. Eddie and I explained to Jalloud that Malta did not believe the allegation regarding the Samsonite bag and therefore we did not claim jurisdiction to try the case. Moreover, if the two suspects came to Malta, the British would apply – probably successfully – for extradition. We made this clear lest it be said at a later stage that we had tricked the Libyans into delivering the suspects. We did not hear anything on the matter from him after this meeting.

The security council proceeded with imposing sanctions against Libya. This included suspending air traffic to the country, which meant Libya was effectively cut off. This made Malta an even more an important link between Libya and the outside world. The island became the extended harbour, as it were, of Libya. Djerba airport in Tunisia was another option, but this involved a difficult drive on bad roads. When the sanctions started to have a negative effect on our trade and on Libya, I mooted the possibility of holding the trial in Malta, provided that the island was given a specific mandate by the security council. But the idea was shot down in Malta before it had time to take off in New York. We applied the sanctions rigorously. I believed, however, that we should still maintain a working relationship with Libya as our southern neighbour. With the blessing of the UN secretary general, I used to go to Tripoli as often as necessary, trying to test the water for possible solutions.

I was consulted on a regular basis by Vladimir Petrovsky, who had been a friend since his days as under-secretary of state of foreign affairs of the

USSR. He was now under-secretary general at the UN and had specific instructions from the secretary general to deal with Libyan affairs. He used to stop in Malta on his way. This Lockerbie affair dragged on till the day I took office as president of Malta on April 4, 1999, but I will return to this subject later.

The US government was very sensitive about our relations with neighbouring countries. We made it clear that we were applying the sanctions rigorously but we were also correct in believing that we should try and keep the door open for a solution to the crisis. I was fully aware that certain governments had their eyes on Gaddafi and were advocating that his regime be brought down. When Eddie and myself later visited the US and met President Clinton and Secretary of State Warren Christopher, we explained the thrust and *raison d'être* of our relations with Libya, saying that maintaining a bridge with that country was in the interests of the international community as a whole. We felt we were right in our stand, but it took a decade for a solution to be found and for our reasoning to prevail. There is no doubt that these were difficult years in Malta-US relations.

At the same time, however, we recognised the positive contribution the US had made to world peace: its role in the two world wars had been decisive. It had also been a determined opponent to Soviet communist expansion in Western Europe. When we criticised the US administration, it was only because we expected them to live up to the prominent role they have played in history.

46

When I mediated between Peres and Arafat

With all this foreign affairs activity, I was spending much of my time abroad in 1990 and 1991. We managed to maintain a strong presence in the CSCE. Speaking at a meeting of the Council of Ministers of Foreign Affairs in Berlin, which had been reunited only nine months earlier, I raised the issue of a new security architecture for Europe, stating that 'security is not only an architectural exercise in the reduction of armed forces, conventional or otherwise. It is based on confidence and trust. Threats to states may come not exclusively from land-based weapons systems. Some states can be reached by sea. All can be reached by air. New perceptions as to the security of small states have to be considered.' In the meantime, through my experience at the UN, I put forward the idea that the CSCE (later to be called OSCE) should become the regional arrangement for peacekeeping under chapter VIII of the UN charter.

An important meeting of foreign ministers was due to be held in Prague in January 1992, but I could not attend because we had a general election in less than three weeks' time. However, my ambassador, Joe Cassar, read out a message on my behalf: 'We believe that the CSCE has now come into its own and should itself ensure a role in providing vision and direction to the other pillars of the architecture of the new Europe that together we plan to shape. Against this background, Malta is convinced that the CSCE procedure is now fully advanced to qualify as the comprehensive regional arrangement – the agency in effect – for the peaceful development of Europe in compliance with Chapter VIII of the United Nations.' This proposal was gaining support. In particular German Foreign Minister Hans-Dietrich Genscher gave it his full backing.

Because of my overseas commitments and heavy ministerial schedule, I did not do any real campaigning, something that can be damaging in an electoral system like ours which requires the continued presence of a candidate. To make matters worse, some of my fellow candidates in my electoral district were telling voters that achievements in foreign affairs did not benefit them and that it was impossible for constituents to find me because I was always engaged. By this stage, home visits were being carried out on a scale never seen before and I had to do in a fortnight what other candidates had been doing for the preceding 12 months.

There were also changes to my electoral districts. Marsa had been removed from Valletta and Floriana and attached to Paola and Tarxien. I was asked by the party to contest this district as well, despite the limited number of Nationalist voters. In my district, I again won more votes than any other member of my party, although the total was lower than that I had won in the previous election. I failed to be elected from the Paola/Tarxien/Marsa district by a few votes. This election taught me a lesson: no matter how dedicated and successful one is as a minister, one has to be there for one's constituents. Apparently Anthony Eden, one of Britain's leading Conservative foreign ministers, used to suffer from a lack of political support and maintained in the face of criticism that his constituency elected him to represent them in the House of Commons and not vice-versa. (Eden was prime minister from 1955 to 1957.)

While this argument appears to be persuasive, I never again repeated the mistake of distancing myself from my constituents. This was the only election in which I had not dedicated myself completely to my constituency. An MP must ensure he is strong in his constituency, since this gives him added relevance in the party structure and when the party is in government.

I think the 1987-92 Nationalist cabinet was one of the best Malta has had since 1921. The only parallel cabinet, which started well but ended up broken up internally, was the Boffa government of 1947. The lesson from that was that, no matter how strong a government is, it will not last long if it is not endowed with cohesion and controlled ambitions. What made the first Fenech Adami administration stand out was its sense of history. We all worked hard together, driven by a common vision of building a new Malta, rich in freedom, with a thriving economy, and active in foreign affairs.

We started our second legislature in 1992 with a three-seat majority, which gave us much greater leeway in the business of the House. Karmenu Mifsud Bonnici had decided to call it a day in the wake of his second defeat. There were two leading contenders to succeed him, Lino Spiteri and Alfred

Sant. I was hoping that Lino would win, since we had been friends since 1966 and I had a lot of respect for his intelligence and clarity of thought. I also believed a Malta Labour Party led by him would be a more constructive opposition. I knew little about Sant, other than he was a studious and intellectually inclined person, always reading books during parliamentary sessions. He had also been associated with some of Mintoff's negative projects in the state economy as well as being involved in limiting entry to university through what was called the 'godfather system'. I followed the leadership election from Dino Marajeni's beautiful castle in Rome. Sant was elected and he had the courage to purge the violent element from the MLP – a characteristic feature of the party under both Mintoff and Mifsud Bonnici. The significance of this move has to be fully understood in order to analyse correctly the events that led up to the 1996 election.

I was again entrusted with the foreign affairs ministry. I relinquished justice and instead took on external trade and countertrade. This gave me an opportunity to follow up my proposal that the OSCE becomes the regional set-up for peacekeeping in terms the UN charter. I pressed the matter and submitted a proposal on May 18, 1992, entitled 'CSCE as a regional arrangement in compliance with Chapter VIII of the Charter of the United Nations'. The proposal underlined the historical significance of the current political transition for security and co-operation in Europe and the growing awareness the CSCE could further contribute towards greater understanding in ensuring security in the region. It went on: 'The participating states declare that the CSCE is the comprehensive regional arrangement for the peaceful development of Europe.'

The Helsinki Summit of June 1992, which Eddie also attended, adopted Malta's proposal. On December 2 of that year the UN General Assembly adopted a resolution entitled 'Co-operation between the United Nations and the Conference for Security and Co-operation in Europe'. Noting the role that the conference plays in promoting democratic values and institutions and human rights, the development of the capabilities of the conference to early warning, conflict prevention, conflict management, and security co-operation including peace-keeping, the general secretary was requested to submit to the General Assembly a report on co-operation and co-ordination between the UN and the conference. Once again Malta had punched above its weight and succeeded. This diplomatic activity was taking place against the backdrop of the conflict in, and break-up of, Yugoslavia.

In June 1991, as the first CSCE ministerial council was held after the signing of the Charter of Paris for a new Europe, the Yugoslav foreign minister, Budimir Loncar, explained the difficult situation developing in his country leading to the potential break-up of Yugoslavia itself. This is what in fact took place. Slovenia managed to sever itself with the least possible bloodshed; but Croatia was not so fortunate, in part because of the sizeable Serbian population in Slavonia. Bosnia Herzegovina was the worst affected. Under Josip Broz Tito's communist regime, which considered atheism as part of the state system, Bosnia Herzegovina was regarded as a federal state mostly based on its religious identity. The story of Islam in former Yugoslavia is perhaps best understood by reading the Nobel Prize winner Ivo Andric's novel *Bridge over the Drina*. The Muslim presence in the region is mainly made up of Serbs, who for their own reasons converted from Orthodox Christianity to Islam. Kosovo is different in that the ethnic Albanian element is also present.

The Yugoslav situation created considerable commotion, especially in the OSCE. I used to have useful discussions with foreign ministers Gianni De Michelis, Hans-Dietrich Genscher, and Douglas Hurd on the breaking-up of Yugoslavia. I maintained that it was not a case of minorities wanting to secede, but of national groupings brought together under the name of Yugoslavia – under the Karageorgevic royal family up to the Second World War and under Tito in the post-war period. For their own reasons, these national groupings sought their independence from the Yugoslav federation. When Slovenia, Croatia, Bosnia Herzegovina, and Macedonia sought independent status, I advised our government to recognise these new sovereign states. De Michelis was rightly concerned about the eruption of civil wars. He told me that with Slovenia things would be easy, with Croatia not so easy, with Bosnia Herzegovina very difficult, and with Macedonia '*è una Macedonia di frutta*' because of the many ethnic groups forming Macedonia itself.

In Bosnia the tragic killings highlighted the weakness of the international community when it came to providing protection for innocent victims. The siege of Sarajevo is today part of history. In one of my meetings with Slovenian Foreign Minister Dimitrij Rupel, I suggested the UN should, through the OSCE in its role of a regional arrangement for peacekeeping, impose a *cordon sanitaire* around Sarajevo and enclaves, such as Srebrenica. We decided to send a letter to fellow foreign ministers through Alois Mock, the Austrian foreign minister, who was chairing the OSCE, with this proposal. Unfortunately there was a lack of political will to make things move. Had our proposal proceeded successfully, the massacre of Srebrenica may have been avoided. Practically everyone knows what the end result was.

Macedonia is also separated from Yugoslavia, though the Kosovo situation is still not politically resolved. The break-up of Yugoslavia is still a contentious issue in some quarters, though the states are now likely to develop closer ties as individual members of the EU.

Slovenia joined the EU with Malta in 2004 and has already adopted the single currency. It has had good political leaders. In particular, its first president, Milan Kučan, managed the transition process with great ability. Croatia's first president, Franco Tudjman, was a powerful personality whose deep sense of nationalism impressed me. He had tears in his eyes as he recounted how, when Croatia declared independence, Malta was among the first countries to recognise its new status. I had good relations with the Bosnian foreign minister, Haris Silajdžic, though at one of our meetings he was feeling down and concerned about his family. I offered them hospitality in Malta if their situation became untenable. It did not turn out to be necessary, though a number of Bosnian children benefited from our offer to host them. I am sure many of them, who are young adults now, have happy memories of the island.

I paid special attention to China, and had an excellent working relationship with the foreign minister, Qian Qichen. When I was in New York for the UN General Assembly, a meeting with the Chinese foreign minister was always on my agenda. I had also decided to appoint a Maltese ambassador for Beijing to enhance our role in international affairs and improve our economic links with a country that is not just rich in terms of population, but also in culture and determination.

In June 1994, I accompanied Eddie on an official visit to China. I had already visited the country as president of the UN General Assembly in 1991 and also in December of that year with Ċensu Tabone during his state visit. Beijing was changing rapidly. While the historic parts were being well preserved, the rest was changing completely. In 1991, the streets were choked with bicycles. Four years later the car had taken over. New and modern buildings were changing the skyline of China's cities. We had a good meeting with President Jiang Zemin, a very pragmatic president who, following Ding Xiaoping, was proposing different economic structures for China, although still maintaining its Communist party political structure. Malta's traditionally solid relations with China were originally started by Mintoff, who, after reaching agreement on the fate of the Nato military base in Malta, visited Mao Tse Tung and Zhou Enlai. In 1972, this was a major and perhaps hazardous step and China does not forget good gestures in difficult moments. The same could be said for my visit to China in 1991, shortly after the Tiananmen Square incident. China's presence in Malta has always been very proper, balancing the practical and the functional. The China Dock at Malta Drydocks was built with Chinese assistance, but some industrial projects were less successful. The Garden of Peace in Sta Lucija is a lasting testament to our political relationship. The Chinese Institute of Culture is an important institution, but I will come back to it later on.

I sought stronger political and economic ties with the Arab world, and gave particular emphasis to our expanding export trade. In spite of the sanctions imposed on Libya, my relations with my counterpart, Azmi Beshara, and later with Foreign Minister Omar Montasser, were solid. The importance of establishing close personal relations cannot be emphasised enough, and never was this more the case as in the difficult years that followed the Lockerbie disaster. Through close personal relations we managed to advance good diplomatic initiatives and keep open important avenues, including contact with the UN secretariat. It was also important for us to steer clear of potential terrorists. This was no easy political feat. It required diplomatic work carried out with skill, intelligence, and awareness. Our ambassador in Tripoli, George Doublesin, made his presence felt. I used to find reading his monthly report always relevant and pertinent. He had a deep insight into situations and could provide good analyses. Our relations with Egypt were very positive. The Egyptian foreign minister, Amr Moussa, was the permanent representative at the UN during my presidency. He is a clever and modern Arab, and one who is acutely aware of Egypt's role in the Arab world. He is moderate but at the same time resolutely defends Arab interests. This helped me to create a strong link with Egypt, which benefited trade and also enabled us to discuss the Palestine issue and relations with Israel.

Our relations with the Maghreb countries were fairly good, though hardly spectacular. We took a structured approach with Tunisia, though a permanent obstacle was the median line between the two countries for offshore oil exploration. We wanted to move forward on other issues, but our efforts were thwarted by the dispute over the median line. Yet the nature of our personal relationship prevented other issues from escalating. The Tunisian foreign minister, Habib Ben Yahja, was a truly accomplished diplomat. When he was ambassador to Washington, banquets held in his honour would be alcohol-free. Yet at the end he would surprise everyone by offering round a box of excellent Tunisian wine. With him in particular, we found a way to stop the median line issue being a stumbling block by placing it at the end of the agenda. In any case, I knew his power on this issue was limited owing to restrictions imposed on him by the president. But it was still important to state each other's point of view and see if there was common ground. We then referred to our immediate superiors. The median line file is quite substantial, though it is clear that both sides understood that nothing should be done to jeopardise the strong friendship that existed between the two countries.

When it came to Saudi Arabia, I wanted to ensure we obtained the best possible terms for our exports. The Malta Export Trade Corporation (Metco) took part in the Saudi International Trade Fair. I had led an official delegation to Saudi Arabia in November 1994. In Jeddah, I discussed with Saudi's accomplished foreign minister, Saud al Faisal, agreements on double taxation on services, as well as cultural and educational cooperation. Riyadh is also the seat of the Gulf Cooperation Council and there I had discussions with the council's secretary general. The Mediterranean figured considerably in our talks.

In November 1994, I returned the visit that the minister of communications of the United Arab Emirates had made to Malta. We had already some connections with Dubai and Metco had been taking part in its business fair for four consecutive years. What impressed me most was the combination of financial and commercial skills available there. I was struck by the great sense of tolerance within the Emirates, where a mixed population of Europeans and Asians, in full respect of the Arab nature of the state, worked in harmony and mutual respect. The Emirates reflect the great potential that lies in the Arab world, yet this is not always correctly directed.

It turned out that 1994 was an important year in our relations with Israel. We had shown the Arab world Malta's strong stance in favour of a Palestinian state, but we repeatedly made the point that the existence of Israel was not under discussion and that, provided Israel was prepared to accept the state of Palestine, discussions could lead to permanent agreements. I visited Israel again in February 1994 for meetings with political leaders, including President Ezer Weizman, whom I respect immensely for his insight and political courage. Shimon Peres is for me, to this day, a man of great vision. He has the commitment and personal charisma to achieve his aims. He recognised the Palestinians as his neighbours and eventual collaborators. Many in Israel consider him to be a dove and a man who has suffered many defeats. Yet a focus on his defeats would be an unfair assessment of one of Israel's best statesmen. Peres believes in Israel but he is also a convinced believer in a new Middle East. He could understand Yasser Arafat and work with him. In his Foundation for Peace, he greeted Palestinians who, in the eyes of his fellow citizens, were terrorists. He was aware of the delicate nature of the discussions with Arafat, who at that time was still in Tunisia working hard to achieve a Palestinian Authority presence in the occupied territories. Peres realised, however, that the work of an extremist on either side could break all the hard work that, day after day, was being put into the peace process. He also told me that the fact that the Golan Heights were in Israeli hands was a constant obstacle in the way of peace with Syria. Peres believed that this stumbling block should be removed in spite of constitutional and political obstacles. He had the courage and vision to say in public, and in private, that there was no political alternative for Israel but to acquiesce to the creation of a Palestinian state. His line of reasoning, which I shared, was that, as I have already remarked elsewhere, in the space of a few years the Arab population in Israel and in the occupied territories would exceed the population of Israel, in spite of all possible immigration. This meant that, if Israel were to maintain its exclusive policy, it would be applying an apartheid policy, which would quite rightly be considered abhorrent.

So the vision of the Middle East was taking shape, particularly through the 1993 Oslo agreement. This was not just the first direct agreement between Israel and the Palestinians; it was the first time that the Palestinians publicly acknowledged Israel's right to exist. It was also a framework for the future relations between Israel and the anticipated state of Palestine, when all outstanding final status issues between the two states would be addressed and resolved. Even though the Oslo agreement was in place, however, much work remained to be done. Arafat and his PLO were still in Tunisia trying to ensure that their presence in the occupied territories would be effective. Within Israel many other forces were working to prevent this agreement taking shape.

Peres knew this, and I made it clear to him that my good relations with Arafat and other Arab world leaders could be put in good use whenever the occasion required. My visit to Israel was a landmark in our relations. I also had the opportunity of seeing Nazareth, the Dead Sea, and the Mount of the Beatitudes. To us Christians the whole land is evocative of the Gospel. We can walk with Christ from the synagogue to the house of Peter.

Before leaving Jerusalem, Peres and I agreed to keep in touch with developments and to be ready to act. Unfortunately, it was not long before this became necessary. An American Jew went on a shooting spree at the

Tomb of the Patriarchs in Hebron, killing 29 Palestinians. The tomb is held sacred by both Muslims and Hebrews alike. The incident, which happened on February 25, 1994, halted the peace process and Arafat felt that his presence in the occupied territories would be seen as little more than cosmetic.

Through his ambassador, Avi Palzner, Peres asked me to go and see Arafat urgently in Tunis and to act as a mediator. Palzner recounts in detail the whole episode in his book *Le Secret d'un Ambassador*. At the time I received the call from Peres, I was in Rome on my way to Paris to meet Foreign Minister Alain Juppé on my return from a visit to Cairo where I was received by the president of Egypt, Hosni Mubarak. President Mubarak has a firm grip on the political situation, fully realising that his stand and relations with the United States are essential for the survival of Egypt as a moderating and persuasive voice in the Arab world and in the Middle East peace process.

As usual, I always find meeting with Ismail Abel Meguid, secretary general of the Arab League, an intellectual experience. His approach is sound and deep. I will never forget his support for Malta's application to join the EU. He told me in no uncertain terms, and repeated it in an interview, that it was in the Arabs' interest that Malta joins the EU. For through Malta's presence in the EU, the Arab world could feel that its point of view was being considered. Also with Meguid we discussed the Middle East situation, which was at a crossroads. Somebody reminded me how often it had been at a crossroads.

In Rome on my way to Paris I met the representative of the PLO who informed me of the grave situation in the occupied territories following the shooting of innocent people praying at the Tomb of the Patriarchs. I was given the impression that Oslo was at stake. In Paris on March 23, 1994, I had a long meeting with Alain Juppé at the Quai d'Orsay. The main thrust of the meeting was Malta's application to join the EU. Through my foreign affairs activities in the Mediterranean, I was showing the role Malta would eventually play in the EU. We were not going to be just a state 'smaller than the city of Catania' but a sovereign state that was prepared to play a role for peace in our region. I informed Juppé that on the following day I was scheduled to go to Tunis to meet Yasser Arafat.

On arrival in Tunis on a direct flight from Paris, I was taken to meet Arafat in his villa. When I explained my mission to him, he said he knew how correct and balanced I had been as president of the UN General Assembly over matters concerning Palestinian issues. He knew of my positive contacts with Shimon Peres, too. Taking part in the meeting with him were Farouk Kaddoumi, his spokesman for foreign affairs, and Palestinian statesman Faisal Husseini, the PLO's representative in Jerusalem, whom I knew beforehand from my visits to Palestine. I told Arafat of Peres's concern at the act of violence at the Tomb of the Patriarchs. The Israeli government had condemned it with no reservations. It was a terrorist act done with a purpose, that of stopping the peace process. I emphasised the point that giving way to the present situation would mean accepting that terrorists on either side would have a decisive say as to whether the peace process was to be on the move or not. Husseini backed me up in my arguments. Arafat was still concerned at the role of the Palestinian Authority in such circumstances. I shared his concern but we could not throw away this chance to bring peace back to the region as agreed upon in Oslo.

At our meeting, held in the dead of night, we ensured the continued observance by the PLO of the Oslo agreement and Arafat's move to Palestine. I do not think Kaddoumi held much hope in the Oslo agreement, still less in a return to Palestine in the existing circumstances. However, in spite of his disagreement, his loyalty to Arafat was absolute and unconditional. In a way I respected Kaddoumi for the tenacity of his views, but I respected him even more for his faith and loyalty to Arafat throughout the years.

47

Stability Pact for the Mediterranean

My mediation between Peres and Arafat gives an insight into the issues that had arisen at the time and highlights the direction the island's foreign policy was taking. There were times when I was advised in the most diplomatic of terms that small states should behave like children, that they should be seen not heard. I made it a point to make my position clear. I intended to make our presence seen and our views heard. Naturally, I was fully aware of our limitations but I feel we have made some good proposals too. For example, I still think that our proposal for a *cordon sanitaire* around Sarajevo, Srebrenica, and similar areas was the right one. The proposal could only have been successfully adopted if it had been taken up by major powers of the CSCE as it was they who could provide the necessary troops. I was not prepared to fall victim to a conspiracy of silence.

I used to make it clear to my colleagues at the ministry that we had to wear shoes that fitted our size. Shoes that were too large made us look like Charles Chaplin but there was nothing more painful than wearing shoes that were too small for our size. For Malta's foreign policy to be respected, it had to be serious, relevant, and well-prepared. It was important, therefore, to have a professional foreign service to back up our foreign policy.

At last we succeeded in seeing through all the necessary procedures for a reorganisation of the service. Victor Gauci, my permanent secretary, contributed greatly towards this end. We opened recruitment for second secretaries to candidates with a university degree. I knew it had to take time for the corps to develop an *esprit de corps*. We had a number of seasoned diplomats, some of whom had served in the former diplomatic service, such as Victor Gauci, and Victor Camilleri. The European Commission had noted the need of ensuring a proper set-up and this strengthened my hand at administrative level. I was envisioning that in 10 years' time we would have a partially-fledged diplomatic service.

In the meantime we wanted to strengthen our link with the United States. The new ambassador, Joe Paolino, succeeded in arranging an official visit to Washington between September 21 and 24, 1994 but no sufficient preparations were made for it. Our meeting with President Clinton at his Oval Office at the White House was interesting but had little depth. Eddie gave a brief but good and interesting account of Malta's foreign policy, underlining Malta's application to join the EU; he emphasised that Malta's membership of the EU would give a sense of security to the central Mediterranean region. He explained well our relationship with Libya, and pointed out that the island's continued links with that country, in full observance of UN sanctions, was in the common interest of the international community in its search for a solution to a difficult situation, which, if not seen to, might have serious repercussions. President Clinton listened and made some interesting comments. I had useful meetings with Secretary of State Warren Christopher and with other officials. We aimed at stimulating a positive attitude from the state department towards Malta in a bid to attract American investment, but I had a feeling they were mostly interested in seeing Air Malta buy Boeing instead of Airbus. Eddie skilfully stayed clear of making any commitment. All in all, the results of our meetings were limited.

Some months before, in June 1994, Eddie and I paid an official visit to China. We met President Jiang Zemin and Prime Minister Li Peng. Like others visiting China at the time, we saw for ourselves the start of the great economic revolution in that country. We had journalists and several businessmen in our delegation. Among the journalists was Fr Joe Borg, who used to say Mass in Eddie's room at the hotel but we had to be discreet about this as the Chinese could have objected. A day will come when this great country will have its glory reflected not only in its economic achievements and its will for world peace but also in its belief in the rule of law and fundamental freedoms.

I had very good working relations with Manuel Marin, the EU's commissioner for external relations, Southern Mediterranean, Middle, and Near East. We had been long discussing the need for the EU to create a link with Mediterranean countries. It was through these and other talks that the Barcelona process started taking shape. Malta's deep interest in Mediterranean affairs made us close participants in this great process. We definitely had to take advantage of this international scenario. The fall of the iron curtain had created a new order in world affairs.

From the very first weeks that I was entrusted with the ministry of foreign affairs, I started voicing the need of a Council for the Mediterranean. At the final Stability Pact Conference in Paris in March 1995, I proposed a stability pact for the Mediterranean. Barcelona was intended to go beyond the concept of a treaty. It was meant to be an ongoing process based on political, economic, and social affairs. I was very much involved in the political side of the process. We worked hard to put the spotlight on the Mediterranean during the third Inter-Parliamentary Conference on Security and Co-Operation in the Mediterranean, held in Valletta. The Malta delegation included Mintoff as a representative of the opposition. We followed a pattern in our collaboration. We first used to discuss an issue, and then work towards reaching a common stand. When a common stand was reached, Mintoff would to turn to me and in his usual figurative language say: 'Now, it's over to you; you do the talking as I might do more harm than good.' We had other IPU meetings in other countries, including Romania and Spain. These gave me the opportunity to understand Mintoff and his thinking from a close distance. We built a bridge of trust between us, which held well for many years. Mintoff remains a difficult person to deal with to this very day.

The IPU meeting in Valletta had entrusted me with the responsibility to put forward in Barcelona a proposal for the setting up of an association of Mediterranean states, made up of government and parliamentary wings, 'to advance and achieve the Mediterranean co-operation prospectus'. In Barcelona, I also focused on the need of a stability pact for the Mediterranean: 'We do not cease being Europeans or Arab or belonging to the Middle East if the Mediterranean is treated as a region with its own personality. We believe that the people of the Mediterranean have an option, either to maintain the Mediterranean as a great divide bordering the sea, with security organisations, but generating suspicion to the other states, or creating the necessary mechanism aimed at enhancing the stability of the Mediterranean. Some still ask, what is the Mediterranean? It is more than a sea, more than a highway.

'Malta was the first country to propose a stability pact for the Mediterranean. We did this in Paris in March 1995 and we reactivated our proposal in international fora, including the UN General Assembly and the Council of Association between Malta and the European Union. We believe that a stability pact for the Mediterranean, by whatever name it might finally be called, would help bring together for discussion parties in dispute. It would also raise for discussion issues that can help pre-empt threats to the security of peoples and states in the region. In other words, a stability pact can well be an exercise in pre-emptive diplomacy. Above all, it would be an alliance in partnership between Mediterranean states.'

I believe my statement was well received. Some months later I circulated to members a document containing my 'Reflections on a stability pact for the Mediterranean', which still serves as a basis in the ongoing debate over the drawing up of a Euro-Med political document. There was a strong air of optimism at the time. Arafat was there too. It was the first international meeting attended by Israel's new foreign minister, Barak. We had the first of a number of meetings together. His presence in Barcelona was not the result of a change in government or a ministerial shake-up, but had come about because, following the assassination of Prime Minister Yitzhak Rabin, Shimon Peres had taken over as premier. I had been with Rabin less than a month before, in New York to mark the fiftieth anniversary of the UN. I remember complimenting him for his statement to the General Assembly.

In Barcelona, we were taken up by our enthusiasm over the work we were doing and perhaps failed to realise the implications of Rabin's assassination. Rabin's murder reminds me of a conversation I had some months before with Syrian President Hafez Assad in Damascus in January, 1995. He received me at his official residence, a very modern architectural structure perched on one of the hills overlooking Damascus. He was in a rather sad mood and took me to see the view of the city from his window. Assad said he felt rather lonely at his official residence and made it a point of going to his office in downtown Damascus every day to feel close to the people.

He also referred to a letter of condolence he had just received from President Weizmann of Israel following the death of his son in a traffic accident. Weizmann told Assad that he too had lost a son. Assad told me he felt 'uncomfortable' answering such a 'considerate' letter because, if he were to do so, he would have to address Weisman as president of the state of Israel, when Syria did not recognise Israel. I raised the Golan Heights issue and asked whether Syria was prepared to recognise Israel if it withdrew from the Golan Heights. Assad was straight-forward in his reply: 'Since when do you compensate a person for returning something that he has stolen from you.' He argued that the Golan Heights were sovereign Syrian territory and their return to Syria had to be unconditional. I tried to explain that in politics one had to be practical and try to find the best solution even if this demanded some sacrifice from a party that was receiving back its due. Assad's reply to this was: 'You want me to make a beau geste in favour of Israel? This is what (Egyptian President Anwar) Sadat did when he went over to Israel and addressed the Knesset. His people could not accept his action. See how he died, killed by his own people. We, Arabs, have our own way to show support or otherwise. In Israel, if Rabin fails to have popular support, he is just voted out of power. We, in the Arab world, kill leaders who act against the people's will. I want to die on my bed.' This brought to an end a conversation pregnant with meaning and devastating in its logic. When Rabin was assassinated, I recalled Assad's words. The irony is that Rabin was killed by a compatriot.

I had also been involved with Eddie in work connected with three Commonwealth Heads of Government Meetings. We went together for the meetings held in Cyprus and Zimbabwe and we had planned to go together to that held in New Zealand too. When I arrived in Sydney, however, I found Eddie at the airport about to fly to Israel to attend Rabin's funeral, and he suggested that I carried on my own and head the delegation to New Zealand. I have been very much a Commonwealth man since my early days as a parliamentarian. The Commonwealth is a positive experience in universality linked by the English language and in most cases having some bond with the United Kingdom.

I had accompanied President Tabone on five state visits: to Italy, India, Australia, New Zealand, and China. President Tabone gave prestige to the presidency. His fatherly figure and his common touch endeared him to people, as perhaps no previous president had succeeded in doing. In 1994 his five-year term was about to expire. The opposition was at one time prepared to consider giving him a second term but it later changed its mind.

Ugo Mifsud Bonnici was approached by Eddie to take up the presidency. I was a bit annoyed in that, being the senior minister in the cabinet, I expected to be offered the post, even though I had no intention to accept. I had one sense of direction, seeing Malta join the EU. All my actions as minister of foreign affairs were directed towards this aim. I used to be in Brussels frequently meeting commissioners and ministers. I was by now a senior foreign minister in the community of foreign ministers. I had been minister of foreign affairs for more than six years.

As I said earlier, the issue was no longer 'if' Malta joins but rather 'when'. Confirmation of this came at a dinner offered by Douglas Hurd to Eddie and myself during an official visit to London. In an after-dinner speech he recounted how his 'friend Guido' had been lobbying him for several years for Malta to join the EU. He explained he had had his reservations but that now these belonged to the past and that henceforth he stood by the decision reached, that is, that negotiations for Malta's membership should start within six months from the conclusion of the IGC. He made it clear that through its active foreign policy Malta was considered their 'eventual positive element' within the EU.

Ugo became Malta's fifth president in April 1994. He brought to the presidency his cultural and intellectual refinement. His excellent personal qualities and his very balanced approach on issues made his absence in the cabinet felt.

The end of the cold war brought about a reassessment of alliances. Nato remained a strong military alliance but had lost its potential enemy. There were new approaches within the alliance, trying to give it a wider dimension. The Partnership for Peace was set up, working alongside Nato but not part of it. It was a partnership made to measure, taking neutral states holding on to their neutrality. The PFP was mainly directed at the Russian Federation and its former components within the Soviet Union context. A new security architecture *à la carte* was being set up. In the PFP, Malta was prepared to contribute to peace-keeping and humanitarian operations. The PFP made specific reference to neutral states; indeed it specifically mentioned that 'these international states, as neutral countries, add breadth to the endeavours of the North Atlantic Cooperation Council and the PFP in building up a climate of co-operation and solidarity in Europe'. I addressed the council in the Netherlands, Brussels, and Berlin. I found that the NACC and PFP had opened up a prospect in security that no other organisation had adequately provided.

At the signing of the PFP framework document on April 26, 1995, I was specific in my commitment: 'In pursuing a policy of non-participation in military alliances, Malta values the basic values and definitions of the Partnership – protection and promotion of human rights and fundamental freedoms and the safeguarding of justice and peace through democracy... For Malta, a particular attraction of the Partnership for Peace lies in its objectives to enhance its capacities of the United Nations and the OSCE in peace-keeping and humanitarian operations.'

I thought that, through the PFP, our limited military forces would get further experience and still be within the context of our neutrality status in terms of the constitution. Unfortunately, the opposition did not agree. It resorted to a scare campaign, claiming, for instance, that we would be sending our soldiers to die for the cause of others.

48

The 1996 election defeat and its aftermath

The year 1996 was a difficult one. To begin with, the government had introduced value added tax. Retailers preferred the old system of taxation at source. Alfred Sant, sensing the retailers' mood, campaigned against VAT, a move that had gone diametrically against the efforts made for Malta to join the EU. All our work to put Malta in pole position in membership talks was at stake.

At the same time, however, Sant did his best to give his party a new image. As I have already remarked elsewhere, he had managed to weed out the violent elements from the party. He moved the party headquarters from Senglea to Blata l-Bajda, close to my house, a step meant to show that the MLP also stood to embrace the middle-class, traditionally Nationalist supporters, besides the people living in Cottonera. He also started a party television station which became very popular among party supporters. In sharp contrast to Mintoff's oratory and to the ranting of Karmenu Mifsud Bonnici, Sant was more down-to-earth in his political speeches. His talk had a refreshing effect and helped in giving Labour the new image it had been seeking. His two deputy leaders also contributed towards this effort by spreading a message of moderation and liberalism. George Vella, a medical doctor from Żejtun, was, depending on his moods, moderate in his views, while George Abela, a lawyer, has a very pleasant personality and enjoys wide appeal.

I realised that our party had to take immediate remedial measures if we wanted to win the elections. I was on government business abroad when the party's executive committee discussed the issue of whether or not the party should have its own television station. I sent in my views in writing – the first time I ever did so – stating clearly we could not rely on the state television network if we wished to put our message across. I therefore strongly argued in favour of having our own station, as shown in the minutes of the executive committee meeting. Unfortunately, though, my voice was not heeded. There was great optimism within the party. Those of us who had reservations about our prospects in the forthcoming election were considered defeatist. Austin Gatt, as secretary general, was efficient and innovative but he ensured that the decision-making process evolved from the centre and, more specifically, from the secretariat, divesting the periphery of power. Richard Cachia Caruana was exercising the same power concentration process at Castille. This went against the leadership style introduced by Eddie who wanted ministers to assume their responsibilities and to work as one team. Cabinet meetings, held on Mondays, were well organised. I used to spend my Sunday afternoons reading cabinet memoranda. The secretaries to the cabinet we had, George Borg, Joe Grima, and Alfred Fiorini Lowell, were all very competent, alert, and highly co-operative.

Richard Cachia Caruana wanted to give the premiership a standing far removed from the concept of *primus inter pares*. As I jokingly used to observe, in his view we had a cabinet made up of a field marshal and a number of sergeant majors. I resented this attitude and my ministry did not succumb to interference. Lest I be misinterpreted, I wish to add that Cachia Caruana is a very competent and well-prepared public officer. His loyalty to Eddie was absolute and his sense of fulfilment was in direct relation to the power he assumed. He gave the impression that his ambition was to be the power behind the throne. This went against the correct concept of cabinet government, which I strongly believe in.

When the police found that Meinrad, son of Brigadier Maurice Calleja, was involved in major drug trafficking, Calleja, whom I had known for many years, mainly as an expert witness in trials involving firearms, sought an interview with the prime minister to discuss his position. For some reason I was not aware of, he did not have this interview granted with the urgency that he expected, so in his distress he came over to see me at my office, without making any prior arrangements. Brigadier Calleja always behaved towards me and towards others in the gentlemanly manner for which he is so well known. I received him immediately. He told me he wished to see the prime minister as he wanted to hand in his resignation in the light of legal proceedings being taken against his son. I told him I was sure the prime minister, whom I knew held Calleja in high esteem, would see him and I advised him to decide about his resignation only after he had met him. Calleja had his meeting with the prime minister some hours later.

What I could not understand was how a meeting that had taken place in the singular circumstances that I have just explained and that concerned a conversation that was innocuous in substance and correct in all its detail, was interpreted by some at Castille, and some journalists, as an act of subversion on my part against the prime minister. I reacted immediately to this and called a press conference, explaining in detail my conversation with Brigadier Calleja. At a later date, a vile attempt on the life of Cachia Caruana was made and Meinrad Calleja was accused of attempted murder. When, on being requested, my daughter Giannella took up his defence, as she was duty bound in terms of professional ethics, the same journalists mounted a further unjustified attack on me. I have given this background for readers to understand the under-currents that existed between Castille and Palazzo Parisio. However, in spite of this, the deep friendship and camaraderie between me and Eddie was not affected.

Meanwhile, Malta was fast gearing up for the general elections. This time I did not leave anything to chance. My standing with the public as minister was high but I did not rely on this. David Casa came over from London, where he worked at our high commission, to take over the running of the campaign. He did a marvellous job. I did a lot of home visits and street parties, which had become very fashionable. After some soul-searching, I had decided to contest, for the first time, the Sliema district too, besides the Hamrun/Valletta one. I had been representing Hamrun uninterruptedly since 1966. Through home visits in my two districts, I could feel the pulse of the nation. The people still believed in the Nationalist Party but memories of the past were already receding. A certain section of the Nationalist press started demonising the MLP leader. I was against this as it is incompatible with the Nationalists' way of doing politics. I made this clear at our daily campaign meetings. The thinking was '*ser ngħadduhom b'20,000*' (we are going to overtake the MLP by 20,000 votes). As part of my campaign, I had a great meeting at the Mediterranean Conference Centre. Eddie came over and in an interview spoke highly of my qualities.

The MLP said that if they were to be elected they would work for a special arrangement with the EU, rather than membership. At this stage I was beginning to doubt our prospects of winning the election. There were those who told me on my home visits that they were not prepared to vote this time because of the introduction of VAT. Others said they were against the Partnership for Peace and feared that, if the Nationalists were to be elected, soldiers sent abroad would return in body bags. The situation had changed drastically since May 1987 and discussion did no longer centre on the state of play between today and yesterday but, rather, on how matters could be improved today rather than tomorrow. In contrast to my personal feelings, others were optimistic. But I was proved right as we were defeated. Eddie called the result 'a photo finish'. I did very well, again obtaining the highest number of votes compared with those of other Nationalist candidates in my districts. The result was even better in my Sliema district, where I also obtained the highest number of votes among Nationalist candidates.

In the light of Labour's victory, such good personal results counted for very little, more so when considering that the MLP was about to dismantle all that we had managed to do to pave the way for Malta's membership of the EU. I had never before experienced the sensation of losing an election when we were in government. The changeover is simple and effective. You are relieved of the practical symbols of power; suddenly, the ministerial car is taken away and my direct telephone lines with Castille, army, and police were removed. I was no longer a minister. I was back in opposition.

There was great ferment and disappointment within the party. Some talked about the need of a change in leadership. I made it abundantly clear from the very beginning that I stood for Eddie. I believed in loyalty, more so when the going was not good, and I also believed that Eddie would lead the party to victory again. The changeover was smooth, without any violence. Within 24 hours of taking office, an emissary from the foreign office was sent to Nato headquarters in Brussels to withdraw Malta's membership from the PFP. By sheer irony of fate, on the same day that Malta withdrew, Switzerland, the neutral state *par excellence*, joined the North Atlantic Council, clearly showing the correctness of our stand and its compatibility with Malta's neutral status.

49

When Mintoff brought the MLP government down

When the MLP took office after winning the general elections, the new foreign minister, George Vella, informed the EU that Malta was freezing its membership application and that the new government planned to propose a new arrangement between the EU and Malta. The island's ambassador in Brusssels, John Vassallo, was removed and his employment with the foreign office terminated. His removal as ambassador was understandable because his posting was a political appointment but, since he had excellent qualifications, I could not understand why his employment had to be terminated. Vassallo later joined General Electric Company where he was equally successful. Our new ambassador in Brussels was my former permanent secretary Victor Camilleri, one of our best diplomats. It was a pity, though also understandable, that we lost the services of Joe Cassar, our permanent representative in New York. Other equally good ambassadors were removed or had their service terminated. Most of my secretariat was disbanded. All in all, however, the transition to the new administration was carried out without any jolts. As a rule there were no acts of violence during the victory celebrations and this gave the general impression that New Labour was indeed different to past Labour administrations. Since the MLP had a majority of only one seat, the MPs had to make it a point to attend Parliament, lest the opposition called for a snap division. Their individual presence in the House was important, more so now when among them, as a backbencher, they had Mintoff.

Besides being the shadow minister for foreign affairs, I was also nominated as a member of the delegation to the Council of Europe. In Strasbourg, I was appointed chairman of the largest political committee, the monitoring committee, which had to ensure that council members abided by the council's statute and lived the principles of democracy and the rule of law. As chairman, I took a leading role, sending representatives to Russia to monitor the situation; to the Ukraine, to report on the capital punishment meted out in that country; to the Baltic republics, to check about the rights of the Russian minorities, and to Croatia. As chairman, I had first-hand information about issues affecting Eastern European countries. Monitoring is not the same thing as policing. One cannot police sovereign states, except in extreme situations, but through this committee the council could give a helping hand to states facing difficulties.

Besides freezing the island's application to join the EU, the government set about dismantling VAT and replacing it with a hotchpotch system, which also required traders to keep the cash registers they thought they had got rid of with the change of government. Those who had foolishly smashed their cash registers during the victory celebrations, thinking they would not be needing them again, were not amused.

Bureaucrats in Brussels could hardly understand the government's decision to freeze the island's EU membership application, more so when negotiations with Malta had been expected to start six months after the conclusion of the IGC. Since the IGC was about to conclude its work, I pleaded with the government to reconsider its stand, or at least to carry on with the negotiations and decide on the basis of the outcome. In my view, Malta was losing its appointment with destiny and denying a great future to the island's younger generation. But the MLP was adamant against membership at that stage and were prepared to revert to the 1970 agreement, the one George Borg Olivier had signed as a first step towards closer union with Europe. I still cannot understand the arguments put forward at the time against membership. In adopting this stand, the MLP earned a negative mark in the island's history, as negative as that they had earned over their integration proposal.

A positive event taking place in Malta at the time, April 15–16, 1997, was the Euro-Mediterranean Conference of Ministers of Foreign Affairs. Although the conference was held in Malta more by default than by any positive action on the part of the government, it was in line with the positive Mediterranean approach successive administrations had been taking. George Vella took an active part but, owing to lack of political will, the conference failed to reach a common stand.

In Parliament the government was facing difficult situations following the presentation of its budget, which in our opinion had no 'social conscience'. Water and electricity rates were raised, a move which, we said, was not justified as there had been no rise in the price of oil. Taking up the challenge, Mintoff denounced the budget, arguing it was against the interests of the working class. Bold in his language, sometimes verging on the vulgar, Mintoff won back the attention of those who had almost forgotten the fiery characteristics he displayed with so much vigour in the past. He held the attention of all, Nationalists and Labourites, whenever he appeared on television. Alfred Sant simply did not know how to tackle him. For a time he chose to ignore him, but this only served to strengthen Mintoff's challenge on behalf of the workers. I had a feeling Alex Sceberras Trigona and Maria Camilleri were on his side. I got to know Camilleri better in our parliamentary sessions at the Council of Europe in Strasbourg. She is intelligent, very dedicated to her work as a teacher, and took her work as MP seriously.

What made the situation politically tense was Mintoff's threat to vote against the government. One day I was in Cape Town in South Africa for a meeting of the Independent World Commission for the Oceans when I received an urgent telephone call from Malta that I was required home as they were expecting to have an important vote taken in House and there was a possibility that Mintoff might vote against the government. Violet had come with me to see her brother, who was the island's consul in Cape Town. On the flight back, our seats were at the back of the plane. Most of the passengers were heavy South African nationals and one sitting next to Violet snored part of the flight away, with his head resting on her shoulder!

I had to pay over Lm1,200 out of my pocket for the flight arrangements. It was early in the morning when we arrived in London, from where we were to take an Air Malta flight to Malta. When I phoned Malta to check about the situation, I was told the crisis had blown over but that we were still required in the House as the situation was uncertain. This was quite understandable but it made our 24-hour stay in Cape Town even more memorable than it would probably have been had we stayed on for the time we had planned.

Faced with Mintoff's revolt, the strong opposition we were putting up, and the somewhat unfavourable reaction from the GWU, Sant withdrew some of the negative parts of the budget. But soon another issue cropped up: the development of a yacht marina in Cottonera. The project had been hastily drawn up and the interests of the people living there, who made use of the area for recreational purposes, had not been taken into consideration. The Nationalist opposition criticised the draft agreement reached with the developers and Mintoff turned the issue into a full-scale battle. When he is on the warpath, Mintoff is usually a formidable warrior. He launched his attack in Parliament but he also sought publicity in the media to press his point home. I am sure he knew he had some support from within the party's parliamentary group but he would not expose them as this would have meant the destruction of their political career.

Mintoff obviously knew how much his vote mattered. Nobody from the government side dared speak to him but I kept my contact with him all the time. My link was possibly the only bridge of communication between our side and Mintoff. We used to meet in his room downstairs at the Palace, where I had my office when I was interior and justice minister. The press was aware of our meetings, which sometimes took place immediately Mintoff spoke to the press. At these press conferences, he would criticise the government for the project and the opposition for not being strong enough in its criticism.

Sant could take it no more. Instead of wisely finding a way of putting off the stand-off until he persuaded Mintoff of the validity of the project, he brought matters to a head, staking the life of his own government in the process. He was wrongly advised to call Mintoff's bluff, and in taking this advice he showed that he did not know Mintoff enough. Mintoff had a penchant for bringing governments down. He had done it to Boffa and to Borg Olivier and he was now at it again. Sant decided, quite unrealistically, to take the issue to the squares. He should have sensed that his party was not behind him in so far as the strategy he had adopted was concerned, more so when he chose to make a frontal attack on Mintoff in Vittoriosa, calling him *traditur* (traitor). Mintoff had never expected this reaction and I was sure he would make Sant pay a high price for it. Meanwhile, in Parliament Sant was bringing me into the picture, hinting that I had been in cahoots with Mintoff in a plot against his government. Imagine Mintoff plotting with me to bring down a Labour government! Obviously the opposition had all the political will to bring down the government on the first opportunity that arose. I still do not know if Sant really believed the 'plot' idea or if it was merely a ploy on his part to keep his team together. It was almost summer and Sant appeared to take the whole affair lightly, telling the people to take their holiday as usual. His famous words were 'go and relax'. However, none could take him seriously.

Sant's master stroke of self-destruction came when he put the Cottonera marina agreement to a vote. Mintoff had insisted for long that he had not planned to vote Sant out of office as this could bring Fenech Adami back in power. He made it clear, however, that Sant should not turn the matter into a vote of confidence as even this would not deter him from voting against it. Sant should have reflected on this and avoided a head-on confrontation with Mintoff, but he unwisely chose to carry on with his plan. Ultimately, the matter was put to the vote and Sant's government was defeated.

There were several within the MLP who considered it political madness for the party to call new elections. One was deputy leader George Abela. Sant believed he could still win the elections and smash Mintoff. In the elections, I contested Hamrun/Valletta and Sliema again. I worked untiringly, and must have gone up and down thousand of stairs on my home visits in Valletta. For the first time ever, Violet also took an active part in the election campaign. Together with Giannella they were very well received in the parts of Valletta that they visited. I made Malta's return in the queue to join the EU the basic point of my election campaign. A few days before the general election, both *The Sunday Times* and the *Independent on Sunday* reported that Malta would be receiving some Lm100,000,000 if Malta joined the EU. At one mass meeting, I read out what the two newspapers had reported from Brussels. The elections were held on September 5, 1998. Mr Mintoff had left everyone uncertain as to whether or not he planned to contest the elections. In the end, he decided not to, ending his long parliamentary career.

On September 6, Violet's birthday, the results gave a clear win to the Nationalist Party. We were back in government. But even more important in so far as I was concerned, our election victory re-opened the way for EU membership.

50

Not a switch-on switch-off affair

As soon as I took the oath of office, I was on the move again. My ministerial car came in with the smoothness that it had left in October, 1996. Within days I flew to Vienna to present to the Austrian chancellor, Wolfgang Schussel, a letter requesting the reactivation of the island's application for EU membership. Austria held the presidency of the union at the time. In my first meeting with Schussel after the elections, I argued that Malta deserved to be put in the same position it held in October 1996, that is, grouped with the countries that were set to become members in the first enlargement. Schussel was not too specific in his reaction but he was pleased that Malta was on the road back to membership.

I started visiting Brussels regularly to lobby on Malta's behalf with the commissioners, and at the General Assembly in New York I made it a point to meet several EU ministers to inform them personally of Malta's reactivation of its membership application. I recall discussing the island's position at length with Commissioner Hans van den Broek whom I knew well since I had been directly involved in the negotiations that had led Malta reach pole position with the other countries set for the first enlargement. The commissioner heard me with his usual courtesy and said that our letter for the reactivation of our membership application would be considered by the commission in due time. I reacted strongly to this, arguing that we were re-elected explicitly on the mandate that we would unfreeze the membership application. Once again, I held that we had already gone far ahead in the membership process, so much so that membership negotiations proper had to start with us within six months after the conclusion of the IGC. The conference had by then been concluded and I argued that we should once again take our place in line for membership.

Van den Broek must have sensed my impatience. He turned to me and said: 'Guido, joining Europe is not a switch-on switch-off affair.' I replied

273

that this had not been the case and that my government was firm in its commitment to see the island form part of the EU. I asked if this was the EU's way of punishing Malta for having frozen the application because, if it were, it would only be punishing those who had sought to put the island back on track. Van den Broek appeared to have understood my impatience, but he did not seem all that convinced by my arguments.

Most EU foreign ministers reacted positively to my plea for Malta to be considered with the rest of the other countries being considered for enlargement. Others expressed reservations and wanted to check the position following the negotiations the Labour government had had with the commission in the 22 months they had been in power. One in particular, the Finnish foreign minister, Tarja Halonen, asked me about Schussel's stand on the matter. When I said I believed he had been very positive, she reacted sharply, saying he should not have done so because of the negotiations the previous Maltese government had had with the commission. I well realised that the way back to the course of joining the EU was not going to be as smooth as I had expected and that we might have to pay dearly for the interruption in the membership process.

When I was in New York for the General Assembly, the American Ambassador to Malta, Catherine Proffitt, and Malta's permanent representative to the UN, George Saliba, had made arrangements for me to meet Tom Pickering, the US under-secretary for political affairs. At the time of my presidency of the UN, Pickering was his country's permanent representative to the UN and he had been against my visit to the Palestinian refugees in 1991. At the meeting, held in the private apartment of the US permanent representative at the Waldorf Towers, Pickering told me that Malta was in breach of the sanctions against Libya and that, unless this stopped, 'we will be applying sanctions against you'. I was taken aback by this categorical statement and argued that the government I represented had been back in power for only a few days and my time had been taken up with the reactivation of the island's EU membership application.

To the best of my knowledge, Malta's relations with the US had been good, and the former foreign minister, George Vella, too, had spoken of our excellent relations with the US. In an equally blunt manner, I told Pickering that, since I had only been foreign minister again for a few days, I assumed he had raised the matter with my predecessor. He said he did not recall doing so but added that the breach of sanctions had been going on for quite some time and that he had planned proposing to the US to impose sanctions against us. If anything, I replied, any sanctions would have to be applied by the UN sanctions committee, with which my party had always cooperated when we were in power. Indeed, I recalled a time when we had asked the committee for advice over the export of shoes to Libya. We had been told that shoes, too, were listed among the goods covered by the sanctions since these could be used by soldiers. Pickering said he was not referring to sanctions by the UN committee but by the US government. I asked Pickering for a report of the allegations to be made in writing and to inform our government of the time when the island allegedly started breaking the sanctions. At this point, Pickering blurted the name of Medavia, a Maltese registered company owned by the Libyan-Arab Maltese Holding Company, Air Malta, and Libyan Arab Foreign Investment Co. I said that, to my knowledge, Medavia had not been involved in breaking any sanctions and insisted that the allegations be made in writing. Despite the highly provocative manner in which Pickering announced his intentions, I remained calm throughout the meeting. I felt Pickering had acted arrogantly, especially when he threatened unilateral sanctions. When I returned to Malta, I asked for an investigation to be made of Pickering's allegations but it turned out that they were unfounded.

During my visit to New York, I had lunch with Abu Zaid Omar Durda, Libya's chief representative to the UN, with whom I had and still have a good working relationship. Durda had worked hard for the removal of sanctions against his country and had eventually succeeded. I had personally favoured a peaceful solution that would take into consideration Libya's responsibilities and the suffering of those who had lost relatives in the Lockerbie bombing. Malta had a direct economic interest in keeping good relations with Libya as, besides its trade with that country, hundreds of workers worked there. Malta had observed the UN sanctions against Libya to the letter, but it had not severed its friendship with the Libyan people.

In my talks with the Italian government and with EU Commissioner Mario Monti, I found genuine support for Malta's application to take its rightful place in the EU. By contrast, a meeting I had in Madrid with Abel Matutes, the Spanish foreign minister and a former EU commissioner, was rather cool. Matutes knew what I had gone through to see Malta reach pole position for membership. He said it was now up to the commission to verify the island's status following the freezing of the membership application, a process that required time. But I argued that the commission had been well aware of what had been happening in

Malta as it was represented on the island. I pleaded for Spain's support so that Malta would not lag behind. It seemed that by the end of the meeting, he began to take a more favourable stance towards the island. I am only giving this background to show how difficult diplomacy can be at times. To make matters worse, we were not even invited to the EU summit to which countries that are given the commission's *avis* are generally invited.

One day in January, Eddie sent for me at Castille and I obviously thought he wanted to be updated about my work over the EU application. However, he spoke to me about the presidency, saying that since the matter of appointing a new president had to come up again in three months' time, he wanted to avoid a repetition of what happened last time when I had not been approached before Ugo Mifsud Bonnici. He wished to know what I thought about the matter, adding that perhaps the best solution was for me to remain foreign minister and the government would try to renew Ugo's mandate, provided the opposition agreed to this. I said my aim was to see the commission authorising the start of negotiations with Malta and to ensure that we were grouped among the countries to join in the first enlargement. The conversation stopped there. I realised that if the opposition were to fail to agree with the government about the renewal of Ugo's term, I could find myself in a position of having to leave the post of foreign minister with my work incomplete. I considered my work would be complete when the island was given the green light to start negotiations.

When King Hussein of Jordan died on February 7, 1999, I was sent to represent the government at his funeral. I recall Shimon Peres telling me at the funeral of the king's vital contribution to the Arab-Israeli dialogue. The king, he said, had had the courage to stand by his convictions. Whenever I found myself abroad, for whatever event, at meetings I had with government leaders, ministers, commissioners, and other politicians, I made it a point of raising Malta's aspiration to join the EU. At times I felt my patience was running out, which is bad in diplomacy. This was particularly so when, during my visit to Amman, I met Van den Broek. When I pointedly asked him about Malta's latest position regarding its application, he again appeared hesitant, saying, for example, that they had been waiting for a report about Malta and reminded me once again that Europe was not a switch-on switch-off affair. I argued Malta's case, pointing out that he had been well aware of the government's commitment to see Malta in the EU and that Malta had been made to wait for its *avis* because of some alleged problems over a Danish referendum.

Malta represented no big problems to the Union. Far from being a switch-on switch-off affair, the Nationalist government had been consistent in its determination to see Malta join Europe for nine years and there had only been a break of two years. Joining Europe, I held, was an ideal which no delay was going to deter the people from reaching. Some bureaucrats in Brussels might have thought that Malta had ruled out membership when the Labour government opted to work out new arrangements with the EU, but they were wrong, as later events had well shown. I am sure Van den Broek did not expect such strong reaction, but there are moments in politics when one cannot leave matters to chance. Later that day, Van den Broek told me he had gone to many working lunches and working dinners before, but not to a working funeral! In fact, I have reason to believe that it had been this 'working funeral' that led the way for Malta to resume the road back to membership with the other candidates. Some weeks later the EU commission advised the European council that Malta be put in its previous position, that reached in the Corfu and Essen summit meetings. The commission also told the council that negotiations with Malta could start immediately the summit meeting approved its advice.

In less than six months I had undone the harm caused to the membership process in the previous two years. The difficult political battle had been won. It was now time for the island to enter into the technical part of the negotiations, for which we had also prepared ourselves well.

In April 1999 a Euro-Mediterranean Conference of Ministers of Foreign Affairs was planned to be held in Stuttgart, Germany and I flew to Cairo, Damascus, and Beirut in an effort to have a strong Arab participation in the conference. In talks with political leaders, we discussed the situation in Palestine and ways to make the Euro-Med process more effective. We particularly discussed how the Arab world could become a prominent participant in the process. I believe it is in Europe's interest to develop a better understanding with the Arab world. I explained to those Arab leaders who were showing distrust in Western advances that Europe was stretching its hand in friendship. The Euro-Med process was one such effort on Europe's part but it had to have a response from the Arab world. Meanwhile, a new government had taken over in Germany and I thought it would be wise to meet the new deputy minister of foreign affairs, Gunter Verheugen who some weeks later was appointed EU commissioner in charge of enlargement.

Eddie had to undergo major heart surgery and for some time I had to take over his work. He was in high spirits before the operation. Very typical of him, the first thing he asked me when he recovered was how we had fared in the local council elections. I used to go and see him almost every day, to keep him company in the difficult recovery period and to keep him informed of developments.

By this time the time had come for the matter of the appointment of the new president to be decided upon. Since Ugo had earned the respect and esteem of the MLP when it was in government, I thought the opposition would agree to the proposed renewal of his term. In the time Eddie was indisposed, talks with the opposition over this were carried out by Lawrence Gonzi. Since I was a potential candidate for the post, we did not think it was correct for me to take a direct part in the talks.

In the meantime I carried on with my work at the foreign office. Walter Balzan, who had been giving such an outstanding service at the ministry and had obtained excellent experience at the UN as deputy head of mission, was appointed permanent representative at the UN. William Spiteri was re-appointed ambassador to Germany where he had given a very good account of himself in the post. He was a hard-working diplomat and had also ensured the smooth transfer of the mission and residence from Bonn to Berlin. His re-appointment was in the country's interests. I posted Joe Cassar as ambassador in Rome. He was the right man for the post, not only because of his diplomatic skills but also because of his deep knowledge of Italian language and culture. He had studied at the Università Cattolica of Milan at an interesting period in Italy's history.

George Bonello du Puis was appointed high commissioner in London. George is a perfect gentleman with whom I had been friends for many years and I thought it was wise to utilise his experience. He was also energetic and there was no question about his integrity. The political appointment of Richard Matrenza, whom I had known since the 1940s, was terminated by mutual agreement at a time when Richard thought it was best for him, taking into account his particular circumstances at the time. We are still friends, even though politically we did not always see eye to eye. From New York Ambassador George Saliba was sent to Washington but I kept Victor Camilleri in Brussels where he did an excellent job. Salvu Borg, another hard-working diplomat, was sent to China where he also did a good job. Michael Bartolo was kept in Geneva and I kept Salvu Stellini as permanent secretary. These are only some of the movements I had to make but I believe they were key appointments to the ministry.

In so far as my secretariat was concerned, I had kept Joe Tonna as my personal secretary. Tonna, whom I have known for over 40 years, is a loyal secretary and I admire his great sense of correctness and dedication to his work. He creates the right atmosphere in the office. David Casa, young and energetic, took a political approach to issues, but he kept in mind that a ministry could not be partisan in its work. Joanna Darmanin was very prepared as a diplomat, excellent at writing memos and briefs. Chris Grima is also an accomplished diplomat and competent in energising the ministry's work; he is now ambassador to Vienna. Jean Paul Grech was a very good coordinator. He was later posted to Vienna where he could continue with his duties on work connected with the OSCE. Today he is our ambassador in Berlin, a much-deserved promotion. In charge of works and minor staff was my 'chiefy', Charles Abela. He is loyal, patient, and efficient. All the staff I had with me at the ministry were always kind to me and worked very long hours without protest. Vincent Camilleri, a former police sergeant, was assigned to me when I first became minister in 1987 and he has been with me as security driver ever since. Lourdes Micallef had first come to work at my office when she was in her teens when I was interior and justice minister. She followed me to the foreign office until October 1996 and came to work at my secretariat again in 1998.

In 1998 the prime minister assigned a parliamentary secretary to my ministry, Dr Joe Borg. Joe was elected to Parliament in a by-election on the resignation of John Rizzo Naudi. He was previously in charge of the European Directorate which he had set up. At the ministry he was mainly in charge of pending accession negotiations and coordinating European issues with other ministries. He does not seek to be a charismatic but he does his work thoroughly. He is a man of substance.

In the talks over the appointment of a new president, the opposition leader disagreed with the renewal of Ugo's term and it appeared too that he did not agree with the government's proposal to have me appointed instead. Dr Sant proposed Dr Edwin Grech, a minister in Sant's administration and father of Karin, the girl killed in the letter-bomb explosion. He was a friend of mine during our student days at St Aloysius College. Not much appears to have been said against me in the talks with Dr Gonzi, except that I had 'plotted' with Mintoff to bring Sant's government down, which is a figment of the MLP's imagination, and that I had been strongly pushing for the island's membership of the EU. I had a feeling the position was therefore at a standstill. The PN's parliamentary group had formally endorsed my nomination for the post and, when the proposal was formally made to me, I accepted in the knowledge that accession negotiations with EU were now imminent. I believed that in my new role I could contribute to further unification.

To stand for the presidency, an MP has to resign from the House because, since the president is elected by the House, he cannot himself be an elector. I had been a member of Parliament for 33 years, spending the best part of my life either on the government or the opposition benches. Resigning from the House was worse than when I had left the legal profession in 1987. At least then I felt there was still a possibility of returning to the profession at some future date, as in fact I did when we lost the general elections in October 1996. It was different this time. Under our system, and in practice if not in theory, when one is elected to the presidency, there is no going back. My last day in Parliament was March 23, 1999. I could hardly believe it. Parliamentary life simply grows on you. I had first been elected when I was 34. My two daughters were eight and six respectively, and my son, not even one year old. Now I was a grandfather of four: Joe was already 17, Gianluca and Angelica 16, and Matthias 11. I had never thought of leaving the House, not even in the worst of times. I had always felt close to my supporters who had voted for me without interruption. I had now become father of the House.

Naturally, I had consulted my wife and my children before accepting the nomination. For the first time since my election to Parliament, my family wished to be present in the House on my last day to hear me make my farewell address. It was an emotional moment for me. That evening the adjournment should have belonged to the opposition but, given the circumstances, they renounced their time so that I could take the adjournment. I was asked by the speaker to adjourn the House at 9 p.m., something I had been accustomed to doing as leader of the House.

This time I was to adjourn the House for Wednesday, March 24, at 6 p.m. When I finished reading the agenda, the speaker, my dear friend Anton Tabone, put the formal question, 'Any remarks?', and gave me the floor. I said that when I had first been elected to the House, Malta had been independent for only a year and a half. There was at that time a great sense of renaissance. For the first time ever, in centuries, we Maltese had become independent. For the first time there was no foreigner ruling over our country. This was the background to the time when I had taken my place in Parliament. The 'young lions' of the time lacked experience but we could follow the example set by our political class since the island had had its first self-government constitution in 1921. Our politics had been very confrontational but even in the worst of circumstances we had always finally managed to find a consensual approach to the most difficult of issues. I brought up the 'break with Britain' resolution which finally saw the main political parties take the road to independence and recounted our recent political experience.

I referred to parliamentarians who had guided us in our early years as MPs, particularly Borg Olivier. He taught us how to turn time to our advantage and how to de-dramatise a situation whenever possible as this leads to the finding of better solutions. I mentioned Giovanni Felice for his wisdom and statesmanship; Ċensu Tabone for his perseverance; Dom Mintoff for his energy and vitality; Anton Buttigieg for his poetic approach to life; Ġużè Cassar whom we all liked and usually called *Żiju Ġus*, and Joe Abela who preferred to resign rather than risk his integrity.

I then put the question: 'Why are we in Parliament?' We were in Parliament to serve, even though we were so very often maligned and hurt. I spoke about idealism in politics. Idealism was not incompatible with realism. While the aim of every party was to be in government, serving in opposition was also a contribution to democracy. I observed how the opposition had co-operated in the setting up of the committees of the House; how through discussions and understanding we had managed to find a solution to the issue over our national day. It was true that five national days were rather cumbersome but solutions were preferable to conflicts. If Malta had a good standard of living, this was also due to the wise guidance of its political class. We owe to Malta's political class the social advancement of Maltese society. What did the Maltese expect from their politicians? Integrity was fundamental. As a rule Maltese politicians had lived up to their reputation.

I also referred to Sir Ugo Mifsud who, in making one of the finest speeches ever delivered in the House in defence of human rights, suffered a heart attack and died two days after. He was defending the right of Maltese who were about to be exiled from their country. These were the kind of politicians who had formed our character. I then spoke about democracy as being an achievement to which members of the House had contributed. On a personal note I asked members of the House to forgive me if I had failed them in some way or other. Nobody needed to ask my forgiveness for I felt that no one had failed me.

The House was charged with emotion. My speech was greeted with applause from both sides. When I left the House, I was surrounded by members from both parties, who came over to congratulate me. Joe Tonna organised a small reception at my office in Parliament. Violet and my children were there. There were tears in their eyes. Leaving Parliament was one of the most difficult moments in my life.

I wrote to Eddie, recalling the times we had worked together for so many years to see that the country enjoyed full democracy and have an acceptable level of prosperity. We had given Malta a sense of direction and an international dimension. We had also put the island on the road to EU membership and helped improve our society. I thanked him for the trust he had shown in me and particularly for his friendship. Eddie answered me that very day:

'I have just received your letter with today's date, where you informed me of your resignation as a member of Parliament, and consequently also as minister. During the 30 years that you have served in Parliament, you worked wisely and with great efforts so that our country moves forward by changing what was bad and reinforcing what was good. You gave a great contribution so that our country strengthened itself in its democracy and in the absolute respect to the dignity of man.

'This work you continued delivering with great generosity and ability at the time you served as a minister. The work that you carried out especially in the field of our country's international relations resulted in our country being regarded with greater respect.

'Your ability and continued advice were of great support to me in the running of our country. For all this, I heartily thank you. I wish you further success in your work in the interests of our people.'

These letters were not just official letters. They expressed our real sentiments for each other. I sent my letter of resignation to the speaker of the House. On March 24, the prime minister gave notice to the clerk of the House of a motion appointing me as president of Malta. The motion came before the House on March 29. Eddie made his first presence in the House after his heart surgery. Lawrence Gonzi, on behalf of the government, moved the motion for my appointment, saying he was sure that Prof. de Marco was the best choice for the post and his appointment had been supported by the majority of the people.

The opposition leader spoke against the motion. He considered me as a bad choice for the presidency since, only up to a few days before, I had been in the thick of the controversy over Malta's membership of the EU. In his opinion, I could not be seen as a person that symbolised unity. Indeed, he felt I was a bad choice as I personified political controversy.

Furthermore, Sant said: 'Prof. de Marco had a prime role in the plot last year which undermined the Labour government and made an early election inevitable.' For the first time in the five elections to the post since the proclamation of the republic in 1974, the opposition moved the name of another candidate, Edwin Grech. The opposition's amendment was defeated, while the motion to elect me was voted for by the House. I had become the sixth president of Malta. It was the 33rd anniversary of the death of my father. I always felt he must have been praying for me all these 33 years I had been in Parliament. That evening I said a special prayer for him.

51

President of Malta

For a few days between my resignation from Parliament and taking over as president of the republic, I went to Rome with Violet to relax and start preparing my inaugural speech. I was 67 and in good health. I wanted to make my speech a mission statement for the presidency, stating my beliefs and highlighting the values that identify us as a people. I particularly wanted to go through the history of our nation to show how it had struggled along the centuries to hold on to its identity. The Maltese who lived during my time have lived a dream. Naturally, I also wished to express my indebtedness to my predecessors in the presidency and to reaffirm my commitment to the country's future.

Before taking over, I had to form my secretariat. I kept Achille Mizzi, who was secretary to the presidency under my predecessor. I also kept Capt. David Mifsud as my ADC. He had also been ADC to Ugo Mifsud Bonnici. I also kept those of the clerical staff who wished to remain with me. I brought Joe Tonna along with me as personal secretary while Joanna Darmanin was my diplomatic officer. Also joining the staff were Lourdes Micallef and Tanya Agius from the foreign affairs ministry. We worked well together, with Tonna, a fatherly figure, being the coagulant between the old and new members of my staff.

I took over on Easter Sunday, April 4, 1999, a most beautiful spring day. The speaker of the House of Representatives and an additional ADC called for me at L'Orangerie in Mile End, Hamrun. I had particularly wished to leave from Hamrun where I had lived for most of my political life. All the family was there to see me off, as were also several of my supporters who had been close to me for years. Some had tears in their eyes as they saw me leave to take up the number one post in the country. At the Palace balcony, Ugo Mifsud Bonnici was taking his last salute and waving back to the crowd in the square. I prayed that when the time came

285

for me to end my term, I would be able to do the same, in full awareness that I would have done my duty.

Sir Anthony Mamo, the first president, Ċensu Tabone, and Ugo Mifsud Bonnici were all at the Palace to see me take the oath of office and of allegiance. Agatha Barbara could not make it that day but she made it a point to call on me some days later. Taking the oath in the Grand Council Chamber was a very solemn moment in my life. Immediately I took the oath, a gun salute was fired and I moved to the centre of the podium to give my inaugural speech. Just before doing so, I glanced for a moment at the audience. On one side, there were members of Parliament, assembled in the chamber as a House. I caught a glimpse of Violet who gave me a reassuring smile. She looked radiant. All this encouraged me to start my speech on the right note.

I first spoke about the president's role, recalling the time when we discussed amendments to the constitution in 1974. 'We wanted to make as few changes as possible to the constitution and we were convinced that, if we left aspects of the presidency undefined, the role would evolve over time according to the historical necessities and the personality of those who occupied this post.' The House had not wanted the president to exercise administrative functions or to duplicate and complicate the functions of the prime minister. It had not wanted the president to be the expression of a political party.

'We wanted a president who could rise above party politics; we wanted a president who, when speaking on behalf of the government of Malta, could reflect the policy of the democratically elected government. We wanted, above all, the president to be the symbol of national unity; we wanted the president to represent us all; to speak on our behalf, because we wanted him to be the president of Malta, of all Malta, not of one part or another of the Maltese spectrum.' I also spoke about Malta's role in the international affairs, saying, for instance, that the island could develop a relevant policy in Europe and the Mediterranean and, in this respect, take the opportunity posed by its size and position to foster peace and stability in the region. I was fully aware of the difficult situation that existed not far from the island's shores.

Another point I made was that in my view Malta had to be valued and used as an instrument of peace, through positive diplomacy, built on moral values and the logic of persuasion. When I reached the end of my speech, the part where I said that 'I have lived my life close to the people, so I intend to remain', the audience burst into applause. Then Violet and I, as well as

Ugo and Gemma Mifsud Bonnici were escorted to the Palace balcony and the crowd in the square greeted us enthusiastically, calling my name over and over again – 'Guido, Guido'.

We were afterwards escorted to the Ambassadors' Room where I received the Companion of Honour decoration and, as required, I was entrusted with responsibility for the Order under *Ġieħ ir-Repubblika* Act. When I left the Palace on my way to the War Memorial for my first official ceremony as head of state, I was once again greeted enthusiastically by the people in the square and in Republic Street. When I laid a wreath at the foot of the monument, my mind raced back to the time when it had been inaugurated and to when my mother used to take us there to see wreath-laying ceremonies.

At San Anton Palace, we were greeted at the door by the palace staff. Some of them were already known to me. Shortly after we arrived, the prime minister and Mrs Fenech Adami called to pay their respects. All the family were invited to lunch at San Anton. My mother's sister, Zia Maria, flew over from Bergamo for the occasion. She reminded me so much of my mother. In the afternoon I went to St Cajetan's church in Hamrun for a thanksgiving Mass said by Fr Joseph Cachia on the 50th anniversary of his priestly ordination. After that, I felt it was time for a coffee at my favourite café, Elia, where I met friends with whom for years I used to enjoy my Sunday mornings. In doing so, I was from the start keeping to the presidential style I had referred to in my speech, that of remaining close to the people. My first day as president was practically over. As we returned home at San Pawl tat-Tarġa, we found that a soldier had been put on guard at the door.

52

Settling in as president

Settling in as president is not as easy as one may think. In the first place it requires a change in *forma mentis*. The political party to which you belonged for so many years is no longer *your* political party. Even in conversation one has to avoid such slips as 'we won' or 'we lost an election'. As president, you cease to belong to a political party. You belong to the nation and you have to behave as such. At some occasions you have to act as spokesperson for the government. When you address the House following an election, the programme of the government is read by the president, but its contents would have been prepared by the cabinet.

When the president is on a state or official visit to another country, he speaks on behalf of the government and he has to project the policies of the government in office. In conversation abroad, he has to explain the government's policies. If there is division in the country, he would be correct in explaining the political situation, but his policy must be that of the government that he, as head of the executive, represents. At home he has to be even more careful and avoid controversies. He has to uphold the democratic nature of society and cannot take sides. He could not, for example, express his personal opinion on whether or not Malta should join the EU. This does not mean that he has no right to raise issues for discussion. There are times when he has to give a voice to the voiceless. Above all, in presiding over the state, the president has to assert his moral authority. Through his statements and personal style, he has to make acceptance of his moral authority an important institution of the state. He has to work for unity and try and bring together all that that makes a nation, its history, its symbols, and its aspirations. He must be in a position to voice the aspirations of the people and promote a common purpose in a spirit of democracy. All this may sound an utopian benchmark, but a president has to do his best to meet the challenge.

Violet and I were very attached to our home, so settling down at San Anton was somewhat difficult, at least at first. Every president adapts the presidential quarters according to his needs and tastes or, to be precise in my case, to my wife's needs and tastes. Violet has very good tastes and I think she contributed to the improvements made to the palace. When we moved in, our two grandsons, Joe and Gianluca, moved in with us. They had been living with us since they were young, so it was natural for them to come with us to San Anton. They settled in in no time.

Violet had to get accustomed to the life of a first lady. She lived the role with competence and ability, and whenever she was required to speak, her speeches were to the point. Violet loved the family, while the Community Chest Fund became her extended family. She took a personal interest in the cases brought to her knowledge. I think the presidency brought us even closer to each other. Since we had to attend quite a number of functions together, we had more time to discuss matters of common interest.

My first appointment abroad was a meeting of the Council of Presidents of the UN in New York in May 1999. It was thanks to my successor as president of the General Assembly, Samir S. Shihabi, that the Council of Presidents was set up. At the time we were all looking forward to the approaching millennium with a sense of adventure and expectation that the unknown usually stimulates. While I was in the United States, arrangements were made for me to see former President George Bush to see if it would be possible for him to fly over to Malta with President Gorbachev for the tenth anniversary of their summit meeting in Malta. I made the invitation on the advice of the US ambassador to Malta, Catherine Profitt, but he could not make it because, I believe, his son, George W. Bush, was contesting the election for the presidency of the US. In New York, I met UN Secretary General Kofi Anan and had other useful meetings.

On my return to Malta, I started my series of meetings with civil society. Meetings with trade union leaders, particularly from the General Workers' Union, the Union Ħaddiema Magħqudin, and other CMTU unions, helped me understand the problems they faced in their work to protect the workers' interests. We met every six weeks and my impression is that they confided in me. On my part, I made it a point to follow up the problems raised and to help in any way I could. I did the same when I met leaders from other organisations, such as the Chamber of Commerce, Federation of Industry, and the GRTU. Schools were in a process of transition at the time, so I thought the best way of learning what was happening was to go right at the place where the action is, the schools.

As is customary for a new president, my first official visit was to the pope. Naturally, meeting a pope is always an event that remains in one's mind. As it happened, my meeting with Pope John Paul II took place at Castel Gandolfo, but the ceremonial trappings of an official visit there, Swiss guards and all, are as impressive as when the pope receives heads of state at the Vatican. The pope greeted me in his study with great affection. A few quotes from my reflections on peace and faith, which I made at my meeting with him may be in order here: 'The Maltese people have shared in the mystery and history of the Christian Faith for almost as long as the great institution of the Church has been in existence. Chronicled in the pages of the Acts of the Apostles... are the acts which brought the message of Christ to our shores, only twenty-seven years after His Crucifixion and Resurrection. St Paul is a symbol of our roots as a people anchored in Christianity, as well as father and inspiration of our actual identity – a people tried through suffering and toil, yet conscious of its role and purpose in building peace – a peace towards each other and those around us. Evangelist and an example to the many peoples he visited, St Paul remains an image followed by so many of our peoples, missionaries, both laymen and clergy, who work for solidarity – in far-away lands – spreading the central message brought to this world by Christ himself – a message of love and dignity.'

I then invited the pope to visit Malta again, particularly in the light of the declaration of attributes of holiness to the Venerable Ġorġ Preca who, among others of our people, had given witness to their faith. In fact, the pope visited Malta less than two years later, and he beatified Ġorġ Preca, Nazju Falzon, and Adeodata Pisani. Although his health was failing him, I was impressed by the clarity of his mind. But the condition he was suffering from restricted his movement. When my family was introduced to him and we were all getting around him for the customary family photo, he had to rely on his *scrittoio* to keep standing upright.

In Rome, I also called on the Italian president, Carlo Azelio Ciampi, whom I had met on other occasions, and on the grand master of the Sovereign Military Order of Malta, Fra Andrew Bertie, at Palazzo Malta in Via Condotti, always a most interesting place to go to when in the Italian capital. Ciampi is a man of great competence and personal charm while Fra Andrew is a learned man. His knowledge of languages, history, and literature is quite comprehensive, but what particularly strikes me is his holiness, which he keeps to himself. I could see for myself that it gives him a great sense of serenity. I fell much indebted to him.

My next overseas trip was to Fiji in the South Pacific to give the first Arvid Pardo Memorial Lecture. It was a most arduous trip; it took me 36 hours to reach Fiji. My stay there was of only 36 hours, after which I had to fly back to Malta, another 36 hours. But I felt it was a duty to give a lecture which bears the name of a Maltese diplomat who had done so much to advance the Law of the Sea at the UN and, particularly, to launch the concept of the common heritage of mankind. In my lecture, 'A permanent trusteeship council – guardian of future generations: Malta's imitative at the United Nations', I spoke of how 'Malta's proposal moved from the realm of utopia, which could be conveniently ignored, to the realm of politics… We had linked our wagon to a star. Some at that time considered our proposal as utopian. Others, perhaps more positively inclined, considered us as idealists, who with subtlety argued that there is a wide gap between idealism and realism. I have always maintained that there is no incompatibility in being both idealistic and a realist at the same time. A realist is an idealist who knows when the time is ripe for his ideals to become a reality. We believe that the trusteeship council must be the focal point for that co-ordination which pre-empts tensions while securing the commonwealth of present and future generations.' Unfortunately, it seems that the reform of the trusteeship council, as suggested by Malta, is still far off from being carried out. I often returned to this subject when I lectured on UN reforms at other times.

The 25th anniversary of the republic fell on December 13, 1999. The national festivities were not all that successful, perhaps mainly because of bad weather. In the days leading to Christmas, we also had very much in mind the new millennium that was dawning, two thousand years from the birth of Christ. That year I celebrated Christmas in Bethlehem, at the invitation of Yasser Arafat. And what an experience it turned out to be! I had with me Violet and Angelica. A number of journalists had joined my delegation, including Joe Mifsud, who had been showing keen interest in the Palestinian cause. A scouts' band gave a display in the main square of Bethlehem and nuns waved to Arafat's wife, Suha, who seemed to be very popular among the people there. Arafat told me later that Suha visited the nuns' convent and schools frequently. Bethlehem looked very much the holy city as described to us in our childhood days. Violet, Angelica, and I found our way to the church of the Nativity. It was crowded, but we had seats reserved for us at the front, just behind Arafat and Suha. Massimo D'Alema, at the time prime minister of Italy, was also there with his wife and children. Mass was celebrated by the Latin patriarch and Fr Joe Borg, who was also part of my delegation, concelebrated. When Mass ended, we were taken to the spot where Christ was born 2,000 years ago. Arafat took hold of my hand and together we went down the steps to the crib. Though Arafat was a Muslim, he believed in a secular democratic Palestinian state. He felt Palestine was the home of the three major monotheistic religions and the place for the children of Abraham, who had the same roots to their belief. The Latin patriarch was Mgr Michael Sabah, a Palestinian who had great faith in Arafat's leadership.

We spent Christmas Day in the city where the Saviour was born; for a time Bethlehem was a city of peace and understanding. Close to midnight, when we preparing to go to bed, Arafat sent me word that he wished to speak to me with some urgency. Since I had been with him only a few hours before, when he made me a member of the Order of Bethlehem, I wondered what he wanted me for at that late hour. After apologising for calling me, Arafat said he knew I had a scheduled meeting with the Israeli Prime Minister Ehud Barak the following day and wished to pass on a message to him. He said he did not mind being continuously insulted in the Israeli press. That was to be expected, but he could not stand seeing the Jewish settlements being trebled instead of being removed. In the face of such open defiance by the Israelis, the Palestinian people were losing faith in his leadership. Arafat felt Israel was doing this on purpose. In effect, this meant he could not negotiate on the Palestinians' behalf and he feared the situation would lead to a second *intifada*. He did not want this to happen as it was not in the interests of his people. Arafat had tears in his eyes as he was telling me this.

So my visit to Barak turned out to be more important than a protocol visit by a head of state. I had known Barak since 1995 when he had first become foreign minister under Shimon Peres. We first met at a Euro-Med meeting in Barcelona. His background was more military than political. Rated as the most decorated Israeli soldier, he was nevertheless gentlemanly in his manners but I did not think he had the same political depth as Shimon Peres. Barak started out explaining his problems in running a cabinet made up of a coalition of parties, including the religious parties. I realised the introduction was a sort of an advance reply to what he assumed I would be telling him following my meeting with Arafat. Then he spoke about the Palestinian issue, and tried to give the impression that he was doing his utmost but the Palestinians were difficult to get round a table.

At this point I passed on Arafat's message about the expansion of the Jewish settlements and of its likely consequences. At first Barak tried to switch to some other subject, but when I pressed on the Palestinian issue, he said the problem was not the number of settlements but the settlements themselves. It was the number of settlers that had increased, not of settlements. When I asked if the increase amounted to a trebling of existing settlements, he did not appear to contest the fact. I said this did not help matters, nor did it help bring Arafat to the discussion table. Barak switched back to talking about his difficulties within his own coalition. I thought I had carried out my mission. Like Arafat, I felt that, unless matters were taken in hand, the Palestinians were heading towards a second *intifada*.

I returned home happy that I had been able to hear Mass at the church of the Nativity and sad about the feeling that war would soon return to the Holy Land. We celebrated the end of the twentieth century and the start of the new millennium at the Independence Arena in Floriana. I was asked to say a few words to mark the event but clearly the people were in no mood to hear any speeches at that hour. With good reason, they were only interested in the future – in their own personal future, in that of their family, and of their country. Most were looking forward to seeing Malta join the EU. It was important to work for a positive conclusion of the membership negotiations without any loss of time. The future beckoned indeed.

Less than a month before the start of the new millennium, on December 7, 1999 to be precise, Fiorella gave birth to her third child, Federica. We wished to baptise her at the chapel in San Anton but there were some problems over this and we had to wait until Easter to get the necessary permission. We even planted a tree to mark the baptism, the first, I believe, to have been allowed to take place at the chapel.

53

Start of the Millennium

My New Year resolution was to speak my mind on major issues without being politically provocative. As head of state, I had to meet the executive branches of the government. Prime Minister Fenech Adami used to inform me of the country's situation at our fortnightly meetings and I also began seeing ministers individually. This gave me an opportunity of getting an insight into particular lines of government work. It was essential, too, to keep in touch with parliamentarians of both sides of the House. In the meantime, I still kept lecturing at the university, keeping alive my interest in criminal law. By now I was getting more interested in the work of the UN and its relationship with regional organisations. In fact I spoke about this at a conference organised by the United Nations Association of Spain.

The role of regional organisations, operating under the aegis of the UN, was gaining in importance as, following the end of the cold war, new regional conflicts were arising, creating tension and strife. It was with this in mind that the Maltese government had proposed that the Organisation for Security and Co-operation in Europe (OSCE) be declared a 'regional arrangement' in terms of chapter VIII of the UN charter. There is formal agreement today between the two that has led to cooperation in many zones of tension. It was a landmark move that led the way to similar agreements between the UN and other regional organisations.

In May 2000 I was given the degree of Doctor of Humane Letters, Honoris Causa, from the University of Bridgeport, Connecticut. In my oration, I spoke of the poverty curtain, a subject I had spoken about in my concluding statement as president of the 45th session of the UN General Assembly. I raised as one of the challenges of the future the freedom from want, the fight against poverty, believing as I did, and still do, that the poverty curtain can, as vigorously as the cruelty of the iron curtain, divide the world.

An event that brought a lot of nostalgic memories to me, for reasons that I have already spoken about earlier in these memoirs, was when I addressed the parliamentary assembly of the Council of Europe in June 2000. At the Council of Europe I used to bring up the need of having the Mediterranean agenda closely followed in Europe. When I addressed the assembly, I picked up where I had left off at the time when I was an active member.

'Europe can have an added relevance in world affairs not only through a sound relationship between the Council of Europe and the United Nations, but through the creation of an ongoing dialogue with the southern Mediterranean neighbours. Malta in this council has been positively insistent on promoting this Mediterranean dialogue for it has been our constant belief that stability in Europe and stability in the Mediterranean are inexorably intertwined. Ignoring this reality can have damaging effects. The Mediterranean cannot be an impenetrable sea-wall. The Mediterranean as a great divide spells disaster for future generations. The Council of Europe, through its ring of Mediterranean states, can be a positive forum for dialogue and understanding in the region, for the Mediterranean is a sea that unites us all in our designs.' The speech was very well received. I discussed the same theme at many other international meetings, including one at the Royal Institute for International Affairs at Chatham House in London.

We needed peace and stability not only in the Mediterranean but also in the Middle East. But peace building is a long and arduous task. Even so, as I remarked in a talk at the Peres Centre for Peace in Tel Aviv, it is a road that we must tread, irrespective of the difficulties peace-makers meet. Twenty-five centuries ago, Sun Sin wrote *The Art of War*. Why can't we write, through our actions, *The Art of Peace*? At meetings with Shimon Peres in Tel Aviv and with Arafat in Ramallah, we tried to make the parties reach some kind of settlement but politics in Israel were hardening and the prospects for peace receding.

Let me break away from this theme for a moment and speak about when Violet and I were received by Queen Elizabeth II at Buckingham Palace in 2000. The queen exuded elegance and charm when she welcomed us. I was given the insignia of honorary knight grand cross of the Order of St Michael and St George, an order originally instituted for service given in Malta and the Ionian Islands. The cushion on which the first knight had knelt when he was admitted to the Order is kept at the Palace in Valletta. The queen loves to say that the only place, apart from the United Kingdom, which she could refer to as her home is Malta where, as a princess, she had lived at Villa Guardamangia in Pietà as the wife of a young naval officer. She used to drive around the island alone, doing the shopping herself and sometimes even going to see a film with her husband at a cinema in Qormi.

A state visit to Tirana in Albania brings me back to my role as president. The Albanian president, Rexhep Meidani, did not belong to any political party. He had been appointed in a bid to put the presidency above party politics. I was then, and still am, anxious to see the presidency in Malta play a more significant role in the country's institutional set-up. Indirectly, the visit also reminds me of the institutional and constitutional tie between the president and the judiciary. In fact, as I once remarked to the judiciary, 'There is a bond because the head of the state represents not only the national unity but he is also the guarantor of the constitution and of the institutions of this country. An independent judiciary that safeguards the right of the citizens is one of the constitutional organs basic for the governance of the country. There is a constitutional bond, not only because the nominations for the judiciary are made by the president upon the advice of the prime minister but also because the president of Malta, through the constitution, presides over the Commission for the Administration of Justice.'

Speaking about the qualities one looked for in a judge, I said: 'It is important for a judge to be an authority and be brilliant in law; it is essential that a judge be motivated in his or her work. It is indispensable that a judge be honest.' My conclusion, which I think is significant in the light of events years later, was: 'You, Your honour, honourable judges and magistrates, live this principle every day. For this Malta is grateful to you. For the other issues and problems that I have just mentioned, there are solutions; for honesty there is no substitution. Honesty is indispensable.'

54

The Pope revisits Malta

The year 2001 was a memorable year for Malta as Pope John Paul II revisited the island on the last leg of a pilgrimage he made in the footsteps of St Paul that also included stops in Greece and Syria. His visit had a profound effect on my inner life. In that year, too, I also made a number of state and official visits to foreign countries and strengthened the links between the presidency and the trade unions. I found that the GWU leaders, Tony Zarb, Manwel Micallef, Salvu Sammut, and Michael Parnis, were really dedicated to the union and to the welfare of the workers in a national context. The same can be said of Union Haddiema Magħqudin's leaders, whom I already knew before my appointment as president, in particular Gejtu Tanti and Gejtu Vella. They, too, were strong believers in the workers' cause; they were firm in their attitude but also able to put the workers' interest within the national needs. A milestone in my relations with the trade unions was when I addressed a UHM conference and, later, a GWU congress. I also continued with my visits to local councils.

In March 2001, the University of Malta conferred on me the degree of D.Litt. (Honoris Causa). My link with the university began in 1947 as an 'occasional student' at the faculty of arts. The university was then in St Paul Street, Valletta. I graduated as a legal procurator in 1950, as a bachelor of arts in 1951, and as a lawyer in 1955. I was appointed lecturer in criminal law in 1967, and a professor in 1982. The D.Litt was given to me mainly for services to the country. At the conferment, I spoke about Malta's vision for the future: 'What will Malta be like in the coming years? What values shall we ascribe to our identity as a people, as a nation? What role for Malta tomorrow?'

When I spoke about Malta's identity, I said: 'Identity does not rest solely on a common language, memory, or tradition. Identity is founded on values. Yet the manner in which we value ideas is perhaps the greatest challenge of the contemporary era. Dialogue about values presupposes that we value them. Values give us anchorage. They give us a point of reference. We denounce war because we have faith in man's ability to settle international disputes without resorting to death and destruction. The ruthless exploitation of labour is intolerable because we cherish the dignity of all human beings. We condemn the death penalty with the same vigour as abortion because we cherish the right to life... Like other people in the region, we are at one and the same time European and Mediterranean. These two aspects of our identity are reflected in our culture, our lifestyle, and our traditions. Neither should prevail at the cost of the other.'

I then referred to the then on-going debate about membership of the European Union as being itself a reflection of our democracy. I spoke about the future: 'I wanted to share with you some of my thoughts on the fundamentals which will set the path of our future. We have to live the future. We have to ensure a future not based on ideologies but on ideas. Our experience with ideologists in the past century has exposed us to conflicts and intolerance. We, as a people, will face the future by making full use of our characteristics; a language that binds us to both sides of the Mediterranean; a Latin culture that identifies us with Europe; the knowledge of an international language, which links us to the world; the continuity of a faith, which binds us to a message of love and universal solidarity... I believe that in the coming years the Maltese people will live a new renaissance. Successive generations, through their hard work, will achieve a higher quality of life. They will make of solidarity their commitment and of bridge-building among peoples their mission. Anchored to our values, the Maltese people shall, with confidence, face the challenges that a wider world to which we belong will demand.'

Some called the speech a sort of a political testament. Well, as it happened, it came very close to being my last will and testament as only two days later I had one of my closest brushes with death. It happened on March 14, the second day of a state visit to Bulgaria, when we were on our way back to Sofia after visiting a shrine dedicated to a Bulgarian hermit in the mountains. The shrine was well worth a visit. When it was over, we stopped at a restaurant for a quick meal as I had to be back in Sofia to give a talk at the University of St Clement Ohridski. We had been back on the road for some time when suddenly a trailer crashed into our car, spinning it out of control. I was on the phone with Violet when the incident happened. She heard the crash and thought the worst but I was not injured. The car was badly damaged. Had it not been an armoured car, we would probably have been killed.

The Bulgarian ambassador who was accompanying me turned white. So did our driver. But there was a greater shock to come. In a domino-like fashion, the trailer hit other cars carrying members of my delegation, killing a young Bulgarian security guard and seriously injuring two, Lino Arrigo Azzopardi, a photographer, and a Bulgarian woman, an interpreter. Others were only slightly injured. The interpreter was injured in her eyes. At first it was thought the accident could have been an attempt on my life but the possibility was ruled out soon afterwards. It is more likely the driver of the trailer had been distracted by the carcade and lost control of his vehicle. Several European television stations reported the incident.

When my staff in Malta went over to San Anton to inform Violet of the accident, she told them she had known about it the moment it happened as she had been on the phone with me. What she did not know was how close it had been to a fatal accident. The Bulgarian government was extremely concerned over the crash. I thought it was best not to over-dramatise the accident and decided to carry on with my programme and go directly to the university of Sofia where people were waiting for my lecture. Naturally, I was still feeling somewhat shocked after the crash, but I managed to give the lecture as planned. That day I spoke about the UN and its future.

Immediately afterwards, President Petar Stoyanov came over to see me. I cancelled an official reception I had planned to give as a sign of respect to the security guard who had been killed and to those members of the delegation that had been injured. Instead, later that night I went to visit the injured in hospital. Arrigo Azzopardi was in a very bad shape and I spoke to his sons who wanted to take him to a Swiss hospital. I also went to see the woman who had suffered serious injury to her right eye. Fortunately, her eyesight was safe. I sent a message to the wife of the security guard, expressing my sincere condolences. I gave a press conference the following day before leaving for Slovenia, the second country we had to visit on this trip. As expected, the reporters were mainly interested in the accident we had on the road to Sofia. Louis Galea, who accompanied me during this trip, showed great solidarity with me and with the injured. Louis and I had done a lot of political campaigning together in the past, so we knew each other well. We had also faced a number of dangerous situations together, but not of the kind we experienced in Sofia.

The three countries I visited on this trip were all engaged in membership negotiations with the EU. My aim was to introduce the island as an aspirant EU country and to work for future cooperation among us. In Sofia before the accident, I had been received with full military honours by President

Stoyanov, who belonged to the Popular Party and, therefore, to the Christian Democratic Movement of Europe. We discussed the EU, the situation in the Balkans, the Mediterranean, as well as the issue of the Bulgarian nurses in Libya, eventually freed in 2007. Stoyanov was doing his best to modernise his country, turn it into a healthy democracy, and boost its economy.

As I said, after our Bulgarian visit, we flew to Slovenia. At Llubjana I was received by President Milan Kučan, whom I got to like because he was a clear-minded person and effective in his work. A former communist, in 1991 he had sought the independence of his country from the Federal Republic of Yugoslavia and, in a seven-day war, managed to do so without passing through the ordeal other republics, such as Croatia and Bosnia Herzegovina, had to go through. He was quick in making Slovenia a democracy and in liberalising its economy. I visited the interesting Postojna caves with its magnificent stalactites and stalagmites. The professor in charge of this historic place had a personal story to tell. His grandfather had been a soldier in the army of the Austro-Hungarian empire in World War I. In the World War II his father had served in the Italian army as at that time the area where he lived was Italian territory. He himself had served in the Yugoslav army and his son was about to serve in the Slovenian army. And his grandson? Well, he might join a European army, he said.

From Llubljana we flew to Bratislava. It was my first ever visit to the capital of Slovakia. The country had passed through two important stages in recent years, the first in 1989 with the birth of a movement for liberation from communist domination. I was in Strasburg when Vaclav Havel came over to the Council of Europe to see his country being admitted as a free and democratic member state. I met Havel in 1991 when I visited Czechoslovakia as president of the UN General Assembly. I had given a talk on the UN at the Carolinum University of Prague. Havel had discussed with me the problems he was meeting in keeping the two parts of the country together. I had also met Alexander Dubcek, leader of the Prague spring, a Slovak. The country joined the EU in 2004. I met President Rudolf Shuster in the beautiful castle at Bratislava.

On my return to Malta, I was handed a letter that I had received from Pope John Paul II about his planned visit. There were great expectations and preparations for his visit but, before greeting the pope in Malta, I had to make another state visit, to Estonia, another EU applicant country. Again, as I may have said before, our relations with the other new EU applicant countries were very limited at the time and therefore it was highly useful for such a small country as Malta to establish new ties with them. The president of Estonia was Lennart Meri, a writer and a film director in addition to being a prominent figure in the uprising that led to his country's independence from the Soviet Union. He was a man of high principles, highly committed to safeguarding independence. In my delegation I had Austin Gatt, who was keen on establishing working arrangements with the Estonian government on information technology. The Estonians were moving fast in this direction.

I gave a lecture on 'Europe: Its values, its future' at the University of Tartu. President Meri honoured me with his presence. I spoke of what makes Europe's common heritage and of the contribution given by great figures over the ages, such as Plato, Aristotle, Cicero, Virgil, St Thomas Aquinas, St Francis of Assisi, Dante Alighieri, Shakespeare, Leonardo da Vinci, Michelangelo, Johann Sebastian Bach, Wolfgang Amadeus Mozart, Voltaire, Monet, Goethe, Dostoevsky, Pirandello, Ortega y Gasset, and Alexandr Solzhenitsyn. Through their endeavours and those of many others, Europe's physical and intellectual environment had been largely moulded into that in which we live today. Their achievements represented an integral aspect of a shared European identity, of our common heritage.

I then drew a parallelism between Malta and Estonia. Both were European countries, acting within relatively different geo-political contexts. The country had re-acquired its independence and had made great strides forward. Estonia was a Baltic country and a European nation, which were complementary to each other. Since its independence, Malta had constantly promoted a Mediterranean agenda in discussions about European security and stability. The island had sought to promote dialogue in a region where differences could hit peace and stability. The Maltese people had a Mediterranean and European heritage, identity, and responsibilities. The two aspects of our heritage complemented each other and helped to enrich the country even further. For what, after all, is a nation? French philosopher and writer Ernest Renan put it this way in a lecture he had given at the Sorbonne in 1882: 'The essence of a nation is that its entire people have a great deal in common and also that they have forgotten a great deal. If we were to apply this to our concept of Europe, its values, its future, we can say that the essence of Europe lies in that all its peoples have a great deal in common and also that they have forgotten a great deal. This is our *maison commune*. Here lies our future.'

Back in Malta, the people were closely following the pope's trip to Athens and to Syria and were particularly struck by his visit to a mosque in Damascus. When I welcomed him on his arrival in Malta on May 8, 2001, he looked frail and exhausted. He could hardly walk up the dais. In my speech of welcome, I said the pope's visit was 'in accordance to what St Paul had revealed to his fellow voyagers, when the angel told him, *"in insulam autem quandam oportet nos devenire"* (We have to arrive to a certain island). It is this *oportet* of Providence that has linked the island of Malta to a faith that is eternal, to a love built on the sacrifice of the Son of Man, to a universality inspired by unity in fullness.' I then quoted from the Acts of the Apostles: 'Once safely on shore, we found that the island was called Malta. The islanders showed us unusual kindness. They built a fire and welcomed us all because it was raining and cold.' I went on to say that: 'For the Maltese people, our faith is our country's greatest asset. In a world which need the building of a warming fire because of the rain and cold, you have, Your Holiness, been a driving force of change.' In a very tired voice, the pope expressed his deep feelings at his coming to Malta, reliving the path of St Paul in his evangelising mission.

When I received the pope at the Palace in Valletta, he had recovered a bit from his travel exhaustion. It seemed to me that the more he was in contact with people, the better he felt. In the Tapestry Chamber, he talked about his trip, making particular reference to his visit to the Syrian city of Quneitra, close to the Golan Heights, that had been almost completely destroyed by Israeli forces in 1974. He told me that Cardinal Sodano, secretary of state to the Vatican, was not in favour of his visit to Quneitra as he feared it could have irritated the Israeli government. The pope saw the cardinal's point but he felt that if he had to send a message of peace, he could choose no better place than a city that had suffered the consequences of war. On a different subject altogether, the pope appreciated the island's stand in favour of the family and its defence of life from its inception.

I then introduced my family to His Holiness. We greatly treasure our memories of that meeting. Federica was just a year and a half. He blessed us all, one after the other. Then he gave me as a present a beautiful Madonna and Child in mosaic. It is kept at the Palace, a permanent message of love to the people of Malta from a great and saintly pope. I keep in my study a picture of the pope presenting me with this 'Madonna and Child' as well as the letter which he had sent me expressing his wish to visit Malta.

The pope had recovered completely by the time he had to go to the Palace balcony to wave to the crowd in the square. The people gave him a most enthusiastic welcome and he reacted warmly to them. He was at his best feeling the mood of a crowd. He later had private talks with the prime minister, with the leader of the opposition, and with members of Parliament. When he left the Palace he made us all feel blessed by his presence. It occurred to me then that, had we not installed a lift at the Palace in time, it would not have been possible to welcome the pope there. Of the many great figures who had been to the Palace in the course of the island's history, kings and queens, Napoleon, Winston Churchill, and President Roosevelt, I had no doubt that the pope's visit would be of lasting memory.

The following day we had the beatification of Nazju Falzon, Dun Ġorġ Preca, and Suor Adeodata Pisani. It was a beautiful spring day, as glorious as a Maltese spring day can be, and the thousands who attended the ceremony enjoyed every minute of it. We wished we could somehow freeze this moment in history for a while for us to be able to savour it a bit longer. My wife and I, as well as the prime minister and his wife received Holy Communion from the hand of the Holy Father. In the afternoon the pope visited the church of the Society of Christian Doctrine, MUSEUM, which is close to my house in Blata l-Bajda. He blessed the remains of Dun Ġorġ, (proclaimed saint in 2007), and met members of the society, which he had founded. It was again a moment of great emotion. From Blata l-Bajda, the pope went straight to the airport for his departure. In his parting message, he said:

'Malta is at the centre of the Mediterranean. You therefore have a unique vocation to be builders of bridges between the peoples of the Mediterranean basin, between Africa and Europe. The future of peace in the world depends on strengthening dialogue and understanding between cultures and religions. Continue in your traditions of hospitality, and continue in your national and international commitment on behalf of freedom, justice and peace.'

I saw in these words a mission statement for the people of Malta. I later saw to it that a commemorative plaque be placed on the outer wall of the Palace alongside others marking Malta's independence, the award of the George Cross to the people of Malta by King George VI, and the Roosevelt scroll. In my farewell address, I said: 'Your stay in Malta has lasted barely thirty hours, but your presence in each and every one of us will last a lifetime. For you, through your presence, through your words, and through your deeds, have made us live the fullness of the faith and the richness of the Church... In your voyage, in the footsteps of St Paul, you have taught us the nobility of asking forgiveness, the sharing in the suffering of those who are denied their rights, the conviction that force will give way to dialogue, and that only peace can bring to peoples trust and prosperity.' By way of conclusion, I then said a few words in Maltese: '*Il-poplu Malti kollu jara fik it-twettiq tal-fidi, f'milja ta' mħabba. Berikna.*' (The Maltese people see in you the wholeness of faith in the fulfilment of love. Bless us.) The ceremony over, I extended my hand to him to help him get down from the dais. I still feel the warmth of his hand holding mine; it was a most wonderful feeling and I have treasured the moment since, and always will.

55

Promoting Malta abroad

The government was now getting deeply involved in negotiations with the EU over our membership application and I was kept informed in great detail of developments as they occurred. Besides my usual meetings with the prime minister, I was also in regular contact with the speaker of the House of Representatives, Anton Tabone, and had visits from Chief Justice Joe Said Pullicino. Joe brought to the law courts his *savoir-faire* and his down-to-earth application of the law. He has a pleasant personality which sometimes belies his firmness of purpose. Before he was appointed to the judiciary in 1966, he was part of my legal office, Guido de Marco and Associates. We knew each other well and I had complete trust in his integrity. The president of Malta chairs the Commission for the Administration of Justice which meets on average once a month. In my time as chairman we drew up a code of ethics for judges and magistrates. It was formally presented on May 11, 2001.

I kept in touch with the diplomatic corps, both those who were accredited to Malta and those who represented the island. I made it a point of presenting letters of accreditation myself as I wished to see the level of preparedness of our representatives. Besides, this also helped establish a closer relationship between the head of state and the ambassadors. I also continued the practice of meeting Malta's ambassadors at their annual reunion in Malta, which I had introduced as foreign affairs minister. At such reunions, I invariably made an address of a political nature, highlighting issues of world affairs that were relevant to Malta.

As president, I received at San Anton quite a good number of important figures, including Prince Philip; prime ministers, including those of Tunisia, Mohammed Ghannouchi; of Greece, Kostas Simitis, an extremely intelligent person and a very distinguished personality; of Slovakia, Mikuláš Dzurinda; of Sweden, Göran Persson; as well as Margöt Wallstrom and

Anna Diamantopoulos, European Union commissioners; Nicole Fontaine, president of the European Parliament; Alois Mock, former Austrian foreign minister and a good friend of Malta in difficult years; Fausto Bertinotti, who was responsible for Rifondazione Communista, and is now president of the House of Representatives in Italy – a man of culture who knows how to give a balanced approach to his extreme left political policy; Hans-Dietrich Genscher, former German foreign minister, one of the foremost foreign ministers of his time and who, together with Chancellor Helmut Kohl, contributed to the reunification of Germany; Pierre Moscovici, French foreign minister; Claudio Scajola, Italian interior minister; and Ioannis Kasoulidis, Cyprus's foreign minister.

Meeting such important people was part and parcel of my duties, which I liked since, besides promoting Malta's interests, I also discussed matters of common interest. But there was another duty that was equally important, meeting local people in their localities. This enabled the president to feel the pulse of the country. A president also has to associate himself directly with the people's feelings. When, for example, vandals struck at Mnajdra temples, I went over to the place to see the damage done and later took part in a protest against the vandal act. It was a hideous attack.

The Chinese never forget a friend; so when I paid a 10-day official visit to China in July, accompanied by Violet and Foreign Minister Joe Borg, we were given a warm welcome. We visited Beijing, Shanghai, and Hong Kong. President Jiang Zemin hosted us at a state dinner at which the highest authorities were present. Zemin prides himself on having a good voice and during dinner he sang some romantic Chinese songs for us. Knowing I liked Italian music, he sang 'O Sole Mio'. Zemin was no lightweight; he followed Deng Xiao Ping, the great reformer of China's economy. He had once explained to me how he had managed to convince Deng Xiao Ping of the importance for China to establish free economic zones on the lines of those in other countries and in Hong Kong, then still in UK's hands. Hong Kong was, and still is today, a major freeport. Zemin was very interested in Malta and when I told him of the island's history, its politics, and of its future in Europe and in the Mediterranean, he was astonished and said he would wish to visit the island one day. Since he was scheduled to visit Europe at the time, I suggested he should stop over in Malta. There and then I rang up Eddie, who immediately agreed to invite Zemin to visit Malta.

One day during our visit we were taken for a trip on a large, beautifully decorated boat. Lunch was served by tall, beautiful Chinese girls in regional costumes. In Beijing, we had talks with the foreign minister, Qian Qichen, one of the finest political brains I met in China. In our free time, we visited the Great Wall of China. We have a photo of Federica, not yet two, running along a stretch of the wall. Fiorella and Paul had come with us on this trip at their own expense but when we returned to Malta I was handed an anonymous letter, which had been sent to the minister of finance, saying that they had travelled to China at the taxpayers' expense. The government had not paid one single cent for them.

Beijing is an ever-changing city and Shanghai is even more so, a fast growing metropolis, very modern, very audacious in its view of the future. Our visit to Hong Kong was a most valuable experience. We arrived there in a rain-storm. I went to pay a visit to Teng Chee Hwa, executive secretary of the special and autonomous region of Hong Kong. China keeps a low-key presence in Hong Kong which has a different political system from that on the mainland and I have a feeling that, in keeping Hong Hong as it is, China is sending a political message to Taiwan. In its quest to reclaim sovereignty over Taiwan, China does not want to substitute the political or economic system there for its own; it is ready to recognise a different political and economic system if that is the will of the people in Taiwan, provided Chinese sovereignty is recognised.

Our honorary consul in Hong Kong, Vivien Chou Chen, is very active and efficient. She is very hospitable to visitors from Malta, too. The visit to China consolidated further our political ties with that country. Representatives of Maltese business, who formed part of my delegation, did their part in trying to find markets for locally-made goods and services. While I was in Beijing, I opened our new embassy and visited the College of Foreign Affairs where I gave a talk and received a doctorate degree, Honoris Causa, from this prestigious university. I had also visited the college on my first visit to China in 1991. It is the place where most of China's diplomats receive their training and diplomatic education.

Zemin kept his pledge to visit the island on his European tour. He did so together with his wife and foreign minister Qian Qichen on July 23, 2001. Part of his large delegation stayed at San Anton, the rest at the Corinthia Hotel, Attard. Our kitchen staff had to make way to Chinese staff that had to meet Zemin's dietary needs on his travels. Zemin was highly impressed by Malta, its culture, history, and high standard of living. He was taken to visit the Neolithic temples and was enchanted by Valletta and Mdina. While he was in Mdina, a Falun Gong woman, Wang Wenyi, managed to get close to him and angrily berated him about the harassment and oppression of Falun Gong practitioners. Zemin told her the Falun Gong were killing themselves. The incident made headlines in newspapers in a number of countries.

Zemin told me he was an atheist but he found it useful to meet religious leaders in China. Even so, he said that every time he heard Schubert's *Ave Maria*, he felt an emotion he could not explain. Zemin also talked to me about the disappointment the Chinese felt when the pope declared saints a number of those who had been killed in the Boxer revolution in 1900. The Church had said these had suffered religious persecution but China had strongly denounced the canonisation. To add insult to injury, the Church had proclaimed them saints on China's national day, October 1. I tried to explain that the pope certainly did not mean to insult the great Chinese nation and that a meeting with the pontiff would clear up the differences, but he was not impressed by my words. At another time, I also discussed with him the possibility of China opening a cultural centre in Malta, pointing out that this could reach out to the Mediterranean. He liked the idea and promised to look into it on his return to China. Thanks to his intervention, we now have in Malta an institute of Chinese culture, which is active and very well equipped to teach the Chinese language and to promote Chinese culture and civilisation.

I used to pass the summer months at Verdala Palace, overlooking Buskett Gardens. Built by Grand Master Verdalle in 1588 as a summer residence, the palace is actually a castle. It is splendid in its simplicity and so relaxing in its surrounding beauty. It has a charm all its own at sunset. The birds come in folds to rest on the trees. I am very non-alcoholic in my drinking but Violet and I used to enjoy staying on the bridge leading to the castle, sipping a gin and tonic with ice.

We looked after Verdala Palace well. One major job there was the restoration of frescoes that had been whitewashed at the time when the island was a colony. The wife of one British governor did not like the frescoes and had them covered. Violet took a particular interest in the castle and saw to it that the place be completely refurbished. She particularly sought to restore the second floor to what it had looked like at the time of Grand Master Vilhena but she could not find in Malta a carpet that fitted the upper dining room at a price that was within our budget. She raised the matter with the Chinese ambassador, Yang Guiron, knowing that the Chinese are excellent manufacturers of carpets. He asked for the measurements and provided her with samples. Violet chose a sample of a carpet that corresponded to those made in Vilhena's times. One fine day the ambassador informed Violet that the carpet had arrived. This beautiful carpet, which has given the dining room an elegant look, was given as a gift from the Chinese people to Malta's first lady to be placed at Verdala Palace.

Violet was also influential in efforts made to have a staircase by Girolamo Cassar restored to its pristine glory. A Public Works Department team removed all the whitewashing that had been applied to the staircase over time, discovering in the process a lovely niche and interesting graffiti of vessels and of prayers inscribed by prisoners who must have been kept in the castle at some time or other. The restoration brought out the beauty of the stone work. We thought that in this day and age the palace ought to have a lift installed but it was difficult getting a permit from the Malta Environment and Planning Authority. It was only installed in the last months of my presidency.

On September 6, 2001, I received the credentials of the newly-appointed US Ambassador to Malta, Anthony H. Gioia at the Palace in Valletta. On the same day, I gave a luncheon in his honour at Verdala Palace. Only five days later, I was having my usual siesta at the palace when Violet jolted me out of my sleep shouting 'An aeroplane has crashed into the Twin Towers in New York… come Guido, come…' She was watching a newsreel of the crash on CNN. Like people from all over the world, I could hardly believe my eyes. In those few minutes, the world assisted to one of the major terrorist attacks in history. There and then I expressed my deep sorrow at the event to the American ambassador and asked him to express my feeling of solidarity with the American people to President George W. Bush. I later sent a written message to President Bush, expressing our strong support to the United States and adding that we stood by the American people in resisting terrorism in all its forms. Three days later, we held a commemoration at the Palace in Valletta, for which the American ambassador attended. The Archbishop, Mgr Joseph Mercieca, said a prayer for the victims of the attack and we observed a three-minute silence. Another commemoration was held in the Palace courtyard three months later.

In November 2001 I paid a state visit to Germany, made in return to that by President Richard von Weizsacker in October 1990. At the time I was president of the UN General Assembly and had attended the Punta del Este Conference in Uruguay on world trade. To be on time to receive the German president in Malta, I had to fly to Malta via Milan almost non-stop. I have always admired Weizsacker and in a way I took him as my model during my presidency. I think that credit for arranging the visit is due to Ambassadors Kunz and William Spiteri. Kunz had to terminate his accreditation to Malta a few weeks before the state visit. But I would like to make an open appreciation of his deep involvement in the arrangements for this visit. Most German ambassadors have been good representatives of German diplomacy. Ambassador Kunz was certainly one of the foremost. Ambassador Spiteri was also very hard working. He had also arranged a state visit for me to Poland, another country to which he had been accredited.

On my state visit to the Federal Republic, I visited Germany's oldest university, Heidelberg, where I gave a lecture on 'The Mediterranean – Europe's reluctant agenda?' I spoke of the history of the area, saying that, since ancient times, 'the Mediterranean Sea has acted as a great trading route, linking littorals and peoples. Peoples interacted, and through a cross-fertilisation of ideas, civilisation flourished. However, through the centuries, this sea of culture and civilisation has also acted as an impermeable frontier among people. A few kilometres of sea have made strangers of neighbours... We have a choice. The Mediterranean Sea can either continue to accentuate the great divide, perpetuate problems and escalate struggles, or it can act as an area of convergence among peoples, among cultures. We have to see in the Mediterranean a *mare nostrum* – our sea – in full respect of cultures of people and the sovereignty of states, creating thereby a *Pax Mediterranea*. Europe cannot afford to be further reluctant in its Mediterranean agenda. There is so much to lose. There is a future of peace and prosperity to gain'.

I had in my delegation Dr Joe Borg; the rector of the University of Malta, Prof. Roger Ellul Micallef; the chairman of Air Malta and of Metco, Louis Grech and Anthony Diacono respectively; the chairman of the Malta Development Corporation, Lawrence Zammit; and the president of the Chamber of Commerce, John Sullivan. They worked hard to promote new business links. As a result of contacts made by me and by members of my delegation, particularly Louis Grech and Ambassador Spiteri, talks were started for Lufthansa Technik to consider setting up shop in Malta, which eventually it did.

In Berlin I was received by President Johannes Rau and his wife Fra Rau at their official residence. Soprano Miriam Gauci, who happened to be in Berlin at the time, was invited by the German president to a state banquet given in our honour. The following day I had an interesting meeting with Chancellor Gerhard Schroeder, an able politician. Schroeder wanted to be informed about the Mediterranean and in particular about Libya. With Malta being so small, in my talks abroad I usually spoke of the island's

Mediterranean dimension in our European context. This is what I had done in Germany, a country of 80 million people, particularly when I spoke to ambassadors at the representative office of the EU.

'Every country, member or applicant thereof, brings to the Union its own particular dimension. The government believes that Malta will be contributing its own Mediterranean dimension, its insight and perspectives which result from a strategic position and geographical location in the region. My government believes that what Malta will add to the Mediterranean dimension of Europe is a sharper focus on those aspects of Mediterranean stability and cooperation which come naturally to us through history and geography; because of our awareness of Mediterranean issues, because of our constant advocacy of Mediterranean affairs, and also because of our sense of service to peoples of the Mediterranean, Malta in the European Union will have a bridging effect to Europe's Mediterranean dimension.' I would like to think that our visit to Germany had a positive effect. Above all, Germany was looking at Malta's bid to join the EU positively and appeared to appreciate the island's Mediterranean policy.

We approached the end of the year with a measure of satisfaction and at the same time apprehension at the fact that the country's future depended a great deal on the decisions that had to be taken in the months ahead.

56

Upheaval in judiciary

In February 2002, I received in a state visit the president of Albania, Rexhap Meidani. Albania and Malta have kept very good relations since my first visit to that country as president of the UN General Assembly. Meidani is a dignified person and had genially tried to give a balancing role to the presidency in Albanian politics. His son was studying at the Mediterranean Academy of Diplomatic Studies at our university at the time. During the state visit, we invited him to stay with his parents at San Anton.

Meanwhile, controversy was building up in the country over the island's application for membership of the EU. Since a referendum on the issue and general elections were already on the horizon, I thought that, in such a moment of great division, I could help in easing the tension by serving as a coagulant. With this in mind, I visited a number of localities, including Safi, Mosta, Cospicua, Msida, Senglea, Paola, Floriana, Pembroke, Rabat, and Valletta.

The drug problem in the country was growing and I set up an open-ended committee to study the matter in detail. They came up with a valuable report, making suggestions for amendments to the laws already in force. In this work I had the co-operation of the director of Caritas, Mgr Victor Grech, a close friend since our university days, the commissioner of police, John Rizzo, and experts from the social services and the medical and health department.

A state visit that has long remained in my mind is that made by Vaclav Havel, president of the Czech Republic, in April 2002. Through much personal sacrifice and dedication, Havel contributed to the return of democracy in his country. The talk he gave when he was conferred with the degree of LL.D. (Honoris Causa) by our university remains impressed in my memory. Law and justice, he said, were sometimes used in substitution of each other. He had been brought before a court of law in his country and accused of having broken the law when he criticised the then dictatorship for denying the people democracy and freedom. The court had sentenced him to imprisonment according to law. But was this justice? For a legal system to be just, laws had to be according to norms of justice. And justice demand a society based on freedom.

In the state dinner I gave in his honour at the Palace in Valletta, I welcomed him with the words, 'You were a convict in the name of freedom. Your actions were criminalised because you believed in the physical, moral, and intellectual freedom of mankind. It was a struggle against totalitarianism, a struggle for freedom from the shackles of an ideology that, during the last century, was transformed into cause and justification for violence and repression.' It was a pleasure conversing with Havel and his lovely wife. We entertained him privately at Verdala Palace. We enjoyed his company very much. After his state visit, he stayed on for a few days, spending the evenings with members of his retinue at a bar, Żmerċ, in Attard, close to the main gate of San Anton gardens. The first time he went to this bar, there was no place at table, but the owner somehow recognised him, or was told about him, and welcomed him enthusiastically. He enjoyed his glass of cold beer in the company of friends and liked mixing with local people.

Another interesting person was President Ferenc Madl, a lawyer by profession, whom I met shortly afterwards during my state visit to Hungary. Budapest is a splendid city and its neo-gothic Parliament is one of the most beautiful I have ever seen. President Madl's state dinner in our honour was given at this building. From the balcony overlooking the beautiful Danube, the scene, with the illuminated Buda castle in the background, has a fairyland touch. Violet and I were greatly impressed.

Malta has many things in common with Cyprus. Like Malta, Cyprus was at the threshold of the EU when I paid a state visit to that country. I paid homage to Archbishop Makarios at the foot of his gigantic statue and had meaningful discussions with President Glafkos Klerides, who did his best to come to an agreement with his Turkish counterpart over the divided island. Both knew each other since they were young. Klerides worked hard to bridge the division but the time was not yet ripe for a solution acceptable to both sides. In Cyprus, we compared notes on the progress made with the EU over membership negotiations. The problem for Cyprus was to make the EU accept the country as a member despite the division of the island, a hurdle that was practically overcome in September 2002.

Greek President Kostis Stephanopoulos, a cultured gentleman and a person whom I treasure as a friend, received me warmly when I visited his country on a state visit. Prime Minister Kostas Simitis, whom I had already met in Malta, received me in his office. After the state visit, our consul in Athens invited me to visit some of the Greek islands on a yacht. Violet enjoyed it indeed, as did Isabel Borg, wife of the foreign minister who was with us. In Malta in October 2002, we had President Milan Kučan of Slovenia on a state visit. I have known President Kučan since the early nineties when I visited his country as foreign affairs minister. He impresses me by his common-sense approach to issues. At the state dinner given in his honour at the Palace, I said: 'What a difference a decade can make, Mr President! From that winter December day in 1990 when your people realised that ages-old dream, a dream so vigorously and so eloquently expressed by France Prešeren, your national poet, for Slovenia to embrace independence, to be able to lead its own destiny and to establish its deserved place among the family of nations, your beautiful country never looked back.'

As I may have already remarked, state visits were politically engineered, as it were, for Malta to get maximum benefit from them. The Czech Republic, Slovenia, Hungary, and Cyprus were all EU candidate countries. Greece was also important as it supported Malta's and Cyprus's applications from the very beginning. Poland, which I had also visited, was also a candidate country. It had made good progress since Solidarnosc started the freedom movement in the country from the Danzig shipyards. The Catholic hierarchy supported the movement to the hilt and Pope John Paul II added his weight to such support. President Aleksander Kwasniewski, who received me in Warsaw, had been a minister of youth affairs under General Wojciech Jaruzelski, but he had adapted to the changes in his country and had become president. He and his beautiful wife showed me and Violet and my delegation around the presidential palace, as well as the chapel where Pope John Paul II had prayed. A marble plaque marks this event. I found the man very knowledgeable in foreign affairs. He had a strong pro-American approach, particularly to Middle East affairs. Kwasniewski saw to it that Poland joined Nato. It was greatly ironic – but good politics – for a country that had given its capital's name to the Warsaw Pact to join Nato, more so when the move was propelled by a former communist! The Warsaw Pact was an organisation of Central and Eastern European communist states, set up in 1955 primarily to meet the potential threat from Nato.

In Warsaw I was struck by the physical memories of World War II. When I laid a wreath at the tomb of the Unknown Soldier, the whole setting, with the destroyed ghetto in the background, and plaques recording the battlefields where so many Polish soldiers had fought and died, brought out the horrors of a war that had in fact started there, in Poland. At the same time, though, I was impressed at the rebuilding that had been done. The Royal Palace, for example, was completely rebuilt. Solidarnosc is not as strong today as it was at the time it led the movement for change in the country but its work had a lasting effect on the history of Poland and sent ripples of change in other countries as well.

Joe Said Pullicino ended his term of office as chief justice on reaching retirement age on January 15, 2002. The new chief justice was Noel Arrigo. Little did I imagine at the time that the changeover was to lead eventually to one of the greatest upheavals in the judiciary in Malta's history. The prime minister gave me the shock of my life when, during an urgent meeting at the Palace in the morning of August 1, he told me that two of the judges, Noel Arrigo and Patrick Vella, were being investigated on charges of corruption and bribery. I could hardly believe it. It had never crossed my mind that such a thing could happen to our judiciary. In my long years in the legal profession, over 50 years, I had seen the judiciary pass through difficult times. I had also come across learned judges, and others who were not so learned, as well as judges of high moral standing and courage and others who did not have, as Manzoni once put it, '*un cuor di leone*'. But I never had reason to believe, suspect, or even think for a moment that any member of our judiciary would fail in integrity. By all accounts, it was one of the worst moments in my public life as it directly challenged the belief I had always had in the integrity of the judiciary.

As it happened, I had been scheduled to visit the head office of the Malta Association of Professional Bodies that day. I kept the appointment and, while I was there, without obviously saying anything about what the prime minister had told me earlier that morning, I spoke of the importance of integrity. In the afternoon I had a meeting of the Commission for the Administration of Justice. As the news had not yet been made public, I could not inform the members of what was taking place. But, at the start of the meeting, I received a telephone call from Noel Arrigo apologising for his absence as he had some business to look after at police headquarters. The commission, too, was shattered when it later learned of the news. The prime minister set in motion the procedure for their resignation as laid down in the constitution. The speaker of the House of Representatives addressed a letter to me in my capacity as president of the Commission for the Administration of Justice to take the necessary action against the two members of the judiciary and, in the light of a precedent set by Ugo Mifsud Bonnici in a case involving a member of the judiciary, I abstained from taking cognisance of the case and a newly-appointed deputy chairman, Acting Chief Justice Joseph David Camilleri, took over in chairing the commission. When Noel Arrigo and Patrick Vella resigned on August 9 and August 12 respectively, the commission abstained from taking further cognisance of the case and the speaker was duly informed. When the two judges came over to the Palace to hand over their resignation, they both looked broken. They had both been my students at university and I had seen them moving on in life. Patrick Vella was jailed for two years on March 13, 2007 after admitting to the charges, while, at the time of writing, the trial of Noel Arrigo has not yet started.

In the meantime, discussions with the EU over the island's membership application were reaching their conclusion and the people were soon to be called to decide on the issue in a referendum. I brought up the subject when, as president, I presented decorations of merit at the annual ceremony marking Republic Day, on December 13, 2002. One point I made then was that 'diversity of opinions, freely discussed and honestly expressed, does not amount to a divide but to a dialogue in a healthy democracy... Fundamental for democracy, however, is that, within a context of divergent opinions, the sovereign will of the people has to prevail. This is democracy; the debate, the vote, the respect for the will of the people.' I touched the same point in my Christmas message: 'In the New Year, the people will be called upon to take important decisions, decisions that affect the future of all of us. We need to live democracy and we do this by being tolerant towards different views. It is only this which is best for our country. Together, we should arrive at our own conclusions. Together, we should be wise enough to respect the will of the people as democratically expressed. This is democracy in which we believe.'

When, on December 31, 2002, Violet and I attended the *Te Deum* at St John's co-cathedral, we felt we had a lot to be thankful for after another year in the service of the people. But our minds were on the future and we prayed for guidance in a year when the country had to take important decisions.

57

Yes to Europe

When the membership negotiations with Brussels were concluded, Eddie Fenech Adami did not let grass grow under his feet and set a date for the holding of a referendum on whether or not the people wanted to see Malta join the EU. I duly signed the proclamation for the referendum to be held on March 8, 2003. As it had been expected, the campaign was keen indeed. The 'IVA' campaign had been well prepared and reached out to the people in very effective terms. The MLP put up an all-out offensive to deny Malta's accession to the EU.

At one point, I found myself at the centre of a controversy when I was attacked by the deputy leader of the MLP over something I had said in the 1998 election campaign. As I have already remarked, I had quoted from reports from Brussels appearing in two newspapers, *The Sunday Times* and *The Independent on Sunday*, that Malta would be receiving Lm100,000,000 following accession. Fenech Adami was a convincing speaker in the campaign; he was indeed the heart and soul of the pro-Europe campaign. The party backed him completely. Alfred Sant worked equally hard to put his party's message across.

On referendum day, my family voted at the polling station in Hamrun. Over 91 per cent of the electorate voted and of those who cast a valid vote, 53.6 per cent (143,094) voted in favour of Malta joining the EU and 43.6 per cent (123,628) voted against, a majority of over 19,000 votes. By Maltese standards, this was a substantial majority. As the Nationalist Party and the thousands who voted 'yes' celebrated the vote for Europe, Sant, using a mathematical argument that defied definition, held they had blocked the way to Europe. This caused a bit of confusion at first but Fenech Adami was not taking any nonsense. He had no doubt the country wanted Malta to join the EU and he felt the referendum result would be confirmed if he were to call a general election. It was clear that there were many non-Nationalists who had voted for Europe and that, if a general election were to be called, these would not risk voting Labour. Only one day after the referendum results were out, that is on March 10, I dissolved the House of Representatives, at the request of the prime minister, and called general elections for April 12.

By a master stroke, Fenech Adami openly challenged Sant at 'his' mathematics. It was a swift campaign. The European ideal, which the PN had worked so hard for, was at stake. A win for Sant would have meant putting Malta's application back on hold. But it was clear that the people were in no mood to accept this. Sant failed to feel the pulse of the nation. It very much looked as if he had shut both eyes to reality. The election confirmed the referendum result and, as president, I called on Fenech Adami to form a new government. A new cabinet was sworn in on April 15 and on April 16 and 17 we were in Athens for the official signing of the treaty of adhesion by the prime minister and the foreign minister. I was seated next to President Stephanopoulos.

On May 24 we had the official opening of Parliament and, in accordance with procedure, I read the speech prepared for me by the government, outlining its programme. Foremost among the bills which the government had planned to introduce was the European Union Act, which was approved by Parliament on July 14, 2003. On July 16, 2003, 13 years to the day that I had presented Malta's request to join the EU, I gave my assent to the bill, marking the end of the country's long journey to Europe. I was one of the country's main protagonists in this long and difficult journey, at least up to 1999. In my young student days at St Aloysius, I remember writing an essay entitled 'Perseverance gains the crown'.

Membership was indeed an exercise in perseverance, insistence, and consistence. There was further reason for me to rejoice. My son Mario was elected in the first general elections he contested. He had decided to contest close to the closing date for nominations and he was elected from the first district, the one I had represented in Parliament for 33 years. It was a personal satisfaction to see Mario in Parliament. As president, I could not show him or give him any support.

But, to go back to Malta and Europe, joining Europe is not a goal in itself. It is a means to an end. Through its presence in the EU, it should not only seek material benefit but also live up to its mission of serving as a bridge for peace between the peoples of the Mediterranean. Having reached the end of the journey, a new one was now starting. This is history in the making, a milestone that will be enjoyed by our children and grandchildren.

58

Common foreign policy

Having gone through such an exciting period, during which Malta had become part of the EU following a referendum and a general election, the political climate in the country started settling down. Alfred Sant, after first resigning, had decided to stay on and live to fight another day. More importantly, the MLP agreed to respect the people's will to be part of the EU. This means that, 40 years after independence, our political parties are following a common foreign policy.

In Parliament there was no conflict in so far as foreign affairs were concerned, save for differences over some nuances here and there. The political parties were pulling their weight together to make a success of EU membership. As to the island's Mediterranean policy, this had been a common aspect of our foreign policy for quite a number of years, as was Malta's support for the United Nations. This gave the presidency a greater opportunity to promote common goals in society.

Through the Community Chest Fund, direct financial help was given for various good causes. At one time, for example, a cheque for Lm6,380 was given to Fr Anġ. Seychell, who turned his home in Żejtun into a hostel, Dar Nazareth, for those needing shelter. The YMCA in Valletta was given Lm6,000 and Caritas at San Blas, Lm10,000. In the years of my presidency, the amount collected for the Community Chest Fund ran close to Lm2 million. One major activity that greatly helped boost revenue for the fund was the television programme *L-Istrina Flimkien*, run by Where's Everybody with the support of Violet, Andrew Psaila, of Public Broadcasting Service, Charles Mansueto, of Maltacom, and many others. The fund received 50 per cent of the money raised. No fewer than 6,788 individuals received nearly Lm1 million in financial help among them. In addition, over Lm220,000 were given to institutions while people having members of their family abroad for medical care received nearly Lm200,000 in assistance.

The fund had as its beginning the August Moon Ball, first held during the governorship of Sir Robert Laycock. It developed into Malta Community Chest Fund under the leadership of Lady Mamo, wife of Sir Anthony Mamo. It has been presided, since the presidency of Agatha Barbara, by the president of Malta. Both Violet and I dedicated a considerable part of our time to the fund. To us both and, no doubt, to all those who have, or who are still involved in it, the fund is an essay in human experience. As one goes through the flow of requests for assistance, one discovers a lot of hidden poverty. Besides, the fund also helps those suffering acute illnesses, the unemployed, those in difficult situations because of a drug habit, victims of usury, or those eager to resettle in society after imprisonment. The setting up of the fund was a great idea as it gave the presidency a human dimension. The donations were handed out at the Palace to ensure that the receivers be given the respect they deserved. I felt somewhat uneasy at first going through such money-giving events but I realised later that these constituted a strong exercise in solidarity. Violet and I still follow the Malta Community Chest Fund with great interest.

Through my links with Caritas and Mgr Victor Grech, I had become greatly aware of the drug problems facing young people today. Victims of drugs were ending up in prison, certainly not the best of places where addicts could shake off their habit. This is why, as I have explained earlier, I set up an open-ended committee to deal with the problem. Mgr Grech was a prominent member of this committee. I admire Victor for his dedication to those suffering from drug affliction. He is a man of God, committed to help those who have fallen by the wayside, as it were, or who have become rejects of society. I remember also Fr Benny Tonna, whom at one stage, together with Mgr Grech, I had asked for advice when we came to identify better those needing help from the Community Chest Fund. Unfortunately, Fr Tonna died when he was still relatively young. The committee did good work and the government went on to carry out some of its recommendations. In fact, changes in the law affecting drug victims were made, particularly one removing the mandatory imprisonment in certain cases. In addition, a better distinction was made between drug-sharing and trafficking. Drug addicts are now considered as persons needing help, not punishment.

Sometimes life throws up incidents when they are least expected. A problem that arose when I visited Tel Aviv for the eightieth birthday celebrations of my long-time friend Shimon Peres threatened to develop into a diplomatic incident. As is the practice, when a head of state visits another country, and the visit is not a state visit, he usually makes a courtesy call on that country's head of state. When I requested to pay a courtesy call on President Moshe Katsav, I was told by Ambassador Gol that my visit to Katsav would not be allowed unless I bound myself not to see Yasser Arafat during my stay there. I replied that, as a head of state, I could not accept such a condition and that, if Israel would insist on the condition, I would not call on President Katsav. In the end the Israeli foreign office backed down although, as it happened, I had no time to visit Arafat. I only managed to call on the Latin Patriarch Michel Sabah at his seat in old Jerusalem. We spoke about Arafat and the future of Palestine, as well as about the difficulties being faced by Palestinian Christians.

In spite of the strong rivalry between them, Shimon Peres and Ariel Sharon held each other in great respect. I could see this for myself in Tel Aviv. Peres held on to his stand for a two-state solution, pointing out that, within a few years, the ethnic component will see the prevalence of Palestinian people over the Israel ethnic segment in the former Palestine. Failure to accept the two-state idea would mean that, in a democratic Israel, the Palestinians would prevail through their demographic superiority, or that Israel would be turned into an apartheid state, which was incompatible with the nature of Israel.

For Shimon Peres's birthday celebrations, there were, among others, President Johannes Rau of Germany, and former American president, Bill Clinton. The girls at the theatre where the celebrations were held gave a hearty welcome to President Clinton, chasing him everywhere for embraces. In his speeches Sharon appealed to Peres to join up with him to give Israel a strong government so that it would to take the right decisions. Eventually, Peres ended up joining the new party that Sharon had decided to start, Kadima. Unfortunately for Sharon, though, he suffered a severe haemorrhagic stroke at the time of the election and Ehud Olmert, his deputy prime minister, took over. I had met Olmert on that occasion. In my conversation with him, he appeared to be very anti-Arafat, which certainly did not bide well for the future.

I received in Malta on state visits President Arnold Rüütel of Estonia and President Vaira Vike-Freiberga of Latvia, two Balkan republics that were about to join the EU together with Malta. President Rüütel, a politician of considerable experience in his country, had succeeded Lennart Meri, though I doubt if Meri considered him as his successor in his political beliefs. Vike-Freiberga had lived most of her life in Canada. On returning to Latvia, she contested the presidency and won with ability and style.

In March 2004, President Kwasniewski of Poland paid a return visit. In the talks and private conversations I had with him, I realised how much the eastern countries of Europe felt indebted to the United States and that this had in fact prevailed over their sense of belonging to Europe. Then, in Budapest, I inaugurated, together with President Madl, the Corinthia Grand Hotel Royal, a classic five-star luxury hotel. Madl received me at his new residence in the old castle city of Buda. Madl and I have many things in common, not least our study of constitutional law.

I had also been invited to give the opening talk at a conference at the House of Commons on 'Wider, deeper, stronger: The Enlargement of the European Union'. With the island's membership of the EU having been approved in a referendum and a general election, I could speak without having to be careful lest I fail to show a balanced approach in the light of the MLP's stand over Europe. In Amman for a World Economic Forum meeting, I paid a courtesy call on the king of Jordan, Abdullah II. He is a very modern king, pulling his weight as a voice of moderation in a difficult world, one that finds it difficult to understand the suffering and humiliation in the Arab world.

Another most interesting person I met was Hosni Mubarak, of Egypt. Notwithstanding the passage of years, and the difficulties affecting his international commitments, Mubarak is still in control of the political situation in his country. This does not reduce the relevance of the Muslim Brotherhood in Egyptian politics. In our meeting, we obviously talked about 9/11 and I remember him telling me how, as a pilot instructor himself, he could not understand how the hijackers could direct their planes with such precision at the Twin Towers. The role of Malta in the EU figured prominently in our talks.

With Amr Moussa at the Arab League, we made an in-depth examination of the political situation both in Iraq and in Palestine. I had also met at the Mubarak Library the former Arab League general secretary Esmat Abdel-Meguid, one of the very first Arab personalities to support Malta's application to join the EU. I had also greatly enjoyed meeting Mohammed Sajid Tantawi, Grand Imam of Al-Ashar. He is a man of great spirituality, embodying the intellectual and spiritual depth of Islam. Violet and I then went on a private visit to Aswan to see the marvel of the dam, and as we made our way on a boat down the River Nile, we stopped to see the beautiful remains and grandeur of the magnificent civilisation that was Egypt.

The year 2003 ended on this high note. We were now in the last three months of my presidency. They were eventful indeed. A highlight of my presidency was my state visit to Italy, and, I may add, with good reason too. We have always had excellent relations with Italy, which has contributed millions of liri to the island's development through financial protocols. As foreign minister, I had been involved in the negotiation of two of these protocols. I had also put in a good word in the right places when the last protocol was being negotiated. Italy had supported Malta's application to join the EU from the very start.

We travelled to Rome on the Italian president's private aircraft. As we were approaching the capital, we were escorted by planes of the Italian Air Force. At Ciampino, I inspected a guard of honour and we were received by Minister Rocco Buttiglione on behalf of the Italian government. From there, we went directly to the Quirinale where we were received with full military honours. President Carlo Azelio Ciampi, a person of charm and erudition, received me with great cordiality. We had known each other for a number of years. We had a private discussion in his study, while Donna Franca looked after Violet, showing her around the palace of the popes and, afterwards, the residence of the Italian royal family.

Donna Franca and Violet got on well together. At the end of this encounter, we gave a joint press conference. From the Quirinale, I left for Montecitorio to be received by the president of the House of Representatives, Pier Ferdinando Casini. In the afternoon, I addressed the Unione degli Industrialisti di Roma, underlining the advantages of investing in our country and the financial services Malta offered. In the evening the Italian president and Donna Ciampi gave a state dinner in our honour in the magnificent dining room of Palazzo Quirinale. It was a grand affair. In his toast to Malta, Ciampi spoke of the good relations between the two countries and, on my part, I quoted what Garibaldi had said when he visited Malta in 1864: '*Amor con amor si paga i maltesi dovrebberò amarmi molto perchè li ho amato, per la loro ospitalità a pro dei fratelli italiani e per il loro eroismo storico.*'

I also recalled Aldo Moro who, on the eve of Malta's independence, had addressed the people of Malta on television: '*Desidero ricordarvi che Malta potrà sempre contare sull'amicizia del Governo e del popolo italiano nell'azione che vorrà compiere per conseguire quei fini di giustizia e di libertà che sono nostro prezioso comune patrimonio.*' I said in my toast: '*Quarant'anni dopo, Signor Presidente, posso dire che l'Italia ha mantenuta la sua parola.*' I then referred to Malta's future as a member of the EU and spoke of how the two countries in Europe would assert the relevance of the Mediterranean to which we both belonged.

The following day, I laid a wreath at the monument of the Unknown Soldier in Piazza Venezia. I was received there by the minister of defence,

Antonio Martino. As I climbed up the splendid stairs to the tomb of the Unknown Soldier, *corazzieri in alta uniforme* stood to attention on both sides and a military band played *Canzone del Piave*, a military song of the First World War. My mother used to sing it to me when I was young; she knew it word for word. At that moment I wished her to be present. She would have loved the moment, seeing her son, as president of Malta, paying homage to the fallen of her country of origin. Before leaving the *Altare della Patria*, I inspected a guard of honour at the foot of the monument.

Later I was received at Montecitorio by Gianfranco Fini, at the time acting prime minister in the absence of Silvio Berlusconi who was indisposed. During the talks, Berlusconi phoned me up to excuse his absence and promising his continued help to Malta. Only a few days before my state visit to Italy, the fifth financial protocol with Malta was signed. Berlusconi was very much involved in the work aimed at ensuring the signing of this protocol. In the evening I hosted a reception in honour of President Ciampi and Donna Franca at the Grand Hotel St Regis. It was attended by the highest authorities in Italy and by members of the diplomatic corps.

The following day, I took leave of President Ciampi before going on visits to Milan and Palermo. I was warmly received in both cities. Before leaving Rome for Milan, I paid a courtesy call on John Paul II. His health had deteriorated further. He could scarcely speak. Yet he continued to inspire us all by his suffering, a message of endurance and hope. His very presence transmitted holiness. The world loved him and through his illness he made us all feel one in his love of Christ. It was my last visit to Pope John Paul II: he died a year later.

In Milan we were received by Mayor Gabriele Albertini and later by Roberto Formigoni in his capacity as president of the Lombardy region. I had known Formigoni since the difficult days Malta faced in the time of the Mintoff administration. I addressed students at Milan's Bocconi University and later took part in a meeting with Milanese industrialists on the advantages of investing in Malta. Apart from Joe Borg, I had in my delegation Michael Bonello, governor of the Central Bank; Roger Ellul Micallef, rector of the University of Malta; Joseph Zammit Tabona, chairman of Malta Enterprise; Marc Bonello, chairman of the Maritime Authority; John Grech, chairman of the Malta Tourism Authority; F.X. Zahra, chairman of the Bank of Valletta; Anthony Tabone, vice-president of the Federation of Industry; and Louis Apap Bologna, president of the Chamber of Commerce. They all contributed to making our stay successful.

From Milan we flew to Palermo, where we had an excellent visit, meeting, among others, the president of the Sicilian Regional Assembly, Guido Lo Porto, at the Palazzo dei Normanni, and the president of the Sicilian region, Salvatore Cuffaro. I was given a doctorate degree, Honoris Causa, in European studies by the University of Palermo, where I gave a lecture on 'Pax Mediterranea'. Before concluding the visit, we went to Monreale to see its famous cathedral, called by some 'the most beautiful temple in the world'. I was also given the honorary citizenship of Monreale and a diploma, Honoris Causa, by the Accademia Siculo-Normanna. I felt my visit to Italy was a success from the political, economic, and cultural aspects. It reflected the high esteem in which Italy looks at its relations with Malta. On our part, we did our best to expand relations even further.

I did not wish to end the presidency without paying a state visit to Libya and to Kuwait. At that time, life had just begun to return to normal in Libya following the lifting of the sanctions. Leaders from the West had lost no time in flying over to Tripoli in a bid to win back contracts they had before the sanctions were imposed. Among the first to visit Libya were Berlusconi, Blair, and Schroeder. The removal of the sanctions, following Libya's decision to give up its programme of weapons of mass destruction, and the opening up of its markets to the West, was all to the good as it was dangerous to isolate that country politically. Isolation could have led Libya to become an extremist Islamic state. My argument all along had been that in the present political scenario the alternative to Gaddafi were the Islamic fundamentalists.

Malta was acting almost as a bystander in these events. Our foreign office had dedicated itself mainly to the challenge of Malta becoming a member of the EU. I could well understand this but in my view politics can never be a one-track approach. Joining the EU should not have meant giving the impression that we were turning our back to the southern Mediterranean. I believe there were several in Libya who viewed Malta's enthusiasm for Europe as an abandonment of the special relationship the island had had with that country for so many years. In very difficult times for Libya, Malta had done its best to press for peaceful solutions as it felt that this was in the interest of the international community. When Malta was about to become a member of the EU, the visa requirement was re-introduced, creating an irksome situation for businessmen. Libya was seen to be making matters a bit difficult in this respect and it appeared we had our failures in this regard, too.

In the light of my contribution towards the strengthening of our bilateral relations, I had the advantage of being seen very positively by the Libyan side. Muammar Gaddafi respected me highly and at one time had entrusted me with ensuring that our relations remained healthy and productive. But, at the beginning of 2004, our relations were at best tepid. On my state visit, we flew to Sirte where Gaddafi was staying at the time. I was received with full military honours at the airport. Immediately afterwards, I was taken to a camp in the desert, from where Gaddafi used to run the affairs of state. The greetings were very friendly. I was seated next to Gaddafi and, in the presence of my whole delegation and his delegation, we started reviewing the international situation. Gaddafi can be very balanced in his views if the occasion so warrants. He felt it was premature to consider Libya as a possible candidate for membership of the Euro-Med process. He did not favour the two-state solution for the Palestinian problem, holding that there was only one Palestine in which the Israelis and the Palestinians have to cohabit in peace. I said that in my view this was not a practical solution. The Israelis would never accept that their state be wiped out and, in any case, the Palestinians, too, felt they had to have a country to call their own.

Our talks drifted to bilateral relations and I explained Malta's role in the EU and its relationship with the Arab world, but he did not express any particular view at this stage. In the evening, we were hosted to a state banquet. Gaddafi and I sat at the head table on our own. My wife and Isabelle Borg sat at a separate table, together with some other women from protocol. Gaddafi appeared keen to create the right atmosphere. He said he was thankful for Malta for keeping its friendship with Libya in more concrete ways than 'the sons of our Arab brothers'. I told Gaddafi how I kept contact with Yasser Arafat, particularly in the time he was being kept under house arrest in what was left of his headquarters following Israeli's bombing, and that possibly I was one of the very few who communicated regularly on the phone with him during his forced isolation. Gaddafi turned towards me and said in English: 'Thank you for what you are doing for Arafat and for keeping in touch with him in this very difficult situation that he is passing through.'

I brought the discussion back to Malta in Europe and how Malta intended raising Mediterranean issues. Gaddafi said he had come to the conclusion that it was also in Libya's interest that Malta joined the EU, for Malta in the EU meant that Libya would have a friend in the EU. Gaddafi conferred on me the highest Libyan honour, and I made him honorary companion of honour of the Order of Merit of Malta. Even though Gaddafi's camp was in the desert, the weather was cold. But the atmosphere between the two sides was warm and we all felt we had put our relations on solid ground again. On the way out, Gaddafi turned to my wife and told her, 'I would like my wife to see you tomorrow in Tripoli.'

On our way to Tripoli the following day, we stopped at the man-made river, an impressive engineering feat. In Tripoli we were housed at the Corinthia Bab Africa Hotel. The changing political climate, the new hotel, and other developments were giving Tripoli a new look. We had fruitful talks with the Libyan prime minister, Shokri Ghanen, and other authorities. My wife and I, and members of my delegation, were taken to see the marvels of Leptis Magna. On our return to Tripoli, the former ambassador to Libya and good friend of my family, Hind Sciala, took us for dinner in a restaurant down-town.

At one moment we were informed that Mrs Gaddafi was going to call on my wife that evening. We were told not to hurry over dinner but to keep her informed, through protocol, when we would be returning to the hotel. We returned close to 11. Gaddafi's wife arrived a few minutes later, together with her beautiful daughter, Aisha. The introductions over, I left Mrs Gaddafi and her daughter in the company of my wife and Isabelle Borg. Violet was positively impressed by Mrs Gaddafi and her daughter. She found the conversation interesting and she greatly appreciated the gesture, considering that in some Arab states the wife does not as a rule take a public role in her husband's public affairs.

We left Tripoli early in the morning the following day, convinced we had helped in strengthening even further the good relations between the two countries. Future generations would have to continue to do this as it is in our common interest. The next day was February 10, feast of the St Paul's Shipwreck, and I could hardly miss going to the feast in Valletta. I had been taking part in the feast since I was a boy and this was going to be the last time for me to attend as president. The pontifical Mass and the panegyric, which in my view take too long, reach their climax in Paolo Nani's antiphony *Sancte Paule*. Every time I hear it, it radiates in me an innermost feeling of belonging to the faith brought to us by the apostle, a faith that we have treasured with great love. After Mass, we unveiled a marble plaque commemorating the pope's 'mission statement', as it were, to the Maltese given before his departure on his last visit to the island. The plaque, next to others on the wall of the Palace, was blessed by Archbishop Mercieca.

In March I was invited to St Petersburg by the Academic Council of the university there to receive a degree, Doctor of Science, Honoris Causa, in recognition of my 'contribution to European integration and the strengthening of the peace process and friendship between countries'. On my way to the city, we stopped at the monument to those who died in the defence of Leningrad during the siege of World War II. We had a young woman as a guide. I remember she was freezing with cold. As I was laying a wreath, I recalled that, like Leningrad, Malta, too, had passed through a siege during the war. After the conferment of the degree, I addressed the faculty of international relations on a 'Second generation United Nations'. As a point of interest, the governor of St Petersburg was Valentina Matviyenko, a former ambassador to Malta in the crucial years of transition from the Soviet Union to Russian Federation. She is very competent and dedicated in her work and, to my knowledge, very close to President Putin. She has contributed a great deal to making the city, which houses one of the world's leading museums, the Hermitage, one of the main cities of our continent. At Mihailovesky Castle, I opened an exhibition on 'Seven Years of Maltese Maritime History'. In my short but interesting stay in St Petersburg, I was assisted by Ambassadors Cassar and Vlasov. Corinthia runs one of the leading hotels there, the Nevskij Palace Hotel, situated in one of the best streets of this imperial city.

My visit to Kuwait had been scheduled for quite some time. It had to be put off twice, first because I had to undergo a minor operation, and then the emir had to go abroad for medical care. When my presidency was about to come to an end, the emir sent over his personal plane to take me and my delegation to Kuwait City on March 13. A friendship had arisen between us ever since the emir had visited New York to plead with the UN General Assembly for the liberation of his country. In fact I was visiting Kuwait just weeks after the liberation when the oil wells were still on fire. The emir, who was staying in a temporary villa at the time, was not in the best of health. Even so, he made it a point to welcome me, and he invested me with the Order of Mubarak the Great. I reciprocated by making him a companion of the Order of Merit. We discussed future oil requirements and the emir explained how they handled their oil revenues, stressing the importance on their part to invest such revenues wisely to ensure the livelihood of future generations. Naturally, we also analysed the situation in Iraq and the Palestinian problem but the emir looked very tired, and the crown prince even more so. Sheik Sabah, the prime minister, who used to be foreign minister in my time as foreign minister, was as active as ever. Equally active was my good friend Sheik Nasser Al Sabah, minister of home affairs.

Within a few months, the *dramatis personae* in Kuwait were to change. The emir died soon afterwards. The crown prince was too ill to be considered for succession. Sheik Sabah al Sabah succeeded the emir and Sheik Nassar al Sabah became prime minister. Kuwait holds on to its political traditions, a blend between the modern style of governance in a democracy and the traditions of the Al Sabah family. I hope the new leaders will hold on to the wisdom of the old emir, giving new hopes to the coming generation.

My last appointment abroad as president was in Spain. I was in Valencia on March 18, 2004 and met the personalities of this beautiful city overlooking the Mediterranean. I was made a member of the Valencia Association of Graduates and Doctors in Journalism. The following day I attended the feast of St Joseph, which is celebrated with great pomp and fireworks. Even though, like most Maltese, I am well used to seeing a great deal of fireworks in summer, I found theirs outstanding. Then I went to Navarres to see the parish where a priest of Maltese origin, Don Vincente Scicluna, had lived. He was shot by the Bolshevists during the Spanish Civil War and was beatified by Pope John II in 2002. I heard Mass at the church where he had served; it was said by the auxiliary bishop of Valencia. The event was made even more interesting as relatives of the Blessed Vincente Scicluna attended. The mayor of Valencia, whose surname is Mifsud, gave me as a gift a name-plate of a street named after Malta, Avinguda Repubblica de Malta. *Avinguda* means 'avenue' in Catalan. The street name was given by descendants of Maltese who had settled in Spain in the late eighteenth century. I placed the name-plate in the drive-way of my home.

Only a week before my visit to Spain, 191 people were killed in train bombings in Madrid. As it happens, that morning, March 18, I was at the Palace receiving the diplomatic credentials of a new Spanish ambassador to Malta. Anyway, while I was on my way to the airport after my visit to Valencia, accompanied by our ambassador in Madrid, Cecilia Attard Pirotta, we received a telephone call from Malta requesting my presence at the state funeral of the victims of March 11 terrorist attack. So I travelled to Madrid for the funeral on March 24. Visiting heads of state and other invitees were received at the cathedral by the king and queen of Spain. The Mass was simple but impressive as was the sermon given by the cardinal of Madrid. The visiting dignitaries sat on the side of the high altar. Spanish Prime Minister José Maria Aznar sat next to the opposition leader, who was about to be appointed prime minister after having won the general elections – a victory to which, I may add, the Atocia Station attack contributed. The royal family and the families of the victims sat in the centre. At the end of the Mass, the royal family met the families of the victims individually down the aisle. My term as president was now nearly over. We were fast approaching April 4, 2004.

59

A private citizen again

Quite naturally, speculation was rife at the beginning of the New Year as to who was going to take over as president after my term. Eddie was not showing any interest in the post and, in any case, he had been saying he had planned to retire on reaching his seventieth birthday on February 7, 2004. He had ruled out accepting the post in a newspaper interview carried at the time. But I could hardly believe Eddie would just call it a day and end up having as his main duty taking his grandchildren to school, as he used to say he would do, possibly in jest, on retirement. It was certainly up to him to decide what was best for him but, in my view, he certainly had the qualities required for this demanding post. The difficulty every new man to the post faces is winning the people's acceptance. I make one exception in this regard: Sir Anthony Mamo, the first president, was immediately accepted by all. Character, style, and circumstances all play a determining part in this.

When Eddie decided to retire from the leadership, the party started proceedings to elect his successor. There were three contestants: Louis Galea, John Dalli, and Lawrence Gonzi. I know the three of them very well, having seen their gradual rise in politics from the start of their careers. Louis and Lawrence were former students of mine at the university and, indeed, I was Lawrence's tutor for his thesis. Louis Galea, a good administrator with excellent foresight, has been a minister since 1987 and has always given a good account of himself. Before the 1987 general elections, he was general secretary of the party, having succeeded me to this post when I was elected deputy party leader in 1977. John Dalli is a person of sound efficiency, not always easy to get along with, but certainly intelligent. Some describe him as a rough diamond. He may be rough, but a diamond he certainly is. As a cabinet minister, he was assertive and Fenech Adami gave him a free hand in the running of his ministry. Lawrence Gonzi is an intelligent and dedicated politician, strong in social welfare affairs. Up to this time, he had preferred keeping a low profile. His great appeal lies in his integrity, and one feels that, with him at the helm, the country and the government are in safe hands.

Louis Galea was eliminated in the first round. In the second, Gonzi got a majority of votes but was short of the required number as required by the party's statute. There was a measure of bitterness in the campaign. A leadership campaign is hardly ever easy as supporters of opposing candidates may not always show the required correctness in the fight for the post. In the leadership contest between Eddie and I, the situation was different in that we felt that democracy was at stake at the time. In the last round of the election for the party leadership, Dalli, though certainly disappointed, voted for Gonzi.

While this important political change was taking place, the prime minister and Mrs Fenech Adami hosted an official dinner in my honour at the Auberge de Castille on March 9, 2004. It was attended by both government and opposition members. The occasion was charged with emotion as both Eddie and I knew that to a certain extent this was going to be one of our last encounters in our political lives. I avoided going nostalgic and I toasted to the country's future.

I reciprocated the invitation by hosting a dinner in honour of the prime minister and Mrs Fenech Adami on March 21 at the Palace, Valletta. Eddie and I have lived the history of our country together for over 30 years. We shared very difficult moments and suffered the turmoil of political violence, the death of Raymond Caruana, the frame-up of Pietru Pawl Busuttil, and the bitter disappointment of remaining in opposition when we had won the absolute majority of votes in 1981. We worked hard together to bring about the necessary constitutional changes to ensure that the party winning the majority of votes takes power.

Eddie presented his letter of resignation as prime minister to me on March 23. He looked artificially buoyant to me and I could somehow sense his inner feeling at divesting himself from the day-to-day running of the country, to which he had dedicated so many years of his life. Some time later I received Lawrence Gonzi to whom I entrusted the formation of the cabinet, on appointing him prime minister. We discussed the cabinet, including his decision to take on finance as well. Clearly, he felt the need to give personal attention to the country's finances, particularly in view of the island's EU membership. John Dalli took the foreign affairs portfolio, while Joe Borg resigned his seat on being appointed EU commissioner. The cabinet was sworn in on the same day. A positive change was the addition of Dolores Cristina as social security and welfare minister. Helen D'Amato was appointed parliamentary secretary for health, with special responsibilities for the aged. The political changeover at the top was a case of the new substituting the old.

Eddie attended the swearing-in of Gonzi as prime minister, and I was happy to see at the ceremony Lawrence's father, Ġiġi, whom I have known since my early days in court where he worked as registrar. Of course Lawrence's mother was there, too. They had raised a wonderful family.

My last official engagements as president were related to the commemoration of *Jum il-Ħelsien*. The year 2004 marked the 25th anniversary and I thought it proper to host a reception at the Palace, Valletta and to plant a tree at San Anton Palace. It was the last time for me to go up to the monument at Birgu, this time with a different prime minister at my side. I always found it somewhat difficult going up the path of cobbled stones, particularly if it was rainy. It requires a balancing act to keep one's dignity. Mintoff told me once the path was made difficult to climb on purpose, to show how difficult it had been for Malta to reach that milestone.

On April 1, I received Lawrence Gonzi and we discussed the strong reasons for the appointment of Eddie as president. He also reported about the political situation and our formal entrance in the EU on May 1, 2004, making me feel very much like Moses leading the Jews to the Promised Land but not reaching it himself. I had been involved in the membership process from the very beginning, living the highs and lows, including the freezing of the island's application by the Sant administration in 1996. But membership of the EU is not something that needs to be associated with an individual or individuals, although there have been a number of individuals who played a key part in the process. Membership came about through the long and dedicated effort of the people at all levels, guided by the Nationalist Party, led by a Nationalist government, mandated by a referendum and a general election, as well as the vote of the House of Representatives.

Before leaving San Anton, I hosted a dinner for my family and close relatives. It was a way of saying thank you for all their help and assistance. I particularly felt indebted to Violet. Although she is very private person by nature, in my view she managed to be an excellent first lady throughout my term. She had also helped to transform San Anton Palace from a modest building into a classical residence and introduced changes in the running of the president's palaces, opening the doors for events and visits by people from all sectors of society, including senior citizens. She was an excellent adviser in matters of organisation and was at her best in her work at the Community Chest Fund. In fact, she often took personal interest in cases of people requiring medical care abroad. On my state visits abroad, she would often go visiting places for children suffering serious illnesses to get an insight into how they dealt with difficult cases. She had tried to find a home where people accompanying sick relatives to London could stay, but was advised that the plan was not financially feasible, at least at that time. It was through her effort that the Community Chest Fund began to take half the revenue raised in the annual television fund-raising marathon. She would ensure that terminally ill patients were given all that was required, including very expensive injections, to help them ease their suffering and perhaps extend their life-span. Yet, through it all, Violet kept a very low profile.

We had now already moved most of our personal effects from San Anton to our home in San Pawl tat-Tarġa. It is incredible how many things one accumulates in five years. A house that is not in use deteriorates fast and looks awfully shabby. Refrigerators and washing machines, for example, do not work, plants run wild, and tree roots create problems.

Leaving San Anton was a poignant moment. When we said goodbye to the staff in the palace courtyard in the morning of April 4, most of them were in tears. They had been our extended family. As we stepped into the car, I saw tears in Violet's eyes but we kept a brave face as we were driven past the palace gate for the last time. At the Palace Square in Valletta, we were greeted by the AFM brigadier and I took my last salute as president. I felt an inner sense of satisfaction at having performed my duty to the best of my ability.

As I went up the staircase to the Palace, I had flashbacks in my mind of times past, particularly of the internal and external difficulties on the road to the island's membership of the EU and of the work that had gone into the effort to further establish the presidency as a national institution, respected by all sections of the population, irrespective of their political allegiances. As I arrived at the Pages Room, I greeted Eddie who was about to start the journey that I was concluding. I wished him well personally and in Malta's interest. I was then asked to take my place with other past presidents. My voyage was over.

338

As Eddie Fenech Adami was taking the oath of office, I became a private citizen again. And, as a private citizen I once again committed myself to contribute as best as I could to the island's future. Five years to the day, I had said in my inaugural speech, 'To be Maltese is to live a dream.' I lived that dream. Becoming a private citizen again did not dampen that dream. Exciting times lay ahead for Malta and I intended to share the new times with the same high spirits that motivated my life in the service of the country.

Index

Abdilla, Paul 192
Abdullah II, king of Jordan 326
Abel, Meguid Ismail 255
Abela, Charles 279
Abela, George 263, 271
Abela, Joe 281
Abela, Lino D. 27
Abela Medici, Anthony 182
Abela, Wistin 171
Accademia Siculo-Normanna 329
Addolorata cemetery 139
Adenauer, Konrad 60, 204
Administrative Council (PN) 108, 116
Asian Peoples' Solidarity
    Organisation 64
Agius, Kalcidon 132
Agius, Lino 134, 146
Agius, Maurice 125
Agius, Tanya 285
Airbus 258
Air Malta 99, 149, 244, 245, 258,
    275, 269, 312
Al Sabah, Jabir 223
Albania 106, 224, 225, 226, 232, 297,
    315
Albertini, Gabriele 328
Alia, Ramiz 226
Allied Newspapers Limited 125
Ali Rezaq, Omar Mohammed 242,
    243
Altare della Patria 328
Amato Gauci, Frederick 95
American investment 258
Amin, Idi 84

Anan, Kofi 290
Andreotti, Giulio 60, 130
Angel 194
Apap Bologna, Louis 328
Aquilina, Canon 28
Aquilina, Ġużè 33, 40
Aquilina, Paul 100
Arab League 255, 326
Arafat, Suha 219, 292
Arafat, Yasser 217, 254, 255, 292,
    325, 330
Arcidiacono 56
Aristocracy of the workers 153
Ark Royal 191
Arrigo Azzopardi, Lino 301
Arrigo, Noel 318, 319
Arvid Pardo Memorial Lecture 292
Ashrawi, Hannah 218
Assad, Hafez 260
Atocia Station 334
Attard Kingswell, Joe 92, 203
Attard Pirotta, Cecilia 333
Attardi, Ugo 41
Attlee, Clement 35
Auberge d'Aragon 47, 96
Auberge de Castille 336
August Moon Ball 324
Austro-Hungarian Empire 302
Avertan, Patri 109
AZAD 126
Aznar, Josè Maria 333
Badoglio, Field Marshal Pietro 31
Baker, James 209, 224
Baldacchino, Alfred 113

Balzan, Walter 177, 208, 278
Bank of Valletta 109, 191, 328
Barak, Ehud 260, 293
Barbara, Agatha 132, 140, 141, 142,
   149, 286, 324
Barcelona process 236, 258
Bardia 22
Bartolo, Michael 17, 208, 211, 230,
   233, 278
Basuto soldiers 31
BBC 227
Beethoven 13
Belgium 15, 236
Belknap 196
Ben Yahja, Habib 252
Bencini, Effie 101
Berisha, Sali 226
Berlin 13, 86, 195, 247, 262, 278,
   279, 312
Berlin Wall 86, 87, 159, 195
Berlinguer, Enrico 87, 129
Berlusconi, Silvio 328
Bernard, Fr 28, 34, 83
Bertie, Fra Andrew 291
Bertinotti, Fausto 308
Bessmertnykh, Aleksandr 227
Bethlehem 8, 218, 292, 293
Birindelli, Admiral Gino 106
Black Monday 125
Blair, Tony 329
Blood Commission 64
Blood, Sir Hilary 64
Blue Sisters 124
Boeing 258
Boffa, Charles 27
Boffa, Sir Paul 39, 76, 102, 186
Bonaparte, Napoleon 16, 46
'Bomb Rome' 23
Bonello, Carmelo 157
Bonello du Puis, George 131, 174, 278
Bonello, Marc 328
Bonello, Michael 328

Bonello, Giovanni 124
Bonello, Vincenzo 48
Bonnici, Manwel 174
Borg Costanzi, Victor 147, 185
Borg, George 264
Borg, Isabel 317
Borg, Joe 200, 235, 238, 279, 308,
   312, 328, 336
Borg, Fr Joe 258, 292
Borg, Maurice 192
Borg Olivier, Alexander 207
Borg Olivier, Eddie 36, 45
Borg Olivier, George 19, 36, 39, 45,
   46, 47, 48, 53, 61, 62, 63, 64, 65,
   67, 68, 71, 72, 76, 79, 80, 82, 83,
   84, 85, 89, 90, 91, 92, 93, 96,
   101, 102, 105, 106, 107, 108,
   109, 110, 111, 112, 113, 115,
   116, 117, 134, 140, 141, 150,
   158, 174, 177, 186, 207, 208,
   268, 270, 281
Bosnia Herzegovina 250, 302
Bottomley, Arthur 83
Boxer Revolution 310
Braine, Bernard 83
'Break with Britain resolution' 62, 65
Brigate Rosse 87
Brincat, Joe 164
British forces 39, 182
British government 17, 18, 46, 47,
   61, 62, 63, 64, 65, 71, 82, 84, 89,
   91, 106
British imperialism 18
British Medical Association 123
British rule 17
British security service 181
Broadhurst 70
Bulgaria 300
Bush, President George 196, 290
Buskett Gardens 310
Busuttil, Fr 27
Busuttil, Pietru Pawl 165, 166, 167,

169, 171, 186, 336

Buttigieg, Anton 72, 80, 85, 110, 131, 281

Cachia Caruana, Richard 264, 265

Cachia, Emanuele 122

Cachia, Joe 109

Cachia, John 125, 162

Cachia, Fr Joseph 287

Cachia Zammit, Alexander 39, 79, 97, 103, 134

Cachia Zammit, Lawrence 97, 101

Calì, Giuseppe 8

Calleja, Alfred 127, 180, 182, 191

Calleja, Brigadier Maurice 264, 265

Calleja, Meinrad 265

Camilleri, Frank 48

Camilleri, Fr Frans 33

Camilleri, Gino 166

Camilleri, Giuseppe Maria 39

Camilleri, J.D. 120

Camilleri, John 115, 116, 173

Camilleri, Josie 46

Camilleri, Victor 203, 208, 257, 267, 278

Camilleri, Vincent 279

Canberra High Commission 205

Canon Law 187

Cape Town 269

Cardona, Wilfrid 127

CARE 61

Caritas 315, 323, 324

Carli, Guido 150

Carolinum University of Prague 302

Carrillo, Santiago 87

Caruana, Carmelo 79

Caruana Curran, Maurice 40, 99, 102, 103, 138, 140, 146, 147, 187

Caruana Demajo, Thomas 113

Caruana, Archbishop Dom Maurus 12, 18

Caruana, Raymond 127, 163, 164, 165, 166, 169, 182, 336

Casa, David 265, 279

Casa Sant Cassia 30

Casaroli, Cardinal Agostino 152

Casino Maltese 110

Cassar, Charles 179, 180, 193

Cassar Galea, Joseph 85

Cassar, George 36

Cassar, Girolamo 311

Cassar, Ġużè 80, 110, 138, 149, 160, 281

Cassar, Joe 208, 230, 247, 267, 278,

Cassar, Mario 158

Cassar Naudi, Joseph 187

Castille Place 34

Catholic Church 23, 187

Catholic marriages 187

Cato 37

Caucescu, Nicolae 106

Cauchi, Lino 127, 182

Central Bank 89, 328

Chamber of Commerce 138, 290, 312, 328

Charter of Paris 249

Chee Hwa Teng 309

China 106, 203, 226, 227, 228, 229, 251, 252, 258, 261, 278, 308, 309, 310

China Dock 252

Chinese Institute of Culture 252

Chou Chen, Vivien 309

Christian Democratic Movement of Europe 302

Christian Workers' Party 65, 68, 95

Christopher, Sister 12

Christopher, Warren 246, 258

Churchill, Sir Winston 17, 22, 34, 35, 305

Church-run schools 151, 152, 153

Church-state relations 64

CID 166

Ciampi, Carlo Azelio 291, 327

Civil marriage 187

Clinton, President Bill 224, 325
CNN 231, 231, 311
Cohn-Bendit, Daniel 87
Cold war 19, 34, 35, 60, 150, 195,
    197, 207, 215, 228, 235, 262, 295
Coleiro, Edoardo 40, 46
College of Foreign Affairs 309
Colombo, Arturo 39
Colonial administration 3, 5, 17, 81
Colonial flag 46
Colonial legal service 46
Colonial Office 47, 62
Comitato Permanente Universitario
    45
Commission for the Administration
    of Justice 133, 134, 178, 297, 307,
    318
Commonwealth and Foreign
    Relations Office 47
Commonwealth Heads of
    Government Meetings 261
Commonwealth Parliamentary
    Association 81, 82, 126, 199
Commonwealth Parliamentary
    Conference 83
Communist Party 195, 251
Community Chest Fund 323, 324,
    338, 390
Confederation of Free Trade Unions
Conference for Security and Co-
    operation in Europe 107, 249,
    295
Connelly, John 83
Constitution 17, 18, 29, 62, 71, 82,
    107, 110, 111, 112, 120, 142,
    146, 149, 150, 154, 155, 161,
    164, 171, 262, 281, 286, 297, 318
Constitutional amendments of 1987
    80, 242
Constitutional court 107, 112, 134,
    140, 154, 161, 186
Constitutional Party 3, 36, 40

Copeland, Fr 28, 29
Corfu Summit 238
Corinthia Hotel 309, 326, 331, 332
Council for the Mediterranean 204,
    259
Council of Association 259
Council of Europe 13, 59, 80, 85, 86,
    87, 88, 139, 195, 199, 204, 236,
    267, 269, 296, 302
Council of Government 2
Council of Presidents 290
Court of Appeal 37, 121, 134, 186
Creasy, Sir Gerald 2
Cremona, John J. 107
Cremona, Ninu 18
Cremona, Paul 149
Criminal Code 53, 69, 123
Criminal Court 69, 70, 121, 123,
    186, 241
Cristina, Dolores 337
Croatia 250, 251, 268, 302
Crown Advocate General's Office 69,
    76, 112, 140, 141, 177
Crown Counsel 76, 77, 141
Crusaders of the Blessed Sacrament
    1, 13
CSCE 107, 215, 227, 236, 247, 249,
    257
Cuffaro, Salvatore 329
Curia 63, 152, 153, 187
Curmi, Giovanni 40
Cuschieri, Anastasio 18
Cuschieri, Gejtu 157
Customs House 21
Cutajar, Lawrence 192
Cutajar, Major 182
Cyprus 200, 236, 237, 238, 261, 308,
    316, 317
Czechoslovakia 13, 230, 302
D'Alema, Massimo 292
D'Amato, Helen 337
Daily Chronicle 17

Dalli, John 174, 335, 336
Dandria, Mgr Enrico 72
Dante 40, 41, 224, 303
Darmanin, Father 28
Darmanin, Ġuże 51
Darmanin, Joanna 279, 285
de Gasperi, Alcide 41, 60, 204
De Michelis, Gianni 200, 231, 250
Debating Society 28, 37, 44
Debono, Joe 192
Debono, Nardu 120, 178
Decolonisation 137, 213
DeGaetano, George 36
De Gaulle, President Charles 91, 107
De Klerk, Frederik Willem 216
Deladier, Edouard 14
Delia, Fr Ġuże 27
Delors, Jacques 235, 237
De Marco, Guido: family history,
    childhood and education 2-14;
    life during the war and in shelters
    3-31; university life 39-41; first
    interest in politics 45-49; marries
    Violet 55-57; Violet 43, 44, 46,
    55, 56, 57, 59, 60, 70, 72, 75, 76,
    77, 96, 110, 119, 120, 157, 161,
    172, 225, 241, 269, 271, 282,
    285, 286, 290, 292, 296, 300,
    301, 308, 310, 311, 316, 317,
    319, 323, 324, 326, 327, 331,
    337, 338, 345; Gianella 75, 110,
    138, 241; Fiorella 75, 119, 161,
    241, 294, 309, 345; Mario 76,
    119, 161, 241, 275, 322; interlude
    with Herbert Ganado's party 67-
    73; elected to Parliament 75-78;
    early years in parliament 79-88; as
    government minister 177-183;
    skin disorder 189-190; as
    president of the UN General
    Assembly 217-234; as president
    of Malta 285-334; accident in

Bulgaria 300-301
Democratic Action Party 39
Democrazia Cristiana 41
Department of Information 77
Desert war 22
Diacono, Anthony 312
Diamantopoulos, Anna 308
Dimech, Manwel 4
Diplomatic corps 95, 203, 205, 238,
    307, 328
Diplomatic incident 194, 324
Diplomatic World Bulletin 211
Divine, Fr 28, 29
Dorman, Sir Maurice 91, 107
DPP vs Beard (1920) 70
Dubcek, Alexander 230, 302
Durda, Omar Abu Zaid 275
Dzurinda, Mikuláš 307
East Berlin 86
E-boats 29
Echard, Fred 208
Eden, Sir Anthony 248
Education Act 153
Edwin Grech 279, 283
Egypt 30, 71, 161, 252, 255, 326
EgyptAir hijacking 187
Eisenhower, General Dwight 30
Elections, 1987 72
Electoral districts 113, 130, 131, 135,
    150, 248
Elia Borg Bonaci Café 96
Elizabeth II, Queen 296
Ellul, Michael 183
Emma, Sister 12
Encounter 41, 51, 60, 71, 86, 225,
    327
England, Richard 90
Enlai, Zhou 251
Essen Summit 238, 277
Ethiopia 9, 14, 230, 231
Euro-Communism 87
Euro-Med process 230, 277

European Convention for the Protection of Human Rights and Fundamental Freedoms 185
European Court of Human Rights 48, 87
European Economic Community 130, 200, 204
European Peoples' Party 85
European Union 72, 107, 200, 201, 236, 237, 238, 239, 259, 300, 308, 313, 322, 326
European Union of Christian Democrats 199
Excelsior Hotel 103
Expropriation 110, 138
Fabian Society 80
Fabriani, Arnaldo 7, 16
Faisal, Saud al 253, 256
Falun Gong 309
Falzon, Michael 174
Falzon, Nazju 291, 305
Fanfani, Amintore 60, 130
Farrugia, Philip 69
Fascism 100, 135
Fascist Grand Council 31
Fascist Repubblica Sociale Italiana 34
Faustino, Padre 8
Federation of Industry 290, 328
Federation of Parent-Teacher Associations 153
Fenech Adami, Eddie 36, 45, 92, 93, 101, 103, 108, 110, 111, 112, 115, 116, 117, 124, 125, 126, 131, 133, 149, 150, 157, 160, 162, 163, 169, 171, 173, 174, 179, 180, 189, 192, 193, 195, 196, 199, 207, 235, 242, 245, 246, 249, 251, 258, 261, 264, 265, 266, 276, 278, 282, 308, 321, 335, 336, 337, 338, 339
Fenech, Joe 51, 175
Ferġha Drammatika, Għaqda

tal-Malti Università 43
Ferro, Colonel 29
Fini, Gianfranco 328
Fiorini Lowell, Alfred 264
First World War 2, 4, 17, 18, 328
Firth, Fr 28, 29
Fisher, Jack 83
Fisher, Nigel 82, 83
Fleri Soler, Tancred 27
Flores, Joseph 41, 146
Floriana 7, 16, 21, 72, 99, 130, 153, 248, 294, 315
Fogarty, Prof. 37, 44
Fontaine, Nicole 308
Foreign Interference Act 140
Foreign Office 95, 200, 205, 206, 266, 267, 278, 279, 325, 329
Foreign Office Review 206
Forensic Laboratory 127, 182
Fort St Elmo 46, 242
Franġisk, Dun 28
Franca, Donna 327, 328
France 5, 14, 15, 21, 22, 34, 105, 107, 130, 236, 317
Francia family 17
Free trade unions 100, 124
Freedom Day 191
Freitas do Amaral, Diogo 86
French Revolution 73, 140
Frendo Azzopardi, Jackie 39
Frendo Azzopardi, Joseph 172
Gaddafi, Muammar 107, 203, 246, 329, 330, 331
Galea Debono, Joe 122
Galea, Louis 116, 131, 157, 163, 173, 174, 301, 335, 336
Galea, Rob. 40
Ganado, Albert 46, 63, 68
Ganado, Herbert 45, 63, 64, 67, 68, 69, 100
Ganado, J.M. 70
Gandhi, Mahatma 137

Garibaldi, Giuseppe 327
Gatt, Austin 264, 303
Gatt, Ċensu 41
Gatt, Lawrence 174
Gauci, Miriam 312
Gauci, Victor 203, 205, 257
Gaza 217, 218, 219, 224, 230
General Assembly of the United
    Nations 199, 206, 207, 208, 210,
    212, 213, 217, 219, 220, 223,
    227, 228, 232, 233, 234, 249,
    251, 255, 259, 260, 273, 274,
    290, 295, 302, 311, 315, 332, 345
General Workers' Union 39, 76, 81,
    92, 100, 124, 142, 159, 203, 269,
    290, 299
Genscher, Hans-Dietrich 247, 250,
    308
George Cross 30, 110, 305
George VI, King 30, 31, 34, 305
Gerada, Mgr Emmanuel 92
Ghannouchi, Mohammed 307
Giacomelli, Giorgio 209, 219
Gieħ ir-Repubblika 287
Gioia, Anthony H. 311
Giovane Malta 17
Glasnost 197, 227
Goethe 13, 303
Gol, Ehud 325
Golan Heights 254, 261, 304
Gonzi, Archbishop Sir Michael 12,
    61
Gorbachev, Mikhail 35, 195, 196,
    197, 227, 228, 290
Gozo Party 40
Grand Harbour 29, 30, 191
Grand Hotel St Regis 328
Grand Master Ramon Perellos 79
Grand Master Verdalle 310
Grand Master Vilhena 310
Grand Master Ximenes 46
Great Wall of China 309

Grech, Edwin 279, 283
Grech, Jean Paul 279
Grech, John 328
Grech, Karin 126, 127, 182
Grech, Louis 312
Grech Orr, Charles 126
Grech, Mgr Victor 315, 324
Grey, Ian 83
Grima, Chris 279
Grima, Joe 264
Grima, Karmenu 125
GRTU 290
Gudja 163, 166
Guevara, Ernesto 'Che' 87
Guido de Marco and Associates 241,
    307
Guiron, Yang 310
Gulf Cooperation Council 253
Gulf crisis 213
Gulia, Oliver 68, 102, 146
Gulia, Wallace 36, 45, 146
Ħal-Far 131
Halonen, Tarja 274
Hansen, Peter 83
Harding, Hugh 36
Harding, William 146
Harley Street 189
Hassan, Prince 219, 220
Havel, Vaclav 230, 302, 315
Haven Bar 6, 24
Headquarters Allied Forces
    Mediterranean 47, 105
Hegel 13
Helsinki 107, 150, 204, 236, 249
Hermitage 332
Herrera, Josè 163
Herrera, Joseph 163
High Court of Justice 190
Hiroshima 35
Hitler 13, 14, 15, 34
HM Naval Dockyard 17
HMS *Edinburgh* 191

HMS *Terror* 23
Hogg, Douglas 245
Holland 15
Holland, Patrick 81, 85
Holy Land 219, 294
Holy Trinity Church 8
Hong Kong 308, 309
House of Commons 61, 82, 248, 326
House of Representatives 7, 177,
    285, 307, 308, 318, 322, 327, 337
House Select Committee 169
Hoxha, Enver 225
Human Rights Day 215
Hurd, Douglas 236, 244, 250, 262
Hussein, King 276
Hussein, Saddam 208, 209, 210, 220
Husseini, Faisal 256
Hyzler, A. 40
Hyzler, George 174
Idris, King 71
Il Corriere della Sera 14
Il-Berqa 22, 70
Il-Biskuttin 7, 8, 11, 21
Illustrious 22, 23
Il-Moviment tal-Malti għat-Tfal 33
Il-Ħajja 125
Il Sung, Kim 204, 227, 229
Imelda, Sister 12
In... Tagħna 122, 165
Independence Arena 72, 294
Independence Day 72, 73, 108, 109,
    113, 117
Independent World Commissiosn for
    the Oceans 269
In-Nazzjon Tagħna 95, 113
Integration 60, 61, 62, 63, 64, 80,
    105, 268, 332
Inter-Governmental Conference 238
International Maritime Law Institute
    175
Inter-Parliamentary Conference on
    Security and Co-Operation in the

Mediterranean 259
Intifada 217, 218, 221, 293, 294
Irish Republican Army 61
Iron curtain 35, 86, 195, 197, 228,
    258, 295
Israeli secret services 194
Italian culture 18, 40
Italian language 16, 18, 28, 45, 278
Italian security service 181
IVA campaign 321
Ix-Xagħra tal-Floriana 72
Iż-Żuż 51, 52
Jalloud, Abdul Salam 245
Japan's surrender 35
Jerusalem 218, 219, 254, 256, 325
Jewish settlements 293
John XXIII, Pope 59
John Paul II, Pope 60, 151, 159, 224,
    291, 299, 302, 317, 328
John's Garage 193
Jones Party 40
Judiciary 76, 129, 156, 177, 178, 186,
    297, 307, 315, 317, 318, 319
Jum il-Helsien 337
Juppé, Alain 239, 255
Kadima 325
Kalkara 134
Kaplani, Mohammed 225
Katim 34
Katsav, Moshe 325
Kennedy, President John F. 195
Khaddoumi, Farouk 220
King George V Hospital 76
King's Own 3
Kingdom of the Two Sicilies
Kiwanuka, Benedicto Kabimu
    Mugumba 84, 85
Klerides, Glafkos 316
Knights of St John 16
Knightshall 77
Kohl, Helmut 308
Kollek, Theodor 'Teddy' 218

Kosovo 250, 251
KSU 45
Kucan, Milan 251, 302, 317
Kunsill Universitarju Nazzjonalista
48
Kunz, Gerhard 311, 312
Kwan, Hung Ng 68, 69, 70
Kwasniewski, Aleksander 317, 326
La Vallette Band Club 3, 4, 44
Labour parliamentary group 160
Latvia 238, 325
Law of the Sea 95, 203, 292
Law Society 36
Laycock, Sir Robert 62, 324
Le mie vicende 37
Leadership election 115, 116, 249
League of Nations 13
Legislative Assembly 2, 18, 40, 62
Leħen is-Sewwa 9, 14, 63
Leningrad 332
Levi, David 218
Liberation 235
Liberation of Kuwait 210, 223
Liberto, Italia 11
Libya 22, 30, 71, 107, 130, 204, 244,
245, 246, 252, 258, 274, 275,
302, 312, 329, 330, 331
Libyan Arab Foreign Investment Co.
275
Libyan-Arab Maltese Holding
Company 275
Licari, Joseph 235
L-Imnarja 138
L-Istrina Flimkien 323
Lockerbie 187, 241, 243, 245, 246,
247, 252, 275
L'Orangerie 109, 120, 285
Lord Carrington 106
l-orizzont 132
Lovelace, Richard 216
Lufthansa Technik 312
Luftwaffe 22, 25, 126

Lungaro Mifsud, Vera 175
Lyceum 7, 33, 153
MacDonald Constitution 29
Macedonia 250, 251
Madl, Ferenc 316
Madrid Peace Conference 224
Maginot Line 14
Maghreb 71, 252
Malta Association of Professional
Bodies 318
Malta Development Corporation 89,
312
Malta Dockyard Corporation 89
Malta Environment and Planning
Authority 311
Malta Export Trade Corporation 253
Malta Government Employees'
Union 124
Malta Hotels and Restaurants
Association 138
Malta in the Making 157
Malta Labour Party 60, 61, 62, 64,
65, 72, 73, 81, 95, 97, 109, 113,
117, 124, 125, 133, 142, 157,
158, 161, 166, 193, 203, 249,
263, 265, 266, 267, 268, 269,
271, 278, 279, 321, 323, 326
Malta Shipbuilding 191
Malta Summit 196, 197
Malta-US relations 246
Maltese nationalism 18, 208
Maltese-EU Parliamentary
Committee 239
Mamo, Lady 324
Mamo, Sir Anthony 69, 70, 107, 110,
112, 146, 286, 324, 335
Mamo, Paul 100
Manchè, Albert 48
Manchè, Richard 127
Mandela, Nelson 216
Mann Borgese, Elizabeth 233
Mannarino, Don Gaetano 46

Mansueto, Charles 323
Marchetti, Savoia 21
Marcuse, Herbert 86
Mare Nostrum 41, 312
Marin, Manuel 236, 258
Marina di Ragusa 137, 138, 140
Marlborough House 68, 71
Marriage Act 187
Marsa Secondary School 153
Marsamxett harbour 23
Martini, Admiral 181
Matrenza, Richard 278
Matutes, Abel 275
Matviyenko, Valentina 332
Mau Mau 46
May, Betty 83
May, Erskine 90
Maxim Gorky 196
Mboya, Tom 83
McNeil, Roy 83
Mdina 91, 101, 119, 309
Medavia 275
Médecins Sans Frontières 231
Mediterranean 17, 31, 35, 39, 41, 47,
     62, 71, 77, 83, 96, 105, 106, 107,
     130, 197, 200, 204, 205, 206,
     213, 224, 235, 236, 237, 253,
     255, 257, 258, 259, 260, 261,
     265, 268, 277, 286, 296, 300,
     302, 303, 305, 308, 310, 312,
     313, 315, 322, 323, 327, 329,
     330, 333
Mediterranean Academy of
     Diplomatic Studies 205, 315
Mediterranean basket 107, 204, 236
Mediterranean Conference Centre
     77, 96, 265
Mediterranean policy 107, 130, 204,
     206, 313, 323
Meidani, Rexhep 297
Mein Kampf 13
Mengistu, Mariam Haile 230

Mercieca, Sir Arturo 37, 45, 72
Mercieca, Manwel 51
Meri, Lennart 303, 325
Micallef, Manwel 299
Micallef Stafrace, Joseph 81
Middle East 194, 204, 213, 216, 219,
     220, 224, 237, 254, 255, 259,
     296, 317
Mifsud Bonnici, Carmelo 18
Mifsud Bonnici, Karmenu 99, 152,
     153, 159, 160, 161, 170, 173,
     248, 263
Mifsud Bonnici, Ugo 36, 53, 79, 91,
     92, 108, 110, 115, 116, 149, 163,
     173, 262, 276, 285, 286, 318
Mifsud, David 285
Mifsud, Joe 292
Mifsud Tommasi, Anthony 178, 180,
     182
Mifsud, Sir Ugo 2, 72, 208, 281
Military base 106, 150, 169, 251
Miller, Reggie 39
Mintoff Dom 39, 46, 47, 53, 60, 61,
     62, 63, 64, 65, 67, 68, 71, 76, 79,
     80, 81, 89, 90, 92, 99, 101, 105,
     106, 107, 108, 110, 111, 112,
     113, 115, 117, 122, 123, 125,
     126, 129, 130, 131, 132, 134,
     137, 138, 140, 141, 142, 149,
     150, 151, 152, 153, 159, 160,
     164, 169, 170, 193, 203, 204,
     249, 251, 259, 263, 267, 269,
     270, 271, 279, 281, 328, 337
Miruzzi, Miss 11
Mitrovich, Giorgio 72
Mitterrand, François 219
Mizzi, Achille 285
Mizzi, Albert 149
Mizzi, Edgar 112, 125, 140, 141,
     150, 157, 160, 170, 244
Mizzi, Fortunato 1, 16, 17, 56, 72,
     141

Mizzi, Nerik 1, 2, 13, 16, 18, 39, 48
Mock, Alois 250, 308
Montanaro Gauci, Anthony 146
Montgomery, Field Marshal 30
Monte di Pietà 24
Montebello, Dennis 133
Montecitorio 327, 328
Moran, Vincent 81, 83
Moran, Willie 100, 102
Moro, Aldo 60, 129, 327
Moscovici, Pierre 308
Mountbatten, Lord Louis 47, 63, 105
Moussa, Amr 252, 326
Mubarak, Hosni 255, 326
Munich crisis 12
Muscat Azzopardi, Godwin 193
Muscat Azzopardi 18
Muscat, Carmelo 36
Muscat, Richard 137
MUSEUM 305
Muslim Brotherhood 326
Mussolini 14, 15, 21, 31, 34
Nagasaki 35
Narvel Garba, Joseph 208
Nasser, Sheik Al Sabah 333
National Congress of Students 46
Nationalism 1, 17, 18, 47, 63, 68,
    208, 251
Nationalist Party 2, 3, 16, 18, 19, 31,
    36, 37, 39, 40, 48, 49, 60, 61, 62,
    63, 64, 65, 67, 68, 77, 79, 84, 85,
    92, 95, 99, 100, 106, 108, 112,
    114, 115, 117, 125, 130, 133,
    134, 135, 137, 138, 141, 142,
    149, 153, 156, 158, 160, 161,
    163, 165, 166, 169, 170, 178,
    181, 186, 241, 265, 271, 321, 337
Nationalist Youth Movement 60, 63
Nato headquarters 105, 266
Naudi, Fr 28
Nazareth 254, 323
Nazism 35, 100

Nehru, Pandit 72
Neolithic temples 309
Neutrality 130, 150, 160, 169, 170,
    262
New South Wales 18
New York 199, 207, 208, 209, 210,
    211, 213, 229, 243, 244, 245,
    251, 260, 267, 273, 274, 275,
    278, 290, 311, 332
Ngala, Ronald 83
Non-Aligned Movement 204, 207,
    212
North Atlantic Association 105
North Atlantic Cooperation Council
    262
North Korea 204, 227, 229, 230
Novetsky Sally 242
Obote, Milton 83, 126
October 15, 1979 125, 134
Ogata, Sakako 210
Ohio 30
Olmert, Ehud 325
Order of Bethlehem 293
Order of St Michael and St George
    296
Organisation for Security and
    Cooperation in Europe 215, 234,
    236, 247, 249, 250, 262, 279, 295
Oslo agreement 217, 254, 256
Ottawa conference 82
Our Lady of Mount Carmel 2, 8, 75,
    109, 200
Oxfam 231
Oxford Studio 12
Pace, Fr 28
Pace, Giuseppe 40
Pace, Joseph 189
Pace, Paolo 85
Palazzo Parisio 205, 207, 208, 265
Palazzo Venezia 15
Palestine Liberation Organisation
    194, 220

Palestinian Authority 254, 256
Palzner, Avi 255
Pantalleresco, Mgr Albert 46
Papakostantinou, Michalis 236
Para-military labour corps 151
Parastatal employees 138
Pardo, Arvid 95, 203, 292, 342
Parliamentary Assembly of the
    Council of Europe 296
Parnis, Michael 299
Parnis, Tony 77
Partit Nazzjonalista 67
Partito Nazionale 67
Partnership for Peace 262, 265
Patto d'Acciaio 15
Pax Mediterranea 312, 329
PCP 65
Pellegrini, Toni 64, 65, 68
Pemphigus 189, 190
Peng, Li 228, 258
Pereira, N.P 83
Peres, Shimon 253, 256, 260, 276,
    293, 296, 324, 325
Perestroika 197, 227
Perez de Quellar, Javier 208
Permanent Commission against
    Corruption 185
Permanent Law Revision
    Commission 186
Persson, Göran 307
Petacci, Clara 34
Petrovsky, Vladimir 227, 234, 245
Philip, Prince 307
Piazza Venezia 327
Pickering, Thomas 210, 274, 275
Pico, Joseph 158
Pincio 16
Pisani, Adeodata 291, 305
Pius XII, Pope 6, 59
Plumer, Field Marshal Lord 18
Poland 15, 34, 159, 238, 312, 317,
    318, 326

Police academy 180, 182, 190
Police Force 73, 105, 117, 121, 127,
    165, 166, 173, 177, 178, 180,
    181, 182, 183, 190, 191, 193, 199
Polling booths 171
Populorum Progressio 59
Potsdam 35
Prague Spring 230, 302
Preca, Saint Ġorġ 291, 305
Presti, Consolata 4
Prison regulations 187
Private schools 138, 153
Pro-Europe campaign 321
Proffitt, Catherine 274
Progress Press 125
Psaila, Andrew 323
Psaila, Dun Karm 7
Psaila Savona, Joe 193
Public Broadcasting Service 323
Public Registry 186
Pullicino, Lawrence 120, 165, 178
Punta del Este Conference 311
Putin, President Vladimir 332
Qian, Qichen 228, 251, 308, 309
Quadragesimo Annum 48
Quirinale 327
Quneitra 304
Rabin, Yitzhak 217, 260, 261
Ragonesi, Victor 112
Rajt Malta Tinbidel 45
Raniolo, Francesco 4, 7, 8, 15, 16
Rau, Johannes 312, 325
Red Cross 22
Rediffusion 33, 62
Refalo, Carmelo 81
Regia Aeronautica 21
Regina vs Falzon 121
Removal of George Borg Olivier
    115, 116, 117
Republic Day 113, 319
Rerum Novarum 48
Rhodesia 82, 84, 89

Rifondazione Communista 308
Rizzo Naudi, John 174, 189, 190,
    194, 279
Roh, Tae Woo 230
Roman Catholic religion 111
Rommel, Erwin 30
Roosevelt, President Franklin D. 34,
    35, 305
Royal Navy 3, 17, 39, 191
Royal Opera House 12
Rule of law 130, 156, 177, 208, 212,
    243, 258, 268
Russian Federation 228, 262, 332
Rupel, Dimitrij 250
Rüütel, Arnold 325
Langer, S. 187
Saar 13
Sabah, Michel 325
Safi 171, 315
Said Pullicino, Joe 241, 307, 318
Saliba, Evarist 203
Saliba, George 274, 278
Saliba, Guido 36, 43, 183
Sammut, Eric 45
Sammut, Salvu 299
San Anton Palace 24, 175, 287, 337
San Anton Gardens 316
San Pawl tat-Tarġa 120, 287, 338
Sandys, Duncan 13, 14, 71
Sang-Ock, Lee 229
Sant, Alfred 166, 248, 263, 269, 321,
    323
Sant, Lorry 92, 132, 138, 171, 173,
    180
Santa Marija convoy 30
Sarajevo 250, 257
Saudi Arabia 123, 162, 253
Saudi International Trade Fair 253
Savona, Father 12
Scajola, Claudio 308
Sceberras, Camillo 72
Sceberras Trigona, Alex 132, 204,

269
Scerri, Vincent 41, 146
Schembri, Carmelo 146
Schembri, Giovanna 4
Schembri, Noel 158
Schroeder, Gerhard 312
Schumann, Robert 60, 204
Schussel, Wolfgang 273, 274
Sciberras, Maria 187
Scicluna, Carmelo 154
Scicluna, Don Vincente 333
Sciriha, Canon George 28
Sea Malta 99
Seaston, Fr Gerald 40
Security at the airport 187
Security Council 207, 209, 210, 223,
    234, 245
Security Council Resolutions 210,
    213, 220, 224
Self-government 17, 18, 29, 31, 39,
    45, 64
Self-government constitution 17, 18,
    281
Selvatico, Furtu 139
Services' rundown 89
Sette Giugno 18, 45, 113
Seychell, Ang. 323
Shangkun, Yang 228
Sharon, Ariel 325
Shevardnadze, Edward 35, 196, 226,
    228
Shihabi, Samir S. 290
Sibtijiet Flimkien 149
Sigmunson Sigmund 208
Silajdižic, Haris 251
Simitis, Kostas 307, 317
Sir Paul Boffa Hospital 76
Sisters of the Little Company of
    Mary 124
Slava 196
Slovenia 238, 250, 251, 301, 302, 317
Smith, Linda 208

Smith regime 82
Soares, Mario 86
Socialist thugs 125, 153, 171
Società Universitaria di Letteratura
   Italiana 41
Society of Jesus 27, 28
Sodano, Angelo 225
Sofia 300, 301
Soler, Denis 189, 190
Soler, Ines 43
Solidarnosc 124, 317, 318
Sorbonne 87, 303
Sovereign Military Order of Malta
   291
Soviet Union 35, 71, 87, 105, 107,
   226, 227, 228, 230, 262, 303, 332
Spanish Civil War 9, 333
Special Action Group 181
Special Mobile Unit 166, 170, 171,
   179
Spiers, Ronald 208
Spiteri, Lino 248
Spiteri, Salvinu 124
Srebrenica 250, 257
Sri Lanka 83
St Aloysius College 12, 27, 28, 33,
   79, 119, 126, 279
St Aloysius Gonzaga 28
St Cajetan Church 33, 287
St Dorothy's School 119
St Francis church 8
St Gaetano Band 33
St Ignatius of Loyola 28
St John's co-cathedral 13, 25, 100,
   319
St Joseph of the Apparition 6, 11
St Joseph School 119
St Joseph's Convent 12
St Joseph's High School 6, 22, 33
St Luke's Hospital 109
St Paul's Shipwreck 331
St Petersburg 332

St Rocco Baths 3, 4, 5
Sta Caterina d'Italia 12, 56
Stability Pact Conference 259
Stalin 34, 35
State Department 210, 258
Statute of Westminster 47, 82
Stella Maris College 153
Stellini, Salvu 278
Stoyanov, Petar 301
Strickland, Lord 186
Strickland, Mabel 40, 60, 65, 68, 153
Strasbourg 13, 85, 86, 88, 174, 178,
   267, 269
Stubbings, David 158
Student Representative Council 1,
   45, 91
Studio Master 138
Stukas 23
Suarez, Adolfo 86
Sudeten 13
Suez Canal 17
Sullivan, John 312
Ta' Ċenċ 90, 120
Ta' Kandja 180, 181
Tabone, Anthony 328
Tabone, Anton 134, 174, 280, 307
Tabone, Ċensu 79, 95, 108, 110, 115,
   116, 162, 173, 174, 199, 204,
   235, 251, 281, 286
Tal-Barrani 161, 162
Tanti, Gejtu 299
Tapestry Chamber 79, 304
Tarxien 164, 165, 248
Teferi Ber 231
Telemalta Corporation 124, 203
Teresa, Mother 224, 225
Terror 23, 352
Testa, Oscar 6
The Bulletin 37
The Daily Telegraph 122
The Independent on Sunday 271, 321
The Palace 3, 4, 16, 34, 79, 100, 117,

173, 175, 177, 180, 270, 285,
286, 287, 290, 296, 304, 305,
310, 311, 316, 317, 318, 319,
324, 327, 331, 333, 336, 337, 338
The Sunday Times 271, 321
The Times 122, 126, 153,
Thomistic philosophy 36, 42
Thomson, George 84
Three Cities 23, 39
Tiananmen Square 226, 252
Times of Malta 14, 70, 91
Tito, Josip Broz 250
Tomb of the Patriarchs 255, 256
Tonna, Benny 324
Tonna, Giuseppe 51
Tonna, Joe 177, 230, 279, 282, 285
Totò 134
Treaty of Rome 60
Truman, President Harry S. 35
Trusteeship Council 233, 292
Tse Tung, Mao 251
Tudjman, Franco 251
Tufigno, Michael 141
Twin Towers 311, 326
Uber Alles 13
Uganda 2, 31, 37, 39, 46, 63, 83, 84,
126
UN 41, 186, 203, 207, 208, 209, 210,
211, 212, 213, 215, 216, 217,
218, 219, 220, 221, 223, 224,
225, 226, 227, 228, 229, 230,
231, 232, 233, 234, 236, 245,
246, 247, 249, 250, 251, 252,
255, 258, 259, 260, 274, 275,
278, 290, 292, 295, 301, 302,
311, 315, 318, 332
UN Charter 207, 213, 220, 227, 247,
249, 295
Unemployment problem 13, 62
UNHCR 231
Unilateral Declaration of
Independence 82

Union Jack 46, 60
Union Ħaddiema Magħqudin 100,
124, 290, 299
Unione degli Industrialisti di Roma
327
Unione Politica Maltese 67
United Arab Emirates 253
United Nations 34, 61, 95, 197, 199,
206, 207, 215, 217, 221, 233,
234, 247, 249, 262, 292, 295,
296, 323, 332
United States 35, 61, 85, 107, 181,
220, 245, 255, 258, 290, 311, 326
Università 16, 37, 43, 278, 357
University of Bridgeport 295
University of Malta 205, 299, 312,
328
University Sports Club 37
Upper St Elmo 182
Uruguay 311
US air raids 220
Valencia Association of Graduates
and Doctors 333
Valenzia, Geoffrey 166
Valenzia, Kenneth 183
Valletta 1, 2, 3, 4, 5, 6, 9, 11, 15, 21,
22, 23, 24, 25, 27, 33, 34, 36, 39,
41, 43, 44, 47, 48, 77, 79, 91, 96,
108, 109, 125, 172, 191, 248,
259, 265, 271, 296, 299, 304,
309, 311, 315, 316, 323, 328,
331, 336, 337, 338
Value added tax 263, 265, 268
Van den Broek, Hans 273, 274, 276,
277
Vanderfelt, Sir Robin 83
Vassallo, John 238, 267
Vatican Council 152
Vatican Council II 59
VE day 34, 35
Vella, Fr Bartolomew 28
Vella brothers 158

Vella, Charles 238
Vella, Gejtu 299
Vella, George 263, 267, 268, 274
Vella Haber, Kelinu 33
Vella, J.J. 103
Vella, Michael 177
Vella, Patrick 318, 319
Verdala Palace 12, 310, 311, 316
Verheugen, Gunter 277
Versailles Treaty 13
Victory Kitchens 30
Vike-Freiberga, Vaira 325
Vilhena Hall 193
Vincenti Buildings 33, 41
Violence 61, 62, 96, 99, 100, 103,
    108, 109, 110, 111, 113, 125,
    126, 127, 131, 133, 135, 137,
    144, 145, 153, 163, 164, 165,
    170, 179, 180, 181, 192, 193,
    256, 266, 267, 316, 336
Virgil Society 36
Vittorio Emmanuele II, King of
    Piedmont and Sardinia 22
Vittoriosa 270
Von Weizsacker, Richard 311
Kaleme, W. 83
Wagner 13
Wallstrom, Margöt 307
War Damage Commission 33, 39
Warsaw Pact 87, 230, 317
Weizman, Ezer 253
Wembley Store 44
Wenyi Wang 309
West Bank 217, 219, 224, 230
Western Alliance 106
Western Europe 86, 159, 246
Westminster Hotel 44
White House 258
Wied id-Dies 143, 145
Wirth, Alfred 102
Work Agency for Palestinian
    Refugees 209

World Commission for the Oceans
    269, 353
World Economic Forum 326
World Summit for Children 211
World War II 9, 137, 302, 317, 332
Xandir Malta 125, 137
Xuereb, J.H. 56
Xuereb, Paul 173
Yacht marina, Cottonera 175, 269
Yalta 34, 35
Yanayev, Gennady 227
Yeltsin, Boris 227, 228
YMCA 323
Yong Nam, Kim 228
Zaegel, Charles 13
Zahra, F.X. 328
Zahra, Giuseppe 76
Zammit, Bernard 34
Zammit Clapp, Emilia 124
Zammit, Duminku 145
Zammit, Lawrence 312
Zammit, Mary 124
Zammit, Michele 4
Zammit, Susanna 4
Zammit Tabona Joseph 328
Zammit, Sir Temi 186
Zarb, Tony 299
Żejtun 79, 101, 161, 162, 171, 179,
    181, 186, 192, 193, 263, 323
Zemin, Jiang 251, 258, 308
Zimbabwe 261
Zuk, Shan 68, 69